ERIK SATIE

Twayne's Music Series

ERIK SATIE

Alan M. Gillmor
CARLETON UNIVERSITY

Twayne Publishers
A Division of G.K. Hall & Co. • *Boston*

Copyright 1988 by G. K. Hall & Co.
All rights reserved
Published by Twayne Publishers
A Division of G. K. Hall & Co.
70 Lincoln Street
Boston, Massachusetts 02111

Copyediting supervised by Barbara Sutton
Book production by Janet Zietowski
Typeset in Century Oldstyle by Compset, Inc.

Printed on permanent/durable acid-free paper
and bound in the United States of America

Library of Congress Cataloging-in-Publication Data

Gillmor, Alan M.
Erik Satie / Alan M. Gillmor.
p.   cm.—(Twayne's music series)
Bibliography: p.
Includes index.
ISBN 0-8057-9472-7 (alk. paper)
1. Satie, Erik, 1866–1925.   2. Composers—France—Biography.
I. Title.   II. Series.
ML410.S196G54   1988
780′.92′4—dc19
[B]   87-37381
CIP
MN

For Donald and Douglas

Contents

About the Author

Alan M. Gillmor was educated at the University of Michigan (B.Mus., M.A.) and at the University of Toronto (Ph.D.). Fellowships from the Canada Council (1969–70 and 1977–78) enabled him to spend extended periods of study in France (Paris and Honfleur) and in England (London and Cambridge) where the major research for this monograph was carried out. In 1972 he completed his doctoral dissertation, "Erik Satie and the Concept of the Avant-Garde," under the supervision of the late Arnold Walter (with external examination by Roger Shattuck).

Professor Gillmor has held positions in the Faculty of Music, University of Houston, and the Faculty of Music, McGill University. In 1971 he joined the Department of Music at Carleton University, Ottawa, Canada, where he teaches courses in nineteenth- and twentieth-century music, opera, contemporary American music, jazz, and music appreciation. From 1980–85 he was the English-language editor of the *Canadian University Music Review/Revue de musique des universités canadiennes,* Canada's leading musicological journal.

In addition to his continuing work in the area of fin de siècle French music, Professor Gillmor maintains an interest in experimental music, particularly that of Canada and the United States. He has published in the *Musical Quarterly, Queen's Quarterly, Contact: A Journal of Contemporary Music,* and the *Canadian Composer/Le Compositeur canadien,* and has contributed articles on Canadian music to the *Encyclopedia International,* the *Encyclopedia of Music in Canada,* and *The Canadian Encyclopedia.*

Preface

Erik Satie remains, more than a half century after his death, one of the most curious figures in contemporary music. It is difficult to imagine another twentieth-century composer—of any stripe—whose appeal has cut so deeply across the social and aesthetic boundaries of our time. Despite his slender creative output Satie remains relevant to large numbers of people from seemingly incompatible sectors of society. On the one hand is the scholarly community, which views the composer as central to any thorough understanding of the *belle époque* and the Parisian 1920s. On the other are the heterogeneous remnants of the counterculture, who see in Satie one of the few "classical" composers outrageous enough to belong in their neo-Dada, anti-Establishment world. Between these poles are the Madison Avenue hucksters, ears forever to the ground, who have seen fit to make use of Satie's whimsical music in their pitches for everything from coffee to feminine deodorant. Hence Satie is one of those relatively rare cultural phenomena, a creative figure embraced both by the Academy and the mass media, a strange, multifaceted personality who continues to delight, confound, bemuse.

A common fate of controversial contemporary composers—Arnold Schoenberg is a famous example—is that their reputations are often based more on glib generalization than on adequate knowledge of representative music. Popular opinion, for example, sees Schoenberg as a cold, cerebral composer, creator of the dreaded System; similarly, Satie emerges as a mere clownish eccentric given to mildly amusing puns, whose often childlike (some would say childish) music finds its ideal service as, at best, a superior form of sonic wallpaper. Such simplifications, of course, do great disservice to two utterly dissimilar composers:[1] the Austrian Jew, frightening his potential audience with a preponderance of late-Romantic Teutonic solemnity in his lofty search for the sublime; and the Frenchman from Normandy, managing to elude total respectability in the eyes of the same public by his very refusal to appear serious, his anti-Romantic rejection of the sublime. If Schoenberg was sometimes guilty of smothering instinct with technique, Satie, never lacking in imagination, almost miraculously transformed his alleged technical incapacities into a virtue, thus creating a unique body of music that succeeded in penetrating the lingering mists of Bayreuth and Parnassus like a beacon, clearing the stage for a truly contemporary aesthetic.

Here we begin to approach the heart of the Satie enigma: by the prevailing canons of classical aesthetic theory Satie emerges quite unequivocally as a seriously flawed composer, one of the second or even the third rank, but one whose effect on the development of contemporary musical thought has been nonetheless profound. Indeed, it is possible to demonstrate that he had a catalytic effect on the emergence of twentieth-century avant-gardism at least the equal of far more celebrated and accomplished contemporaries such as Debussy, Stravinsky, and Schoenberg. How is it that a composer of such seemingly limited scope and slender technical resources has become accepted as one of the truly significant precursors of modern aesthetic tendencies?

One of the first important facts to emerge is that Satie was the first French composer of major significance whose career began entirely beyond the pale of the Wagnerian ethos. Even Emmanuel Chabrier, one of the strong musical influences on the formation of the Satie style, struggled all his creative life to rid himself of the powerful Wagnerian influence. And it has been well documented that Debussy recklessly flirted with "the old sorcerer" before venturing onto his inimitably French path. Although many general surveys of contemporary music, in recognition of Debussy's revolutionary musical language, begin with a discussion of French Impressionism, it is apparent that the Impressionist aesthetic (if not the idiom) is a clear extension of the Romantic sensibility, that musical Impressionism is an exquisitely refined and peculiarly Gallic form of a movement deeply rooted in Teutonic soil. In this context the anti-Impressionist Satie emerges, in the harsher light of the postmodern era, as a more forward-looking figure than many a more famous and polished contemporary.

Throughout his life Satie eventually rejected each group of young composers that gathered around him. In this way he managed to remain continuously in the vanguard, his frequent alliances with younger people explaining, in part, the infantine and artless nature of the man. He was fond of pointing out that he would gladly start over again if he were shown anything new. Writing in Jean Cocteau's ephemeral broadsheet, *Le Coq,* he declared that "THERE IS NO SCHOOL OF SATIE. Satieism could never exist. I would oppose it." And he went on to explain that "there must be no slavery in art. I have always tried to throw followers off the scent by both the form and content of each new work. It's the only way, for an artist, to avoid becoming the head of a 'school'—that is to say a pundit."[2] It was Satie who, in 1917, christened Les Nouveaux Jeunes, soon to become known as Les Six, thus beginning an association that would greatly enhance his fame. It was not long, however, before relations between several members of the group and the irascible composer became strained. Of the three composers most allied to the Satie-Cocteau aesthetic, Georges Auric and Francis Poulenc managed to run afoul of Satie by early 1924, leaving Darius Milhaud alone on good terms with him to the end.

Les Six had always been more a figment of a journalist's imagination than a unified group, and as the talents of these composers ripened and flowered along individual lines in the immediate postwar years, Satie found it necessary once again to switch allegiance to a younger, and ultimately less talented, coterie of musicians—the short-lived École d'Arcueil—led by Henri Sauguet, and including such minor talents as Maxime Jacob, Henri Cliquet-Pleyel, and Roger Désormière. Satie never did discover a young composer to whom he could subordinate himself; it was not in the nature of the man. As a result, both Les Six and École d'Arcueil rallied around the older man, probably somewhat to his amusement, considering him their artistic progenitor.

To the year of his death in 1925 Satie was a seminal influence on a variety of vanguard movements, some ultimately important, others decidedly removed from the mainstream of contemporary artistic evolution and consequently short lived. His relationships with such notable contemporaries as Diaghilev, Cocteau, Picasso, Picabia, and Clair allowed him to become one of the few musicians of his time involved in such progressive artistic trends as Cubism, Dadaism, and Surrealism. Through his alliance with filmmaker René Clair, Satie emerges as a pioneering figure in the history of film music. His score for Clair's film Entr'acte—the outrageously anarchistic intermission feature of the Satie / Picabia ballet Relâche (1924)—is preceded by a mere handful of original film scores by notable composers, chief among them Saint-Saëns's Opus 128 for strings, piano, and harmonium, written expressly for Henri Lavedan's L'Assassinat du Duc de Guise (1908), Honegger's score for Abel Gance's La Roue (1923), and George Antheil's well-known Ballet mécanique (1924), written originally for a film production by the painter Fernand Léger and the American cameraman Dudley Murphy.

Neoclassicism is another contemporary artistic temper with which Satie's name is intimately connected. Most of the composer's champions—

even many of his detractors—consider *Socrate* (1918) to be among his finest works and a landmark in musical neoclassicism. No less a personality than Stravinsky, the greatest spokesman for the new classicism, warmly recognized the touching simplicity and dignity of *Socrate,* especially the austere and moving final scene depicting the death of the great philosopher, and he in turn dedicated one of his charming—and very Satiean—*Three Easy Pieces* for piano four hands to Satie. In such works as the *Sonatine bureaucratique* (1917), based on Clementi, and the Dada stage-work *Le Piège de Méduse* (1913), scored for clarinet, trumpet, trombone, violin, cello, double bass, and percussion, Satie anticipated some of the principal distinguishing features of the neoclassical style: the use of pre–nineteenth-century models, and the substitution of small ad hoc combinations of solo instruments for the large Romantic orchestra..

Finally we should note the influence the Satie spirit has continued to exercise on the contemporary musical scene, from the urbane Franco-American reveries of Virgil Thomson to 1960s rock (Blood, Sweat and Tears) and John Cage's controversial magical mystery tours. Thomson admired the French composer for his Gallic playfulness, for the guileless simplicity of his musical language, and for the vigor with which he denied the virtues of Germanic art. He taught him that the best thing Western music could do was to stop taking itself so seriously. Cage, from the moment he discovered Satie, admired his extraordinary abnegation of the will and sensed a profound humanism aimed at liberating men and women from the artificial barriers with which they shut themselves off from life.

In 1945, Rollo Myers, Satie's second biographer and one of the composer's great champions, solemnly declared that "it is obvious that a musician who enjoyed the friendship and admiration of men like Debussy, Stravinsky, Picasso, Roussel, Koechlin, Cocteau, Milhaud, Honegger and many others cannot possibly be dismissed as either a *fumiste* [practical joker] or still less as a nonentity."[3] To date the overwhelming majority of the composer's critics have followed Myers's lead in their grave assumptions that his cryptic behavior was a kind of mask for an underlying seriousness prevented from surfacing because of a monumentally deficient technical ability. Utilizing the canons of a predominantly Anglo-Germanic critical tradition, Satie's critics have seemed reluctant to concede that the composer *was* at heart a *fumiste* and a *fantaisiste*—in a venerable Gallic line, it might be noted, stretching from François Villon and Rabelais through Ronsard and La Fontaine to Alphonse Allais, Alfred Jarry, and Léon-Paul Fargue—and that this, contrary to making of him a nonentity, is of primary significance to the development of the avant-

garde ideal and consequently to the evolution of twentieth-century aesthetics. "It is not surprising," Rosette Renshaw has perceptively noted,
"that his enemies have striven to emphasize his idiosyncracies which,
according to them, outweigh his talent. If only Satie had erected a barrier
between his personal life and his work as a musician, if he had been
content to joke about everything except the sublime domain of music,
'serious' people would have forgiven his buffoonery."[4] But Satie's irreverent attitude toward art and life, his very refusal in fact to differentiate
the one from the other, is the primary quality that defines his importance
and explains, to a great extent, his relevance and his ultimate historical
significance. If the composer did in fact wear a mask, as many would
claim, its function was not to conceal his own alleged inadequacy, but
rather, in the words of Peter Dickinson, "to cloak a spiritual crisis which
Satie sensed well before this century."[5]

Satie's creative career spanned one of the most fertile and volatile
periods in Western cultural history. It was a time of enormous flux and
disintegration of traditional values on all fronts—a period of exhilarating
creative exploration and freedom for some, of despair and disillusionment
for many more, a *belle époque* for the privileged few. The ripeness of
decay was in the air, but also the hardy seeds of the brave new world to
come. Like all the arts, but in a subtler and more abstract way, music
mirrored the decline of the old order with prophetic accuracy, and as the
underlying principles of tonality came under attack—beginning most
forcefully with Wagner—the system, like the society that created it, began to break down under the stress of expansion until the inevitable point
of disintegration was reached sometime shortly before the outbreak of
that malignant scourge we insist upon calling, with artless sophistry, the
Great War. Western man became a victim of the very ideology of progress he invented to deliver him from an earlier crisis of values, and the
dynamic of progress, so vividly reflected in the pathological urgency of
much late-Romantic music, was rather suddenly replaced in the period
around World War I with a vibrant jangle of artistic movements arising
from confused notions of Marxism and Freudianism mingled with an ata-
vistic urge to recall the imagined simplicity and homogeneous complete-
ness of a preindustrial age. Thus the stage was set for the advent of
modernism, a veritable orgy of experimentalism in the arts, which, in its
most virulent forms, denied the validity of the seemingly immutable laws
that had governed the evolution of the classical tradition over the past
three centuries.

Satie has become almost an icon in the jagged landscape of contemporary musical aesthetics. His anti-Romantic rejection of the sublime, his glorification of the homely and the commonplace, his highly refined sense of the absurd and the whimsical are the primary qualities that have endeared him to the more iconoclastic members of the critical fraternity. A parody of the bohemian dandy, the strange little man from Normandy emerges as the quintessential modernist.

Stylistic analysis is, of course, fundamental to any critical evaluation of a composer's oeuvre, but with an artist of Satie's strange and fanciful nature there is a strong temptation to substitute anecdote for analytical perception. Consequently the composer's musical achievement has been obscured by a plethora of fascinating documentation concerning his life and times, his literary activities, and his connections with sundry painters, poets, and men and women of the theater. This is an understandable tendency, for, like most progressive music composed between 1890 and 1920, Satie's music resists traditional analytical methods. Despite its deceptive simplicity his music—as much as Debussy's or Ives's— requires its own analytical framework, one that recognizes the fragile juxtaposition of multiple layers of aesthetic meaning.

We can accept as a generality that the truth we seek about an artist is revealed largely, though not exclusively, through his creative work. But with an artist of Satie's kind, the problem takes on an added dimension, for in one very important sense art and life for Satie—as for his staunchest American disciple John Cage—become very nearly one and the same thing. It is important to recognize the fact that Satie was more than simply a musician. The recent publication of his considerable body of writings[6] shows him to be a literary figure of some importance and unquestioned individuality. His whimsical drawings and striking calligraphy have received nearly as much attention. And when these literary and artistic fantasies are married to the musical, as in the quintessentially Satiean *Sports et divertissements* of 1914, we have a score that properly belongs as much on the walls of an art gallery as on the shelves of a music library. Satie's is an exceedingly fragile art form, a delicate interweaving of individual strands of artistic experience suspended in exquisite balance, and any attempt to define this elusive art is like trying to dissect the proverbial butterfly. As the composer Lothar Klein has noted: "It is useless to comment on any specific work, for Satie's work eludes musical analysis. One must contemplate the whole oeuvre and the thought behind it; comprehending this, the swerving movements of modern music can be followed more easily."[7]

Satie was in some ways the most progressive French composer to appear on the Parisian musical scene following the death of Hector Berlioz in 1869. Many of the reasons for his peculiar attraction for several generations of artists remain obscure and require further exploration. Most attempts to decode the Satie enigma have fixed inevitably on the bizarre personality while failing to locate Satie's creative achievement in the new forms of aesthetic experience that have dramatically altered the morphology of art in the technocratic society. The rich variety of Satie's creative activity takes on meaning, not as an isolated phenomenon, but principally in the context of post-1870 French nationalism, which saw the marriage of art and anarchism and the birth of the modern. Viewed as such—in his several capacities as composer, littérateur, wit, and artistic agent provocateur—Satie emerges with reasonable clarity as a singularly powerful catalyst in the birth of the avant-garde in France. He was a truly original musician who did more to incorporate material from the other arts and enlarge the experiential boundaries of musical form than possibly any other musician of his time.

Alan M. Gillmor
Carleton University

Acknowledgments

The cooperation and assistance of numerous people have made possible the successful completion of this book. A special debt of gratitude is owed to Roger Shattuck and Nigel Wilkins, inveterate Satieans both, for their careful reading of the manuscript in its entirety and for their constant encouragement over a period of many years. I am equally indebted to Ornella Volta, not only for her splendid contributions to the Satie literature, but for her generous assistance in numerous matters pertaining to fact and interpretation. I would also like to single out Steven M. Whiting, who kindly read a draft version of chapters 1–3 and made a number of valuable suggestions for improvement.

In addition, I should like to thank the many others who kindly responded to requests for information or assisted in other ways too varied to enumerate; among them, Istvan Anhalt, the late Elaine Brody, John Cage, Terry Clark, Hélène Couture MacTavish, Joseph Dallett, David Diamond, Tom Gordon, Jacinthe Harbec, Wayne Howell, Helmut Kallmann and the staff of the music division of the National Library of Canada, Christopher Marsden, Prue Neidorf, Ernst Oppenheimer, Wendy Roche, R. Wayne Shoaf, and Donald A. N. Wallace.

To Michel Gaulin, who helped clarify countless fine points of translation from French sources, I offer my deep appreciation. And to my colleagues in the music department at Carleton University—Patrick Cardy, Bryan Gillingham, Elaine Keillor, David Piper, and John Shepherd—my eternal gratitude for their patience, good humor, and expert advice.

For generous financial assistance during several stages of the research and writing of this book I express my deep gratitude to the Canada Council, the Social Sciences and Humanities Research Council of Canada, the Ontario Arts Council, and Naomi Griffiths, Dean of Arts, Carleton University.

Finally, my heartfelt thanks to my wife Susan, artist, friend, and companion, for her unflagging patience and quiet encouragement.

*　　*　　*

For permission to quote copyright material, grateful acknowledgment is extended to the following: G. Schirmer, Inc. & Associated Music Publishers, Inc., and Éditions Salabert for permission to quote excerpts of Satie's music published by Éditions Salabert and Éditions Max Eschig; European American Music, for permission to quote excerpts of Satie's music published by Universal Edition; MCA Music Publishing, for permission to quote an excerpt of Satie's music published by Le Chant du Monde; Ernst Eulenburg Ltd., for permission to quote excerpts of Satie's prose works from Nigel Wilkins's *The Writings of Erik Satie* (London, 1980); and Harvard University, for permission to quote excerpts of unpublished Satie manuscripts in the former Dumbarton Oaks Research Library collection of Satie material now held by the Houghton Library.

ERIK SATIE (1866–1925)
Reproduced by permission of Alexandre Istrati and Natalia Dumitresco,
sole legatees of Constanin Brancusi.

Chronology

1866   Birth of Eric Alfred Leslie Satie, 9 A.M. 17 May, no. 90, rue Haute, Honfleur (Calvados), son of Alfred Satie and Jane Leslie Anton, born in London of Scottish parents. Baptized in Anglican Church (September).

1867   Birth of sister Olga.

1869   Birth of brother Conrad.

1870   Satie family moves to Paris.

1872   Mother dies. Sent back to Honfleur to live with paternal grandparents, Jules and Eulalie. Enters Collège d'Honfleur. Rebaptized in Roman Catholic Church.

1874   Begins music lessons with Vinot, pupil of Niedermeyer and organist at church of Saint-Léonard.

1878   Grandmother dies. Rejoins father in Paris, no. 2 rue de Constantinople.

1879   Father marries Eugénie Barnetche, pupil of Guilmant and Mathias, and establishes himself as music publisher in the boulevard Magenta. Enters preparatory piano class of Émile Descombes, Paris Conservatoire (8 November).

1880   Piano examination (January); described by Descombes as "gifted but indolent." Piano examination (June).

1881   Piano examination (January); jury includes Descombes, Thomas, Sauzay, Duvernoy, Diémer, Fissot. Piano examination (June). "Laziest student in the Conservatoire" (Descombes).

1882   Piano examination (January). "If he continues to work, he will surely arrive!" (Descombes). Piano examination (June). Fails to impress examiners. Dismissed from Conservatoire.

1883   Enters Antoine Taudou's harmony class as auditor (4 December).

1884   *Allegro*, first extant composition (Honfleur, 9 September, signed "Erik Satie").

1885   Passes preparatory examination at Conservatoire (6 November) with performance of Chopin *Ballade*. Accepted into intermediate piano class of Georges Mathias. *Valse-ballet* and *Fantaisie-valse*.

1886   Piano examination (January). "Insignificant and laborious" (Mathias). Piano examination (June). "Worthless. Three months just to learn the piece. Cannot sight-read properly" (Mathias). *Ogives*. Meets Spanish-born poet José–Maria Patricio Manuel Contamine (pseud. J. P. Contamine de Latour). *Trois mélodies* ("Les Anges," "Les Fleurs," "Sylvie") on poems by Contamine de Latour. *Élégie* (Contamine de Latour). Acquires nickname "*Monsieur le Pauvre.*" Leaves Conservatoire (early November). Volunteers (15 November) for military service (33rd Infantry) and departs (9 December) for Arras (Pas-de-Calais). Reads Flaubert and Péladan.

1887   *Chanson* (Contamine de Latour). Hears Chabrier's *Le Roi malgré lui* (May). *Trois Sarabandes*. Moves to no. 50, rue Condorcet, Montmartre, near Cirque Médrano. Frequents Chat Noir, no. 12, rue de Laval (later rue Victor Massé). Engaged as second pianist at Chat Noir (November / December?). Meets Dynam-Victor Fumet and Alphonse Allais.

1888   *Trois Gymnopédies*.

1889   Visits Universal Exposition. *Gnossienne* ("No. 5"). *Chanson hongroise* (fragment). Moves (or early 1890?) to tiny room at no. 6, rue Cortot, Montmartre, not far from Sacré-Coeur.

1890   Meets Joséphin Péladan, "Sâr" of the Order of the Catholic Rosy Cross, the Temple and the Grail. *Trois Gnossiennes*. Appointed "chapelmaster" for Péladan's Rosicrucian sect. *Danse* (for small orchestra), later incorporated into *Trois Morceaux en forme de poire* (1903).

1891   Quarrels with Rodolphe Salis and leaves Chat Noir for Auberge du Clou, no. 30, avenue Trudaine. Friendship with Debussy. *Gnossienne* ("No. 4"). *Première pensée Rose + Croix (Marche antique pour la Rose-Croix?)*. Incidental music for Péladan's *Le Fils des étoiles*. *Hymne pour le "Salut Drapeau"* for Péladan's *Le Prince de Byzance*.

1892   Performances of *Le Fils des étoiles* at first Rosicrucian Salon
        (March). Presents candidacy to Académie des Beaux-Arts (to
        succeed Ernest Guirard). *Sonneries de la Rose + Croix.*
        Quatre Préludes: (1) "Fête donnée par des Chevaliers Nor-
        mands en l'Honneur d'une jeune Demoiselle"; (2) "Prélude
        d'Eginhard" (1893?); (3) "Premier Prélude du Nazaréen"; (4)
        "Deuxième Prélude du Nazaréen" (nos. 3 and 4 composed June
        1892 for Henri Mazel's *Le Nazaréen).* Rupture with Péladan
        (letter to editor of *Gil Blas).* *Uspud,* "ballet chrétien en trois
        actes" (with Contamine de Latour).

1893   Founds Église Métropolitaine d'Art de Jésus Conducteur. Fre-
        quents Nouvelle Athènes in Place Pigalle. Liaison with Suzanne
        Valadon (January–June). *Danses gothiques.* "Épître de Erik Sa-
        tie: Première aux Artistes Catholiques et à tous les Chrétiens,"
        Le Coeur, no. 6 / 7 (September / October) with facsimile of
        second *Gnossienne* (titled, however, *6ème Gnossienne* and dated
        April 1893).

1894   *Prélude de La Porte héroïque du ciel* for "esoteric drama" by
        Jules Bois. Presents candidacy a second time to Academy (to
        succeed Charles Gounod). Indignant letter (17 May) to Saint-
        Saëns *(Le Ménestrel).* Meets Ravel at Nouvelle Athènes.

1895   *Pages mystiques*: (1) "Prière"; (2) "Vexations"; (3) "Harmonies"
        (1893–95?). *Messe des Pauvres.* Publishes two issues of *Le
        Cartulaire de l'Église Métropolitaine d'Art de Jésus Conducteur*
        (May and June) in which he denounces Lugné-Poë, Des-
        champs, and Gauthier-Villars ("Willy").

1896   Presents candidacy a third time to Academy (to succeed Am-
        broise Thomas).

1897   *Gnossienne* ("No. 6"). Premiere of Debussy's orchestral ver-
        sion of *Gymnopédies* (nos. 1 and 3) at Salle Erard (February).
        Pièces froides: "Airs à faire fuir"—"Danses de travers." *Caresse*
        (1897?).

1898   Moves to no. 22, rue Cauchy, Arcueil-Cachan (October).
        Known as "Velvet Gentleman." Frequent visits with Debussy
        in the rue Cardinet.

1899   Accompanist / arranger for chansonnier Vincent Hyspa in
        Montmartre cabarets and at society soirées (ca. 1899–1905).
        Jack in the Box, pantomime on scenario by Jules Dépaquit

(1899–1900). Witness (with Pierre Louÿs and Lucien Fontaine) at Debussy's marriage to Rosalie Texier (19 October).

1900   *Geneviève de Brabant,* miniature opera for marionettes on libretto by Contamine de Latour (ca. 1900). Numerous cabaret songs arranged and composed for Hyspa, Paulette Darty, and others, most unpublished, many incomplete (ca. 1897–ca. 1909): *Tendrement, Chez le docteur, L'Omnibus automobile, Un Dîner à l'Élysée, Le Veuf* (Hyspa); *Je te veux* (Pacory); *La Diva de l'Empire* (Bonnaud & Blès); *Légende Californienne, Imperial-Oxford* (Contamine de Latour); *Allons-y Chochotte* (Durante). Music-hall dances: *Poudre d'or* and *Le Piccadilly. Rêverie du pauvre. Petite ouverture à danser. Petite musique de clown triste. Verset laïque et sompteux.* "Les Musiciens de Montmartre,"*Guide de l'Étranger à Montmartre.*

1901   *The Dreamy Fish,* music for a story by Lord Cheminot (Contamine de Latour).

1902   Receives 76 centimes from Society of Composers for performance rights.

1903   *Trois Morceaux en forme de poire.*

1904   Physically attacks critic "Willy" at Chevillard concert at Cirque d'été (10 April).

1905   *Pousse l'Amour* (fragments), operetta in collaboration with Maurice de Féraudy and Jean Kolb. Enrolls in Schola Cantorum.

1906   *Chanson médiévale* (Mendès). *Passacaille. Prélude en tapisserie. Douze petits chorals* (1906–8). *Musiques intimes et secrètes* (1906–13). *Six Pièces de la période 1906–1913:* 1. "Désespoir agréable" (1908); 2. "Effronterie"; 3. "Poésie" (ca. 1913); 4. "Prélude canin" (ca. 1910); 5. "Profondeur"; 6. "Songe-creux" (1906–8).

1908   Obtains Diploma in Counterpoint (15 June) from Schola Cantorum ("Avec la mention *très bien*") signed by d'Indy and Roussel. *Aperçus désagréables* (1908–12). Attends Radical-Socialist meetings in Arcueil. Participates in Patronage laïque d'Arcueil, a nonreligious charitable organization under directorship of P.-A. Templier, father of his first biographer.

1909   Receives *Palmes Académiques* from Mayor of Arcueil for services to community (4 July). *Vin d'honneur* in his honor at no.

43, rue Émile Raspail, Arcueil (7 August). Contributes column "Quinzaine des Sociétés" to local newspaper *L'Avenir d'Arcueil-Cachan.* Gives *solfège* lessons on Sunday mornings.

1910   Resigns from Patronage laïque. *Nouvelles Pièces froides* (1910–11). *Deux Rêveries nocturnes* (1910–11). *Carnet d'Esquisses et de Croquis* (1897–1914). Meets Roland-Manuel.

1911   Ravel performs second *Sarabande, Le Fils des étoiles* (act 1 Prelude), and third *Gymnopédie* at concert of Société Musicale Indépendante (16 January). Debussy conducts orchestral version of *Gymnopédies* at concert of Cercle Musical in Salle Gaveau (25 March). *En Habit de cheval.* Publication of *Sarabandes, Trois Morceaux en forme de poire,* and *En Habit de cheval* by Rouart-Lerolle.

1912   "Mémoires d'un amnésique" begin to appear in *Revue musicale S.I.M.* (April–July / August–November). Literary contributions to *L'Oeil de veau* (February–May / June). Meets Pierre Bertin and Stravinsky. *Préludes flasques (pour un chien). Véritables Préludes flasques (pour un chien).*

1913   Meets Georges Auric. Further installments of "Mémoires d'un amnésique" (January–February). *Le Piège de Méduse,* comedy in one act (with Seven Monkey's Dances). *Descriptions automatiques.* Ricardo Viñes premieres *Véritables Préludes flasques* (Salle Pleyel, 5 April) and *Descriptions automatiques* (Conservatoire, 5 June). *Embryons desséchés. Croquis et agaceries d'un gros bonhomme en bois. Chapitres tournés en tous sens. Vieux sequins et vieilles cuirasses. Enfantines*: 1. *Menus propos enfantins*; 2. *Enfantillages pittoresques*; 3. *Peccadilles importunes. Trois Nouvelles enfantines. Les Pantins dansent.*

1914   Viñes performs *Chapitres tournés en tous sens* (Salle Erard, 14 January) and *Croquis et agaceries d'un gros bonhomme en bois* (Salle Pleyel, 28 March, and Salle Erard, 21 April). *Choses vues à droite et à gauche (sans lunettes).* Further installment of "Mémoires d'un amnésique" (February). Meets Valentine Gross (later Hugo). *Sports et divertissements. Heures séculaires et instantanées. Trois valses distinguées du précieux dégoûté.* Assassination of socialist leader Jean Jaurès (31 July). Joins Socialist Party (1 August). Meets Diaghilev. *Trois Poèmes d'amour* (Satie).

1915   Meets Cocteau. *Cinq Grimaces pour "Le Songe d'une nuit d'été." Avant-dernières-pensées.*

1916   Meets Poulenc. Conference of Société Lyre et Palette (18 April). *Trois mélodies* (Fargue, Godebska, Chalupt). Granados / Satie concert at Madame Bongard's, rue de Penthièvre (30 May). Collaboration with Cocteau and Picasso on *Parade.* "Les Animaux dans la Musique," talk given at school of Professor Lucien Flagny, no. 26, rue de la Tour (2 November).

1917   Begins work on *Socrate,* commissioned by Princesse Edmond de Polignac (née Winaretta Singer). Premiere of *Parade* (Théâtre du Châtelet, 18 May). Lawsuit by critic Jean Poueigh (pseud. Octave Séré) for defamation of character following scandal of *Parade. Sonatine bureaucratique.* Concert at Théâtre du Vieux-Colombier (11 December) organized by Jane Bathori. Formation of *Les Nouveaux Jeunes.*

1918   Rupture with Debussy. Viñes performs *Sarabandes, Gymnopédies,* and *Gnossiennes* at third Festival "Montjoie!" (20 February). "L'Éloge des Critiques," talk given at concert of *Les Nouveaux Jeunes* (Théâtre du Vieux-Colombier, March). Death of Debussy (26 March). Cocteau publishes *Coq et l'Arlequin.*

1919   Performance of *Socrate* at Adrienne Monnier's Maison des Amis des Livres, no. 7, rue de l'Odéon (21 March). Witness (with Cocteau) at marriage of Valentine Gross to Jean Hugo (7 August). "Notes sur la Musique," *L'Humanité* (October). *Cinq Nocturnes. Trois Petites pièces montées.* "Musique et les Animaux," talk given at concert "Pour les Jeunes" (Salle de l'Étoile, no. 17, rue de Chateaubriand, 18 December). Meets Jean Wiéner.

1920   Public premiere of *Socrate* (Société Nationale, 14 February). Premiere of *Trois Petites pièces montées* (Comédie des Champs-Élysées, 21 February). Introduces (with Milhaud) *Musique d'ameublement:* (1) *Chez un Bistrot;* (2) *Un Salon* (Galerie Barbazanges, 8 March). First performance of orchestral version of *Socrate* at Festival Erik Satie (Salle Erard, 7 June). Literary contributions to *Le Coq* (May–June–July / August / September–November). *Premier Menuet. La Belle Excentrique* (for Mlle Caryathis). *Quatre petites mélodies* (Lamartine, Cocteau, Anon., Radiguet).

1921   Joins Communist Party. "Les Enfants musiciens," talk given at
       "Soirée pour les Jeunes" (Salle de l'Étoile, no. 17, rue de Cha-
       teaubriand, 17 February). Visits Brussels and Ghent to hear
       first Belgian performances of *Socrate* (April). Meets E. L. T.
       Mesens. "Conference sur les Six" (Brussels, 11 April). "Fes-
       tival Erik Satie" (Brussels, 12 April). Public premier of *Le Piège
       de Méduse* (Théâtre Michel, 24 May). Premier of *La Belle Ex-
       centrique* (Théâtre du Colisée, no. 38, avenue des Champs-
       Élysées, 21 June). Literary contributions to *Le Pilhaou-
       Thibaou* (July), *Action* (August), and *L'Esprit nouveau* (Decem-
       ber). *Sonnerie pour réveiller le bon gros Roi des Singes (lequel
       ne dort toujours que d'un oeil)* (*Fanfare*, 1 October).

1922   "Préambule," talk given at concert of Marcelle Meyer (Salle de
       La Ville-l'Évêque, 17 January) at which *Premier Menuet* is pre-
       miered. Dada Congress (Closerie des Lilas, 17 February). Pre-
       miere of *Sports et divertissements* (Salle de La Ville-l'Évêque,
       22 February). Literary contributions to *Fanfare* (January), *Les
       Feuilles libres* (February–June / July–October / November),
       Catalogue (March–April–May–June–October–November), *Le
       Coeur à barbe* (April), and *L'Almanach de Cocagne*.

1923   Formation of *L'École d'Arcueil* (Sauguet, Jacob, Cliquet-Pleyel,
       Désormière). Literary contributions to *Les Feuilles libres*
       (March / April–September / October) and *Vanity Fair* (August).
       Ludions (Fargue). *Musique d'Ameublement: 1. Tenture de cab-
       inet préfectoral* (1923); 2. *Tapissierie en fer forgé* (1917-23); 3.
       Carrelage phonique (1917-23). "Quelques Jeunes Musiciens,"
       talk given at "Séance d'Avant-Garde" organized by Cercle in-
       ternational des Étudiants des Nations Alliées et Amies de la
       France (Collège de France, no. 13, rue Champollion, 14 June).
       Works on setting recitatives for Gounod's *Le Médecin malgré
       lui*. Meets Robert Caby. Premiere of *Ludions* (Salle des Agri-
       culteurs, 21 December). Rupture with Fargue.

1924   Travels to Monte Carlo for performance of *Le Médecin malgré
       lui* (5 January). Rupture with Auric and Poulenc. Denounces
       Auric, Poulenc, and critic Louis Laloy in *Paris-Journal* (Feb-
       ruary). Second lecture / concert tour in Belgium (Brussels and
       Antwerp). "L'Esprit musical," talk given in Brussels at Confer-
       ence organized by La Lanterne sourde (Salle Delgray, 15
       March) and in Antwerp (Cercle artistique et littéraire français,

21 March). Literary contributions to *Les Feuilles libres* (January / February), *Création* (February), *Sélection* (April), *391* (June–July), and *Le Mouvement accéléré* (November). Premiere of *Mercure* (Théâtre de la Cigale, 15 June). Collaboration with Rolf de Maré and Francis Picabia on *Relâche*. Shooting begins for René Clair's film *Entr'acte* (June). Cancellation of scheduled premiere of *Relâche* (27 November). Premiere of *Relâche* (Théâtre des Champs-Élysées, 4 December).

1925   Rapid decline in health. Moves to Grand Hôtel, Place de l'Opéra. Moves to Hôtel Istria, Montparnasse. Hospitalized at Hôpital Saint-Joseph, rue Pierre-Larousse, Cirrhosis of the liver diagnosed. Dies, 8 P.M., 1 July.

1

Ars Gallica:
Sources of a Style

The early achievement of Erik Satie appears quite remarkable in view of the social and cultural milieu of the early years of the Third Republic. The Franco-Prussian War of 1870–71 had left a prostrate France in a state of artistic, as well as political, confusion. The persistent domination of Austro-German music joined forces with a renewed French nationalism to produce a grave conflict in French musical affairs, a kind of cultural schizophrenia that was clearly exemplified by two events: the founding of the Société Nationale de Musique in 1871 and the publication from 1885 to 1888 of the *Revue wagnérienne.* Satie's primary importance to the early development of modern French music is due in large part to the fact that he was the first significant French musician of his generation to reject completely and from the outset the dominant Austro-German style and the powerful Wagnerian stimulus. Most of the well-known French composers active in the 1880s and 1890s—Chabrier, Chausson, Delibes, Massenet—either gallicized the Wagnerian musical language then predominant throughout much of Europe or continued earlier French Romantic traditions in the form of lyric opera.

Despite the eclecticism of much French music of the 1880s, when the Wagnerian cult had reached it zenith, the musical avant-garde had its tentative origins at this time. In the sister arts progressive trends multiplied so rapidly in the decades following the debacle of 1871 that a historian of the period was prompted to say that "the twentieth century could not wait fifteen years for a round number; it was born, yelling, in 1885."[1]

The Franco-Prussian War
and the National Society of Music

On 19 July 1870 France declared war on Prussia. In less than two months the antiquated French army fell to superior Prussian forces and with it disappeared the Empire of Louis Napoleon Bonaparte, bringing to an end in France monarchism and Bonapartism. Paris withheld the Prussian siege and bombardment for another four months until the inevitable armistice of 28 January 1871. Through an ignoble military defeat France was forced unwillingly into a new age.

Following the brief but bloody period of the Commune and the establishment of a provisional regime, which endured for nearly five years, republican aspirations were confirmed, in February 1875, through legislation carried by a majority vote of one. It is significant that France suppressed monarchist aspirations only reluctantly and by the narrowest of margins. Throughout the nineteenth century the French mind reveals itself as rationally republican but emotionally royalist. In the aftermath of the Franco-Prussian conflict, as the savage suppression of the Paris Commune made abundantly clear, French society remained fundamentally as conservative as before, yet another dramatic proof of Alphonse Karr's famous dictum apropos of revolutions that the more things change the more they stay the same. Once again in the capricious chronicle of French political life in the Romantic age new actors appeared but the play remained very much the same.

If the passing of the Empire seemed to affect the political and social climate of France very little, the artistic revolt against the philistinism and smug bourgeois values of nineteenth-century French society had begun long before 1870 with the cultivation in the early part of the century of *l'art pour l'art* or Art for Art's Sake, an aesthetic creed that not only dominated the artistic climate of the Romantic period but played a major role in defining the elusive concept of romanticism itself. The proponents of Art for Art's Sake cultivated a purely aesthetic, as opposed to ethical, view of art, becoming in the process the prototypes of the decadent aesthete, the Byronic outsider, the alienated connoisseur of beauty who withdraws from a world of bourgeois banality into a realm of unhampered aesthetic contemplation. In its most elaborate form Art for Art's Sake divorced art entirely from a social context and absolved the artist from all laws beyond those imposed by the art form itself. The champions of Art for Art's Sake shared with the anarchists—their radical brethren on the barricades—an intense hatred of the bourgeoisie, the undeniably cunning exemplars of successful mediocrity. Perhaps the Romantic artist saw in the anarchists' "propaganda of the deed" an echo of his own creed, and doubtless he willingly would have applauded the poet Laurent Tailhade's celebrated slogan: "What do the victims matter, provided the gesture is fine?" Thus it was that the seeds of the new, postwar order had begun to germinate long before 1870. Accordingly, that date can be considered a decisive one in French cultural history only in the sense that the disaster of the war with Prussia had inflicted a psychological shock on France that ultimately became a catalyst for the splendid artistic achievements of the *belle époque*.

Before the war of 1870 there had been little outlet for the performance of French symphonic music. The aspiring symphonist had first to deal with the insatiable French appetite for grand opera and the dazzling virtuosity of the kitsch merchants who flooded the Parisian salons of the mid-century. On a more exalted plane he came smack up against the Austro-German classics, which, since the 1830s when Beethoven's orchestral music was introduced to France, reigned supreme on the more serious levels of French concert life. Such were the conservatism of French audiences and the pro-German sympathies of the organizers and directors of French musical activity throughout nearly the entire nineteenth century that a native composer of symphonic music—especially if he possessed talent and originality—quickly learned to expect little or no sympathy from his countrymen. The distressing career of France's greatest Romantic composer, Hector Berlioz, stands as dramatic testimony to this sorry state of affairs.

It was not until 25 February 1871, at a time when Prussian troops were marching down the Champs-Élysées, that an organization devoted to the performance and propagation of French music was created under the proud and imposing banner of "*Ars Gallica*." The principal architects of the Société Nationale de Musique were Romain Bussine, a professor of voice at the Paris Conservatoire, and Camille Saint-Saëns, the most celebrated French composer of the time. Almost immediately the society's ranks were swelled with the admission of other prominent French musicians, among them César Franck, Jules Massenet, and Gabriel Fauré.

The principal aim of the society was to encourage the publication and performance of serious French music, and even a partial enumeration of works premiered under the auspices of the National Society of Music reveals the great debt modern French music owes to the organization: almost all the late works of Franck, the symphonies and symphonic poems of Saint-Saëns, Debussy's *Prelude to the Afternoon of a Faun* and his String Quartet, d'Indy's *Symphony on a French Mountain Air,* Dukas's *Sorcerer's Apprentice,* Ravel's *Shéhérazade,* Debussy's orchestral version of Satie's *Gymnopédies,* and a host of lesser works. In its attempt to promote a true *ars gallica,* the National Society opposed the prevailing French obsession with operatic music—especially the Italian legacy of Rossini, Bellini, and Donizetti—as well as the longstanding and pronounced influence of German music, above all that of Wagner (although here the Society found itself split into opposing camps, such was the fascination that Wagnerism held for French intellectuals of the fin de siècle).

The cause of French symphonic music was further advanced by the appearance of the Colonne Concerts in 1874, which over the next three decades presented over eight hundred concerts performing the works of about three hundred composers, of which at least half were French. A renascence was under way in French music not unlike that which would soon occur across the channel in England.

Wagnerism in France

So the disaster of the war with Prussia had served to regenerate the artistic spirit of France; but *ars gallica* was destined to run head on into Wagner, Germany's "great master of intellectual eroticism,"[2] to borrow Philippe Jullian's felicitous phrase. It is one of the supreme ironies of French musical history that the toxic Wagnerian virus should have infected France precisely at the moment when young French musicians were declaiming the virtues of Gallic art. It is paradoxical, too, that with few exceptions the charter members of the National Society of Music spent varying periods of their careers grappling with the specter of Wagner. All of the important French composers of the closing decades of the nineteenth century made the obligatory pilgrimage to the Festival Theater in the small Bavarian town of Bayreuth, which continues of course to this day as the principal Wagnerian shrine. Saint-Saëns was there for the grand opening in 1876; Ernest Chausson and Vincent d'Indy went in 1882 for *Parsifal;* even the quintessentially French Fauré made the journey in 1883, followed by Debussy in 1888 and again in 1889, and Chabrier and Guillaume Lekeu also in 1889.

Debussy's flirtation with "the ghost of old Klingsor" has been well documented. Perhaps not quite so well known is the fact that Wagner's genius plagued, in varying degrees, composers as disparate as Chabrier,

Chausson, Duparc, d'Indy, Lalo, Lekeu, Massenet, and, to some extent, the Belgian-born César Franck, even though he did feel compelled to scribble the word "poison" on his score of *Tristan and Isolde.* Although the direct musical effect of the Wagnerian idiom on French music of the fin de siècle was enormous, more pervasive still was the influence of Wagner's immense philosophical system, which succeeded in penetrating nearly every sphere of intellectual activity in France and indeed most of Europe and even beyond.

It was to further Wagner's thought in France that a group of young intellectuals, led by Édouard Dujardin, a fellow student of Debussy at the Paris Conservatoire who had abandoned a musical career for literature, met in Munich in 1884, not many months after Wagner's death, to plan the *Revue wagnérienne.* Dujardin was supported in this ambitious endeavor by a number of devout Wagnerians, prominent among them Houston Stewart Chamberlain, the anti-Semitic Englishman who would gain the distinction of becoming the master's son-in-law through his marriage to Wagner's daughter Eva, Léon Leroy, one of the first critics to champion Wagner's art in France, Théodore de Wyzewa, a music historian of Polish origin whose many articles on Wagner and on the Symbolist aesthetic were published in book form in 1895, and Antoine Lascoux, a music-loving lawyer whose Paris home in the rue de l'Université became a meeting place for the "Petit Bayreuth," a loose confederation of ardent Wagnerians that had been organized by Lascoux as early as 1876 after the first complete performance of the *Ring* cycle in Bayreuth.

From February 1885 until its demise in July of 1888 the *Revue wagnérienne* functioned as the principal organ for the dissemination of Wagnerian thought in France, attracting to its pages the artistic elite of Paris. The poets Mallarmé and Verlaine were represented, as were the painters Odilon Redon, dreamer of luxurious Symbolist dreams, and Henri Fantin-Latour, an artist noted at this time for his lithographs on Wagnerian themes, which, not surprisingly, sold particularly well in Germany. Also pressed into service were the most influential Parisian music critics of the day, among them Alfred Ernst, author of several books on Wagner, and Johannès Weber, onetime secretary to the great Meyerbeer and until 1895 critic for *Le Temps,* one of France's most distinguished newspapers from 1861 to 1942.

After the demise of the *Revue wagnérienne,* the Wagnerian gospel was spread by a variety of journals, such as *La Vogue, Le Décadent, Le Symboliste, La Plume,* and *La Revue blanche,* the leading Symbolist reviews of the late 1880s and 1890s, and many others, some ephemeral, others lasting well into the twentieth century. Alfred Ernst, from 1891 to 1895 music critic for the influential *Revue blanche*—a journal for which Debussy became a critic in 1901—devoted nearly every one of his columns to a discussion of Wagner, as if no other musical activity were taking place in the Paris of the 1890s. By the last decade of the century Wagnerism had infiltrated every corner of French artistic life. In the words of novelist and critic Romain Rolland—who spent a good part of his life attempting to reconcile German and French culture—"the whole universe was seen and judged by the thought of Bayreuth."[3]

A further blow to the cause of *ars gallica* was dealt by Charles Lamoureux, a violinist-conductor who for eleven years beginning in October 1881 presented his Concerts Lamoureux in Paris. Although he did present a wide variety of music, including that of young French composers, his overriding passion was Wagner (he was a charter member of the "Petit Bayreuth" group), and more so than any other individual Lamoureux succeeded in converting the Parisian public to the Wagnerian cause. The literati, however, needed no persuading. The fanaticism with which the Parisian intelligentsia worshipped Wagner is evident from Frederick Brown's numinous description of a Lamoureux concert:

Charles Lamoureux conducted Wagner's operas every Sunday during the summer in the Cirque d'été, like a priest conducting mass. When he mounted the podium, his audience turned its eyes inward and observed a sacerdotal trance till the last note sounded. Even Mallarmé, and for that matter all the symbolists, attended these dominical rites.[4]

Although Wagner's influence on French music was felt well into the first decades of the twentieth century, by 1890, the year of César Franck's death, there were signs of a revolt, a movement away from the ubiquitous Wagnerian vogue. Two organizations were founded in the 1890s with the express purpose of studying and performing the masterpieces of the past. In 1892 Charles Bordes, a pupil of Franck and organist of the church of Saint-Gervais in Paris, created the Chanteurs de Saint-Gervais for the performance of old polyphonic music and Gregorian chant. In addition to editing and publishing old church music, Bordes pioneered in the investigation and publication of French folk music, some of which he used as a basis for his own compositions. In 1894 Bordes, along with Vincent d'Indy and the organist Alexandre Guilmant, founded the Schola Cantorum with the intention of reviving interest in the music of the past, perpetuating the teaching of Franck, and encouraging contemporary composition. In January 1895 the *Tribune de Saint-Gervais,* the monthly bulletin of the Schola Cantorum, began publication, and by 1908, the year in which Satie was graduated from the institution, the Schola had 320 pupils and was a strong rival of the Conservatoire as a training ground for composers. In spite of all this native activity, it would take an invasion of Russian dancers and another Franco-German war to destroy the last vestiges of Wagnerism in France.

Satie: The Formative Years

HONFLEUR, PARIS, AND THE CONSERVATOIRE

Erik Satie's importance to the evolution of the Gallic muse in the fin de siècle is due primarily to the fact that he never succumbed to the widespread Wagnerian idolatry of the time. He was known in the 1890s only to a small band of connoisseurs, which included Debussy and the young Ravel, but in his strange and eccentric way he sowed the seeds of the modern spirit, seeds that lay largely dormant until the sudden climatic changes of 1914–18. Probably more has been written about Erik Satie than about any other composer of comparable stature. Although he was decidedly removed from the mainstream, his bizarre personality and innovative musical experiments have left their stamp indelibly on the arts of this century. One searches almost in vain for Satie's musical ancestors. Like his great contemporary Debussy he was drawn more readily to painters and poets than to other musicians, and it seems likely that his personality was shaped in large part by the motley bohemian contacts of his formative years in Montmartre, then in its heyday as the vibrant center of Parisian artistic life.

Eric Alfred Leslie Satie was born of a Scottish mother, née Jane Leslie Anton, and a French father, Jules Alfred Satie, at nine o'clock on the morning of 17 May 1866 in the Normandy coastal town of Honfleur. Although he set foot on the soil of his maternal island only once, and then as a small child of one year accompanying his parents on a summer holiday trip to Brighton, Satie seems to have maintained a mysterious spiritual tie to the British Isles throughout his life. He took great delight—to the eternal consternation of his translators—in lacing his correspondence (as well as his conversation) not only with sly puns but with strangely improbable expressions in English, which suggests at least a passing acquaintance with the language. Even his adoption of "Erik" in preference to "Eric" may have been a whimsical concession to his northern ancestry.[5] As a final curious observation it might be noted that Satie's parents were married in London, on 19 July 1865 at St. Mary's Church,

Barnes, Surrey, and that they are known to have honeymooned in Scotland, under whose gray skies Erik was, in all probability, conceived, sometime in the early weeks of August 1865. However tenuous Satie's connections with Britain, and Scotland in particular, it seems that a number of the composer's friends had a keen awareness of his inscrutable northern origins. George Auriol, for example, a crony from the Montmartre days, reported that "Erik came to us from the north in a leather bark manned by a crew of trolls."[6] If Scotland remained a kind of spiritual home to Satie, it was Honfleur that nurtured him through the impressionable years of his early childhood and young adolescence.

The ancient fishing port of Honfleur, rising gently on the west bank of the Seine estuary in the northeast corner of Calvados, has changed very little since Satie wandered its narrow streets over a century ago. The lovely old town—immortalized in the Impressionist canvases of Corot, Dufy, Monet, and many other less celebrated artists—is still dominated by the picturesque inner harbor, the Vieux Bassin, a colorful jumble of fishing boats and pleasure craft surrounded by tall, narrow, mostly slate-colored houses. Rising over the gray rooftops to the west is the slender spire of the church of Sainte-Catherine, a remarkable late–fifteenth-century edifice constructed almost entirely of wood, which miraculously has survived the ravages of time. A few blocks to the north of the church the rue Haute, one of the longest and most charming streets of the old maritime quarter of the town, departs from the Place Hamelin and runs westward parallel to the seafront. Here, at no. 90, stands the Satie birthplace, an ancient half-timbered structure that faintly recalls a time when the rue Haute housed Honfleur's wealthy merchants and civic leaders.

After the Franco-Prussian War the Satie family settled in Paris, but upon the tragic death of his mother in her twenty-ninth year in 1872, six-year-old Erik, together with his younger brother Conrad (born 1869), was sent back to Honfleur to live with his paternal grandparents, Jules and Eulalie Satie; their sister Olga (born 1867) remained in Paris with her father. In that same year Satie entered boarding school at the Collège d'Honfleur, where he proved to be an undistinguished student (except for notable successes in history and Latin). Two years later, in the spring of 1874, Satie's grandfather, well known in Honfleur as a ship-broker, municipal councillor, and captain of the fire brigade, introduced his grandson to the organist of the church of Saint-Léonard, one Vinot, a graduate of the celebrated École Niedermeyer in Paris.

The Swiss-born Niedermeyer had settled in Paris in 1823 after a peripatetic career in Austria, Italy, and Switzerland. Failing as a composer of opera, he found his true vocation in the study, performance, and composition of church music. He founded a short-lived journal of church music, published a much-criticized method of accompanying plainchant, and composed a voluminous body of sacred music, much of which is still in use in French churches. Although he could claim the great Gabriel Fauré among his pupils, Niedermeyer was also responsible for nurturing the minor talents of André Messager and Edmond Audran, purveyors of fluffy operettas that enchanted an entire generation of vaudeville audiences in the 1880s and 1890s.

The École Niedermeyer specialized in placing its graduates in church positions in the provinces, and in 1873 a jury headed by Charles Gounod awarded the post of organist and choirmaster at Honfleur's Saint-Léonard to Vinot, who headed a field of twenty candidates. The church of Saint-Léonard has had a violent history. Situated on the near-east side of town, Saint-Léonard was destroyed during the Hundred Years' War, rebuilt at the end of the fifteenth and beginning of the sixteenth centuries, partly burned in 1562, and mutilated in 1594 during a period of religious strife. From that time the main bay, the nave, and the facade survive. The remainder of the structure dates from the early seventeenth century, with the exception of the squat octagonal belfry, which was added in 1760. Here in the gloomy confines of Saint-Léonard and around the corner from the church in Vinot's studio at no. 32, rue Bourdet, the young Satie was initiated into the beauties of old church music, in particular, Gregorian chant. Thus we see the first signs of a preoccupation with the medieval world in general and medieval music in particular. The diatonic modal lines of medieval monody, the serenity and haunting simplicity of plainchant, are never far beneath the surface of Satie's music, most obviously the overtly neomedieval works of his so-called Rosicrucian phase of the early 1890s, but no less the postwar *Socrate* and even certain pages of the late piano works and the ballets.

In July 1878 Vinot relinquished his post at Saint-Léonard for a similar position at Lyon. That same summer Satie's grandmother died, and it was decided that the boy should rejoin his father, Alfred, in Paris at no. 2, rue de Constantinople. Sometime during the following year Satie acquired a stepmother by the name of Eugénie Barnetche, while his newlywed father proceeded to establish himself as a music publisher in the boulevard Magenta. In the autumn of that year, on 4 November 1879, the thirteen-year-old Erik, along with thirty-seven other candidates, sat for the piano examination at the Paris Conservatoire. His performance of a Dussek concerto movement did not qualify him for a place in the main piano classes, but on 8 November he was accepted into the preparatory class of Émile Descombes. For the next seven years he sat most of the biannual piano examinations—with generally indifferent success. The Conservatoire records for that period (1879–86) provide a series of fascinating glimpses of Satie's progress. At his first examination in January 1880 he played the F-sharp Minor Piano Concerto, op. 69, of Ferdinand Hiller for a jury that included his teacher, Descombes, and Ambroise Thomas, the director of the Conservatoire. Descombes's description of his pupil at that time as "gifted but indolent" would be a recurring refrain throughout Satie's unhappy studentship. The following June he appeared again before the committee, this time with Henri Herz's Piano Concerto no. 5 in F Minor, op. 180, and although Descombes noted a certain grace and beauty of tone in his young pupil's playing, he underlined (quite literally) the fact that Satie was the only student in the class who did not work hard enough. His next recital, in January of the following year, featured the C Major Piano Concerto, op. 87, of Ignaz Moscheles, and temporarily raised Descombes's hopes, for he noted some improvement in Erik's work habits and once again made special reference to his lovely keyboard touch. But the other examiners—Thomas, Sauzay, Duvernoy, Diémer, Fissot—were not impressed: "passable," "mediocre," "feeble," was all they could muster for the occasion. By June, after hearing Satie's performance of the first movement of Mendelssohn's D Minor Piano Concerto, op. 40, the exasperated Descombes reported that Satie was quite simply the laziest student in the Conservatoire; but he softened the blow by referring once again to the lovely sound his delinquent student managed to coax from the piano, concluding that he had considerable talent, which, however, only hard work would properly develop.

Satie's final year in Descombes's class showed some small improvement. His performance in January 1882 of one of Mendelssohn's *Characteristic Pieces* brought him a modicum of praise from his sorely tried teacher: "If he continues to work, he will surely arrive!" Descombes exulted. But the other examiners remained singularly unmoved. For his last examination on 15 June 1882 Satie played the finale of Beethoven's A-flat Major Piano Sonata, op. 26. The general response once again was, at best, lukewarm. Thus, having consistently failed to impress his examiners, Satie became a victim of the Conservatoire's Article 60, which stated that a pupil was to be dismissed if, after three years, he was not recommended for the institution's annual piano competition, which usually took place in July.

Satie's activities for the next eighteen months remain unclear. His Conservatoire career was not yet at an end, however, despite his repeated failure to gain admittance to the main piano classes, for his name reappears in the Conservatoire register for 4 December 1883, the date of his acceptance as an auditor into the harmony class of Antoine Taudou. Taudou, a Prix de Rome winner in 1869, had just that year joined the Conservatoire staff, and although he is entirely forgotten today as a composer, his distinguished contemporary Gabriel Fauré considered him to be the finest teacher of harmony at the Conservatoire during that period. It would appear that Satie remained in Taudou's class until the end of the academic term the following June. We can speculate that Taudou's instruction awakened a new interest in the young musician, for upon his return to Honfleur for the holidays, Satie sketched out a four-line *Allegro* for piano (dated Honfleur, 9 September 1884), his first groping attempt at composition. We can speculate further that he spent a goodly portion of the following year assiduously practicing the piano in yet another attempt to bring his performance skills in line with the Conservatoire standard for regular admission. Once again, on Friday, 6 November 1885, Satie, now aged nineteen and a half, appeared for the piano examination, having prepared a Chopin *Ballade.* This time he passed with a simple majority of three of the five votes cast in his favor and accordingly took his place in the intermediate piano class of his stepmother's former teacher, Georges Mathias. A professor of piano at the Conservatoire from 1862 to 1893, Mathias had been a piano pupil of Kalkbrenner and Chopin, and a composition student of Jacques Halévy. Like his colleague Taudou, he is completely forgotten today as a composer—despite a rather large body of compositions in most of the prevailing academic forms of the period—but he did distinguish himself as a teacher. Among Satie's fellow pupils in Mathias's piano classes were Paul Dukas, universally known as the composer of *The Sorcerer's Apprentice,* and the conductor Camille Chevillard, who succeeded his father-in-law Charles Lamoureux as director of the famous Concerts Lamoureux.

It seems that Mathias was able to inspire his pupil in a way that Émile Descombes could not, for whereas Satie's absenteeism in the preparatory piano classes in 1881 was considerably above the class average— seven absences in December alone—his record of attendance with Mathias was quite respectable from November 1885 through the end of 1886. Mathias, however, does not seem to have shared Descombes's charitable disposition. His response to Satie's performance of Mendelssohn's *Rondo Capriccioso,* op. 14, was flatly negative—"insignificant and laborious," an opinion generally shared by all members of the jury. Six months later, in the June examination, Satie played a Mendelssohn Prelude in D Major (probably the last of the *Three Preludes,* op. 104) with equally mediocre results. Most critical of all was his teacher Mathias: "Worthless," he reported. "Three months just to learn the piece. Cannot sight-read properly." The other members of the committee—which still included Ambroise Thomas—while not quite so harsh, nevertheless recorded similar opinions. Many years later Satie related, laconically, that Taudou insisted he should devote his time to the piano, while Mathias, with equal insistence, told him that his real talent lay in composing. It is not surprising that Satie left the Paris Conservatoire in early November of 1886 with unpleasant memories that would haunt him the remainder of his life.

Although the Conservatoire records do not confirm it, there is circumstantial evidence that Satie may have studied solfège (perhaps privately) with the distinguished theorist and musicologist Albert Lavignac, perhaps best remembered for his famous *Encyclopedia of Music,* which he founded and edited from 1913 until his death three years later. Other claims that Satie may have attended, in the early 1890s, some of the composition seminars of Ernest Guiraud—the American-born composer who earned a fleeting glimpse of immortality for his musical settings of the spoken recitatives from Bizet's *Carmen*—cannot positively be substantiated, and it is likely that his Conservatoire training came to an abrupt halt in the autumn of 1886 when he left Paris to begin a year's voluntary military service to avoid the risk of five years of compulsory service.

Although Satie's extended period of study at the Conservatoire ended in failure, one fact clearly emerges that tends to modify the accepted view of him as an ill-trained bungling amateur. If in his fourteenth and fifteenth years Satie was playing—even badly—concerto movements from the virtuoso repertoire of Hiller, Herz, Moscheles, and Mendelssohn, and if, a few years later, he could perform a Chopin *Ballade* sufficiently well to be admitted into Mathias's intermediate class, we must recognize that he possessed a technical ability of considerable scope. Moreover, flashes of praiseworthy comment and encouragement do occasionally leap from the pages of the Conservatoire record, rendering less harsh the recurring lament over his chronic indolence. Satie would later recall the Conservatoire as a "vast, uncomfortable, and rather ugly building; a sort of penitentiary with no beauty on the inside—nor on the outside, for that matter."[7] As if seeking revenge on his former teachers and judges, upon the death in 1896 of the Conservatoire's venerable director Ambroise Thomas, Satie, at that time a complete nonentity eking out a living in Montmartre night spots, boldly and irreverently applied for election to Thomas's vacant seat in the Académie des Beaux-Arts. Years later, in February 1912, he contributed a sarcastic reminiscence of Thomas to the short-lived little review *L'Oeil de veau,* a conscious echo, perhaps, of Chabrier's famous witticism acknowledging three kinds of music: "the good, the bad, and that of Ambroise Thomas." And as if that were not enough, injury was added to insult in 1920 when fragments of Thomas's once celebrated opera *Mignon* figured prominently in Satie's first experiment with "furniture music," or Muzak as we might call it today—a decidedly unflattering gesture. Finally, in the summer 1922 issue of *Les Feuilles libres* Satie ridiculed a passage in Lavignac's book *Music and Musicians* as part of an amusing and occasionally vitriolic attack on the most coveted academic prize in French musical life, the Prix de Rome, concluding his diatribe with a broad swipe at the Paris Conservatoire that unequivocally sums up his dim view of officialdom:

> People in general seem convinced that only the Official Establishment in the rue de Madrid can inseminate musical knowledge.
> Good for them; but I still ask myself—with hands clasped—why we musicians are obliged to receive a State education when painters and writers are free to study as and where they want.
> I have always said that there is no such thing as Artistic Truth—no single Truth, I mean. The one imposed by Ministers, a Senate, a Chamber and an Institute revolts me and outrages me—even though basically I feel indifferent about it.
> With one voice, I cry: Long live Amateurs![8]

In the mid-1880s, while still living with his father and stepmother, Satie began to make certain literary discoveries that would reinforce his already noticeable nonconformist tendencies. He became a voracious reader, and while still in his early twenties he encountered a curious mixture of literary personalities: among them, Alexandre Dumas *père,* prolific master of romantic melodrama; Eugène Vachette (pseud. Chavette), writer of novels and vaudevilles that, in their egregious buffoonery, suggest a kinship with the gentle absurdity of Satie's literary fantasies; Joseph Méry, satirical writer of marked macaronic tendencies whose works prefigure Dada by half a century; the German-born aphorist and satirist Alphonse Karr; and, above all, the Danish master of the fairy tale,

Hans Christian Andersen. The homely Dane, son of a poor shoemaker and a washerwoman, who—like a character out of one of his own tales—came to be welcomed into the aristocratic drawing rooms of Europe, was to remain one of Satie's favorite authors to the end of his life. Like Satie, Andersen was a master of irony and an artist who possessed the rare gift of being able to enter into the mind of the child with such conviction and lack of sentimentality as to appeal to the child in all of us. Referring to Satie's love for Andersen and to his later discovery of Flaubert, Roger Shattuck notes the "unusual combination of tastes which suggests that he discerned in both writers their veiled yet deep-seated religious preoccupation. It is what makes Flaubert at his most earnest often read like an author of fairy tales, and Andersen like an author of stories not at all for children but for unbelieving adults."[9]

Satie undoubtedly saw much to admire in the bohemian life-styles of many of these literary figures, and quite consciously he may have modeled something of his own unconventional behavior on the eccentric careers of such men as Méry, Vachette, and Karr. Karr's free-spirited existence, for example, suggests such striking parallels with Satie's career that it is tempting to speculate that the composer had read the account of Karr's life hidden away in the massive *Mémoires* of Dumas *père*. Karr, who eked out a living as a journalist and as an assistant master at the Collège Bourbon in Paris, for a time lived in a meagerly furnished hut in a little wooded area on the Butte Montmartre at a time when it was largely an undeveloped rural district on the outskirts of the city. Here he wrote his first novel. Later in his career he lived in a sixth-floor flat in the rue Vivienne, where he resided until his retirement, first to the south of France and later to a Normandy fishing village. Joanna Richardson has provided a fascinating portrait of Karr that could very nearly be a vignette of Satie when he entered his "Velvet Gentleman" stage in the poor working-class suburb of Arcueil:

In the winter he used to dress exclusively in black velvet; in the summer, he dressed exclusively in nankeen. He cultivated a moustache and a goatee—or mazarine beard—and he had his hair cut short like velvet pile. This created a sensation, since the current fashion was to wear long flowing locks over the shoulders. . . . He hung his attic bedroom [in the rue Vivienne] with black, and had violet-coloured glass let into the windows; and there he lived, without tables or chairs, wearing a Turkish robe and a Greek cap of Morocco leather embroidered in gold. It was said that he used to sleep fully clothed on his divan (a legend which raised doubts of his cleanliness). On the walls he hung pipes, foils and skulls: the regulation Bohemian bric-à-brac. He hired a mulatto servant whom he dressed in scarlet from top to toe. The mulatto carefully addressed him as Messié instead of Monsieur (no doubt with some blasphemous connotation), and exercised his huge Newfoundland dog.[10]

In a very short time Satie would cease to live the bohemian life vicariously through the pages of strange plays and novels; he would himself soon become part of the legend that is fin de siècle Montmartre.

THE FAMILY MUSIC BUSINESS

Since he did not derive his musical style from Wagner via Franck as did the vast majority of his contemporaries, nor from the tradition of French lyric opera, the sources of Satie's style must be sought elsewhere. The only major musicians he is known to have admired in the 1880s were Bach, Chopin, Schumann, and Chabrier; and, characteristically, he preferred the operettas of André Messager to all of grand opera.

Although Satie had an aversion to his stepmother from the beginning, it seems probable that her music, as well as that of her husband, had some influence on the development of his musical tastes. Eugénie Barnetche was an accomplished pianist who had been a pupil of Georges Mathias and of Alexandre Guilmant, the famous organist of La Trinité, many of whose compositions for his instrument have won a permanent place in the repertoire. But more to the point, Madame Satie-Barnetche was a composer of pallid salon pieces à la Cécile Chaminade at her least adventurous. Her works, all for piano solo, appeared between 1882 and 1897, and although Alfred Satie was her first publisher, she appears to have had a variety of publishers, including Heugel, Gérard, Choudens, Schott, and even Beer & Schirmer in New York, which suggests a considerable demand at the time for her particular brand of parlor entertainment. Since Satie did not permanently vacate the home of his parents until late in 1887, it seems highly probable that he would have heard a great deal of the music of his father and stepmother in the family circle. Eugénie Satie-Barnetche specialized in the kind of popular genre pieces to be found in great quantity in every middle-class music room at the end of the last century. In addition to the inevitable *valses de salon,* among her ten extant works in the Bibliothèque Nationale are such charming trifles as *Evening Breezes* (1883), billed as a nocturne; *Première mazurka* and *Boléro,* both from 1884; *Lamentation,* a "song without words" also from 1884; and, the pièce de resistance, a marvelously (but no doubt unintentionally) silly *Witches' Round* (1882), a sterling example of the campy treasures frequently encountered on Victorian piano racks.

If one accepts the doubtful authenticity of the opus numbers assigned to Barnetche's pieces (they range from op. 66 to op. 96) as well as the accuracy of the advertisements that appear on the back covers of two of the scores, Eugénie Satie-Barnetche was a fairly prolific composer. It is possible, even probable, that the advertised works (which seem to have disappeared without trace) existed only in the mind of Alfred Satie as he sought to promote his wife's music. If, on the other hand, the existence of these works is to be believed, the appearance among them of two sonatas—one for two pianos—and an *Andante* for two pianos (or string quartet) suggests that Madame Satie-Barnetche occasionally ventured onto rather ambitious ground in her compositional activity. At least two of her works—*Scherzo* (1883) and the salon waltz *Las Estrellas* (1887)—are known to have been reprinted as late as 1897 by the firm of E. Baudoux and Sons of the boulevard Haussmann. A final curious note: on the back cover of the *Scherzo*—now retitled *Minuetto*—is an advertisement for Erik Satie's *Le Fils des étoiles* (1891), but no other piece of his stepmother's appears among the host of nondescript names, and quietly she passes beyond the fringes of music history into oblivion.

Satie's father is an equally shadowy figure as a composer. Very little is known of his career. After obtaining his baccalaureate from the Collège de Lisieux, not far from Honfleur—where one of his classmates was the brilliant historian and fellow *honfleurais* Albert Sorel—he indulged his interest in foreign languages by traveling abroad, spending a year in Lübeck, to the northeast of Hamburg, and a year in Milan. Upon his return to France he enrolled in courses at the Sorbonne and at the Collège de France and resumed his association with his former classmate, Sorel, who was becoming well known in academic and diplomatic circles and who, in 1893, would be elected to Hippolyte Taine's vacant seat in the Académie Française. One concludes, therefore, that Alfred Satie was a man of not inconsiderable culture. Evidence of formal musical training, however, is lacking, and judging from the quality of his music, it would appear that he was largely self-taught in composition.

Whereas Madame Satie-Barnetche composed exclusively for the piano, Alfred's modest talent leaned toward the music-hall song. Although he left a handful of piano solos—including a "polka-mazurka" called *Souvenirs de Honfleur* (1883); a waltz, *Olga* (1888), dedicated to his daughter; and another "polka-mazurka" called *Connubial Bliss* (1890), whose English title suggests a rather belated homage to his late wife even though the song is dedicated to another lady—his real forte was the chanson. Alfred's extant songs were published between 1884 and 1888 under his own imprint at no. 26, boulevard Magenta. The songs are all in the direct tradition of the French music hall, which was entering into its golden age in the closing decades of the century. The titles alone sufficiently define the genre: *Le Dévot buveur* (The Pious Drinker), *C'est aussi rare qu'un merle blanc* (It's as Rare as a White Blackbird), *Y a vraiment d'quoi vous suffoquer* (It's Enough to Make You Choke), and so on. The songs invariably copy the same simple thirty-two-bar strophic design that has served the popular song to this day, with topical texts usually couched in working-class slang or the vernacular of the streets. The pattern would be repeated tens of thousands of times in the bistros and music halls of fin de siècle Paris.

In addition to the works housed in the Bibliothèque Nationale, Alfred Satie is also represented once in *Le Mélomane,* a musical journal published from December 1885 to January 1889 under the editorship of Henri Garrigue. This magazine, which offered prizes for the best compositions submitted, contains a variety of salon pieces by a number of obscure and forgotten composers. The only near-notable musician represented in *Le Mélomane* is Henri Duvernoy, who won the majority of the prizes, and who, it might be recalled, was a member of Erik's piano jury at the Conservatoire in the early 1880s. If there had been a prize for the most arcane title of the series, it is tempting to think that it might have gone to Alfred Satie, for in the issue no. 13 for Saturday, 30 June 1888, Alfred appears as the creator of a *Picking-Clause Polka.* This time Alfred's tentative knowledge of idiomatic English seems to have failed him.

A significant aspect of the Satie style is the popular *café-concert* idiom that he would cultivate assiduously off and on for the remainder of his career. Satie's first known effort at composition, the tiny *Allegro* of 1884, reveals the slender musical resources of the salon composer, and his *Valse-ballet* and *Fantaisie-valse* of the following year, as well as the *valses chantées* written around the turn of the century for the music-hall singers Paulette Darty and Vincent Hyspa, are unquestionably cut from the same cloth as the humorous and sentimental songs of his father and the shallow salon pieces of his stepmother. And although he liked to refer to his Montmartre waltz-songs as *rudes saloperies* (uncouth rubbish), "deep in his heart," Pierre-Daniel Templier quite rightly suggests, "he probably loved them."[11] The popular origin of Satie's art would leave its mark on his entire output, and echoes of the cabaret and the music hall resound in such works as *Trois Morceaux en forme de poire, Jack in the Box, Geneviève de Brabant, La Belle excentrique,* and the late ballets *Parade, Mercure,* and *Relâche.* It was precisely this aspect of Satie's style—the cabaret sprightliness and the elegant simplicity—that was championed by Jean Cocteau and praised by *Les Six* after World War I.

It should be noted, too, that Satie's strange and humorous titles and subtitles bear a direct kinship to those common to the cabaret and music hall. Titles such as *Avant-dernières pensées* and *Valses distinguées du précieux dégoûté* lose a great deal of their exclusivity when confronted with the likes of *C'est aussi rare qu'un merle blanc* and *Picking-Clause Polka;* moreover, Satie's penchant for unusual subtitles—"ballet instantanéiste," "poses plastiques"—would appear to be offshoots of the inevitable "caprice caractéristique" or "chanson bachique" of the salon and the music hall.

An essential part of Satie's musical style derives from the ephemeral popular arts that richly embellished his bohemian youth in Montmartre. Had he been content, however, to follow in the footsteps of his father and stepmother and countless other minor tunesmiths of the day, he would have failed to earn a place in the chronicle of contemporary music. A significant aspect of Satie's originality derives from the important fact that he managed to absorb the sound of the Parisian music hall and make it an essential component of his own peculiar musical grammar. As with Connecticut's iconoclastic Yankee, Charles Ives, it is the unique coalescence of traditionally antagonistic musical idioms that opens a path to the future and raises both composers far above the commonplace into the realm of genius. It would seem, too, that Satie's roots in the popular idioms of his day provided him with additional immunization against the pandemic Wagnerian infection then sweeping France and much of Europe.

SATIE AND CHABRIER

Emmanuel Chabrier and Erik Satie were among the most important pre-Debussy contributors to a renewed *ars gallica* and Chabrier has the distinction of being the only musician of stature whose influence can be felt in the works of Satie. Chabrier emerges as a transitional figure in post-1870 French music who, even though he expended a great deal of his creative energy trying to become a kind of French Wagner, produced in his smaller works an antidote to Wagnerism and Wagnerian solemnity. A cursory examination of Chabrier's oeuvre reveals the opposing tendencies prevalent in serious French music of the time: strongly colored Wagnerian harmonic progressions and orchestral timbres contrasted with Latin vitality, wit, and joie de vivre. It is the latter side of Chabrier's musical personality, of course, that provides the link to Satie. A cameo portrait of Chabrier by Constant Lambert might be of Satie, so perfectly do the two personalities blend into one inimitably Gallic figure: "He [Chabrier] was the first important composer since Mozart to show that seriousness is not the same as solemnity, that profundity is not dependent upon length, that wit is not always the same as buffoonery, and that frivolity and beauty are not necessarily enemies."[12] Here is something of the spirit of Jannequin and the French madrigalists, of Couperin and the *clavecinistes,* and of Bizet and the rich tradition of *opéra comique.*

Chabrier's three-act comic opera *Le Roi malgré lui* opened in Paris on 18 May 1887 at the Opéra Comique. Satie saw Chabrier's opera at this time and was so enthralled with it that, after one of the performances, he presented the composer's doorman with a manuscript copy of a work (probably the *Ogives* of 1886) inscribed in his peculiar calligraphic hand in red ink and Gothic script. Unfortunately Chabrier did not return the compliment; he made no reply. Although there is no record of a meeting between the two musicians, Satie may have met the older man in the late 1880s at the home of the composer Ernest Chausson. During most of that decade Chausson's elegant townhouse at no. 22, boulevard de Courcelles was the frequent meeting place of progressive artists of the time, and it has been recorded that both Satie and Chabrier figured among the invited guests. Even if they had met on one of these occasions, Chabrier, who withdrew from society in 1891 owing to serious ill health and who died three years later in September 1894, could hardly have been much aware of the struggling bohemian, although for his part Satie remained a devoted admirer of the creator of *España.*

There are at least two aspects of *Le Roi malgré lui* that must have delighted Satie: the advanced harmonic idiom of portions of the score, and its high-spirited good humor. After his heavily scored Nordic music drama *Gwendoline,* possibly the most Wagnerian of all French operas, which had premiered in Brussels the previous year, Chabrier's *Le Roi malgré lui,* with its lilting waltz and mazurka rhythms, came as a welcome return to the boisterous exuberance of the famous *España* of 1883. It is an interesting coincidence that 1887 was also the year of the first Paris performance of *Lohengrin,* for which Chabrier was engaged as choral director under Lamoureux. But although Wagner would remain one of Chabrier's idols, the Gallic side of the composer happily dominates *Le Roi malgré lui,* a convoluted tale of political and amorous intrigue revolving around the short reign of Henri de Valois, youngest son of Catherine de Medici, as the reluctant king of Poland before he became Henri III of France in 1574 upon the death of his elder brother Charles IX.

Le Roi malgré lui is a representative work that manages a successful fusion of seemingly disparate elements. In some respects it continues the line of sparkling operettas of the Offenbach variety that lit the stages of Second Empire Paris. But it goes significantly beyond the range of the Offenbach school in the richness of its harmonic language, the novelty of its orchestration, and the delicate refinement of its melodic invention. Its true ancestors are Weber, Berlioz, and Bizet, with a strong overlay of rich harmonic texture distilled from Wagner. Chabrier's opera was an influential work in its day, principally because of the composer's daring harmonic language. Maurice Ravel was fond of telling Francis Poulenc that "the première of *Le Roi malgré lui* changed the direction of harmony in France,"[13] and he generously acknowledged his own debt to Chabrier, whose musical inspiration finds an echo in nearly every page of his music. Ravel knew *Le Roi malgré lui* by heart, spoke ecstatically of the *Dix pièces pittoresques*—especially the fourth piece "Sous-bois"—and left his own affectionate homage to the composer in the form of the little 1913 piano piece *À la manière de Chabrier.*

Ravel also recognized a debt to Satie, whom he saw as a kind of intermediary between Chabrier and himself and Debussy. Chabrier's *Le Roi malgré lui* opens, not with the usual effervescent overture, but rather incongruously with a short passage of solemn music derived from the conspiracy scene in the second act, which itself is a parody of the "Blessing of the Swords" from act 4 of Meyerbeer's *Les Huguenots.* The short prelude contains in abundance daring sequences of unprepared and unresolved ninth chords that sound a new note in late-nineteenth-century French music:

Example 1. Chabrier: *Le Roi malgré lui* (1887), prelude, measures 15–19

In fact the score abounds in the kind of unorthodox harmonies and harmonic progressions—chords of the added sixth, sequences of seventh and ninth chords, unexpected modulations—that became primary features of the Impressionist style in music. Although he never embraced the Impressionist aesthetic, Satie's early works reveal, at a kind of embryonic stage of development, much of the harmonic vocabulary of

Impressionist music. Chains of unprepared seventh and ninth chords—later to become major stylistic features of the *Rose-Croix* music—are first used methodically in the three *Sarabandes* for piano, completed in September 1887, four months after the premiere of *Le Roi malgré lui.* Comparison of example 1 with excerpts from the *Sarabandes* (ex. 2) suggests an unmistakable musical connection between Chabrier and Satie.

Example 2. Satie: *Trois Sarabandes* (1887)

(a) *Première Sarabande,* measures 1–4

(b) *Deuxième Sarabande,* measures 17–22

(c) *Troisième Sarabande,* measures 67–70

In 1890 Chabrier published *Six mélodies* for voice and piano. Four of the songs—"Villanelle des petits canards," "Ballade des gros dindons," "Pastorale des cochons roses," and "Les Cigales"—the composer referred to as his "little barnyard suite."[14] In view of the direction Satie's art was to take, it would seem probable that he knew and relished the *Six mélodies,* appearing as they did only three years after the premier of *Le Roi malgré lui.* Chabrier's farmyard portraits, sketched with wit, cool irony, and a mocking realism, are clearly the forerunners of such zoolog-ical vignettes as Ravel's *Histoires naturelles* of 1906; and in their droll simplicity they prefigure the denuded style and the parody of much of Satie.

The second of the *Six mélodies,* the "Ballade des gros dindons" ("Ballad of the Big Turkeys"), composed to a text by the distinguished creator of Cyrano de Bergerac, Edmond Rostand, has perhaps the greatest kinship to the Satie manner. The sparse, rocking accompanimental figure and the singsong simplicity of the melodic line (ex. 3) find echoes in "Sur une lanterne" from Satie's *Descriptions automatiques* (1913) and in the "Au-bade" from his *Avant-dernières pensées* of 1915 (ex. 4).

Example 3. Chabrier: *Six mélodies* (1890), no. 2, "Ballade des gros dindons," measures 1–12

Example 4. Satie

(a) *Descriptions automatiques* (1913), no. 2, "Sur une lanterne," lines 2 and 3

(b) *Avant-dernières pensées* (1915), no. 2, "Aubade," lines 1 and 2

Moreover, Chabrier's inexplicable quotation of a fragment of the famous Serenade from Mozart's *Don Giovanni* as an instrumental refrain between verses of the song is in much the same vein as Satie's own affectionate parody of Chabrier in his "Españaña" from *Croquis et agaceries d'un gros bonhomme en bois* of 1913. Satie must have delighted, too, in the wonderfully sardonic texts of the "barnyard songs." Chabrier's biographer, Rollo Myers, has caught to perfection the implicit anthropomorphism of the verses and Chabrier's musical treatment of them:

. . . Chabrier looks at his ducks and pigs and turkeys with a humorous twinkle in his eye, and sees them as individuals—the waddling ducks like rather simple

country bumpkins, the naïve little rosy pigs with their corkscrew tails and beady
eyes reminding one of a *galatin* [fop], and the pompous turkeys resembling nothing so much as a bevy of self-important aldermen or rather shady business men
in conference.[15]

A final irony remains to be explored briefly. It is somewhat paradoxical
that a man who adored Wagner all his life, who came away from performances of his works in tears, and who expended prodigious amounts of
energy attempting to compose "Wagnerian" operas, should have written
a quadrille for piano duet on themes from *Tristan and Isolde.* Chabrier's
Souvenirs de Munich, composed in 1885–86 at the height of the Wagner
craze and dedicated to Antoine Lascoux, the founding member of the
"Petit Bayreuth," is made up of the five traditional figures of the quadrille,
each of them based on themes from Wagner's great epic of love and
death. Quadrilles were generally based on popular tunes of the day, quite
often famous operatic arias, so that Chabrier's use of *Tristan* for his purpose, though an unorthodox choice, was in keeping with the tradition. It
is possible that the quadrille retained sufficient popularity in the 1880s
for Chabrier to feel no disrespect in making use of Wagner's opera in
such a manner. Or perhaps it was a harmless attempt to purge himself
of the Wagnerian fever that had so long infected him. Whatever the explanation, the composer must have realized that the result would strike
at least the more pious Wagnerians as a grotesque joke in the worst
possible taste. Actually, Chabrier's piano duet does have an important
forerunner, the *Souvenirs de Bayreuth,* a quadrille composed about 1880
by Gabriel Fauré in collaboration with André Messager, and it is almost
certain that Chabrier knew of the work since he was a frequent visitor in
the late 1880s to the home of Chausson, where Fauré and Messager
used to play their duet (and possibly Chabrier's) for a circle of young
Parisian Wagnerites.

Émile Vuillermoz, one of the more progressive critics of his time and
a champion of both Fauré and Debussy, has claimed in his account of the
genesis of *Souvenirs de Bayreuth* that Fauré and his friends intended no
harm to their idol, but found a necessary emotional release in such apparently irreverent acts. "There was," he wrote, "no sarcasm, and no
trace of impiety in this naive outburst of good humor which relieved the
emotional pressures of these young artists. It was for them a way of
having fun and throwing their hats into the air, in front of the statue of
their god."[16] Vuillermoz's explanation has the slightly desperate air of an
apologia. If, as he states, this band of French Wagnerites intended no

disrespect to the German master, if sarcasm were indeed entirely absent from their work, it is difficult to explain why the *Souvenirs de Bayreuth,* Fauré's only excursion into musical parody, was withheld from publication, as was Chabrier's *Souvenirs de Munich,* which did not appear in print until 1911, seventeen years after the composer's death.

Although Wagner himself established the precedent for placing his operatic themes in trivial contexts—his *Albumblatt,* "Ankunft bei den schwarzen Schwänen" (1861), for example, is based on a motive from Elisabeth's "Dich, teure Halle" from *Tannhäuser*—the absolute incompatibility of mood between Wagner's yearning chromatic lines and the sprightly, bouncing rhythms of Chabrier's *Souvenirs de Munich* results in a caricature of *Tristan* par excellence. In this sense both the Chabrier and Fauré quadrilles must be considered significant precursors of the Satie aesthetic. It is not known for certain whether Satie heard Chabrier's piece when it first made the rounds, but he most surely would have been aware of it after its publication in 1911. In any event, Chabrier's bumptious fantasy would doubtless have delighted the composer who could write with such delicious sarcasm: "Anyone who does not love Wagner does not love France . . . Didn't you know Wagner was French?—from Leipsick [Picardy]. . . . But of course. . . . How could you forget? . . . So soon? . . . You? . . . a patriot? . . . "[17]

Like Satie, Chabrier was more or less self-taught in composition and as a consequence his musical language occasionally reveals the coarseness of the amateur. It is, however, the inspired clumsiness of a Mussorgsky, of an artist who proceeds more by instinct than by reason. Indeed, Chabrier freely—even proudly—admitted that he was virtually self-taught and belonged to no school, that he possessed far more temperament than technique. A characteristic statement in an 1886 letter to his publisher Georges Costallat strikes a prophetic pose—in the breezy manner of a Cocteau / Satie aphorism—and reveals Chabrier as the true godfather of *Les Six* and *l'esprit nouveau*: "What can I do to dumbfound the gallery?" he writes. "There's your enemy. . . . Down with the *gniou-gniou!* Never the same shade! Variety, form, life above all, and *simplicity* if possible, and that's the hardest thing!"[18]

2

Monsieur le Pauvre

Satie's first known composition is an *Allegro* for piano; the autograph manuscript is dated Honfleur, 9 September 1884.[1] Although this slight first effort reveals the hand of the rank amateur, the consistent enrichment of the harmony through seventh chords and the chain of secondary sevenths in the fourth and fifth measures effecting a modulation to the dominant indicates a degree of harmonic sophistication in excess of that apparent in the naive salon products of his parents.

Example 1. Satie: *Allegro* (1884), measures 1–6

An unusual feature of this tiny piece is the asymmetrical phrasing (3 + 3 + 3),[2] which the composer would later exploit with some consistency. But the most telling feature of the sketch is revealed in measures 6 and 7. Here Satie makes an unsuccessful attempt to propel the music forward by providing new and contrasting material to balance the effect of the opening six-bar period. Significantly, the passage is scribbled out, and the inexperienced composer resigns himself to a lame repetition of the first phrase, which rounds off the little sketch back in the tonic G major. Here we see something of the composer's mind in action, a vain striving for a varied extension of the initial musical idea. Very soon in his career Satie would turn this deficiency to his own end, and we can speculate that his very inability to transform his material with traditional skill contributed to the frozen immobility and static repetitiousness of the *Rose-Croix* or Rosicrucian music of the early 1890s.

Satie's earliest published compositions, composed in 1885, appeared on 17 March and 28 July 1887 in musical supplements of a publication called *La Musique des Familles.* We must assume either that the young composer's whimsical sense of humor is already in evidence—for the first of the two piano miniatures in question is designated op. 62 (!)—or, more likely, that we are dealing with another example of the suspect marketing practices of Alfred Satie, who seems to have specialized in assigning improbably high opus numbers to his own publications.

The two salon waltzes, although not without a certain pallid charm, are almost indistinguishable from similar efforts of Alfred and Eugénie Satie and need not detain us long. The first piece, *Valse-ballet,* a standard ternary form with the central section in the dominant key, rarely ventures beyond the confines of the basic three-chord pattern typical of the genre at its simplest. Its diatonic melody unfolds over a simple chordal accompaniment in a series of predictable four-bar phrases. Again, as in the 1884 *Allegro,* Satie seems to have some difficulty providing variation and achieving a sense of smooth harmonic transition from one episode to another.

The second piece, *Fantaisie-valse,* is dedicated to J. P. Contamine de Latour, a poet of Spanish origin whom Satie met about 1886. The *Fantaisie-valse* is marginally more interesting than its companion piece despite its similarily restricted formal and harmonic framework. Near the end of the opening D-flat major section, for example, Satie adds a rather unexpected and agreeably sentimental touch by shifting momentarily into the parallel minor mode just before the cadential phrase rounds off the section back in the tonic major. Once again, however, the little piece is creaky at the joints. The transition into the central A-flat section is handled clumsily; rather than the more usual dominant preparation, a tonic D-flat pedal leads rather abruptly into the new key and the secondary melodic idea.

Though of little intrinsic musical interest, these products of Satie's nineteenth year clearly reveal his musical roots in the middle-class parlor music idioms of his time. Of considerably more interest than the music itself is the publicity blurb that introduces these youthful efforts. Another of Alfred's merchandising ploys no doubt, it dismisses the waltzes in a few lines as graceful and elegant works full of feeling, and then goes on to mention the *Trois mélodies* of 1886, making prophetic reference to the composer's "tendency to depart from the rigid laws of rhythmic symmetry." The first of the *Trois mélodies,* "Les Anges," reveals a decidedly four-square structure so that Satie's departure from "the rigid laws of rhythmic symmetry" undoubtedly refers to "Les Fleurs" and more particularly to "Sylvie," the third of the songs and the first of his works to dispense with time signatures and bar lines.

Five Songs

Satie's first collaborator was the dedicatee of the *Fantaisie-valse,* J. P. Contamine de Latour, the pseudonym of José–Maria Patricio Manuel Contamine. Little is known of this very minor poet and short-story writer beyond the fact that he was born in 1867 in Tarragona, near Barcelona, that he published his *Cinq nouvelles* in Paris in 1889 (the first of which, *Miriam,* is dedicated to Satie), and that he was given to a bizarre posturing, claiming among other things to be a descendant of Napoleon. Accordingly, Satie nicknamed his friend "Le Vieux Modeste" and began a series of strange and fanciful collaborations with him that would continue into the early years of the new century.

When Satie met Contamine de Latour, the poet was already under the sway of the mystical writer Joséphin Péladan, with whom Satie would become associated in the early 1890s. Contamine de Latour undoubtedly reinforced Satie's own budding inclination toward a naive religious mysticism; more directly he provided the young composer with the texts for his first five songs, published under the imprint of Alfred Satie.

At the time of Satie's death in 1925 a large poster, inscribed in red and black Gothic script, was found in his lodging at Arcueil. Designed by the composer for the promotion of his songs, it was written in the stilted, pseudomedieval French that he was to favor during his Rosicrucian phase:

In this Dwelling one will find the Very charming and Most gracious Songs of Messere Erik Satie, exalted Master of the Art of Music, player of the organs in the Saintly Chapel of Our Lord the King, with words by Messere I.-P. Contamine de Latour, writer of high fantasy, poet, Maker of stories, Tales, Chronicles and many other charming things.[3]

Three of these early songs—"Les Anges," "Les Fleurs," and "Sylvie"—
were published in 1887 as *Trois mélodies,* op. 20. The remaining two
songs were published separately as "Élégie," op. 19, and "Chanson," op.
52. The *Trois mélodies* and the "Élégie" were composed in 1886, the
"Chanson" the following year. Fortunately for the student of Satie, the
"Chanson" was the last of his works to be assigned an opus number,
spurious or otherwise.

Contamine de Latour's rather insipid and jejune verse deals with the
perennial themes of disillusioned young love and the transience of earthly
beauty. The five poems range in mood from gentle melancholy ("Élégie")
to banal sentimentality ("Sylvie" and "Chanson"). On a slightly higher
poetic plane are "Les Anges," whose overrefined images of "angels floating in the ether like lilies" and "lutes shimmering in divine harmony"
strike a fashionably decadent pose, revealing a debt to Baudelaire and
the Symbolists, and "Les Fleurs," which—again in true fin de siècle
style—equates the transitory beauty of blooming flowers with the fleeting happiness of love.

With the exception of the commonplace "Chanson" of 1887, the five
songs may be considered preliminary exercises in the static chordal style
that would typify the *Rose-Croix* works of 1891–95. They are constructed on essentially the same principle: a slow, steady progression of
triads, sevenths, ninths, and even eleventh chords supporting an arioso-
like vocal line. Strip away the melodic line and the remaining vertical
sonorities provide a glimpse of Satie's mystical Rosicrucian world, with
the difference that the songs still cling to a functional harmonic
framework.

Several characteristic traits are observable in these early songs, chief
of which are the composer's fondness for modal ambiguity and avoidance
of the tonic key. Three of the songs begin with functionally identical harmonic sequences:

Example 2. Satie: Contamine de Latour songs (1886)

(a) "Les Anges," measures 1–4

D: V   ii$_7$ V$_7$

(b) "Les Fleurs," measures 1–2

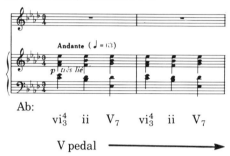

Ab:

$$vi_3^4 \quad ii \quad V_7 \quad vi_3^4 \quad ii \quad V_7$$

V pedal ⟶

(c) "Élégie," measures 1–4

Eb: $\quad vi \quad ii_7 \quad V_7 \quad vi \quad ii_7 \quad V_7$

What follows these harmonically pregnant opening gestures either avoids the expected tonic altogether ("Élégie") or postpones it, either to the end of each verse ("Les Anges") or to the end of the entire song ("Les Fleurs"). Thus we see a gradual dissipation of harmonic function, the three songs emerging as a kind of microcosm of Satie's harmonic evolution.

In "Les Fleurs" the composer comes very close to negating the sense of tonal center altogether, not however through the usual means of extended post-Wagnerian chromaticism, but, more prophetically, through a kind of protominimalist process. The song's twenty-six measures extend, or perhaps more accurately suspend, the implied tonic A-flat by means of a hypnotic repetition of a simple chordal pattern that functions exclusively as an extended dominant pedal, finding release only in the final tonic chord. Also of interest in this song are the modal inflections (especially the flatted seventh) and the subtle fluctuations of phrase lengths reinforced by a number of slight but telling metric shifts.

The "Élégie," a melancholy little piece that shows an awareness perhaps of Massenet, maintains the same suspension of home key as "Les Fleurs," but carries it a step further by avoiding the implied tonic altogether. Its opening measure (see ex. 2c) would appear to be a simple tonic-subdominant progression in C minor. The dominant seventh chord on B-flat in the next measure, however, clearly implies an E-flat key center. As in "Les Fleurs," a short pattern of continuous dominant-function harmony is reiterated (measures 5–8), effectively holding in abeyance the implied E-flat tonic. In place of the more traditional organic development and extension of material Satie provides contrast by sliding a variant of the opening phrase up a half-step into the unlikely region of F minor (measures 9–12), which key, however, is quickly negated by a return to the opening gesture (measures 14–15) in preparation for the next verse, where the entire procedure is repeated.

Example 3. Satie: "Élégie" (1886), measures 5–14

"Sylvie," a song about a girl of such exquisite beauty that even the angels are jealous, is dedicated to Satie's sister Olga. It has the distinction of being the first of his works to dispense with time signature and bar lines. The result is a degree of rhythmic flexibility and suppleness only hinted at in the previous songs. "Sylvie" is also the most harmonically advanced of the 1886 songs, and its great variety of altered chords, as well as its unorthodox cadences (the final cadential progression is V_9–vi_2^4–vi_7–I), contribute greatly to a weakening of functional tonality.

The last of the Contamine de Latour songs, "Chanson," is in most respects the least characteristic of the set. It does not attempt to go very far beyond the naive music-hall confections of his father and stepmother in its symmetrical four-bar phrases and simple diatonic harmony. To compound the problem, the lively allegretto tempo, the marchlike oompah accompaniment, and the expansive C major melodic line all seem to work against the poet's bittersweet lament on the fleetingness of youth and love, beauty and gaiety. Only the persistent use of unresolved dominant seventh chords in the piano accompaniment (ex. 4) tips the hand in favor of the son rather than the parent. And it is here, interestingly enough, that we find a strong prefiguration of the famous *Gymnopédies,* whose composition was less than a year off. Change the meter from duple to triple, cut the tempo in half, and smooth out the contours of the vocal line, and we desert the music hall for a Frenchman's vision of the dance in ancient Greece.

Example 4. Satie: "Chanson" (1887), measures 1–4

And so we can observe several salient characteristics of Satie's mature style in these little-known early works. Already we note the refusal (or inability) to develop and manipulate musical material along traditional lines, the flexible and often asymmetrical phrase structures, the rhythmic suppleness and occasional metrical ambiguity, the diminishing sense of functional harmony, the fondness for unresolved dissonances, and—as a legacy of the salon and the music hall—a kind of objective clarity and a great simplicity of texture.

The Gothic Influence

Partly through the influence of Contamine de Latour, Satie began, about 1886, to affect a pseudomystical posture. He spoke a great deal at this time of "his religion" and began to assume an air of such great humility that his companions nicknamed him *"Monsieur le Pauvre."* In conjunction with his pietistic behavior he immersed himself in a study of plainsong and Gothic art, spending hours of each day—no doubt to the detriment of his studies at the Conservatoire—meditating in the gloom of Notre-Dame Cathedral or devouring books on medieval subjects at the Bibliothèque Nationale.

An important discovery for Satie at this time was the architectural writing of Eugène-Emmanuel Viollet-le-Duc, the controversial Paris-born medievalist responsible for the preservation and restoration of many of France's most glorious ancient monuments—among them Notre-Dame de Paris, the Abbey of Saint-Denis, and the Cathedral of Amiens. Though much maligned even today by purists resentful of his nineteenth-century copies of medieval statuary, Viollet-le-Duc must be given credit for almost single-handedly reversing centuries of neglect and rescuing a good part of France's remarkable Gothic heritage from decay and potential oblivion. Few who gaze in wonder at the grace and beauty of Notre-Dame de Paris today are aware that the present slender spire was designed by Viollet-le-Duc less than a century and a half ago as a replacement for the original, which, at the end of the eighteenth century, had been declared structurally unsound and therefore demolished; or that the great architect effaced what he called the cathedral's "toothless grin" by restoring the Gallery of Kings on the main facade, a series of twenty-eight statues of ancient Judean monarchs unceremoniously pulled down by revolutionary mobs under the mistaken impression that they represented French royalty; nor is the modern tourist likely aware that he is being observed by nineteenth-century gargoyles from the workshops of Viollet-le-Duc, the originals having been removed in the sixteenth century, ostensibly because they were sagging dangerously, but more likely because they offended the neoclassical sensibility of the age.

It is interesting to note that a pupil of Viollet-le-Duc began restoration work on Sainte-Catherine, the Satie family parish church in Honfleur, about the time Erik left the town to take up residence with his father in

Paris. The refurbishing of the apse and the two chancels of Sainte-Catherine was carried out over a period of eight years beginning in 1879, and it is tempting to speculate that Satie would have made a point of checking the progress of the restorers on his occasional return visits to his birthplace in the early 1880s. In any event, we know that Viollet-le-Duc's important work helped nourish Satie's incipient medievalism. His fascination with the medieval world, sparked perhaps by his old teacher Vinot, would expand greatly over the next few years and manifest itself not only in some of the strangest music written up to that time but also in a series of whimsical drawings and sketches of ancient castles, old manor houses, suits of armor, fortified towns, and the like, that almost certainly owe something to Viollet-le-Duc's profusely illustrated books on the art and architecture of the Middle Ages.

The first musical manifestation of Satie's neomedieval obsession were the four *Ogives* of 1886, his first overtly "Gothic" work. The medieval flavor of the pieces is implicit in the title, with its reference to pointed Gothic arches. The first *Ogive* is dedicated to Contamine de Latour, the fourth to his brother Conrad. The second *Ogive* is inscribed to Charles Levadé, like Contamine de Latour a shadowy figure from Satie's youth. A pupil of Massenet at the Conservatoire and a Prix de Rome winner in 1899, Levadé was very close to the Satie family in the late 1880s, even to the extent of having some of his student efforts published by Alfred Satie in 1887. That Satie thought highly of him can be inferred from the fact that a number of early works were dedicated to him, including—besides the second *Ogive*—"Les Anges" from the *Trois mélodies* and the third *Gymnopédie*. As for his part, Levadé, who died as recently as 1948, published a sympathetic reminiscence of his old friend in which he claimed to have "corrected" Satie's early songs and to have taught him harmony for a brief period in 1887, just before—as Levadé reports—Satie graduated from dandyism to bohemianism and disappeared in Montmartre's flourishing artistic underground "to work out his fantasy."[4]

The four *Ogives,* each a mere four lines of barless notation, are the first works of Satie to reveal the marked influence of plainsong. The conjunct modal melodic lines of the *Ogives,* as well as the quasi-antiphonal effect resulting from abrupt changes of texture and dramatically alternating dynamic levels, suggest not only the texture and style but also the practice of early church music. Modality and rich chordal textures are apparent in the early songs and in fact help to weaken their functional tonal base; but in the *Ogives,* strict parallel chordal movement and a pervasive modality are systematically exploited, resulting in a dramatic pre-figuration of the Rosicrucian music soon to appear.

Each of the *Ogives* is constructed in an identical fashion: a modally ambiguous melody given out in octaves (A); the melody repeated fortis-simo as a series of common chords (A^1); the melody harmonized in simple triadic fashion and stated softly (A^2); and finally an exact repetition of A^1.

Example 5. Satie: *Première Ogive* (1886)

Modal ambiguity, already apparent in the *Trois mélodies,* is further exploited in the four *Ogives.* The tonal center of the first *Ogive,* for example, seems to shift between G major (or E Aeolian)((first phrase) and D Dorian (second phrase). Of greater interest is Satie's further exploitation of structural asymmetry. Taking the quarter-note as the basic unit of time, the first *Ogive* consists of a ten-beat antecedent phrase and an elongated fourteen-beat consequent phrase. Similarly the second *Ogive* juxtaposes a nineteen-beat pattern with one of twenty-one beats. Or, as in the fourth *Ogive,* the sequence may be reversed—twenty-one beats followed by a slightly telescoped eighteen-beat phrase. Here we see a conception of musical form as a function of time or duration, in direct opposition to traditional tonal thinking, with its explicit notions of dynamism and progressive linearity. Satie's lifelong preoccupation with what might be termed chronometric form provides us with one of the principal keys with which to unlock the secret of his elusive sound structures. We find in Satie's music a concentration upon unfamiliar relationships of time and space that relate to certain pre-Renaissance (and non-Western) conceptions of musical form while at the same time looking forward to the early music of John Cage and the hypnotic sound world of the minimalists.

Sarabandes, Gymnopédies, and Gnossiennes

In early November of 1886, exactly one year after he had enrolled in Mathias's piano class, Satie severed all ties with the Conservatoire. On 15 November of that year he enlisted in the 33d Infantry Regiment, which was stationed to the northeast of Paris in the town of Arras. Apparently the young musician soon discovered that the discipline of army life was no more to his liking than the oppressive atmosphere of the Conservatoire, for within weeks of his arrival in Arras, Satie, along with two companions, began a self-imposed regimen of cross-country running. The deliberate exposure to the winter cold resulted in a severe case of bronchitis and a three-month period of convalescence. During his recuperation Satie added Gustave Flaubert and Joséphin Péladan to the growing list of his literary discoveries. He was delighted with *Salammbô,* Flaubert's exotic tale of ancient Carthage and the Punic Wars, later claiming it as the inspiration for his *Gymnopédies;* the same author's *La Tentation de Saint-Antoine,* inspired by Breughel's picture of the Temptation of Saint Anthony, also stimulated his fertile imagination. The strange Péladan's influence on Satie was more direct and extensive and will be explored at length in chapter 4.

It was in May of 1887, as we have noted, that Satie first encountered Chabrier's opera *Le Roi malgré lui*. The famous *Sarabandes* began to appear four months later. Many critics consider the *Sarabandes* to be a landmark in the development of French music. At a conference of the Société Lyre et Palette[5] held on 18 April 1916, Satie's friend and disciple Roland-Manuel said, with some justification, that "these *Sarabandes* mark a date in the evolution of our music: here are three short pieces of an unprecedented harmonic technique, born of an entirely new aesthetic, which create a unique atmosphere, a sonorous magic of complete originality."[6] What particularly intrigued Satie's early admirers were the chains of unprepared and unresolved seventh and ninth chords that typify the *Sarabandes*. In accord with Roland-Manuel, the critic Henri Collet saw the characteristic unresolved dissonances and the modality of the *Sarabandes* as sufficient evidence to proclaim a musical revolution. With understandable Gallic pride (he was also writing in 1916) Collet noted that the *Sarabandes* contained "all the marks of a great musical revolution."[7] The French do not stand alone, however, in perhaps overstating the importance of these works as witness the comments of an English admirer, W. Wright Roberts, to the effect that Satie's three dances were more important to the evolution of contemporary French music than either *Le Roi malgré lui* or Debussy's *La Damoiselle élue* of 1887–89.[8]

Still, the historical significance of these early Satie works should not be minimized. Whereas Chabrier injected occasional splashes of seventh- and ninth-chord harmony into an otherwise strongly tonal framework as a kind of exotic coloring agent, Satie's three archaic dances flood the atmosphere in a gentle haze of unresolved dissonances. And although the *Sarabandes*—like Debussy's Pre-Raphaelite *Damoiselle* with its similarly rich harmonic vocabulary—still cling to tonal centers (defined by their respective key signatures—A-flat, D-sharp, and D-flat), their undulating modal lines, underpinned by grave processions of sevenths and ninths, imbue the music with a timeless calm that comes very near to denying the constraining demands of the functional tonal system. These remarkable pieces, with their subtle evocation of accompanied plainsong, initiated a style of writing that colored the music of an entire generation of French composers, some, to be sure, of minor significance, such as Alfred Bruneau, whose opera *Le Rêve* caused something of a stir at its premiere in 1891 owing in part to its declamatory melody and bold harmonic language, others, such as Debussy and Ravel, figures of international importance, whose revolutionary works led modern music into rich new realms of thought and feeling.

The manuscript of the *Trois Sarabandes* reveals a few interesting facts not disclosed by the published score. In the published version, for example, only the second *Sarabande* carries a dedication; however, the manuscript indicates that Conrad Satie was the dedicatee of the first *Sarabande,* and it also suggests that Satie had some difficulty deciding on a dedicatee for the second, for the name of one Arthur Dodement is crossed out in blue pencil and replaced by that of Mlle Jeanne de Bret. But by 1911, the year that saw the publication of the three *Sarabandes,* the composer had again changed his mind, for the published version of the second dance bears the distinguished name of Maurice Ravel, a gesture no doubt prompted by the fact that Ravel had played that piece, as well as the third *Gymnopédie* and the first-act Prelude to *Le Fils des étoiles,* on 16 January 1911 at a concert of the Société Musicale Indépendante. Also worth noting is the fact that tempo markings do not appear in the original published score even though ♩ = 84 is clearly indicated in the manuscripts of both the first and the second piece. Extensive indications of phrasing and dynamics appear only in the manuscript of the second *Sarabande,* although such editorial markings were added to all three pieces in the 1911 Rouart-Lerolle publication. On a less prosaic level of interest is the Contamine de Latour verse that appears in the upper left-hand corner of the first *Sarabande;* inscribed, probably in the poet's hand since it does not appear to be Satie's, is a strange epigraph of marked Symbolist flavor. Not surprisingly it was deleted from the published version, so out of character does its vivid imagery seem:

> Soudain s'ouvrit la nue et les maudits
>   tombèrent
> Hurlant et se heurtant en un lourd
>   tourbillon;
> Et quand ils furent seuls dans la nuit
>   sans rayon,
> Ils se virent tout noirs. Alors ils
>   blasphémèrent.
>   —J. P. Contamine de Latour
>   ("La Perdition")[9]

The *Trois Sarabandes* are the first of a long series of works to reveal Satie's penchant for composing in threes. In addition to the early *Sarabandes* and *Gymnopédies,* most of the piano suites, from the two sets of *Pièces froides* of 1897 to the *Avant-dernières pensées* of 1915, were conceived in a tripartite form, a statistic that prompted the French pianist and pedagogue Alfred Cortot to speak of "a symbolic allusion to the virtues of the Trinity."[10] The composer himself proffered a more droll explanation:

> I invent an absolutely new form. The piece I write seems good to me. But might that not just be luck? If I compose a second and a third piece along the same lines but with different melodic ideas, and if these pieces are still good, then the form I have invented is good in itself.[11]

Compared to such later works as the *Gymnopédies* and the *Pièces froides,* the melodic ideas in each of the three *Sarabandes* are quite different from one another. Nevertheless Satie provides a subtle unity among the dances by allowing characteristic motivic fragments to reappear from time to time in new contexts. A rather obvious example is the figure from the first *Sarabande* (ex. 6a) that is simply transposed from A-flat major to D-sharp minor for its reappearance in the second *Sarabande* (ex. 6b):

Example 6. Satie: *Trois Sarabandes* (1887)

(a) *Première Sarabande,* measure 11

(b) *Deuxième Sarabande,* measure 45

To an age obsessed with Wagner and Austro-German symphonic music, the *Trois Sarabandes* must have seemed strange indeed. Nevertheless, the three miniatures had a far greater importance to the emergence of the French avant-garde than most of the fatuous and largely forgotten French imitations of Wagnerian music drama and Austro-German symphony that exhausted the energies of an entire generation of French composers. Abraham Skulsky has perceptively noted that "the *Sarabandes* . . . may be considered not only an anti-Wagnerian manifestation, but also as a move toward bringing back into French music a purity of melodic line and harmonic texture that could then not be found in the works of any other living composer."[12]

Satie's *Trois Gymnopédies,* which he began to sketch during his short-lived army days, are deservedly among his best-known works, having served more than any other of his creations to make him known to the general public. One can imagine the secret delight of the originator of *musique d'ameublement* (or furniture music) could he have known that one day his slender "Greek" dances would serve, in countless arrangements, as sonic backdrops for numerous television commercials and as theme music for a number of films (a particularly effective marriage of music and imagery is French director Louis Malle's *Le Feu follet* (1963), which uses Satie's music throughout; in his more recent American film *My Dinner with André* (1981) the *Gymnopédies* are heard over the closing credits); and most assuredly the irreverent composer would have heartily approved of Dick Halligan's 1969 jazz-rock fusion arrangement of the first *Gymnopédie* for the rock band Blood, Sweat and Tears, an act of homage largely responsible for elevating Satie to cult status with the youth culture of the early 1970s. A little more than a decade later James Galway and Cleo Laine, two of the most dazzling entertainers of the eighties, collaborated in a vocal arrangement of the first *Gymnopédie,* and the adaptations continue apace, as these inimitable products of Satie's youth penetrate the mass consciousness, becoming a fixed part of the contemporary soundscape.[13]

Since 1897, when Debussy produced his delicate impressionistic symphonic versions of the first and third *Gymnopédie,* the tiny works have received numerous orchestrations, among the more exotic several for brass band and at least one for saxophone quartet. In addition to these somewhat bizarre versions, there exist several orchestrations of the second *Gymnopédie* in a Debussyan manner intended to complete the set. Among the more faithful of these is that made by Satie's friend and champion, Roland-Manuel. The *Trois Gymnopédies* have also seen service as ballet music, most notably Sir Frederick Ashton's *Monotones II,* first performed by the Royal Ballet at Covent Garden on 24 March 1965. Ashton makes use of the orchestral versions by Debussy and Roland-Manuel for his *pièce d'occasion,* which is performed by three dancers (two male, one female) in white leotards against a plain black backdrop, with no additional décor other than sensitive lighting. A similarly stark and deliberately "classical" conception was choreographed by Grant Strate for his interpretation of the *Gymnopédies* (in their original piano version), a pas de deux performed in 1970 by the National Ballet of Canada.

Although Satie claimed, according to Roland-Manuel, Flaubert's *Salammbô* as the extramusical inspiration for his *Gymnopédies,* the title would imply that vague thoughts of classical Greece filtered through the young composer's mind at the time. Rollo Myers and others have suggested that Satie's title was quite probably derived from the Greek word indicating a yearly festival, mentioned by Herodotus, Athenaeus, and others, in honor of fallen warriors, at which naked youths engaged in dances and gymnastics. In her study of the dance in ancient Greece, Lillian Lawler describes dances performed at the Gymnopaedia festivals of Apollo at Sparta and elsewhere under the name of the *anapale.* "In this dance," she writes, "nude boys moving gracefully to the music of flute or lyre, displayed postures and movements used in wrestling and boxing."[14] The German musicologist Grete Wehmeyer was the first to point out that Satie's evocative titles found their way into Contamine de Latour's poetry,[15] for in the issue of *La Musique des Familles* for 18 August 1888—the same publication that printed Satie's earliest compositional efforts the previous year—the following verse by Satie's poet friend appears:

> Oblique et coupant l'ombre un torrent
>   éclatant
> Ruisselait en flots d'or sur la dalle
>   polie,
> Où les atomes d'ambre au feu se
>   miroitant,
> Mêlaient leur sarabande à la gymnopédie.[16]

However the title may have entered Satie's mind, it is worth noting that the composer was not entirely ignorant of the Greek language. As a youth he had been forced to study both Greek and Latin with one Monsieur Mallet, a professor from a local Jesuit school who, in exchange for piano lessons for his daughter, made weekly visits in the late 1870s to the Satie residence in the rue de Constantinople in order to enlighten his indifferent pupil.

The manuscript of the three *Gymnopédies* gives February 1888 as the date of the first piece (April is first written in the manuscript but scribbled out), March 1888 for the second, and 2 April 1888 for the third. Although Mlle Jeanne de Bret appears as the dedicatee in the published version of the first *Gymnopédie,* no such indication is made in the manuscript. And in lieu of the published dedication of the second *Gymnopédie* to his brother Conrad, "À mon ami Arthur Dodement" appears on the manuscript. Both the manuscript and the published version of the third piece name Satie's composer friend Charles Levadé as dedicatee. Finally it might be noted that all three pieces were written on the stationery of Alfred Satie, Éditcur de Musique, 66 boulevard Magenta, Paris.

Although the *Gymnopédies* are harmonically simpler than the *Sarabandes,* the modality, the irregular phrase lengths, and the "cubistic" viewing of a single musical idea from slightly varying perspectives remain. Essentially, the *Gymnopédies,* like the *Sarabandes* before them and the later *Pièces froides,* are one piece written three times—cast in the same mold as it were, but with the most subtle variations in phrasing, harmonic coloring, and balancing of the parts.

Repetition and juxtaposition of musical ideas was to remain a Satie compositional technique, serving for him, as for Debussy in some respects, as a substitute for dramatic development. It should be pointed out here, however, that although Satie was to retain his trinitarian obsession throughout his career, few of the later sets reveal the obvious internal melodic similarities of the early works, quite often being, in fact, of an entirely contrasting character. Hence Constant Lambert's comparison of Satie's music to a sculpture, which can be viewed from any angle while remaining a plastic whole,[17] applies mostly to the nineteenth-century works, although near the end of his career Satie revived his "sculpturesque" view of music in such works as the *Cinq Nocturnes* of 1919.

The structural coherence of the *Gymnopédies* arises from the repetition and placement of the modal diatonic lines—characterized here by the lowered leading tone—in fresh relationships with one another as they trace, with cool impersonality, fragile arabesques of sound over a gently swaying succession of triads, sevenths, and ninths that create in their timeless and slowly shifting progressions a slightly dissonant and pungent harmonic background. A modal tonic for each piece is clearly implied by the almost incessant root movement by fifths, but the feeling for a particular tonal center is inevitably obscured by the shifting modal cadences. In the *Gymnopédies,* as elsewhere in Satie's music, a single musical idea becomes not only the stimulus for compositional activity but the basis for

the entire set of pieces. And since strong contrast is deliberately suppressed, the tiniest deviations become meaningful.

A subtle variety is achieved in the *Gymnopédies* through the principle
of extension whereby the melodic phrases go through a process of elon-
gation upon repetition, as in the first *Gymnopédie:*

Example 7. Satie: *Première Gymnopédie* (1888)

(a) First phrase (measures 5–12)

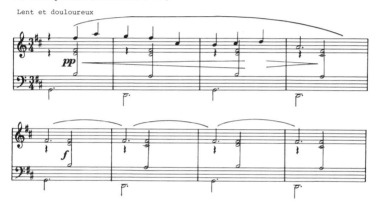

(b) Second phrase (measures 13–21)

Occasionally the melodic phrase structure will remain constant upon repetition, variety being achieved through the calculated alteration of one or
two notes, usually at the end of a phrase:

Example 8. Satie: *Deuxième Gymnopédie* (1888)

(a) First phrase (measures 5–8)

(b) Second phrase (measures 9–12)

Satie's variation technique results in a curiously circular melodic motion that tends to negate any sense of forward motion. Rarely do the conjunct melodic lines advance more than three steps in one direction without turning back on themselves. The effect is further enhanced through a process of melodic inversion whereby characteristic fragments appear in retrograde in subsequent phrases. This can be seen, for example, in the second *Gymnopédie* by comparing the second measure of phrases one or two with the analogous measure of the third phrase:

Example 9. Satie: *Deuxième Gymnopédie* (1888)

(a) Measure 6   (b) Measure 16

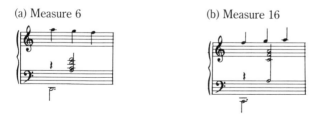

Although Satie's concept of *musique d'ameublement* was to be a much later development, the tendencies already apparent in the early dance suites—the total suppression of rhetorical gesture and the profound impersonality—suggest that most of the composer's music falls into the category of "furniture music." The haunting simplicity of these pieces worked against their immediate acceptance by a generation of musicians swept up in the heady swirl of Wagnerism. The total lack of pretension, the languid charm of the modal (mostly Mixolydian with Dorian and Aeolian inflections) lines, and the delicate chordal accompaniment (mostly root-position triads and sevenths) lend these three grave dances an air of timeless mystery, which is simply another way of concluding, somewhat helplessly, that they are inimitably Satian. Debussy's attraction to the *Gymnopédies* has been well documented, and it is probable that he admired them for much the same reason that he admired the "primitive" freshness of Mussorgsky's music. As Léopold Dauphin, one of Satie's fellow musicians from the Chat Noir days, once quipped: "The *Gymnopédies* seemed to have been written by a savage with taste."[18]

In 1889, at a time when a struggling *ars gallica* was in grave danger of being submerged in a sea of Wagnerism, fresh sounds drifted in from the east, and the ears of French musicians were once again diverted by a new, but this time much more exotic, world of sound. The Universal Exposition of 1889, a grand celebration of the centenary of the French Revolution (and, by implication, the young and shaky Third Republic), placed on display for all the world to see a century of French artistic and scientific achievement, a glorious record symbolized, above all else, by the controversial 984-foot Eiffel Tower, long since the most splendid and famous landmark of one of Europe's most beautiful capitals. For a generation of impressionable young French musicians still in search of a distinctive national voice, the Universal Exposition was an ear-opening experience that served to direct serious French music into new and largely unexplored channels of musical expression.

Between May and November 1889 an estimated thirty-two million visitors flocked to the great exhibition to marvel at the inventiveness of French technology—like some Jules Verne fantasy come to life—as well as to absorb a dazzling array of strange sights and sounds imported from all over the world. Here Parisians encountered a colorful display of exotic music and dance, ranging from Scandinavian and Slavic folk styles to the art traditions of North Africa, the Near East, and the Orient.

The influence of eastern music—in particular the Javanese *gamelan* orchestra—on the development of Debussy's style has been often noted. There is much less general awareness of the fact that Satie too found a stimulus in the strange new music. The composer's first biographer, Pierre-Daniel Templier, was the first to suggest that the Romanian folk ensembles in particular intrigued Satie, and he went on to describe the *Gnossiennes* of 1890 as a "curious mixture of Orientalism and Gregorian mysticism."[19] Jean Roy, writing thirty years after Templier, goes so far as to state that Satie actually incorporated fragments of a Romanian dance into his *Gnossiennes.*[20] Whatever the case, it is undeniable that the Lydian mode, with its prominent tritone, the frequent skips of the augmented second typical of the so-called Gypsy scale, the occasional wholetone coloring, and the ornamental grace notes, all found in varying degrees in the *Gnossiennes,* in some measure contribute to a vaguely Balkan effect.

It seems likely that once again ancient Greek culture was the source of Satie's rather odd title, this time the allusion being to the Cretan Palace of Minos at Knossos, which had recently come very much into the news through the explorations and excavations of the brilliant German archeologist Heinrich Schliemann.

Much has been made of Satie's notational innovations, and it should be noted that the absence of bar lines, which, it will be recalled, began with the song "Sylvie" in 1886 and which after 1890 becomes the norm, does not, excepting perhaps certain of the *Rose-Croix* works, destroy metric regularity; in most instances the bar lines could easily be supplied.

With the appearance in 1968 of three hitherto unpublished Satie works, the number of *Gnossiennes* was increased to six. Robert Caby has edited three piano pieces from 1889, 1891, and 1897, numbering them respectively the fifth, fourth, and sixth *Gnossienne.* Thus the fifth *Gnossienne* was actually the first of the six to be composed, having been completed on 8 July 1889, a few months before the appearance of the original *Trois Gnossiennes* of 1890. The fourth *Gnossienne* is dated 22 January 1891 and therefore coincides with the appearance of the first *Rose-Croix* works. The sixth *Gnossienne* dates from January 1897 and accordingly it has more in common stylistically with the *Pièces froides* of the same year than with its companions.

The six *Gnossiennes* have not figured in as many arrangements as the ubiquitous *Gymnopédies,* although the first three were orchestrated in

1966 by John Lanchbery for Sir Frederick Ashton's ballet *Monotones I.* The earliest arrangement is Francis Poulenc's 1939 orchestration of the third *Gnossienne,* while Robert Caby has done similar service for the last three pieces.

The three *Gnossiennes* of the regular canon do have the distinction of having inaugurated the witty verbal commentary that has become one of the most discussed features of the composer's style. Satie's celebrated verbal wit appears in the original *Trois Gnossiennes* in embryonic form, confined to occasional facetious outbursts of never more than a few words. Not until the "humoristic" works of 1912–15 would the commentary expand into the continuous Dadaistic monologue for which the composer has gained a great deal of notoriety. In the *Trois Gnossiennes* the instructions to the performer vary in intelligibility. Some, such as "postulez en vous-même" ("wonder about yourself"), "sur la langue" ("on the tip of the tongue"), "sans orgueil" ("don't be proud"), and "ouvrez la tête" ("think right"), are clearly nonsensical; others, such as "très luisant" ("shining") and "avec étonnement" ("with amazement"), are rather expressive and vaguely meaningful, while still others—"plus intimement" ("more intimately"), "avec une légère intimité" ("lightly, with intimacy"), and "enfouissez le son" ("muffle the sound"), though eminently French, are virtually within the bounds of the standard nineteenth-century vocabulary of expression markings.

Satie employs the same general compositional procedure for the *Trois Gnossiennes* as govern the earlier *Gymnopédies:* short, conjunct melodic lines of irregular phrase length spun out over a slowly shifting harmonic accompaniment, in this case a simple vocabulary of tonic, dominant, and subdominant root-position triads. Perhaps basing his melodic style on Romanian folk melodies, Satie introduces a mildly exotic element into the *Gnossiennes* through the use of whole-tone and other quasi-Oriental scales, which give rise to the pronounced use of augmented seconds and fourths.

The fourth *Gnossienne* has been so named by Caby. The autograph manuscript is untitled and carries only the marking "Lent" at the head of the score. The title is apt, however, since this piece further exploits the melodic and harmonic peculiarities of the earlier pieces in the set. Again the augmented second figures prominently in the melodic line, which now becomes somewhat more florid as it unfolds over a simple arpeggiated accompaniment:

Example 10. Satie: *Quatrième Gnossienne* (1891), line 3

The accompaniment consists entirely of arpeggiated root-position triads: minor chords on E, D, C, and B, and a major triad on F-sharp. A D–minor tonal center predominates, with occasional movement (always by step) onto E, C, and B. The F-sharp major triad appears only twice, the second time as the penultimate harmony, which somewhat elliptically slides onto an E-minor triad, thus effectively negating the feeling for D minor that hitherto had prevailed.

The circular melodic motion of the *Gymnopédies* has been noted. In the fourth *Gnossienne* Satie has transferred this orbicular movement to the underlying harmonies. Despite frequent movement to the other tonal planes, the D-minor triad returns with great persistence, dominating the other harmonies in the ratio of two to one. Thus the cadential F-sharp to E progression produces a curiously ambiguous effect, suggesting the same kind of formal open-endedness that characterized the *Sarabandes* and the *Gymnopédies*.

It is tempting to interpret the scribbled-out passage on the third page of the manuscript as a reluctance to return to the opening material. But since new melodic variants are not forthcoming, the inevitable repetition occurs. Again, as in the *Allegro* sketch of 1884, the composer seems incapable of progressing beyond a single musical idea. From the outset, therefore, repetition replaced organic development for Satie and thereby he provided, no doubt unwittingly, an antidote to more than two hundred years of Germanic variation technique while at the same time anticipating by nearly a century certain compositional procedures of Terry Riley, Steve Reich, Philip Glass, and others, whose hypnotic minimalist or trance music has emerged as one of the predominant aesthetic tendencies of the 1980s.

The simple accompanimental style is again exploited in the fifth *Gnossienne,* but the sinuous theme with its ornamental thirty-second-note flourishes sets this piece apart, not only from its companions, but from anything else the composer ever wrote. There is a rhythmic suppleness in this piece that makes it at the same time more "Oriental" and less Satiean than the remaining five pieces of the set. The compositional procedure, however, is inimitably Satiean. It has its parallel in the collage techniques of the Cubists, whereby bits and pieces of familiar material are juxtaposed in new and fresh relationships.

The opening nine measures of the fifth *Gnossienne,* with an irregular phrase structure of 4 + 3 + 2, provide the motivic material for the entire piece:

Example 11. Satie: *Cinquième Gnossienne* (1889), measures 1–9

The formal structure of the piece, based on nearly exact returns of the opening motive, might be charted as follows:

A(1–14)	A^1(15–23)	A(24–37)	A^2(38–41)
14	9	14	4

The composer begins an exact repeat of the opening material at measure 15; but this time in lieu of the second phrase (measures 5–7) he inserts a transposed version of measures 10–11, which itself is a variant of measures 1–2; this is followed by a transposed version of measures 6–8. Thus the basic motivic ideas appear on new tonal planes as well as in a different sequence, altering the phrase structure of the second part (A^1) to 4 + 2 + 2 + 1. The third section of the piece (measures 24–37) is an exact repeat of A, while the closing section (measures 38–41) is a truncated repetition of A, using only the first phrase (measures 1–4). The final E minor cadence serves to underline the modal and tonal ambiguity of the piece (G major–E minor), which by 1890 could be considered a Satie mannerism.

Again the almost complete absence of motivic development in the traditional sense stands out, and, as with the *Sarabandes* and the *Gymnopédies,* there seems to be no reason the *Gnossiennes,* in theory, could not turn back on themselves ad infinitum, repeating the simple motivic materials in ever new and subtle juxtapositions.[21]

The sixth *Gnossienne* of 1897 is closer in style to the "Airs à faire fuir" from the *Pièces froides* of the same year. The opening of the piece reveals Satie's continuing interest in the exploitation of augmented melodic intervals, but the marked degree of chromaticism confirms the later date. Unlike the earlier works, the sixth *Gnossienne* indulges in little exact repetition. Instead the motives are continuously repeated on new tonal levels and in slightly different forms, so that the piece conveys the impression of being through-composed.

Satie's early dance suites, written on the eve of his meeting with Debussy and Ravel, remain not only his most widely known works, but in many ways his most remarkable achievement. It is arguable that he would never again capture the vernal freshness of these three sets of slow, grave dances, which have a historical significance far in excess of their slender musical resources. Outside of certain Chabrier piano works, which he quite probably knew and cherished, there was virtually nothing on the Parisian musical scene in the late 1880s comparable to Satie's strange little pieces. In their deceptive simplicity they breathed fresh air into the decadent humidity of the fin de siècle, resurrecting the quintessentially Gallic virtues of Rameau and Couperin while looking ahead to the clean and uncluttered neoclassicism of the 1920s.

3

Montmartre
and the Chat Noir

Late in 1887, following a quarrel with his parents about an alleged *liaison amoureuse* with the family maid, Satie left the middle-class comforts of his father's house and installed himself at the foot of the Butte Montmartre at no. 50, rue Condorcet, near the Cirque Fernando (later—after 1900—the Cirque Médrano) in the boulevard Rochechouart. Having been officially discharged from the army, the young composer was now free to seek entrance into bohemia. He began to frequent Rodolphe Salis's famous Montmartre cabaret, the Chat Noir, which Salis, an indifferent student at the École des Beaux-Arts, opened in December 1881 at no. 84, boulevard Rochechouart in premises formerly leased by the post office department. Less than four years later, in June 1885, Salis moved the Chat Noir away from the vicinity of the increasingly noisy and disreputable Élysée-Montmartre dance hall to much larger quarters at no. 12, rue de Laval (later rue Victor Massé), leaving the original establishment, rechristened Le Mirliton, to his friend the poet-singer Aristide Bruant who, with his broad-brimmed hat, blue-black hair, red muffler, black jacket, and high boots, was to achieve a certain immortality through the famous posters of Henri de Toulouse-Lautrec, that "dwarf of genius" whose pitiless and haunting images of nocturnal Paris have become part of the collective consciousness of that colorful age, so near to our time, yet so far away.

Within a short time Salis's "artistic cabaret" became famous as a meeting place of poets, painters, musicians, and curiosity-seekers of all kinds, gaining a great deal of notoriety through a series of farcical publicity stunts, including, among the more noteworthy capers, a mock coronation wherein Salis had himself crowned king of Montmartre: "God made the world, Napoleon instituted the Legion of Honor, and I," he boasted, "created Montmartre." This was, of course, the heyday of the hilly northern district that very quickly became the greatest symbol of bohemian freedom in one of the freest cities on earth. For little more than three decades, Montmartre, in the 1890s still a semirural area with remnants of farms and fruit orchards, ruled over Parisian night life as a kind of diminutive kingdom of illicit pleasure. In October 1889 the Moulin Rouge opened its doors, and here, at a specially reserved table, sat Toulouse-Lautrec, obedient to the conspicuous painted command, *"Consommations Obligatoires,"* absorbing, two or three nights a week, the rowdy and erotic images, especially the high-spirited dancers—La Goulue, Valentin-le-Désossé, Grille-d'Égout, and perhaps the most famous of them all, La Folle, or La Mélinite, the slim, red-haired corybant of indeterminate sexuality better known as Jane Avril. Outside in the garden of the Moulin Rouge, on a stage carved out of the belly of an enormous plaster and cardboard elephant, Joseph Pujol, or Le Pétomane, the man with the "musical anus," convulsed audiences with his highly unusual brand of Rabelaisian virtuosity. This strange man's uncanny ability to pass wind at will drew incredulous audiences from beyond the borders of France—including at least one crowned head of Europe—who journeyed to Paris for the express purpose of witnessing one of Montmartre's most bizarre spectacles. Freakish exhibitions and racy peep shows, naughty postcards, striptease acts, opium, absinthe and cheap wine, prostitutes for all tastes and budgets—here is a gay and gaudy image of another Paris, a secret Paris, that lingers to this day in the memories of foreign visitors to the French capital.

Bruant and the *Chanson Réaliste*

Whereas the great dance halls such as the Élysée-Montmartre and the Moulin Rouge tended to cater to a rather fashionable crowd of slumming pleasure-seekers from the city below who, as Guy de Maupassant observed, journeyed to the Butte to enjoy "vulgar, noisy fun which was a little squalid and slightly depraved,"[1] the centers of working-class life in fin de siècle Paris were the *cafés-concerts,* or *caf' conc's,* where a new genre of popular song flourished, the *chanson réaliste,* a musico-poetic form rooted in the low-life experience of the bottom rungs of Parisian

society. For behind the glitter and the gaiety Paris was home to a large
population of derelicts and drifters and desperately poor working-class
citizens.

At the beginning of the Third Republic the city could boast a hundred
or so *cafés–concerts,* where musical entertainment was in constant demand, a demand so handsomely met that it is estimated that well over a
million chansons of a popular type have been composed in France since
the 1870s, some individual authors credited with having produced five or
six songs in a single day, four or five thousand in a career.[2] Satie's father
Alfred was in this respect only one of a veritable army of tunesmiths
whose wares flooded the market.

The immediate ancestry of the *café-concert* song can be traced to the
patriotic airs spawned by the Franco-Prussian conflict and the ignomin-
ious French defeat. War songs such as "Vous avez pris l'Alsace et Lorraine" ("You have taken Alsace and Lorraine") and "Le Clarion" ("The
Bugler") by Paul Déroulède and Émile André became so popular in the
1870s they were distributed on postcards.

The last third of the nineteenth century was, of course, the great period of *naturalisme* in French literature, a style of documentary realism
pioneered by the brothers Edmond and Jules Goncourt and developed to
epic proportions in Émile Zola's monumental Rougon-Macquart series,
with its sprawling cast of pimps and prostitutes, alcoholics and beggars,
exploited workers and petty thieves, the very dregs of fin de siècle
French society, twin victims, inescapably, of heredity and environment,
drawn—one is tempted to say photographed—with sympathy and com-
passion. It is out of this plebeian world that a new "poetry of the pave-
ment" was born, a poetry rich in working-class argot or slang that, with
poignancy and irony, sang of the life of the streets and the slums.

Of the many singer-poets of "the other Paris" who emerged in the last
decades of the century, two achieved something near to what today we
would call stardom: Yvette Guilbert, who by the mid-1890s had become
the darling of fashionable society and an international celebrity, and Aristide Bruant, the flamboyant entertainer of more local fame whose inimitable fusion of mocking wit and bitter cynicism virtually defined the genre
chanson réaliste. And it is the colorful Bruant who carries us back to
Salis's Chat Noir, for it was there, in 1883, that he appeared as a poet
and singer of satirical and slanderous songs before striking off on his own
two years later as the proprietor of Le Mirliton. Raymond Rudorff has
sketched a vivid account of a characteristic Bruant performance:

With his thick black hair, high forehead, burly figure, fierce eyes and bitter smile, Bruant was an impressive figure who commanded respect. He invariably wore the same costume for his performances: black corduroy jacket and trousers, a bright red flannel shirt, black neck-scarf and black boots. He fully believed in audience participation. Before reciting one of his songs, he would gaze disdainfully at his audience for a few moments and then announce the title of his next number: "Now, I'm going to sing you *à Saint-Lazare!*" After a dramatic pause, he would repeat: *"A Saint-Lazare!"* and then exhort his listeners to join in: "As for you, herd of camels, try to bray together in tune, will you?" He would usually sing from ten or eleven at night until two in the morning, walking up and down or sometimes standing up on a table as he did so.[3]

The songs almost invariably have the same form: duple meter, a four-bar introduction (which also serves as a ritornello between verses), followed by a sixteen-bar verse in either a two-phrase (A A^1) or four-phrase (A A B A^1) structure. *À Saint-Lazare!*, a melancholy tale of a street girl writing to her pimp from the police hospital at the Saint-Lazare prison, is typical of the genre. The simple, triadic, diatonic melody of *À Saint-Lazare!* is atypical only in that its range of a tenth exceeds the more usual fifth (or even third) of these unadorned, conversational tunes. Characteristically, the verse is couched in a working-class patois that virtually defies idiomatic translation.

Example 1. Aristide Bruant: *À Saint-Lazare!* (from *Dans la rue,* vol. 1, 1889)

cla - re, N'em - pêch' qu'au - jour - d'hui j'suis dans

l'tas, A Saint - La - sa - re!

ii

Mais pendant c'temps-là, toi, vieux chien,
   Quéqu'tu vas faire?
Je n'peux t'envoyer rien de rien,
   C'est la misère,
Ici, tout l'monde est décavé,
   La braise est rare;
Faut trois mois pour faire un linvé,
   A Saint-Lazare!

iii

Vrai, d'te savoir comm'ça, sans l'sou,
   Je m'fais eun'bile! . . .
T'es capab' de faire un sal'coup,
   J'suis pas tranquille.
T'as trop d'fierté pour ramasser
   Des bouts d'cigare,
Pendant tout l'temps que j'vas passer,
   A Saint-Lazare!

iv

Va-t'en trouver la gran'Nana,
   Dis que j'ai prie
D'casquer pour moi, j'y rendrai ça
   A ma sortie.
Surtout n'y fais pas d'boniments,
   Pendant qu'je m'marre
Et que j'bois des médicaments,
   A Saint-Lazare!

v

Et pis, mon p'tit loup, bois pas trop,
   Tu sais qu't'es teigne,
Et qu'quand t'as un p'tit coup d'sirop
   Tu fous la beigne;
Si tu t'faisais coffrer, un soir,

Dan' eun'bagarre,
Ya pus personn' qui viendrait m'voir
A Saint-Lazare!

vi

J'finis ma lettre en t'embrassant,
    Adieu, mon homme,
Malgré qu'tu soy' pas caressant,
    Ah! j't'ador' comme
J'adorais l'bon Dieu comm' papa,
    Quand j'étais p'tite,
Et qu'j'allais communier à
    Saint'-Marguerite.[4]

The Chat Noir

By the time the Chat Noir reopened in the rue Victor Massé in 1885 it had become one of the chief attractions of bohemian Montmartre, home for a motley band of eccentrics whose droll antics drew late-night crowds of spectators from all classes of society, but especially the beau monde, who, with amused condescension, seemed to take a certain masochistic delight in being the disdainful objects of scornful antibourgeois tirades from the splenetic tongues of Bruant and his uninhibited colleagues. The sign of the Chat Noir, designed by Adolphe Willette, was a heraldic black cat (Art) holding a terrified goose (The Bourgeoisie) under one paw, and to one side of the imposing entrance of the "queer, black, whimsical structure"[5] was inscribed the legend, "Passant, sois moderne" ("Passerby, be modern"). Much later, in 1896, Théophile Steinlen's hieratic black cat became the predominant symbol of the cabaret and the chief reminder today of its fin de siècle glory.

The main room of the tavern was decorated with elaborate walnut panels in the style of Louis XIII, complete with a gigantic ornamented fireplace, massive oak chairs and tables, and liveried waiters satirically outfitted in the impressive green-brocaded uniforms of the French Academy. Stained-glass windows by Willette, hanging lanterns by Eugène Grasset decorated with cat motifs in the form of snarling gargoyles, murals by Puvis de Chavannes, Carolus-Duran, Antonio de la Gandara, and Henri Pille, masks of poets, woodcuts, imitation tapestries, copper and pewter utensils, a motley collection of arms and armor, and swarms of cat imagery completed the strange décor. Separated from the main hall

by a counter and a heavy curtain was a smaller back room, magnilo-
quently nicknamed the Institute, where Salis's inner circle met to imbibe
and to listen to poems and satirical songs. The second floor of the cabaret
contained a series of meeting rooms with pompous names—the State
Room, the Lord's Room, the Guard Room, the Oratory—while the third
floor, called the Salle des Fêtes, was the site of the enormously successful shadow plays presided over by the Symbolist landscape painter
Henri Rivière and Emmanuel Poiré, better known as Caran d'Ache.

Among the forty-three plays performed in the decade between the
inauguration of the shadow theater in late 1886 and the demise of the
Chat Noir in 1897 we encounter an odd mixture of themes ranging from
burlesque comedy to historical epic and biblical legend. *The Epic* (1886),
a creation of the caricaturist Caran d'Ache, was based on episodes from
the Napoleonic Wars, complete with elaborate battle scenes; *The Temptation of Saint Anthony* (1888), with drawings by Rivière and music arranged by Albert Tinchant, was derived in part from Flaubert's famous
treatment of the subject, which had appeared in print just thirteen years
previously; *Phryné* (1891), to music by Charles de Sivry and drawings
again by Rivière, was a Greek tragedy by Maurice Donnay, a dramatist
whose fluffy comedies of Parisian life eventually earned him a place in
the esteemed Académie Française; *Saint Geneviève of Paris* (1893),
billed as a "mystical legend," was a collaborative effort of the poet-com-
posers Claudius Blanc and Léopold Dauphin, with drawings once again
by Rivière; the *The Journey to the Star,* one of the most celebrated productions, first seen in 1890, was a sentimental Nativity play with poem
and music by Georges Fragerolle, one of the regular musicians at the
Chat Noir, and shadowy tableaux by Rivière. With dramatic narrations,
usually delivered by Salis himself, against simple keyboard accompaniments provided by the cabaret's fluctuating stable of pianists and assorted percussion effects added by Rivière and his associates for scenes
of a particularly onomatopoeic nature—or, for more lavish productions,
a small theater orchestra, sometimes with added chorus of a dozen or so
singers—the shadow plays were performed behind a lighted glass screen
to the acclaim of Paris's "top 400," which on one occasion or another
would have included such notable patrons as Paul Verlaine, Anatole
France, Sarah Bernhardt, and Jules Verne. Such was the vogue of the
Montmartre tavern in the 1890s that the term "Chat Noir style" came to
be applied for a time—usually in a derogatory sense—to any contemporary painting exhibiting a neo-Gothic imagery.

Within a month of the founding of the cabaret Salis began publishing a little journal, *Le Chat Noir,* which until its demise in 1899 served as a ready outlet for many young radical artists and writers. Under the editorship of Émile Goudeau and later Alphonse Allais and the artistic direction of Rivière and the poet and illustrator George Auriol, *Le Chat Noir* became an important source of social and political satire in the new climate of political and artistic freedom tolerated by the young Third Republic. In its pages the art of Daumier and Grandville was revived in the work of Willette, Caran d'Ache, Jean-Louis Forain, Jacques Villon, and above all, Steinlen, the Swiss-born artist of pronounced socialist views who arrived in Paris in 1881, settled in Montmartre, and issued a steady stream of lithographs and illustrations for books, little reviews, sheet music—including Bruant's two-volume song collection *Dans la rue* (1889–95)—and a variety of journals and newspapers, among them the socialist weekly *Le Chambard socialiste* and *Gil Blas illustré* which, for the insignificant price of one sou (five centimes), offered stories, drawings, and even printed songs by some of the best talent then active in Paris.

With the slogan "shock the bourgeoisie" as his guide, the red-haired Rodolphe Salis, who with mock pomposity liked to refer to himself as the Seigneur de Chat-Noir-Ville, presided over the nocturnal proceedings, playing host from 1881 until his death in 1897 to about everyone of importance in Parisian arts and letters. By the late 1880s the Chat Noir had become the unofficial headquarters of Parisian bohemianism.

It was into this vibrant and more than slightly neurasthenic bohemian microcosm that Satie wandered late in 1887. According to his friend Contamine de Latour, Satie was presented to Salis by the obscure plumber turned humorist Vital Hocquet (or Narcisse Lebeau as he waggishly preferred to be called) who introduced the young musician as "Erik Satie, gymnopédiste!" to which Salis replied with a ceremonious bow, "That is a most noble profession!"[6] Sometime in November or December 1887 Satie was engaged as "second pianist" at the Chat Noir. The new freedom he found there was a revelation to him and transformed him completely. "It was in this milieu," Contamine de Latour recalled many years later, "so different from the one in which he had grown up, that Satie, till then shy and reserved, gave free rein to the hoard of wild good humor that lay dormant in him."[7] In keeping with the ambience of his new place of employment, Satie grew his hair and his beard, literally destroyed his conventional wardrobe, and began to practice the sartorial arts with great panache. Many of the odd characters he is known to have met at the Chat Noir have already been mentioned, and it seems reasonably clear that a process of radicalization was begun there that would rapidly transform the young and impressionable conservatory dropout into the puckish and irascible protohippie he became.

There were the painters and illustrators—Marcellin Desboutin, Georges de Feure, the Spaniards Santiago Rusiñol and Ignacio Zuloaga, all of whom left portraits of Satie. Among the literary figures we find Émile Goudeau and the remnants of *Les Hydropathes,* that society of faded Symbolists whose members included Jean Moréas, Edmond Haraucourt, Marie Krysinska, and, most notably, François Coppée, whose plebeian balladry earned him the appellation "poète des humbles." There were poets of the stature of Charles Cros, Albert Samain, and Jean Richepin, some of whose picaresque *Chansons des Gueux* or "beggars' songs" were transformed into popular *café-concert* ballads. Then there were Satie's fellow Normans, Guy de Maupassant; Albert Tinchant, a melancholy absinthe addict of limited literary and musical talent who ostensibly collaborated with the composer on an unrealized three-act opera whose anti-Wagnerian posture is blatantly exposed in its title, *The Bastard Son of Tristan;* and Alphonse Allais, an inveterate punster who, characteristically, christened his fellow *honfleurais* "Esotérik Satie." Finally we note the musicians: chansonniers such as Jules Jouy, Paul Delmet, Xavier Privas, Léon Xanrof, Dominique Bonnaud, Vincent Hyspa, Maurice Mac-Nab, Marcel Lefèvre, Pierre Trimouillat, Eugène Lemercier, Gabriel Randon (*dit* Jehan Rictus), and of course Aristide Bruant; and Satie's fellow pianists, minor talents such as his erstwhile collaborator Tinchant, Paul Viardot, Georges Fragerolle, Dynam-Victor Fumet, and the capricious Charles de Sivry, brother-in-law of Verlaine, friend of Chabrier, dabbler in the occult sciences, and professional wag. Sivry, who for many years played piano and conducted the small orchestra at the Chat Noir, was, according to one source:

. . . a small black-haired young man with long drooping black moustaches that gave him a slightly oriental air. He was popular for several reasons: for his rank (he was a Marquis, a fact to which he never referred); for his talent (he had arranged many folk-songs and composed light music with contemptuous ease); but specially for his high spirits and affability. He used never to leave his bed until early afternoon, which may partly explain his increasing brightness as evening succeeded afternoon and night evening. By the small hours he was the life and

soul of the party—any party, he was not particular so long as he was at one. At
. . . musical gatherings he would begin soberly enough, accompanying the singers, singing himself, and improvising dutifully, but as time went on . . . the mischievous in him bubbled out and practical jokes became the order of the evening.
The decorous disappeared and the rest gave themselves over to fun with the
lively little De Sivry as ringleader.[8]

Fumet

The question of "creative influence" is always a vexing one, causality a
fluid concept difficult to pin down. When we probe more deeply Satie's
prentice years in Montmartre and examine more closely the many contacts he made there, however, we can point to at least two early encounters that shed further light on the genesis of his aesthetic
experience.

Dynam-Victor Fumet was the regular pianist at the Chat Noir when
Satie was hired in 1887 to replace Fumet, who apparently was relieved
of his duties because, as an intransigent young man of high ideals, he
indignantly refused a request to play what he considered to be a particularly idiotic popular tune,[9] a rather odd claim considering that such a
post would surely have required more than an occasional involvement
with musical inanity and that, moreover, Fumet himself did not disdain
to contribute to the genre with a number of vacuous trifles of his own,
some of which were published in the 1890s.

It is true, however, that Fumet had far loftier musical ambitions than
the majority of his Chat Noir colleagues. He studied for a time at the
Conservatoire under Franck and Ernest Guiraud but was forced to dis-
continue his formal education because of his political activism. Apparently
it had come to the attention of the authorities that the young student
spent a good many of his evenings in the manufacture of bombs for the
anarchist cause, a rather serious offense considering that the young
Third Republic was besieged in the last two decades of the century by a
glut of terrorist bombings under the banner of "Vive l'anarchie!" It is
known that Fumet was in the 1880s a follower of the Russian Peter Kro-
potkin, one of anarchism's chief theoreticians, and that he contributed
verse to the anarchist journal La Révolte. It is clear that he shared the
anarchists' hatred of bourgeois society. Nevertheless, he seemingly
abandoned the anarchist cause and began to drift, in true fin de siècle
fashion, into a curious mixture of occultism and spiritualism, while grind-

ing out a living of sorts at the Chat Noir. After a suicide attempt, he became further engrossed in mysticism, even to the point of devising his own cabalistic religion. Finally, under the powerful influence of the fanatical Catholic mystic Léon Bloy, Fumet eventually came full circle and reembraced the Roman faith, spending the last thirty-nine years of his life quietly (he died in 1949) as organist and choirmaster of the church of Sainte-Anne in Paris.

In a 1954 memoir of his father, Stanislas Fumet confirms that Satie met the elder Fumet at the Chat Noir in 1887 or 1888, perhaps earlier. Satie, he claims, was infatuated with Fumet's music at that time, and he suggests that his father's piano improvisations in particular may have directly inspired such works as the *Sarabandes* and *Gymnopédies,* that both young composers were striving for "an intentional spirit of poverty, for simplicity of thought, in a word, for purity."[10] Although a firm musical connection between the two composers is tenuous and difficult to establish with any degree of certainty, we can speculate that Satie would have been attracted to Fumet the man—"a politico-religious freak"[11] in the opinion of one critic—who may have reinforced his own radical and mystical tendencies, preparing the way for his later association with Péladan and his mysterious society of Rosicrucians. Fumet *fils* has drawn attention to the fact that both composers greatly admired the cool neoclassical canvases of Puvis de Chavannes, and it is entirely possible that the utter simplicity and emotional neutrality of Satie's music derives at least in part from Fumet. Most certainly the two young cabaret pianists had some opportunity to exchange ideas and to hear each other's performances, and it seems reasonable to suggest that Satie would have responded enthusiastically to Fumet's keyboard improvisations, which by all accounts were most impressive.

Stanislas has singled out his father's early work, *Les Enlisements d'en haut,* for comparison with Satie's works of the same period, claiming that it contains, "in abundance, those things that appear to be so new in the *Sarabandes.*"[12] Although the standard sources list *Les Enlisements d'en haut* as a piano solo dating from 1885, two years before the appearance of Satie's *Sarabandes,* the published version of the score carries the subtitle "Andante de Symphonie en si mineur" and the date 1897;[13] it would appear, then, that this work is a piano reduction of the slow movement of a symphony which, if it exists, remains unpublished.

Fumet's work does invite comparison with Satie's compositions of this period. There is a mystical air about *Les Enlisements d'en haut* suggestive of the quasi-religious compositions of Satie's *Rose-Croix* period.

Example 2. Dynam-Victor Fumet: *Les Enlisements d'en haut* (1885–97?), measures 1–35

The stately procession of seventh and ninth chords that opens the work recalls the fascination that dissonant vertical sonorities held for both composers. The unusual time signature suggests that Fumet might have dispensed with bar lines altogether, as Satie had done as early as 1886 in his "Sylvie," for it would appear that he was striving for a fluid, metrically amorphous effect.

It is in the midsection of the piece, however, that Fumet moves beyond the pale of the Satie aesthetic.

Example 3. Fumet: *Les Enlisements d'en haut,* measures 73–95

The impassioned lyricism and the intense chromaticism of this statement reveal the essential eclecticism of Fumet, suggesting more the luxurious melos of Franck or Wagner than the glacial archaism of Satie. The inscription at the head of the score—"*L'âme qui aime le Beau mange le Ciel*" ("The soul that loves the Beautiful hungers for Heaven")—serves to remind us that Fumet was a pupil of Franck, and although he was one of the more audacious disciples of the venerable Pater Seraphicus, his music, like that of most of the Franckian school, never entirely freed itself from "the red specter of Wagner."

In his discussion of his father's sacred compositions, Stanislas suggests a musical style of purity and great simplicity, deriving in part from Gregorian chant. According to him, the intense chromaticism of his father's secular orchestral works is replaced in the sacred music by a kind of modal homophony; his description of this music strongly suggests the Satie of such works as the *Mass for the Poor* of 1895:

> If we consider the harmonies [of the sacred works] we notice that they are rarely chromatic. These chords, by themselves, would be poor indeed. For he aspires to create grandeur from sparseness. . . . Each chord was a complete entity, a summit, the termination of a melodic inspiration.[14]

Laurence Davies, in his study of the Franck circle, has summarized his contribution to the Satie-Fumet problem in these words:

> The style displayed in most of [Fumet's] offerings has been described as "anachronistic modernist"—which is only another way of saying that the composer was trying to adapt his zest for plainchant to the discoveries of the post-Wagnerian

world. His love of chromatics marks him out as a faithful follower of both Franck and Wagner, yet there is a constant striving for concision in his music which cannot be attributed to either influence. It is more like the Satiean habit of *dépouillement,* but differs in not being quite so ruthless.[15]

And here the matter must rest until such time as more of Fumet's music is known. What we can say with certainty is that time has dealt more kindly with the composer of the *Sarabandes* and *Gymnopédies* than with his "capricious, independent and lovable"[16] comrade from the balmy days of Salis's Chat Noir.

Allais

One of the endearing habitués of the Chat Noir during Satie's tenure there was the humorist Alphonse Allais. "Allais," in Sacha Guitry's amusing words, "was never drunk, but he always seemed not quite sober. This latter state suited him so well that he remained in it. There he found his natural equilibrium and kept himself balanced."[17] Aptly described as a *"fumiste* (perpetrator of tall tales and hoaxes) and short-story writer with the mixed talents of Poe and Mark Twain,"[18] Allais is still remembered in France for his light verse and farcical tales, droll little sketches whose subtle blend of irony, whimsy, and fantasy we somehow recognize as inimitably Gallic.

For the last two decades of his relatively short life (he died in 1905 in his fifty-second year) Allais contributed a steady stream of humorous pieces to a variety of little reviews and newspapers at the rate of two or three a week. These were invariably written in various cafés and bars at the eleventh hour, apparently without any great amount of premeditation, and always with a delicious sense of the absurd. "If he wrote a sentence that displeased him or seemed badly put, he would add quotation marks and, in brackets, the name of some third-rate author and the word *sic.*"[19] Among Allais's earliest efforts were the humorous monologues and sketches he wrote for the Chat Noir and the numerous items he published in *Le Chat Noir* between 1888 and 1896. As resident pianist of Salis's establishment in the late 1880s, Satie could hardly have avoided almost daily contact with Allais and his droll antics. The two *honfleurais* share a remarkably similar aesthetic vision, and we can speculate that the young composer honed and refined his own innate sense of the absurd through the influence of his melancholy and phlegmatic friend.

Students of art history will be delighted to learn that Allais was a pioneering figure in the evolution of contemporary painting. Prefiguring both the Suprematists (Malevich) and the Conceptualists (Rauschenberg), not to speak of the minimalists, Allais unveiled a series of abstract paintings between 1882 and 1885 at the annual Expositions des Arts Incohérents, the brainchild of Jules Lévy, a member of Goudeau's *Hydropathes,* who had the idea of mounting a series of art exhibitions "for people who did not know how to draw." Three of these historic canvases might be singled out to illustrate the range of Allais's artistic sensibilities: one was a completely black painting entitled "Negroes Fighting in a Cave at Night," another a completely white painting entitled "Anaemic Young Girls Going to their First Communion through a Blizzard," while a third was a completely gray painting entitled "Drunkards Dancing in a Fog." One wonders, too, if John Cage was aware of Allais's single—and singular—contribution to musical composition, a *Funeral March,* composed for the last rites of a distinguished deaf man, consisting of twenty-four bars of music manuscript, entirely blank, except for the whimsical tempo marking, "Lento rigolando."[20]

The world of science and technology also owes a debt to Allais, for in addition to his important experiments in color photography, which he carried out with his friend Charles Cros, Allais has enriched our lives with a number of ingenious inventions worthy of the legendary Rube Goldberg. Here we might mention the necromobile—or corpse-car, as he called it in English—a hearse powered by the simultaneous cremation of the corpse en route to the cemetery. Or the lighthouse fitted with a gigantic vaporizer designed to blow powerful smells—perhaps the scent of a good local cheese—out to sea so that a sniff would be sufficient navigational guide to a ship's captain in inclement weather. Other less salutary inventions include a combination fishing rod / bicycle pump, sweat-free spectacles, a combination saltcellar / cigar holder, an improved combination meerschaum pipe / police whistle, a bullet-proof knapsack, and a method of teaching animals to play music. This last item would have been of particular interest to Satie, whose preoccupation with "intelligence and musicality in animals" has been well documented.[21] The composer may also have had his inventive friend in mind when he created his "cephalophones," a family of absolutely unplayable musical instruments, among which we find such Hoffnungian contraptions as piston flutes, slide clarinets, keyboard trombones, even a chromatic tub in B, and an alto overcoat (in C). Mention should be made also of Satie's experiments in "philophony" or "phonometrology," a science that includes the measurement of sounds with a phonometer, the observation of sounds with the aid of a phonoscope (a B-flat of medium size is a revolting sight), the weighing of sounds with phono-scales (an ordinary or garden variety F-sharp registers ninety-three kilograms), and even the cleaning of sounds (a filthy business), and the exploding of sounds (pyrophony).[22] Satie's monologues, like Allais's, prefigure the free association modes of Surrealist writing. The short narratives unfold in a kind of stream-of-consciousness manner, constantly shifting between direct discourse and interior monologue. These loose collages are kept from collapsing altogether by means of motivic repetition in the form of intrapsychic asides or parenthetical digressions that recur with rondolike predictability and thus serve to maintain a fragile sense of formal balance. Both authors liked to mix high-flown ornate French with low slang and sprinkle their narrations with fashionable English expressions, and of course both men were incurably addicted to the pun and the leg-pull.

Allais tells the story of a man who took his fire insurance policy so literally that he claimed compensation for all his household combustibles—firewood, candles, even his cigars—only to have the insurance company launch a countersuit against him for arson. In another sketch, called appropriately, "The Imprudential Assurance Company," Allais makes the case for lawbreakers' insurance. Burglary, he argues, is a high-risk profession very much in need of the same kind of protection available to honest enterprises. So great is this injustice in Allais's view that he registers genuine surprise that the brotherhood of thieves has never called a general strike to protest the oversight, and he concludes, with a gentle dig at Proudhon, that such a strike would create certain rather awkward problems:

As we all know, "property is theft." Ergo, if there were no more theft, there would be no more property. Which would mean no more landlords, no more concierges, no more rent! Can you imagine? Not to mention what chaos there would be in the law courts, with everyone having to be acquitted, all judges having to retire and thousands of unemployed lawyers being set loose to roam the streets. It does not bear thinking about.[23]

The memory of another famous compatriot is evoked in this characteristic aside: "(Ah, well—which famous French writer was it said: 'I think, therefore I forget'? I don't remember off-hand.)"[24] Finally, we might reproduce two of the choicer items from Allais's inimitable "Personal Column":

"To Mademoiselle Nina Pack of the Opéra Comique—Your letter is charming, mademoiselle, but your anthropology leaves a little to be desired. If a man is of average height it does not necessarily follow that he is the product of a giant father and dwarf mother."

"To the Marquise de F. . . . of Blois: Yes, madame, you are absolutely right: the gentleman in question was indeed myself. I was not nearly as drunk as you make out, though."[25]

In many ways Satie's numerous writings can be considered a verbal counterpart, a kind of literary realization, of his musical ideals. A glance behind the jesting facade of his Dadaistic ramblings reveals with great clarity a penetrating critical insight and a delicious irony aimed at all that the composer found pretentious, stuffy, and conventional in a world of music controlled, as he saw it, by pompous and unimaginative academicians and a pedantic critical fraternity. "Mediocrity and lack of ability," he declared in 1921 with characteristic mock gravity, "are never found in critics." And he went on to explain:

A mediocre critic, or one who lacked ability would be the laughing-stock of his colleagues; he would find it quite impossible to continue his profession, his ministry, I mean, for he would even have to leave his native country, and all doors would be closed to him; his life would just be one drawn-out agony, and terribly monotonous.

The Artist is really just a dreamer; the critic, on the other hand, has a sense of reality, especially his own. An artist can be imitated; the critic is inimitable, and priceless. How could anyone imitate a critic, I wonder? Besides, it would be of little interest, very little. We have the original, THAT IS ENOUGH FOR US.[26]

A comparison of the writings of the 1920s with the mysterious pronouncements in the pages of the ephemeral *Cartulaire* of thirty years before is revealing. One would expect the careless exuberance of youth to give way to the confident wisdom of age. But despite the diversity of his writings, they reveal a fundamental unity of tone and inspiration. His peculiar mock-serious brand of humor, the incisive wit and harsh invective, the irony and subtle—and occasionally not so subtle—ridicule of enemies real or imagined, the highly refined sense of the absurd—all this remained constant to the very end.

That Satie's literary style and droll wit owe something to Allais seems clear enough. No less an authority than Jean Cocteau saw in Satie's quirky prose sketches the lineal descendents of Allais's tall tales.[27] Both men moved in the same bohemian literary circles that floated around Montmartre in the waning years of the century: the short-lived *Hirsutes* and *Zutistes,* and especially Émile Goudeau's (*Goût d'eau*) society of *Hydropathes,* decadents and *fumistes* all of them, for this was, to an excessive degree, a period of punsters and pasticheurs. Colette, whose first husband Henri Gauthier-Villars, the notorious Willy, was himself one of Paris's most celebrated wags and an occasional contributor to the pages of *Le Chat Noir,* wrote in her memoirs of the period:

> It should be said that the practical joke was in high favour at that time, enjoying a popularity that now seems incomprehensible. . . . The years 1890–1895 had their official, their licensed "wags"; Vivier, Sapeck, led to Salis, foretold and prepared the way for Allais and Jarry. With the decline of leisure, practical-joking changed, became over-subtle, over-delicate and finally died, leaving the throne to heirs who were able to take material advantage of a gift that their predecessors had exploited for its own sake.[28]

The aphorism, the epigram, the pun, the *bon mot*—we recognize something quintessentially Gallic. Here is the language of Villon and Coquillart, La Fontaine and La Bruyère, Voltaire and Chamfort, Cros and Allais, Fargue and Cocteau. Sisley Huddleston, for many years in the early part of this century Paris correspondent for several British and American newspapers and a man who understood the French as well as it is possible for a foreigner to understand this singular race, made a courageous attempt to reveal in a single paragraph something of the essence of *l'esprit gaulois.* Compared to Anglo-Saxon humor, he observed:

> French wit . . . is more dependent on verbal felicity. It ranges from a mere happy accident of a similar sound—the pun—to a shrewd criticism of society—the epigram. Always is it dependent on brilliance of language, on concise and sharp-pointed phrases. It thrusts like a rapier, and it is generally cruel. It wounds and mocks: it laughs at its object.[29]

So in the larger sense Satie simply takes his rightful place among the *fantaisistes* and epigrammatists of his race; in the narrower sense he was a product of Montmartre, his alma mater not the austere Conservatoire but the lively Chat Noir. Here on the ancient hill of the martyrs was a ramshackle world of absinthe and indigence, a community of street singers and street walkers, political subversives, mystics, caricaturists, farceurs, and assorted buffoons, whose virulently antibourgeois idealism must be considered a vital—perhaps *the* vital—factor in the formation of Satie's eccentric personality, a personality markedly less idiosyncratic when viewed in the context of the perpetual sideshow that was fin de siècle Montmartre.

4

The Rosicrucian Adventure

Sometime in late 1889 or early 1890 Satie moved from the rue Condorcet further up the slope of the Butte to no. 6, rue Cortot, where he settled in a tiny room of an old house, not far from the church of the Sacré-Coeur. Although he had come under the spell of Joséphin Péladan's strange writings as early as 1886, it was not until late 1890 while performing at the Chat Noir that Satie actually met the man, possibly through Contamine de Latour, or through the painter Desboutin, and came directly under his influence. After hearing Satie play at Salis's cabaret, Péladan invited him to join his newly formed Rosicrucian brotherhood as official composer to the Order, and, perhaps recognizing a kindred spirit in the mysterious Péladan, or, perhaps sensing a potentially useful alliance with a man who was already the talk of Paris, he accepted. Thus began one of the strangest liaisons of Satie's career, one that resulted in the first stylistically unified body of work—the so-called *Rose-Croix* music of 1891–95.

Latin Decadence

Joseph-Aimé Péladan—whose Christian name was modified in honor of the poet Joséphin Soulardy, a family friend from his childhood and adolescent years in Lyon—came by his colorful and complex nature quite directly, inheriting his predisposition to hermeticism and mystification from an eccentric but talented and industrious family. His father, the Chevalier Adrien Péladan, a Bourbonist royalist and ultramontane Catholic, was a right-wing journalist and scribbler of plaintive verse à la Lamartine, the author of a number of mystical religious tracts, and, from

1883 until his death in 1890, editor of a monthly journal called *Les An-nales du surnaturel,* while his precocious elder brother, Dr. Adrien Pé-ladan *fils,* author of several arcane medical studies and something of a philologist specializing in ancient China and Assyria, also displayed a marked interest in occultist matters, reinforcing his brother's mystical proclivities until his untimely accidental death in 1885 from strychnine poisoning.

Not long after his arrival in Paris in 1882, Péladan came under the influence of the royalist, ultra-Catholic writer and critic Jules Barbey d'Aurevilly, who later contributed prefaces to two of his novels. Like Barbey d'Aurevilly, Huysmans, Villiers de l'Isle-Adam, and other fin de siècle decadents, Péladan strongly reacted to the vulgarity and corrup-tion of the fledgling Third Republic as well as to the scientific materialism and Darwinian determinism of his age by plunging into a world of occult-ism and aestheticism. Early in his career he proclaimed himself a seer, took the royal Assyrian title "Sâr" ("Priest-King")—or, on occasion, "Sâr Mérodack," after a character in his first novel *Le Vice suprême* whose name in turn was derived from the biblical Babylonian king Mérodack-Baladan—grew a long and unkempt beard, wore flowing oriental-style robes, designed his own coat of arms, and posed as a spiritual descendent or reincarnation of Babylonian-Assyrian monarchs. Even in an age when eccentric behavior among aesthetes was the norm, Péladan must have cut a rather extraordinary figure in Parisian society. Knowing something of Satie's own pietistic tendencies and his fascination with the Gothic world, it is not difficult to see why the impressionable young bohemian was attracted to the Sâr, whose spiritual message resonates sonorously, if abstrusely, through orotund and windy prose such as this:

We believe in neither progress nor salvation; for the moribund Latin race we are preparing a final explosion of splendour to dazzle and mollify the barbarians who are approaching. The last enthusiasts of this world, we come among the tavern crowds braying the *Marseillaise* to intone a final hymn to the Beauty which is God, and thus earn the right to gaze one day upon the mystic rose.
My lust for the ideals of the past has violated the tombs in which the miracles lay sleeping, and my debauchery has had knowledge of some very young ideas which will not develop for another century.[1]

Péladan's many novels, written in a flamboyant and colorful style, are a strange mixture of erotic dream, sensualism, supernaturalism, fantasy, and strict Catholic dogma. His principal work consists of a series of twenty-one novels which appeared between 1884 and 1925 under the general title of *La Décadence latine.* As implicit in the title of the series, Péladan's central theme revolves around the conviction that religious decay and declining faith were leading inexorably to the decadence of the Latin race. Each novel features a seer with a Sumerian or Babylonian name who, as a Rosicrucian prophet, preaches a return to faith. In his study of the literature of the period Alfred Carter states that the characters in the many volumes of *La Décadence latine* "all divide their time between over-heated boudoirs and the Parisian slums, either painting their faces or seeking 'l'ignominie des moeurs décadentes' in the dives of the capital,"[2] and by way of conclusion he describes the entire series as a combination of "lascivious mysticism and Platonic hocus-pocus."[3] In a less vituperative vein George Ross Ridge interprets Péladan's message in these terms:

Modern man as a cosmopolitan, he [Péladan] warns, is doomed because he has succumbed to the great harlot, Babylon. She has seduced him from nature, from the ways of righteousness. Thus man has passed from his holy communion with nature to the cult of artificiality, of anti-nature, in idolatrous harlotry. And life without nature, he warns, is ultimately sterility—death without resurrection.[4]

This was, of course, an age of intense fascination with occultism, theosophy, and spiritualism. Romanticism, having turned further inward to explore the interior landscapes of the mind, underwent a subtle metamorphosis and reemerged in the autumnal twilight of the century as Symbolism. Here was an art born of Parnassus, of Baudelaire and Poe, but also of Wagner and Nietzsche, an overrefined and precious art most brilliantly typified by the bejewelled Byzantine visions of Gustave Moreau and Joris-Karl Huysmans's remarkable and influential *À Rebours,* a strange and haunting book that lies close to the psychological core of fin de siècle decadence.

In 1884 the Marquis Stanislas de Guaïta, a decadent poet and occultist of Hungarian descent, was drawn into Péladan's circle through his encounter with the latter's mystagogic novel *Le Vice suprême,* a work heavily indebted to Flaubert's *Temptation of Saint Anthony* and *Salammbô,* that greatly impressed him. Four years later Guaïta and Péladan joined forces to create the Cabalistic Order of the Rosy Cross, ostensibly a revival of Rosicrucianism, a secret society of mystical initiates which, like its sister society Freemasonry of which it seems to be a stray branch, claims a very ancient origin in the mists of time. Although Rosicrucianism may have its roots in the twelfth-century Order of Sion and its militant arm the Knights Templar, ancient guardians of the Holy City of Jerusalem, the first incontestable documents of the society date only from the early seventeenth century, beginning with the publication in 1614 of the *Fama Fraternatis of the Meritorious Order of the Rosy Cross,* a weird allegorical romance, attributed to the German theologian and alleged Grand Master of the Priory of Sion Johann Valentin Andrea, devoted to the life and work of the visionary Christian Rosenkreuz (1378–1484), considered by all but the most devout believers to be a figure of doubtful historicity.

By 1890 Péladan, resenting what he perceived to be the anti-Catholic tendencies of the group, broke with Guaïta in what became known as The War of the Two Roses and founded a new order of Rosicrucianism which he called the Order of the Catholic Rosy Cross, the Temple and the Grail and which he defined as "an intellectual brotherhood of Charity, dedicated to the realization of works of mercy according to the Holy Spirit from which the members gather strength to multiply the Glory and prepare the Kingdom."[5] Péladan ruled over his theocracy like some ancient biblical patriarch. He drew up an elaborate ecclesiastical hierarchy, which included "commanders" and "dignitaries," "archons," "aesthetes," and "grand priors," and proceeded to fight The War of the Two Roses with a series of bizarre "episcopal decrees" or *mandements,* wherein he "excommunicated" enemies of the faith for crimes of "sacrilege and iconoclasm."[6] Further accusations were exchanged between the two Rosicrucian groups in the press. The schism was complete.

Like most Symbolist literary figures, Péladan idolized Wagner, not only as a musician of intoxicating power, but as a philosopher of the new art. He is known to have attended performances of *Parsifal* in Bayreuth in the summer of 1888, and, like so many of his generation, he responded deeply to the lofty idealism of the German master's "sacred festival drama," with its unique synthesis of poetry, music, and drama, and above all its overriding "Christian" message. That Péladan had an intimate knowledge of Wagner's operas is inferable from the title of his book, *The Complete Theater of Wagner, the XI Operas, Scene by Scene, with Biographical and Critical Notes,* which appeared in 1895 with a dedication to Judith Gautier.

Wagnerism and Catholicism, Zoroastrianism and Greek tragedy, antirepublicanism and anti-Semitism, androgyny and Lesbianism, tradition and hierarchy—here is a heady brew that carries us to the very heart of that subconscious world of chimera and dream that seems the very es-

sence of the French decadence. Although it is impossible to determine
precisely what attracted Satie to Péladan and his Rosicrucian sect, there
can be little doubt that the rebellious composer saw in the bizarre personality of the foppish Sâr something of a kindred spirit and that he found
the colorful ceremony and eccentric trumpery of his quasi-medieval Rosicrucian rites appealing for a time. In addition to the almost certain amusement with which he must have viewed the Order's fustian ritual—much
to the point is Rodolphe Salis's declaration that "mysticism and hoaxes
go well together"[7]—Satie doubtless appreciated the opportunity which
his official position with the organization afforded for the performance of
his music. Certainly the climate of taste was in favor of Satie's turning to
Péladan at this time. Here was a hothouse atmosphere fed by spiritism,
artifice, and a pervasive neurotic mysticism. Writing immediately after
World War I, Rudhyar Chennevière, or Dane Rudhyar, as he later preferred to be called—himself a rather eccentric composer with more than
a streak of mysticism in his makeup—succeeded admirably in capturing
something of the essence of Péladan's crumbling fin de siècle world:

It was at the time when neo-mysticism and symbolism gushed forth from the
solemn fount of *Parsifal*. The influence of the English Pre-Raphaelites had penetrated the youthful artists of France. The Sâr Péladan was seeing visions, de-
ciphering the hermetic arcanas of the Chaldean magi. The souls of the cathedrals
were being discovered. It was the epoch of long stations in minster naves im-
pregnated with the glow of stained-glass windows of symbolic design. . . . These
artists, weary of the "grand gesture" of romanticism, saddened by national defeat, incapable of understanding the meaning and grandeur of a civilization of the
future, heralded by the noise and tumult of machinery, took refuge in the Past,
in the mysticism of the Middle Ages. They allowed themselves to be lulled to
rest by the religion of their childhood, by all that it offered them in the shape of
atmospheric distance and revery, seeking to find the true well-spring of this faith
shrouded in the mists of passing centuries, in order to drink forgetfulness of self,
and of their incurable nostalgia, and to lose themselves voluptuously in the oblivion of its waters.[8]

The Rosicrucian Salons

Although Satie's relationship with Péladan and Rosicrucianism was to endure for only about two years, the music he wrote between 1891 and
1895 reveals a stylistic unity and is therefore usually grouped under the
generic heading *Rose-Croix*.

   An untitled work for piano—edited and orchestrated by Robert Caby

and published by Salabert in 1968—is Satie's first *Rose-Croix* composition. Caby has given it the title *Première pensée Rose + Croix*. The manuscript (B.N., Mus., Ms. 10.051 [1]) is dated 20 January 1891, two days
before the fourth *Gnossienne*. Like the earlier *Ogives* and *Gnossiennes,*
the *Première pensée Rose + Croix* is devoid of time signatures and bar
lines, a practice that becomes the norm for Satie beginning with the *Rose-
Croix* works.

This short work consists of eight phrases, each consisting of eight
beats, with the exception of the last two, which are reduced to six beats
each. Unlike the later *Rose-Croix* works, the *Première pensée* reveals a
distinct separation of melody and harmony throughout. As harmonic support to a conjunct diatonic line, whose triplet figurations provide the only
relief from an otherwise steady stream of quarter notes, Satie utilizes a
tritonal accompaniment based on a juxtaposition of root-position triads:

Example 1. Satie: *Première pensée Rose + Croix* (1891), beginning

Following is a harmonic synopsis of the work:
    Phrase 1: b–F–b
    Phrase 2: e–B-flat–e
    Phrase 3: b–F–b
    Phrase 4: F-sharp–G–F-sharp–c-sharp–F–b
    Phrase 5: F-sharp–G–F-sharp–c-sharp–F–b
    Phrase 6: d–A-flat$^+$–d
    Phrase 7: G–D-flat$^+$–G–C$^+$
    Phrase 8: d–E–F–b–d
Three aspects of the work are worth noting: (1) the predominantly tritonal relationship between chords, (2) the almost constant fluctuation of
mode, and (3) the abrupt transposition of phrases, usually at the interval
of the fourth. The appearance of augmented triads in phrases 6 and 7
underscores the tritonal relationships, the most distinctive feature of Satie's first Rosicrucian work.

The first titled work Satie is known to have written for Péladan is the incidental music for the Sâr's play *Le Fils des étoiles* (1891), first performed at the Durand-Ruel Gallery on 17 March 1892 during Péladan's first Salon de la Rose-Croix, which ran from 10 March to 10 April. Largely owing to the generosity of Count Antoine de La Rochefoucauld, a minor Symbolist painter and Grand Prior of the Order of the Catholic Rosy Cross, Péladan was able to hold a series of six Salons de la Rose-Croix between 1892 and 1897.

Péladan's stated artistic aim, as set forth in 1891 in the twenty-seven (a mystical trinitarian number—3 to the power of 3) "Rules of the Salon de la Rose-Croix," was "to *ruin realism*, reform Latin taste and create a school of idealist art."[9] Accordingly, Realism, as typified for example by the "ignoble" paintings of Courbet, was rejected, as was the new Impressionism—"aesthetic anarchy" in Péladan's view. The "Rules" go on to specify the banned subject categories, among them historical, patriotic, and rustic scenes, still lifes, seascapes, landscapes (except in the manner of Poussin),[10] and all humorous subjects. On the other hand, in order to foster the mystical Catholic Ideal, the Order strongly encouraged subjects drawn from myth, legend, allegory, and dream. The twenty-seventh and last rule is of particular interest to the musician, for it states that the Rosicrucian Salon will open with a Solemn Mass of the Holy Ghost, preceded by three fanfares for harp and trumpet composed by Erik Satie expressly for the Order, this ceremony to be followed by selections from *Parsifal* by "the superhuman Wagner."[11]

Between 1892 and 1897 a total of 231 artists exhibited at Péladan's Salons. All but a handful of these "dreamers of decadence" are more or less forgotten today. Conspicuously absent from the exhibitions were the giants of the Symbolist movement—Gustave Moreau, Odilon Redon, and especially Puvis de Chavannes, for a time Péladan's favorite artist, a "transcendent idealist" whom the Sâr praised lavishly for his dream landscapes and allegorical themes.

Péladan had first offered *Le Fils des étoiles* to the Odéon and the Comédie Française and was rejected by both theaters, the director of the Comédie Française, Jules Claretie, informing him that the play, although written in a fine scholarly language, was too much like literary music and would appeal only to a few initiates. And so, rejected by the Establishment, Péladan, again with the financial backing of La Rochefoucauld, opened his own Théâtre de la Rose-Croix as an adjunct to his Rosicrucian exhibitions, and there until the demise of the Salons in 1897 he produced six of his esoteric dramas, two of which were provided with incidental music by Satie.

Le Fils des étoiles was presented on three occasions in March during a series of five Rosicrucian soirées. It was badly received, an expensive fiasco that precipitated a break between Péladan and his patron La Rochefoucauld. We can glean something of the Sâr's musical tastes by noting that each of the soirées was consecrated to the memory of a different composer. The first program on 17 March was dedicated to Palestrina, and, along with the premiere of Péladan's play, Palestrina's *Pope Marcellus Mass* was performed by a choir of forty under the direction of one Bihn Grallon. The second concert, conducted by the great Lamoureux, was devoted to the music of Wagner and featured selections from the operas—including a nearly complete performance of the third act of *Parsifal*—and was introduced by a eulogy of the master by Péladan. The third soirée, under the direction of Vincent d'Indy, was a memorial concert for the recently deceased César Franck, not surprisingly a composer greatly admired by the Sâr. On the fourth evening the last two string quartets of Beethoven were performed in strange conjunction with a *Marche antique pour la Rose-Croix* by the obscure Grallon,[12] while the fifth and last concert, again directed by d'Indy, was dedicated to the pupils of Franck.

A complete piano score of Satie's incidental music for *Le Fils des étoiles,* together with Péladan's autograph scenario, exists in two manuscripts (B.N., Mus., Ms. 10052 [1] and 10052 [2]). Until 1973, only the Preludes to the three acts of the play had been published, although a *Gnossienne* used in act 1 turned up later in almost its original form as the opening of *Three Pieces in the Shape of a Pear.* Although the three Preludes are generally classified with Satie's piano works, the program for the first performance suggests that the original instrumentation called for an unspecified number of harps and flutes. The subtitle "Wagnérie Kaldéenne" ("Chaldean Wagnery") that appears in the published version of the Preludes would appear to have been an afterthought, for the manuscript omits any reference to Wagner, using only the subtitle "Pastorale Kaldéenne" ("Chaldean Pastoral"). Certainly there is nothing overtly Wagnerian about Satie's music, although the characteristic "timelessness" of all the *Rose-Croix* music is curiously much closer to Wagner than one might think. Péladan's play, on the other hand, clearly exploits the arch Wagnerian theme of redemption through compassionate love. On the fly-leaf of the score Satie has written the following dedication in the peculiarly stilted dialect he cultivated throughout his *Rose-Croix* period:

> Without prejudice to the observances of my cousins, the powerful sorcerers, I offer this work to my peers. In doing so, I claim no glory for myself.

I invoke upon my fellows the mercy of the Father, creator of things visible and invisible; the protection of the Majestic Mother of the Redeemer, Queen of Angels; along with the prayers of the heavenly hosts. May the righteous indignation of God crush out the proud and the unholy.

Erik Satie

The story is set in Chaldea about 3000 B.C. and concerns the young and androgynous poet-shepherd Oelohil, a true "son of the stars," who, like Tannhäuser, is torn between profane and spiritual love, between eros and agape. During his secret initiation into the Chaldean priesthood he proves himself worthy of the high office by resisting the temptation of the flesh, thus earning the right in the end to wed the young daughter of the high priest Goudéa, the chaste and pure Izel.

The three Preludes carry the following descriptive titles: act 1: *The Calling* ("Chaldean Night"); act 2: *The Initiation* ("The Lower Room of the Grand Temple"); act 3: *The Incantation* ("The Terrace of *Patési* [i.e., Priest-King] Goudéa's Palace"). The general mood of the act 1 prelude, and indeed of the *Rose-Croix* music in general, is suggested by the verbal inscription "En blanc et immobile" ("White and motionless") (line 1) and "Pâle et hiératique" ("Pale and hieratic") (lines 5 and 11). The opening motif, a four-note figure consisting of slowly moving fourth chords in parallel motion, provides the musical material for the entire prelude. Through transposition, variation, and development, the initial motif undergoes a series of thematic transformations:

Example 2. Satie: *Le Fils des étoiles* (1891), act 1, prelude (motivic transformation)

(a) Initial motif

(b) Variation

(c) Development

(d) Variation

The form of the prelude is defined by the juxtaposition of the motifs in the order (a) (b) (c) (d) (b) (c). The arpeggiated nature of motifs (b) and (d), suggestive of the harp sonorities of the original version, relieves the static chordal texture of motifs (a) and (c). The triadic harmonies (largely 5/3, 6/4, and seventh chords) of motifs (b), (c), and (d) provide further contrast to the stark quartal harmonies of the opening. As in the *Première pensée Rose + Croix* Satie prefers motivic transposition at the fourth or the fifth.

The four-note motif of the first prelude (ex. 2a) undergoes further transformation to provide the material for the second-act prelude. The harmonic vocabulary of the second prelude is richer than that of the first. In addition to further use of fourth-chords, Satie uses chains of sevenths and ninths reminiscent of the *Sarabandes*:

Example 3. Satie: *Le Fils des étoiles* (1891), act 2, prelude

The strictly parallel chordal movement of the first prelude gives way to a mixture of parallel and contrary motion. The juxtaposition of motifs— (a) (b) (c) (b) (c)—all of which are derived from the motifs of the act 1 prelude, provides a formal scheme almost identical to that of the first prelude. Again Satie breaks the regularity of the chordal texture with a contrasting arpeggiated motif and favors motivic transposition at the fourth or the fifth.

The prelude to act 3, the longest of the three, contains the greatest degree of motivic, textural, and rhythmic variety. Chains of major, minor, and augmented 5/3 chords and major and minor 6/3 chords are juxtaposed with stark passages of parallel fourth-chords and fanfarelike passages in octaves:

Example 4. Satie: *Le Fils des étoiles* (1891), act 3, prelude

(a) Major, minor, and augmented 5/3 chords

(b) Major and minor 6/3 chords

(c) Parallel fourth chords

(d) Fanfarelike motifs

It was inevitable that many writers would see in *Le Fils des étoiles* the influence of plainsong. Certainly there is a vaguely antiquarian quality to the three preludes that defies accurate definition; the strangely immobile and seemingly illogical chord sequences have something of the flavor of organum. Typically pertinent is Wilfrid Meller's remark that "Satie saw in the impersonality, the aloofness, the remoteness from all subjective dramatic stress of this music [i.e., plainsong] qualities which might, with appropriate modifications, approximate to his own uniquely lonely mode of utterance."[13] Once again the crucial limitations of Satie's technique resulted in a negation of the temporality characteristic of tonal music—a feeling that the music occupies space but not time.

Although the early compositions—especially the *Ogives* and *Sarabandes*—prefigure much that was to come, the music for *Le Fils des étoiles* may be considered the model that best served Satie throughout his brief *Rose-Croix* period. The techniques and the harmonic vocabulary would vary slightly from work to work, but all the *Rose-Croix* works, from the *Première pensée Rose + Croix* of 1891 to the *Messe des pauvres* of 1895, reveal Satie's obsession for vertical sonorities in strange and incongruous contexts. In his sketchbooks of this time can be seen numerous unorthodox scales of his own invention and series of chord progressions showing many different ways of harmonizing various melodic steps. These early sketches became the raw material from which he constructed his Rosicrucian legacy. He seems to have been intent on creating an invocatory effect through reiteration, juxtaposition, and accumulation of sonorities rather than through any kind of traditional harmonic logic. Tonality and rhythm as such did not concern him. His aim was to create a vague, floating "Puvis de Chavannes" atmosphere, an ideal he held up to Debussy when the older composer was working on his Maeterlinck opera. In the *Rose-Croix* music Satie invented the kind of music that Leonard Meyer, three-quarters of a century later, was to call "anti-teleological"—a nongoal-oriented music, a music that is simply *there,* a kind of quasi-religious "furniture music" before the fact.[14]

The last *Rose-Croix* work to date from 1891 (the manuscript—B.N.,

Mus., Ms. 10053—is dated 2 November) is the curious *Hymne pour le "Salut Drapeau,"* written for Péladan's five-act drama *Le Prince de Byzance* and the only extended vocal work of the *Rose-Croix* period. Robert Caby edited the hymn in 1968 in versions for voice and piano and for unison female chorus and orchestra. In order to facilitate performance, Caby has added a metronome indication (♩ = 48), time signatures, bar lines, and expression markings.

It is interesting to note that the intervallic structure of Satie's strange vocal melody (C-sharp D E-flat F-sharp G A-flat B C-sharp) conforms to the chromatic genus of the ancient Greek Mixolydian mode, a scale he used again the following year in his ballet *Uspud*. This scale, with its prominent augmented second (E-flat–F-sharp), yields only two "plain" triads, one major (G–B–D) and one minor (B–D–F-sharp). The remaining five triads derived from the mode are dominated, in nearly equal ratio, by augmented and diminished intervals, which serve to undercut any tendency toward functional harmonic progression. The underlying harmonies of the *Hymne pour le "Salut Drapeau,"* however, consisting of chains of major, minor, and diminished 6/3 chords, conform only partly to the mode. Whereas the melodic line is faithfully doubled in the top line of the accompaniment, the remaining chord members frequently step outside the mode, resulting in a variety of peculiar false relations:

Example 5. Satie: *Hymne pour le "Salut Drapeau"* from *Le Prince de Byzance* (1891), measures 5–9

Following is the rather pompous ode Péladan provided for his young composer:

> Langes de tous les fils
> Manteau de tous les pères
> Suaire des héros
> Étoffe teinte à la veine d'un peuple
> Salut Drapeau!

Ta hampe est le grand mât de l'Argo national
Ta hampe est la colonne où un peuple s'appuye
Il est mort si tu penches, si tu tombes, avili
Salut Drapeau!

Voile gonflée par toutes les poitrines
Orgueilleux labarum
Aile éployée des foules palpitantes
Tu portes dans ton vol le destin d'une race!
Symbole généreux
Idéal collectif
Salut Drapeau![15]

It is impossible to determine whether the strange clumsiness of this piece was, for some inexplicable reason, deliberate, or, as is more likely the case, simply a by-product of Satie's experimentation at this time with exotic scales. His fascination for odd harmonic progressions seems in this instance to have overridden any concern for structural coherence. A certain unity is provided by the recurring accompanimental figure ♪♪ ♩ but its repetition seems random and therefore unpredictable, in keeping with the similarly ambiguous metrical structure of the piece as revealed by the editorial time signatures. The work's most glaring structural deficiency, however, is its peculiar text / music relationship. In order to utilize the first-stanza music for the longer second and third verses, Satie simply spread these two verses over three repetitions of the opening music, resulting in an awkward staggering of the strophic form. This would clearly suggest that the music was composed in advance of Péladan's verse and only later superimposed on the text. A piece such as this lends credence to Contamine de Latour's assertion that Satie was, with his limited technical resources, still groping for a distinctive style, rather "like a man who, knowing only thirteen letters of the alphabet, is nonetheless determined to create a new literature with these limited means rather than confess his own inadequacy."[16]

The year 1892 saw the composition of the three *Sonneries de la Rose + Croix,* the posthumously published *Quatre Préludes,* and the three-act ballet *Uspud.* The *Sonneries de la Rose + Croix* were originally printed in red and illustrated with a fragment of Puvis de Chavannes's *La Guerre.* The three *Sonneries,* or fanfares, subtitled "Air de l'ordre," "Air du grand maître," and "Air du grand prieur," were originally intended, on the strict order of Péladan himself, for performance only at meetings of the Rosicrucian brotherhood.

Each of the *Sonneries* is constructed on a principle somewhat similar to that of the *Ogives,* although here we find a degree of internal complexity conspicuously absent from the earlier work. Like the *Ogives,* the *Sonneries* are monothematic, achieving variety through dynamic and textural means. For example, the "Air de l'ordre," marked "Lent et détachée sans sécheresse" ("Slow and detached without dryness"), opens with a chain of major, minor, augmented, and diminished root-position triads, the basic material for the entire piece. This chain of 5/3 chords (A) is followed by a fanfarelike elaboration of the opening chords (A^1) and, after an exact repetition of (A), a subsequent union of the vertical structure (A) with the linear structure (A^1), which can be designated (A^2):

Example 6. Satie: "Air de l'ordre" from *Sonneries de la Rose + Croix* (1892)

(a) Chain of 5/3 chords (A)

(b) Fanfarelike elaboration (A^1)

(c) Union of vertical and linear elements (A^2)

What follows this exposition can only be described as a slight development section based on contractions of (A^2) and (A). An exact (except for octave transpositions at the beginning and end) repetition of (A^2) serves as a brief recapitulation. The "Air du grand maître" (Péladan) and the "Air du grand prieur" (La Rochefoucauld) are both constructed on the same principle.

If the *Hymne pour le "Salut Drapeau"* is structurally diffuse and indeterminate, the *Sonneries de la Rose + Croix* reveal, for the first time in Satie's oeuvre, a subtle proportional balance, the precise mathematical formula and arcane significance of which may have been passed on to him through Péladan and his Rosicrucian teachings or through Debussy, whose acquaintance he also made about this time.

Numerological symbolism in music has surfaced at every stage of Western music from the time of the ancient Greeks to the present day. Analysts have long known of the rich vein of number symbolism imbedded in the music of Bach. Studies of Mozart and Masonic symbolism have yielded equally fruitful results in this respect. It would appear that Haydn and Beethoven also had connections with Freemasonry. Several recent studies have subjected the music of such composers as Berg, Stockhausen, and Nono, as well as Dunstable and Obrecht, to numerical analysis, often with fascinating results. Considering Debussy's well-known interest in occultism and his affinity for Symbolist aesthetics, it does not come as a complete surprise that Roy Howat, in a recent study, should have managed to demonstrate beyond a reasonable doubt that the composer was involved in esoteric number symbolism at least as early as 1885.[17] Although unassailable evidence is lacking, Debussy may have been elected, in this same year, Grand Master of the Rosicrucian Priory of Sion, a highly secret organization reputed to be the administrative power behind the Knights Templar. If this is true, it would place Debussy at the very heart of fin de siècle French occultism and go a long way toward explaining the mystical sources of numerological symbolism in his work, in particular his use of the Golden Section, a mathematical ratio used from ancient times in art and architecture and discussed extensively in the theoretical writings of the French Symbolists with whom the composer was closely allied in his early years.

Although it is generally assumed that Satie did not meet Debussy until 1891, and then at the Auberge du Clou where Satie had established himself as a pianist after quarreling with Rodolphe Salis and severing his ties with the Chat Noir, it is quite possible that the two composers would have encountered one another earlier at the Chat Noir where Debussy is known to have preceded his younger colleague as an accompanist in the early 1880s. The Auberge du Clou had opened in December 1883 at no. 30, avenue Trudaine, not far from the second Chat Noir in the rue Victor Massé, and by the early 1890s it had become one of the chief rivals to Salis's establishment, even to the point of mounting its own shadow plays.[18] Satie was only one of a number of Chat Noir habitués—others included Tinchant, Hyspa, and Desboutin—who eventually deserted Salis to take up residence in the rival cabaret. Coincidentally, it was here, on the second floor of the Auberge du Clou, that Guaïta and Péladan held the early meetings of the Cabalistic Order of the Rosy Cross, beginning in 1888. At least one source has suggested that Debussy may have been a member of this secret society and that it may have been he who introduced Satie to Péladan rather than vice versa.[19]

Whatever the chronological details of the encounter between Debussy and the young bohemian whom he described in 1892 as a "gentle medieval musician who strayed into this century to give joy to his best friend, Claude Debussy,"[20] it would appear to be more than coincidental that Satie, in that same year, should have tried his hand at organizing a piece of music utilizing the structural proportions of the Golden Section, the "divine number" known since the time of Pythagoras from whence it was absorbed into numerous esoteric traditions, including Rosicrucianism.

The Golden Section can be expressed in mathematical terms as $\dfrac{b}{a} = \dfrac{a}{a+b}$, a ratio, a little under two-thirds, whose exact value is irrational but approximates to 0.618034. Since the *Sonneries de la Rose + Croix* are devoid of bar lines, the basic temporal unit of the three pieces is the beat, in this case the quarter note. Accordingly, a proportional analysis of the first *Sonnerie* would reveal the following structure: an "exposition" (see ex. 6) consisting of (A—36 beats), (A^1—36 beats), (A—36 beats), and (A^2—36 beats), followed by "developments" of (A^2) and (A) (21 + 6 beats and 20 + 6 beats, respectively), and a restatement of (A^2—36 beats), giving a total of 233 beats. The Golden Section of 233 (233 × 0.618034) is 144.00192 or 144 rounded off to the beat; the "exposition" of the first *Sonnerie* is exactly 144 (36 × 4) beats long. The Golden Section falls, therefore, precisely between the "exposition" and the truncated statements of (A^2) and (A) we have called the "development" section.

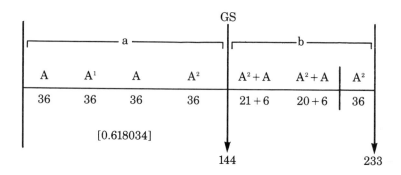

The third *Sonnerie,* although more condensed, is proportionally a kind of mirror image of the first *Sonnerie.* Again it opens with a string of 5/3 chords (A—34 beats), followed by a fanfarelike elaboration of the same harmonies (A^1—34 beats), a union of the two textures (A^2—71 beats), which is expanded in a kind of "development" section, and a restatement of (A—34 beats), for a total of 173 beats. The Golden Section of 173 is 106. Reading the score back to front—that is, in the order (A) (A^2) (A^1) (A)—(A^1) begins precisely on beat 106. In other words, the ratio between the first two statements (A + A^1—68 beats) and the last two (A^2 + A—105 beats) is a Golden Section, with the shorter portion appearing first rather than last.

Perhaps there is some veiled symbolism in the fact that the second *Sonnerie,* the one dedicated to the Grand Master Péladan, conforms only marginally to the proportions of the Golden Section and then only if its "development" section (106 beats) is considered as an interlocking value attached to both the "exposition" (147 beats) and the "recapitulation" (49 beats). If the 106-beat "development" section is figured into the equation twice, the total number of beats (253 + 155) is 408, the Golden Section of which is 252, an acceptable margin of error of one beat.

A	A^1	A^2	A^2	A
49	49	49	106	49

253

155

This is clearly stretching the point and it is of course entirely possible that the presence of Golden Section proportions in any of the three *Sonneries* is purely fortuitous. However, considering the circumstantial evidence as well as the fact that two of the three *Sonneries* conform exactly to the system, it would seem reasonable to speculate that Satie, who relentlessly eschewed "traditional" means of formal organization in almost all of his work, found in the Golden Section a means of structuring his music that was at once elegant and in tune with the arcane numerological systems in vogue at the time, particularly among the Symbolists.

The austere *Préludes,* published posthumously in 1929, go under the following imposing titles: (1) "Fête donnée par des Chevaliers Normands en l'Honneur d'une jeune Demoiselle"; (2) "Prélude d'Eginhard"; (3) "Premier Prélude du Nazaréen"; (4) "Deuxième Prélude du Nazaréen." There is some evidence to support the view that Satie may have conceived the first of the *Quatre Préludes* as early as 1884, for on the reverse side of the manuscript of his first known work, the *Allegro* of 9 September 1884, there is a four-line sketch of the beginning of "Fête donnée par des Chevaliers Normands en l'Honneur d'une jeune Demoiselle," marked "Lent (XIe siècle)." In the right-hand margin of the manuscript (B.N., Mus., Ms., 10050 [1]) the name "Saint Ambrose (340–397)" is inscribed in pencil in the composer's hand. No doubt Satie would have found much to admire in the life of Saint Ambrose, Bishop of Milan from 374 to 397, who by all accounts led an exemplary life of extreme humility and self-denial in his devoted service to humanity. One can only imagine, however, what the young bohemian's response might have been to the venerable Bishop's veritable obsession with chastity as revealed by his treatise *De lapsu virginis consecrate* (Concerning the Fall of the Consecrated Virgin).

Although the "Fête donnée par des Chevaliers Normands" may date in part from 1884, there is no question that the two "Préludes du Nazaréen" were composed in 1892, while the "Prélude d'Eginhard" may date from as late as mid-1893. The seven-page manuscript of the "Deuxième Prélude du Nazaréen," dated 12 June 1892, carries the title "Prélude pour 'Le Nazaréen' d' H. Mazel," and would thus appear to have been intended as incidental music for the play by Henri Mazel, poet, critic, and mystic who, like Péladan, was imbued with the lofty religious idealism of the period. By now Satie's Gothic imagination was in full flower and, like some medieval scribe, he decorated his manuscript with fanciful black-ink drawings of whimsical Gothic castles as well as with pencil-drawn caricatures of himself.

Patrick Gowers, in a detailed study of the technical vocabulary of the *Rose-Croix* works based on an examination of Satie's sketchbooks, has demonstrated that these strange "Rosicrucian" pieces, fabricated almost entirely from streams of disjunct chordal progressions juxtaposed occasionally with severe monophonic lines of a pronounced Gregorian flavor, were synthesized from numerous melodic and harmonic "exercises" consisting of unorthodox scalar structures and unusual four-part harmonizations of various melodic intervals, a modus operandi which, in Gowers's view, tends "to confirm the impression of a calculating, theory-conscious and therefore somewhat abstract composer. . . . "[21] A case in point is the first of the *Quatre Préludes,* the basic musical material of which is synthesized from a series of motivic ideas arising from ten different harmonizations of melodic intervals—seven seconds, one third, and two fifths—which are strung together in a seemingly random pattern to form the entire basis of the piece. The resulting progression, a slow thirty-nine-chord sequence of mostly 6/3 and 6/4 chords, is darkly colored by a preponderance of diminished and minor chords which lend this knightly Norman feast in honor of a young noble woman an air of grave solemnity and timeless mystery. The unorthodox and unpredictable harmonic progressions, floating free from the exigencies of functional tonality, sound remote and disembodied, like a faint echo from some dark Gothic crypt.

The Metropolitan Church of Art of Jesus the Leader

Although he was to compose in a "Rosicrucian" style until 1895, Satie's association with Péladan was destined to be short-lived. A few months after the first performances of *Le Fils des étoiles* in March 1892, about the same time he was putting the finishing touches on the incidental music for Henri Mazel's *Le Nazaréen,* the composer began to show signs of impatience with Péladan's strict and solemn Order. And in August of that year he launched his literary career with an open letter addressed to the editor of *Gil Blas* in which he announced his break with the Sâr, claiming in the flowery and pseudoarchaic language he affected at the time, that the "good Master Joséphin Péladan . . . has in no wise exercised authority on my Aesthetic independence. . . . Inasmuch as I am the pupil of anyone," he declared, "Methinks this anyone can but be myself."[22]

Thus it was that Satie dissolved all ties with Péladan and set himself up in opposition to him by founding his own "church," the Metropolitan Church of Art of Jesus the Leader. There is extant a strange document in the composer's ornate calligraphy which outlines the "program" of the new church. Satie's Congregation of the Poor Knights of the Holy City, we are informed, are "pious skeletons," involved in the most profound mysteries, whose sacred mandate is to defend Christianity and maintain the public peace. Like their ancestors the Knights Templar and the Hospitalers of St. Lazarus of Jerusalem, ancient guardians of the Holy Sepulchre, these humble penitents, white-robed and adorned with the double red cross, lead a most austere life, having renounced the material goods of this world and taken the monastic vows of obedience, poverty, and chastity.[23]

From his tiny, windowless room—really no more than a closet—in the rue Cortot, now christened "Our Abbatial," Satie launched a series of fantastic attacks on the literary and musical world with the aid of his privately printed journal, the *Cartulary of the Metropolitan Church of Art of Jesus the Leader,* which he was able to support for a very short time with a small inheritance received upon the death of his father in 1892. Operating from his sparsely furnished quarters, Satie began to act out his fantasies, giving free rein to his capricious imagination and assuming in the process a role that combined the traits of the cynical intellectual and the Montmartre wag. He appointed himself Parcener and Chapel Master of his new church and estimated that his disciples—divided into an elaborate ecclesiastical hierarchy—would number in the hundreds of millions! He had in mind a figure of 1,600,000,000 for his black-robed and gray-hooded "Peneants noirs convers," while the "Peneants noirs profès," robed in black and white, would number 8,000,000, the "Peneants gris," a mere 40,000, the "Peneants blancs," 200, the "Cloistriers," 50, and the "Définiteurs," 10. Each of these groups would be distinguished by the color scheme of its vestment. The Parcener himself would be attired grandly in a crimson robe with violet hood, and the official vesture of the church was to be "cowl, sleeves, and leggings of mail; hooded robe; conical helmet with nosepiece; and gloves of mail"; its arms, "a large battle sword and a lance five meters long."[24] At its peak, the Metropolitan Church of Art of Jesus the Leader enjoyed a total membership of one, with Satie himself in the triple role of founder, high priest, and sole adherent of the sect.

Through a series of published declarations and printed pamphlets which appeared before the publication of the *Cartulary,* Satie explained that the aim of his new church was "to restore the Holy Religion trodden underfoot by sinners, and the Arts which are its most sublime expression."[25] He was clearly aping, more likely mocking, Péladan's misanthropic ideas in his proclamations aimed at those responsible for "the aesthetic and moral decadence of our time."[26] It is odd that very few of Satie's critics to date have seen fit to view the Metropolitan Church as a vast travesty of Péladan's Rosicrucian Temple. Coming as it did on the heels of his association with the Sâr, it is hard not to see Satie's fanciful organization, with its astronomical numbers, its elaborate hierarchical structure, and its pseudopious aims, as a deliberate and extravagant parody. Even the composer's stilted literary style can be construed as a caricature of Péladan's bombastic prose, and his practice of "excommunicating" his enemies—real or imagined—recalls the Sâr's episcopal decrees during The War of the Two Roses. Moreover, Péladan by this time was increasingly subject to ridicule from many quarters—including the pages of *Le Chat Noir, La Plume,* and *Le Figaro*—so that Satie was by no means alone in exposing the foibles of this effete poseur who by the end of the century had become a shabby and rather ludicrous figure. All the more ironical in this context is the indignant statement of Wilson Lyle, a practising Rosicrucian who declared most emphatically as recently as 1981 that Satie was *not* a Rosicrucian because, in Lyle's opinion, "he utterly lacked the artistic alchemy, mental as well as mystical, to reach out and grip the hearts and minds of the musical audiences"[27] as certain of his contemporaries—Franck and Debussy, for example—had succeeded in doing.

Apparently there were to have been eight to ten issues of the *Cartulary,* but only two numbers appeared, those for May and June 1895. On the surface it is paradoxical that Satie's main targets at this time were such forward-looking creative people as Aurélien Lugné-Poë, actor, producer, and from 1893 to 1929 director of the experimental Théâtre de l'Oeuvre, Alfred Valette, founder (in 1890) of the progressive monthly *Le Mercure de France,* Alexandre Natanson, cofounder of the influential *Revue blanche,* Léon Deschamps of the fortnightly Symbolist review *La Plume,* which ran from 1880 to 1904, and above all the notorious novelist and journalist Henri Gauthier-Villars, music critic for a number of important newspapers and magazines, including *Gil Blas, Art et critique,* and the virulently right-wing *Écho de Paris.*

In a brochure dated 8 March 1895 entitled "Intende votis supplicum" Satie brought to task Lugné-Poë, Valette, Natanson, and Deschamps for unspecified "execrable practices," concluding that the Metropolitan Church considers them "to be evildoers speculating on human corruption" and therefore condemns them "to the hatred of righteous persons and will use all means to precipitate their moral downfall."[28] Satie's severe censure of Lugné-Poë, whose experimental theatrical activities were warmly praised in the pages of *Le Mercure de France, La Revue blanche,* and *La Plume,* may point to a fairly conspicuous streak of xenophobia in the composer's makeup, for the director's only "crime" would appear to be his marked preference for foreign playwrights. During the first two seasons of his Théâtre de l'Oeuvre (1892–95) productions of native plays were significantly outnumbered by foreign works, with the Scandinavians—Ibsen, Björnson, Strindberg—commanding the greatest attention.

It was, however, the pompous Gauthier-Villars, or Willy, as he preferred to be called, who was to receive the lion's share of Satie's spleen, and a good part of the first number of the *Cartulary* is aimed at the bemused critic, who plastered the Parcener's "excommunications" on the walls of his apartment at no. 93, rue de Courcelles. Colette, who was married to Gauthier-Villars from 1893 to 1906, has left a revealing portrait of her first husband. Willy, it seems, depended on a troupe of collaborators in order to meet the deadline for his weekly column, which appeared under the curious title "Les Lettres de l'Ouvreuse" ("Notes of an Usherette"). Colette described the hebdomadal ritual as follows:

> For the big Sunday concerts a corps of despatch-riders was mobilised, carefully picked men [among them, according to the author, such rising stars as Alfred Ernst, Émile Vuillermoz, Claude Debussy, and Vincent d'Indy] who galloped from Colonne to Pasdeloup, from Pasdeloup to the Conservatoire, exchanged stalls, snatched a seat from beneath the confederate who had been mounting guard. . . .[29]

Apparently Willy suffered from a not uncommon writer's disease characterized by Colette as "a sort of agoraphobia, . . . a nervous horror of the blank page,"[30] and she closes the "case against M. Willy" in a rather backhanded manner by concluding that "he was a born critic, although even the opinions on which he based his judgements were borrowed from other people."[31] Willy's columns (whatever the precise origin of their authorship) were typical of the epoch—witty, sarcastic, cynical, given to outrageous puns and startling neologisms. Although, according to Debussy, Willy was musically illiterate, this gregarious charlatan set himself up as a champion of avant-garde music—Wagner's in particular—probably more for the publicity value of such a stance than for any deeply held musical convictions.

Two of Satie's most vicious (and amusing) diatribes were directed at the pretentious critic who, in his opinion, had "blasphemed in passing judgements on Wagner" and therefore was commanded "to languish in grief, in silence and in painful meditation."[32] Willy rose to the bait and, mimicking the heavy-handed solemnity of the Parcener's "liturgical" prose, answered the charges in his newspaper column, dismissing Satie as a trashy composer and inconsequential buffoon. The composer's reply was swift and rang with a stinging invective of libelous intensity: "Your breath stinks of lies, your mouth spreads audacity and indecency. Your depravity has caused your own downfall; it has made your incomparable crassness clear to even the most limited of intelligences."[33]

This was but the opening skirmish in a *guerre de plume* that would continue into the early years of the new century. Salis's *Le Chat Noir* gleefully reported the Satie-Willy affair, and the acid-tongued critic continued his ridicule of the composer in his numerous columns. In a letter of 31 March 1898, written in large Gothic script and adorned with an ornate ogival window drawn in red, Satie adopted a more characteristic mock-conciliatory tone toward his despised adversary: "To think that We mistook you for a stupid barbarian," he wrote, "for a coward, for a rather silly and pallid reject of Literature! How wrong We were, honored Sir; how wrong. A regrettable mistake!"[34] The conflict finally came to a head on 10 April 1904 during an orchestral concert at the Cirque d'été. During the performance of a Beethoven symphony Satie confronted Willy about the harsh treatment he was being dealt by the critic in the press. By way of response Willy attempted to dismiss the composer with a supercilious comment, whereupon Satie set upon him with his fists only to be beaten off by Willy's walking stick and ignominiously dragged off to the police station.

In 1892 Satie launched one of his most sustained capers: on three occasions he boldly presented his candidature to the distinguished Institut de France. Upon the death of Debussy's master Ernest Guiraud on 6 May 1892, Satie, with unflappable temerity, applied for membership in the Institute's Academy of Fine Arts. The eccentric bohemian accordingly made a series of official visits to the Institute's offices in the Palais Mazarin where he placed in the committee's hands a grossly inflated account of his musical achievements. Not at all surprisingly the Academicians lost no time in snubbing the little-known Montmartre cabaret pianist, although at least two members of the committee, Ernest Reyer, one of the leading French Wagnerians, and the painter Gustave Moreau, favorite of Debussy and creator of chimerical Gothic visions reminiscent of the restorations of Viollet-le-Duc, showed some consideration for him. The taciturn and misogynic Moreau, although a respected master of the

Symbolist style, displayed an utter contempt for success and an intense preoccupation with the occult which might account for his courteous treatment of the obscure young composer on this occasion.

The death of Charles Gounod on 18 October 1893 gave the undaunted composer yet another opportunity to invade the sanctuary of the academic world, and early in 1894 he applied for Gounod's vacant seat at the Academy. Again he was, of course, ignored. But this time he was prompted to reply to his judges, and on 17 May 1894—his twenty-eighth birthday—he sent a letter to *Le Ménestrel* addressed to the jury president Camille Saint-Saëns in which he threatened the illustrious composer with "the flames of Hell" for his "incomprehension of the ideas of Our Time" and his "ignorance of God."[35]

Satie's third and last attempt to gain an official seat came in 1896 upon the death, in February of that year, of Ambroise Thomas. The result of this third endeavor need hardly be recorded. In asserting his illusions through these mocking and mystifying actions, the young composer gave visible form to his fantasies while indulging in one of the favorite pastimes of the artistic avant-garde. It was, he said with his jesting, "laughing eyes," an attempt to make the guardians of tradition, the perpetuators of sterile academic formularism, aware of the beauty of a "living and genuine art."[36] Years later, in 1912, he devoted an entire installment of his *Memoirs of an Amnesiac* to an account of his attempts to storm the redoubtable Academy and sway "the crafty worthies of the Palais-Mazarin."[37] Time, of course, has provided the final irony, for whereas Satie's name is now known throughout the world, the successful candidates on these three occasions—Émile Paladilhe, Théodore Dubois, and Charles Lenepveu—have lapsed into well-deserved obscurity.

Last Rosicrucian Thoughts

About 1893 Satie began to frequent the Nouvelle Athènes in the Place Pigalle. Here his bohemian spirit continued to flourish in the congenial company of poets and painters united in their deep scorn of official art, including many of his old cronies from the Chat Noir and the Auberge du Clou. Among the habitués of the Nouvelle Athènes during Satie's tenure there was a tempestuous young painter, one year older than the composer, who was to become the only woman ever to break into the mysterious inner circle of his life. Suzanne Valadon, at the time of her meeting with Satie early in 1893, had already achieved a certain success as an artists' model—much in demand by Renoir, Degas, Toulouse-

Lautrec, and others—and later as a painter in her own right. Although still highly respected as an artist, her Impressionistic nudes and landscapes are today overshadowed by the superb paintings of her son Maurice Utrillo, who was born in 1883 in Suzanne's eighteenth year. The paternity of the boy is uncertain, although Puvis de Chavannes, for whom Utrillo's mother often posed, is a prime candidate for the distinction, even though the boy was named after another of his mother's numerous lovers, the Barcelona-born art critic and engineering student Miguel Utrillo, whose actual acknowledgment of paternity was frequently supported by Suzanne herself, quite truthfully it now appears.

On 14 January 1893 Satie and Suzanne Valadon met, probably at the Nouvelle Athènes; that same evening the composer proposed marriage. "It was my last chance," he later reflected. "It was then three o'clock in the morning—an impossible time to get to the *mairie*. After that it was always too late. She had too many things on her mind to get married; so we never brought up the subject again."[38]

Even though Suzanne was at this time the mistress of a wealthy young lawyer, Paul Mousis, she soon took up with Satie, moving into a studio next door to him in the rue Cortot. Like all the composer's relationships the Valadon affair was to be volcanic and transitory and not without an element of the bizarre. The sensuous young woman and the impecunious cabaret pianist spent idyllic days together sailing toy boats in the ponds of the Luxembourg Gardens; often he would buy her necklaces of sausages and send bouquets of flowers to her ten-year-old son, and once on her birthday he brought her a paper sack "with all the wonderful smells of the world in it."[39]

Satie explained to his friends that Suzanne, even though ignorant of music, nurtured his musical inventiveness. "She will never get a rapt expression on her face like a spaniel of a critic," he observed, "and she has a tender little belch which is often inspiring."[40] The composer and his companion, who was affectionately known as "Biqui," often slept wrapped in blankets on the bare floor of her studio, and it was here that Suzanne painted her first picture in oils, a portrait of the bearded composer in bohemian dress. In return Satie presented her with a song fragment entitled "Bonjour, Biqui, Bonjour," dated Easter Sunday 1893 and adorned with an "authentic portrait" of Suzanne in pen and ink. An intimate letter of 11 March 1893 carries us behind the jesting facade for a rare glimpse of the composer's innermost feelings. "Dear little Biqui," he wrote, "impossible to stop thinking of your whole being; I am completely full of you; wherever I go I see nothing but your lovely eyes, your gentle

hands and your tiny feet." One wonders if Suzanne was already cuckold-
ing him, for he concludes this letter with a note of quiet despair: "For me
there is nothing but icy loneliness which makes my head go empty and
fills my heart with sadness. . . ."[41]

The relationship between painter and composer was uncertain and
sometimes violent. The end came on 20 June and soon after Suzanne
moved back with Mousis, only to settle with him several doors from Satie
at no. 2, rue Cortot. In order to soothe his injured pride the composer
posted a series of placards on the street side of his door in full public
view denouncing the virtue of Suzanne in the vivid prelatical terms soon
to be familiar from the pages of the *Cartulary*. Speaking of the rupture
in later years to one of his disciples, Satie recalled in terms that may be
only slightly exaggerated:

The Master was the most melancholy of humans. He bawled and he threw himself to the floor to weep bitter tears. Suzanne was the only one in the world from
whom he could draw the spirit his soul required. She was the anchor to his sanity.
If she left him, all would be lost. He sobbed and fainted.[42]

On the eve of his meeting with Suzanne Valadon, Satie conceived one
of his most bizarre works. If the Metropolitan Church is construed as an
elaborate parody of the Order of the Catholic Rosy Cross, the fantastic
stage-work *Uspud*, "A Christian ballet in three acts," would appear to be
a preposterous burlesque of the Sâr's Rosicrucian novels and dramas.
This curious piece, dating from November 1892, was composed to a
strange teratogenic scenario by Contamine de Latour, who later recalled
a visit he and Satie made to the Paris Opéra where the composer boldly
challenged the Director, Eugène Bertrand, to a duel because he had
failed to acknowledge receipt of the score, which had been submitted to
the Opéra on 20 December 1892. After receiving a number of strongly
worded letters from the composer berating him for rejecting a work he
had never properly examined, Bertrand finally agreed to consider it, but
at this point Satie assured the failure of his mission by making the outrageous demand that the ballet be submitted to a special committee of
forty musicians, of whom half were to be chosen by the authors.[43] No
more was heard of *Uspud* until 1895 when two brochures were issued,
one under the auspices of the Metropolitan Church, dated 9 April 1895,
which contained four extracts from the music of the ballet along with a
stinging denunciation of the chief editor of *La Revue blanche,* Alexandre
Natanson, the other a complete scenario of the stage-work followed by

an announcement that *Uspud* would be succeeded by a one-act ballet, *Ontrotance,* already in preparation, and, God willing, *Corcleru,* a ballet in three acts, a two-act work, *Irnebizolle,* in which, Satie proclaimed, no single person would appear on stage, and, finally, another three-act ballet with an even more outlandish title, *Tumisrudebude.*[44]

Like so many of Péladan's plays and novels, *Uspud* is a phantasmagorical Christian allegory, and it seems likely that both authors—Péladan and Contamine de Latour—might have derived inspiration from Flaubert's surreal *Temptation of Saint Anthony,* with its hallucinatory overtones of sadomasochism and Oriental pantheism.

The ballet features a single stage character, the pagan Uspud, who, dressed in Persian garb, appears on a deserted beach by the sea where he sees a vision of a very beautiful woman clad in gold with a dagger piercing her breast—a personification of the Christian Church. Uspud repulses her embrace whereupon he is attacked by all manner of monsters and demons with human form, but with the heads of animals— jackals, lynxes, unicorns, baboons, boars, crocodiles, etc. The beautiful woman reappears, snowy white and crystal clear, and plunges her dagger into the breast of Uspud causing him to fall into a trance wherein the vision of a gigantic crucifix appears to him against the seraphic background of a heavenly choir hymning the power and dominion of the Almighty. His conversion is complete. Weeping, he prostrates himself before the cross in prayer and receives the blessing of the Holy Spirit. The voices of the Holy Saints summon him to martyrdom; he commends his soul to the Lord and is torn to pieces by a swarm of demons as the angels escort his soul to the heavenly regions and into the resplendent arms of Christ.

Given Satie's abstract working methods at this time, it comes as little surprise that the music of *Uspud* bears absolutely no dramatic relationship to the stage action. "Music and libretto," in James Harding's words, "are like two trains which pass in opposite directions."[45] Indeed, it would appear that Contamine de Latour's scenario was grafted onto Satie's emotionally neutral music after the fact, or vice versa. *Uspud* is a compendium of the composer's by now familiar "Rosicrucian" devices: chains of 5/3, 6/3, and 6/4 chords, sevenths and ninths (and occasional higher extensions), fourth-chords, and monophonic fanfarelike passages. In all there are twelve distinctive motivic ideas in *Uspud,* of which eight are exposed in the first Act. They seem to be juxtaposed in a random order, although the opening monophonic statement that frames the ballet appears ten times—both in its original monophonic texture and in simple harmonized versions of 6/3 and 6/4 chords—thereby providing a fragile sense of unity and stability in an otherwise structurally diffuse and harmonically complex score. Other motifs undergo a more subtle process of transformation. For example, the second motif to appear, a strange harmonization of the same Greek chromatic mode used the previous year in the *Hymne pour le "Salut Drapeau,"* appears in the following guises:

Example 7. Satie: *Uspud* (1892)

(a) Original motif

(b) Rhythmic variant with slight harmonic alterations

(c) Rhythmic variant with altered voicing

(d) Monophonic variant of (a)

(e) Rhythmic variant and contraction of (b) with motivic repetition

(f) Rhythmic variant of (b)

(g) Harmonic variant of (a)

(h) Harmonic variant of (a) with motivic repetition

(i) Rhythmic variant and contraction of (b) with motivic repetition

Other motivic ideas undergo similar transformations, while still others reappear without alteration (or, in two instances, simply transposed to the fifth). Five of the twelve motifs are derived from the Greek mode, and the sheer persistence of these gestures, with their predominant augmented and diminished intervals, lends a strange "atonal" coloring to *Uspud.* Its harmonic novelty, momentarily intriguing, soon induces in the listener a mystifying and stultifying sense of boredom, granting authority to Contamine de Latour's assertion that *Uspud* was "a compendium of foolish things designed . . . to dumbfound the public."[46]

At the height of his affair with his beloved "Biqui," Satie composed the strange *Danses gothiques,* which he subtitled "Neuvaine pour le plus grand calme et la forte tranquillité de mon Âme" ("Novena for the greatest calm and tranquility of my Soul"). The work is dated 23 March 1893. The long titles given to several of these nine short "dances"—"À l'occasion d'une grand peine" (On the occasion of a great sorrow"), "En faveur d'un malheureux" ("On behalf of a poor wretch"), "Où il est question du pardon des injures reçues" ("Where there is question of forgiveness for insults received")—would seem to point to the impending rupture with Suzanne Valadon, already hinted at in the letter of 11 March quoted above.

On a purely musical level there is nothing really new in these pieces; the formula is becoming wearisome. The pieces have no individual character. The same rhythmic idea ♫ ♩ (or its augmentation) runs obsessively throughout the entire suite, which again is constructed from the motivic juxtaposition of plodding chains of triads, sevenths and ninths, with an occasional touch of added-sixth harmony adding a certain lush warmth to an otherwise rather austere series of harmonic progressions.

The only work to date from 1894 is the *Prélude de La Porte héroïque du ciel,* written for an "esoteric drama" by Jules Bois, a mystical writer known for his studies of satanism and magic and for a series of occult dramas after the fashion of Péladan. His *Les Noces de Sathan* (1892), for example, for which Debussy briefly considered writing instrumental music, has been described as "sacrilegious and effusive garbage."[47] Like *Uspud* it is a drama of redemption, featuring the conversion of Satan, the fallen angel, by Psyche, symbol of Christian devotion and goodness. Satie's *Prelude to The Heroic Gate of Heaven,* which the composer coyly dedicated to himself, can perhaps be seen as an ironic study of religious sentimentality. The entire piece consists of sequences of luxurious modal harmonies, punctuated six times by a six-beat (3 + 3) phrase that functions as a kind of plagal cadence, thereby providing the work with a fairly strong sense of formal cohesion. The cadential formula (ex. 8) appears on five different tonal levels— (C–G), (E–B), (B–F-sharp), (C-sharp–G-sharp), (F-sharp–C-sharp)— reaching its farthest distance from the "tonic" (C–G) in its fifth appearance (F-sharp–C-sharp) before coming full circle on a repetition of (C–G). Moreover, it describes a kind of arch form by its appearance at intervals of 11, 23, 33, 40, 23, and 6 beats (taking the quarter note as the basic temporal unit).

Example 8. Satie: *Prélude de La Porte héroïque du ciel* (1894), cadential motif

There is far less harmonic disjunction between the twelve identifiable motivic ideas of this piece than in previous works of the period, and this, along with the relatively simple harmonic vocabulary (mainly triads and sevenths) as well as the rather loose "tonal" framework defined by the circular cadential pattern, perhaps accounts for the relative accessibility of the piece, considered by the majority of the composer's critics to be the most attractive of the *Rose-Croix* works.

If the *Prélude de La Porte héroïque du ciel* is the most appealing of the *Rose-Croix* works, the most famous (or infamous) is the second of a group of three pieces edited by Robert Caby from scraps in Satie's notebooks and published in 1969 as *Pages mystiques* with a suggested date of 1893–95. The first of these fragments, entitled "Prière," would appear to be a parody of a standard chorale harmonization such as a student of composition might be required to do; the third, simply called "Harmonies," offers three examples of the kinds of exercises Satie often imposed upon himself in his search for new and strange harmonizations of scales of his own invention. It is the second of the *Pages mystiques*, for decades buried in obscurity, that has become the composer's most celebrated work due to a peculiar set of performing instructions which states that if one wishes to play the piece 840 times in succession, it would be advisable to prepare oneself in advance, in the most profound silence, by a period of serious immobility. The theme of "Vexations," a curious chromatic line of thirteen beats made up of all the notes of the chromatic scale save G-sharp / A-flat, is first given out in the bass. Two harmonizations of the theme in three-part texture follow—separated by a repetition of the cantus firmus—the second of which simply reverses the disposition of the two top parts. The majority of the harmonies are diminished 6/3 chords, but the second one of each section is an augmented triad, and there are also two augmented sixth chords with a bass note of F. As was often to be the case Satie's notation, with unusual and confusing enharmonic spellings, is needlessly complex and seems to bear little relation to the actual sounds heard.

Since John Cage's historic "complete" performance of "Vexations" in New York in September 1963, an eighteen-hour-and-forty-minute marathon now reverently enshrined in the pantheon of experimental music folklore as well as the *Guinness Book of Records,* a veritable cult has grown up around the piece, which has received numerous performances in North America and abroad. It is not surprising that most performers and audiences who have experienced "Vexations" in its entirety have reported some form of expanded consciousness akin to the spirit of Zen, although at least one pianist, Peter Evans, who attempted an uncut solo performance of the piece in 1970, rebelled at the fifteen-hour mark (at repetition 595), claiming that the piece was gradually wearing away his mind to the point where he began to experience frightful hallucinations.[48] Such is the nature of "Vexations," with its extreme chromaticism and predominantly tritonal coloring (only one of the seventeen chords in each system does *not* contain the interval of the tritone) that a number of performers have remarked on their inability either to memorize the piece or to retain its sounds accurately in the memory even after twenty-four hours of continuous exposure to the piece. Perhaps it is this very unpredictability that makes "complete" performances of "Vexations" possible at all.

It is arguable that "Vexations" just may be one of Satie's grandest leg-pulls.[49] It is therefore ironic that the little work's contemporary champions—most of whom come from the ranks of high-culture experimental music—should approach this most mystical of Satie's pages with a pious reverence of almost Péladanesque fervor. When Gavin Bryars refers to "Vexations" as a kind of poor man's *Ring of the Nibelung* one is inclined to believe in his utter sincerity.[50] But regardless of how one approaches Satie's Zen-like performing instructions, the fact remains that "Vexations" has had an enormous impact on contemporary experimental music, most obviously as a kind of *Urtext* for the influential minimalist school.

The last of Satie's *Rose-Croix* works and perhaps the fullest realization of the composer's carefully cultivated Gothic dream is the *Messe des pauvres* of 1895, fragments of which were published in June of that year in *Le Coeur,* a short-lived review of Catholic-occult tendencies financed by Péladan's erstwhile collaborator Antoine de La Rochefoucauld and edited by Jules Bois.[51] The same issue contains an effusive article by Conrad Satie extolling the virtues of his brother, a "Christian idealist" in his view, who "professes only disdain for the realism which has clouded the intellect of his contemporaries." His brother, Conrad went on to say, "prefers to live with his thoughts in poverty than without them in prosperity; his works are written solely for art's sake."[52] Satie's Mass has no precedent in organ literature, although among its progeny might be numbered certain works of Jean Langlais, Jehan Alain, Virgil Thomson, and Olivier Messiaen.

The *Mass for the Poor* is scored for organ (or piano), with unison high and low voices which, however, are called for only in the "Kyrie eleison" and the "Dixit domine." Not surprisingly the work does not follow the plan of the Catholic Mass. The opening "Kyrie" (and its tiny appendage the "Dixit domine") are followed by a series of short movements of Satie's own invention:

"Prière des Orgues" ("Organs' Prayer")

"Commune qui mundi nefas"

Chant Ecclésiastique" ("Ecclesiastical Chant")

"Prière pour les voyageurs et les marins en danger de mort,
    à la très bonne et très auguste Vièrge Marie, mère de
    Jésus" ("Prayer for travellers and sailors in danger of
    death, to the very good and august Virgin Mary, mother of Jesus")

"Prière pour le salut de mon âme" ("Prayer for the salvation of my
    soul")

The "Prière des Orgues" and the "Commune qui mundi nefas" are sprinkled with a number of those inimitable performance instructions that Satie was in the habit of employing, here including such things as "Très chrétiennement" ("In a very Christian manner"), "En dedans" ("On the inside"), "Avec un grand oubli du présent" ("With great forgetfulness of the present"), and "Presqu' invisible" ("Almost invisible").

In keeping with the previous *Rose-Croix* works the harmonic vocabulary of the *Mass for the Poor* is characterized by much parallel movement of triads, sevenths, and ninths, and occasionally, as in the last section, chords built of superimposed fourths. Once again motivic repetition and juxtaposition is the operative principle. In one instance repetition occurs between movements: the "Prière pour les voyageurs et les marins en danger de mort, à la très bonne et très auguste Vièrge Marie, mère de Jésus," despite its imposing title a mere two lines of music, is simply a reharmonization of the second half of the preceding movement, the "Chant Ecclésiastique." Two of the movements reveal a formal symmetry unusual in Satie's music of this period. The "Prière des Orgues" is a simple ternary structure with identical 61-beat streams of 5/3 chords (A) framing a 78-beat (39 + 39) central section (B) of mixed triads and sevenths. Similarly, the "Prière pour le salut de mon âme" consists of 38-beat (A) sections (19 + 19) framing a 60-beat central (B) section, which itself is a small ternary form (a b a) with a symmetrical phrase structure of (10 + 10) (10 + 10) (10 + 10).

It would be wrong to conclude that Satie's Rosicrucian adventure was nothing more than an elaborate hoax. Cynical and misanthropic, bruised by his brief and stormy affair with Suzanne Valadon, he may have sought escape for a time in his own peculiar brand of religious mysticism. Indeed, very near the end of his life, long after he had abandoned his Metropolitan Church fantasy, he still maintained an intense interest in spiritual matters and eagerly engaged in serious theological discussions with the neo-Thomist philosopher Jacques Maritain. As for his part Maritain found in Satie a man of great moral integrity and a composer of clear aesthetic vision who managed to cleanse and purify music of all pretension while avoiding a sterile neoclassical formalism by assuring that his creative self did not become estranged from the existential world of his immediate environment. In the (not always reliable) testimony of Jean Cocteau, it was Maritain who was chiefly responsible for Satie's "Christian death."[53] "You know," the dying composer allegedly confessed to Cocteau, "I'm not so anti-God [*antibondieusard*] as all that. When I am well again I'll turn over a new leaf, but not right away so as not to shock my friends. And anyway, I've always made my sign of the cross every morning. . . ."[54]

Still, it is prudent to approach the popular perception of the humble, self-effacing Monsieur le Pauvre with some circumspection. In the early 1890s Satie subscribed to two newspaper clipping services, carefully preserving every scrap of information about his career to reach the press. Here we find announcements of his candidacy for the Academy of Fine Arts, reprints of his denunciation of Lugné-Poë from the *Journal de dé-*

bats and the Belgian journal *Art moderne,* and mention of the Satie portraits by Desboutin, Feure, and La Rochefoucauld. One other curious item in the composer's scrapbook deserves mention: an advertisement for a haberdashery in the Faubourg Montmartre with the chic name of La Maison du High-Life Tailor, reminding us of the arty velvet suits that became the most visible trademark of a man soon to be known as the Velvet Gentleman. Such zealous surveillance of his own progress from nonentity to public figure at least slightly tarnishes the image of the saintly and ascetic recluse unconcerned with worldly matters. Moreover, we have it on the authority of the writer Francis Jourdain, who was acquainted with the composer and his bohemian circle in the 1890s, that "toward 1895 Satie was more celebrated as a farceur than as a musician; . . . the practical joke was for a long time the only thing that he took at all seriously."[55] Whatever the extent of any genuine religious impulses that may lie imbedded in the pseudotheocratic lucubrations of the Metropolitan Church of Art of Jesus the Leader, there is surely a far greater element of hype and self-aggrandizing puffery, barely beneath the surface of which one senses a deep disgust at the pedantry of the academy and the platitudes of bourgeois existence.

5

The Velvet Gentleman

The decade between 1896 and 1905—the year of his entry into the Schola Cantorum—has until recently remained the least explored period of Satie's career.[1] The Rosicrucian fantasy had more or less run its course and the composer seems to have been groping for a new direction, while maintaining for a time his close association with the Montmartre cabaret scene. One of Satie's intimate friends during his last few years of permanent residence in Montmartre was Augustin Grass-Mick, a caricaturist noted for his whimsical and anecdotal views of a number of now famous artists of the *belle époque*.[2] In a short reminiscence of the period he claimed that Satie's last two years in the rue Cortot were years of reflection and creative inactivity: "What did he do? Absolutely nothing whatever. . . . Between 1896 and 1898, the year when, desiring a change of scene, he made his escape from the Butte, I never saw him work nor write nor take notes."[3] In company with Grass-Mick and Henry Pacory—author of the verse for Satie's *valse chantée* "Je te veux"—the composer made the daily rounds; the three bohemians frequently dined together and even more frequently drank together, a favorite watering place being the Auberge du Clou where they could often be found in the company of a number of now legendary denizens of the Butte, among them—in addition to old Chat Noir acquaintances such as Allais and Auriol—Georges Courteline, revered Prince of Humorists, whose numerous comic sketches amply reflect his philosophy—"that of taking nothing seriously";[4] and the caricaturists Georges Delaw and Jules Dépaquit, the latter the first mayor of the "free commune" of Montmartre and a *fumiste* of extraordinary inventiveness who collaborated with Satie on a little ballet called *Jack in the Box*.

Grass-Mick was not too far off the mark, for the year 1896 is conspicuously blank in Satie's chronology, although the following year did see
the composition of the sixth *Gnossienne* and the two sets of *Pièces
froides.*

On 20 February 1897 in the Salle Erard, Debussy's orchestral versions
of the first and third *Gymnopédie* were premiered at a concert of the
Société Nationale, the first public exposure of Satie's music since the
unsuccessful performances of *Le Fils des étoiles* at Péladan's first Rosicrucian Salon in 1892. The conductor was Gustave Doret, a Swiss musician who, a little over two years previously, had given the world
premicre of Debussy's *Prélude à l'après-midi d'un faune.* The *Gymnopédies* were extremely well received and although the victory may have
belonged mostly to Debussy, Satie lost little time in expressing his pleasure at the success of the occasion. Three days after the concert, on 23
February, he penned a flowery letter to Ernest Chausson, the President
of the National Society of Music, in which he profusely thanked the members of the committee "for the welcome given by them to My *Gymnopédies* orchestrated by the Venerable Claude A. Debussy."[5] A week later,
on 2 April, he wrote a similar letter to Doret, to whom the Satie / Debussy *Gymnopédies* were dedicated: "I embrace you my Brother. May
my embraces, through their petrifying -and consoling properties, pre-
serve for Me the faithful companion that you are."[6]

Cold Pieces

The *Pièces froides* (Cold Pieces) of 1897 mark not so much a new direction for Satie as a return to the simplicity and linearity of the *Gymnopédies*
and *Gnossiennes.* The two sets of pieces—"Airs à faire fuir" ("Tunes to
Make You Run Away") and "Danses de travers" ("Crooked Dances")—
again reveal the composer's trinitarian obsession, each set of three
pieces, like the *Sarabandes* and *Gymnopédies,* being in effect one piece
viewed, as it were, from three angles.

Not surprisingly the "Airs à faire fuir" are very close in mood and style
to the sixth *Gnossienne* of the same year—a thin melodic line, inflected
by occasional augmented seconds, sounding over a rocking left-hand accompaniment of mildly dissonant harmonies. The three "Airs à faire fuir"
taken together outline a perfectly symmetrical ternary form with 187-
beat A sections flanking a 108-beat central B section. The symmetry is
further enhanced by the fact that the majority of the motivic ideas in the
outer sections have a predictable foursquare phrase structure. The

third piece utilizes the same eleven motifs as the first in precisely the same order, except for the final cadence. The first and third pieces are otherwise nearly identical except for their opening statements, which in the third piece appear in transposition, mostly to the fourth (fifth), after which the piece is an exact duplication of the first until the final cadence.

The rather loose structure of these pieces is tempered by the repetition of a motif (ex. la) that functions as a cadence by virtue of the fact that it has a strong harmonic movement (V^6_4–i), appears with much greater frequency than any other motif, and closes the first piece—although here we have a characteristic Satiean twist as the final "tonic" E minor chord of the cadence slyly shifts up a semitone to land unexpectedly on an F major chord, which fresh sonority, the composer presumably felt, had a certain "purity" (ex. lb):

Example 1. Satie: "Airs à faire fuir" (1) from *Pièces froides* (1897)

(a) Cadential motif

(b) Final cadence

The second of the "Airs à faire fuir" is constructed from just two closely related ideas (ex. 2):

Example 2. Satie: "Airs à faire fuir" (2) from *Pièces froides* (1897)

(a) Motif "A"

(b) Motif "B"

Although the phrases follow a classical tonal plan in its simplest form (tonic / dominant–tonic / tonic), the phrase structure itself is characteristically Satiean in its quirky asymmetry (8–7 / 9–10). The transposition of the motifs to submediant and dominant tonal levels outlines a simple ternary structure as follows:

A		B		A¹		Coda
C major	C major	A major	G major	C major	A major	transition
a a¹	b b¹	a a¹	b b¹	a a¹	b b¹	to III
8 7	9 10	8 7	9 10	8 7	9 10	6

Again, as in the first piece, the surprise comes in the coda, which unexpectedly slips onto a C-sharp pedal, ending the little piece, "in the most profound silence," on an unresolved viiᵒ₉ chord (ex. 3) which in turn slides awkwardly into the opening G minor chord of the third piece:

Example 3. Satie: Airs à faire fuir" (2) from *Pièces froides* (1897), coda/
transition

The three "Danses de travers," taken as a whole, have neither the
formal symmetry nor the motivic variety of the "Airs à faire fuir." The
opening gesture—a supple melodic line imbedded in a gently swaying
arpeggiated accompaniment—is the sole musical inspiration for all three
pieces. As with the *Gymnopédies,* the second and third pieces "cubisti-
cally" view the prime musical idea from slightly varying perspectives:

Example 4. Satie: "Danses de travers" from *Pièces froides* (1897)

(a) 1, beginning

(b) 2, beginning

(c) 3, beginning

The shifting harmonies (at regular two-beat intervals) outline a narrow tonal structure based mostly on mediant relationships framed by D minor:

1	2	3
D minor/A minor	F major/D minor	F major/(B minor)D minor

The one bit of sly Satiean humor appears at the end of the suite; the seemingly random chord sequences of the third piece have carried the music from its F major opening to a strong B minor cadence. Although, in the earlier music, Satie's whimsical performance directions and wry verbal commentary rarely seem to bear an obvious relationship to the music, here we have a foretaste of the subtle musico-poetic humor that would later reach fruition in the piano suites of 1913–14. It is tempting in this instance to speculate that the composer recognized that he had, as it were, painted himself into a corner by ending his piece in the remote tonal region of B minor, a tritone away from the opening tonality. This would explain the coy comment "Très loin" ("Very remote") and the sudden and clumsy shift—by way of the flatted leading-note—to D minor, thus bringing the tonal journey of the little suite of "Crooked Dances" full circle:

Example 5. Satie: "Danses de travers" (3) from *Pièces froides* (1897), final cadence

Hyspa

One October afternoon in 1898 Grass-Mick and Pacory accompanied Satie on foot to the grimy Parisian suburb of Arcueil-Cachan where the composer rented a room over a dingy café at no. 22, rue Cauchy. At first he spent only a few nights in his new quarters, complaining of the mosquitoes, deliberately sent to plague him, he was quite certain, by the Freemasons, and the disgusting smells emanating from a nearby tannery. But soon he removed his chattels from the rue Cortot, and late in 1898 the thirty-two-year-old composer, pushing a wooden handcart containing his worldly goods, descended the Butte, crossed the Seine, and arrived in the southern reaches of the great city where he was to live out the remainder of his solitary existence. His room in the rue Cauchy was on the third floor of a gaunt triangular building known locally as "Les Quatre Cheminées," a rather shabby structure surrounded by four tall chimneys belonging to neighboring factories and situated at the intersection of several streets in a bleak working-class district brightened only by the nearby Parc d'École d'Arcueil. The room itself was considerably larger than his Montmartre closet, more easily accommodating his bed, a trunk, a bench, a chest of drawers, and a few pictures, prominent among them the colorful Impressionist portrait of himself by La Rochefoucauld.

"Les Quatre Cheminées" has changed little from the time of Satie. Still in existence is the ground-floor café where the composer spent many hours jotting down his eccentric ideas over frequent glasses of cognac. The drabness of the establishment is only slightly relieved by the presence of a rectangular bronze plaque situated on the third-floor level of the building's west side indicating that Satie had lived there from 1898 until his death.

The composer now entered into what some commentators have described as the period of "The Velvet Gentleman," a reference to his rather restricted wardrobe which consisted of a dozen identical gray (or beige) velvet (or corduroy) suits—opinions vary as to the exact color and nature of the fabric—and in this attire, which he purchased with the money remaining from his small inheritance, he became known and eventually accepted into the dreary community where "one feels . . . the mysterious presence of Our Lady of Lowliness."[7]

These were discouraging years for the composer. Debussy was beginning to enjoy the fame that would elude his "gentle medieval" friend during most of his lifetime, but still Satie clung to the older man, finding in him comfort and consolation. "If I did not have Debussy," he wrote, ". . . I do not know how I would manage to express my poor thoughts, assuming that I still express them at all."[8] Theirs was a stormy relationship, with the irascible Satie as the fickle partner, a kind of Rigoletto-like figure playing the role of the wretched jester in Debussy's court, alternately envious of the older man's success and awestruck by his genius.

Almost daily Satie made the six-mile journey, usually on foot, from the rue Cauchy to his old Montmartre haunts where he managed to eke out a living accompanying cabaret singers.[9] The wee hours of the morning would find the mysterious bohemian wending his way back to Arcueil, a hammer in his pocket for protection on the long nocturnal journey, and, we are told, usually more than a little alcohol coursing through his veins. For some years after his move to Arcueil, Satie maintained his Montmartre connections. In addition to his association with the Chat Noir, the Auberge du Clou, and the Nouvelle Athènes, he is known to have frequented the Divan Japonais in the rue des Martyrs, a cabaret noted for its "oriental" décor, its poetry readings, and its chansonniers, notable among them Yvette Guilbert, then on the threshold of a brilliant career. Later, after 1904, Satie may have been engaged as a pianist at the Lune Rousse, a *cabaret artistique* founded in September of that year by Dominique Bonnaud and Numa Blès, a team of chansonniers with whom the composer collaborated on "La Diva de l'Empire," one of his most charming music-hall confections.[10]

Satie's most fruitful collaboration during these lean years was with Vincent Hyspa, a one-time student of philosophy from the southeastern town of Narbonne, midway between Montpellier and the Spanish border, who arrived in Paris in 1887 ostensibly to study law. For Hyspa, as for many other ambitious young émigrés from the provinces, Montmartre proved a stronger attraction than the university and soon he became known at the Chat Noir as a contributor of verse to the house journal and eventually as a chansonnier in his own right. It was probably here that Satie met Hyspa, in 1887,[11] and it seems likely that he provided piano accompaniments for him at the Chat Noir and later at the Auberge du Clou.

Until 1895 Hyspa toured the provinces in the summers with Salis's Chat Noir troupe. That same year, after an unpleasant and much publicized break with Salis, Hyspa, in company with five other disgruntled performers from the Chat Noir, became involved in the creation of a rival cabaret situated near the Tuileries Gardens and appropriately named the Chien Noir. Soon Hyspa's fame had spread southward to the Left Bank and the Latin Quarter, where he appeared for a time at a cabaret called the Noctambules in company with the Algerian-born *café-concert* singer Eugénie Buffet, whose specialty was performing the earthy ballads of Bruant and others dressed in the shabby costume of a *pierreuse* or Parisian street-walker of the poorer districts. By late 1898 Hyspa was being described in the pages of *Le Gaulois* as "the most astonishing poker-faced joker one can imagine,"[12] and by the early years of the new century he was widely known throughout Paris for his *chansons d'actualité* or topical songs, which documented with dry and mocking humor the numerous political scandals that rocked the young Third Republic.

For most of the year 1899 Satie accompanied Hyspa during his rounds of the cabarets and at fashionable private soirées for which engagements he borrowed suitable clothing from his brother Conrad and arranged numerous piano accompaniments for Hyspa's chansons, the tunes of which were more likely to be borrowed from other chansonniers or from the world of operetta as newly composed. However, among the newly composed Hyspa songs we find at least five with music by Satie: "Tendrement," "L'Omnibus Automobile," "Chez le docteur," "Le Veuf," and "Un Dîner à l'Élysée," all composed around the turn of the century (ca. 1899–1906), the last-named appearing in Hyspa's printed song collection *Chansons d'humour*, published by Enoch in 1903 with a preface by Maurice Donnay and whimsical drawings by Jules Dépaquit, Georges Delaw, and others. Of the remainder, "Tendrement" was published shortly after its composition (ca. 1902) and subsequently reissued several times, while "Chez le docteur" and "L'Omnibus automobile" first appeared in March 1906 in a special issue of *L'Album musical* dedicated to Hyspa. "Le Veuf" remains unpublished, although its principal tune was incorporated into the *Three Pieces in the Shape of a Pear* of 1903.

Among the Satie manuscripts in Harvard University's Houghton Library collection are numerous sketches for popular songs of the *café-concert* type, many of them fragments of less than eight measures or so. Of the melodies that exist in a more or less complete state, at least twenty-eight have been attributed to Satie, while forty-one other songs in the collection are probably tunes from other sources which the composer copied into his notebooks for the express purpose of making transpositions (where necessary) and piano accompaniments for Hyspa and others.[13]

The Hyspa songs taken as a whole are no better nor worse than countless similar music-hall products of the period, although "Tendrement" ("Tenderly"), the best known of them, does reflect the chansonnier's sentimental doggerel—"The Roses have bloomed / In the garden of my heart, / But these roses of love are not as pink / As your wonderful, full-blown lips"—with a gentle waltz-tune of considerable charm and polish. The form of "Tendrement," familiar from thousands of popular songs written before and since, is the standard thirty-two-bar refrain (A) followed by a thirty-two-bar verse (B) in the dominant key, the two verses of "Tendrement" swelling the structure in this instance to A B A B A plus an eight-bar introduction and coda.

Of lesser musical interest but more typical of Hyspa's satirical talents are the topical songs. "Un Dîner à l'Élysée" ("A Dinner at the Élysée") is a song about an official banquet at the Élysée palace during the presidency of Émile Loubet (1899–1906) in honor of the Society of French Artists and the National Society of Fine Arts. An innocuous tune in a diatonic G major is punctuated during the refrain by improvised snatches of *La Marseillaise,* a satirical reference perhaps aimed at the staid academicians of the Society of French Artists and certainly a reminder that Loubet was a liberal republican of peasant stock whose presidency was repeatedly undermined by anti-Semitic, ultraroyalist elements during the stormiest years of the Dreyfus debacle.

The butt of the joke in "Chez le docteur" ("At the Doctor's") is Émile Combes, an elderly radical senator who succeeded René Waldeck-Rousseau in 1902 as prime minister. The "little father," as he was familiarly known in reference to his seminarian background, rapidly accelerated the policies of his predecessor and launched a vigorous anticlerical offensive, in harsh repudiation of his former faith, resulting in the introduction of a bill in 1904 calling for the separation of church and state. Combes's attempt to force passage of his bill through the Chamber of Deputies is rather ungraciously compared by Hyspa to a gastrointestinal disorder resulting in a severe case of intestinal blockage. Exploratory surgery is in order and, through six of the eleven verses, we are taken on a grand tour of Combes's interior—with distressing results. Poor Combes is in bad shape: he has a sprained spleen and galloping consumption, his belly is awfully empty and his heart much too small, his lungs appear to be breathing in something other than holiness, his small intestine is a rather revolting sight, he is full of beans—in short, the doctor declares that he has never before seen such a mess. This bizarre biological journey is set to a sprightly C major tune made up of two pairs of four-bar phrases (a a b b) with a four-bar introduction and a one-bar tag by way of a final cadence. Throughout, the piano maintains a thumping 6/8 meter with two chords per bar marking the strong beats. Whether or not to Hyspa's distress but certainly to the Vatican's, the Separation bill became law on 9 December 1905, almost a year after the forced resignation of *le petit père* Combes and the fall of his government.

Songs such as these along with hundreds of other topical songs of the period have, by their very nature, lost their currency, even in France. Far more enduring—and of greater historical importance—are Satie's flirtations with the ragtime idiom. He may have the distinction of being the first French composer, possibly the first European composer, to adopt the saucy syncopated American music that took Paris by storm in the very first year of the new century when the John Philip Sousa band appeared at the Universal Exposition of 1900. That same year Parisians were gaily strutting to the rhythms of the cakewalk, considered by most authorities to be the immediate ancestor of ragtime.

There are in Satie's music notebooks a fairly large number of sketches in a marked ragtime rhythm, revealing an extensive involvement with a genre that would later find an echo in the "Steamboat Ragtime" from *Parade*. Only two of these have been published, an *intermezzo américain*, "La Diva de l'Empire," and a march, "Le Piccadilly," both of which combine insouciant ragtime rhythms with the French vogue for fashionable English expressions.[14]

"Le Piccadilly" follows the standard ternary form of the march (whether Sousa or Joplin) with the central trio section in the subdominant key. In addition to the four-bar introduction, Satie adds a four-bar vamp before each sixteen-bar strain.

"La Diva de l'Empire," composed for a Bonnaud / Blès revue called *Dévidons la Bobine* which toured a number of seaside resort towns in 1904, was dedicated to Paulette Darty, a well-known chanteuse of the day who was billed as the "Queen of the Slow Waltz." A statuesque, ample-bosomed blonde, Darty must have cut an enticing figure as the Diva "with velvety eyes and the flash of a smile under the great Greenaway hat," circling the stage "showing the wiggling of her legs and her pretty frilly underwear," to the voyeuristic delight of "the gentlemen and all the Piccadilly dandys"—all this to the then exotic (and to many lascivious) ragtime rhythms of Satie, thumped out on a piano or alternatively conveyed in the piquant and coarse timbres of a small *orchestre de brasserie* or cabaret band.

Less adventuresome but more in keeping with Darty's patented stage image is "Je te veux" ("I Want You"), like "Tendrement" a *valse chantée*. An early postcard advertisement for "Je te veux" carries a striking photograph of Darty,[15] who remained closely associated with the song, performing it in October 1909, some years after its composition, at a charity concert in Arcueil with the composer at the piano, much to the delight of Satie's fellow Arcueillais. Like most of the published cabaret songs, "Je te veux" is available in alternate versions for voice alone, voice and small orchestra, small orchestra alone, or solo piano. The instrumental versions of "Je te veux" add a new ternary trio section (C D C) to the standard A B A (refrain / verse / refrain) of the sung version, expanding the structure to A B A C D C A B A, thus making it identical in form to "Poudre d'or" ("Gold Dust"), a charming instrumental waltz in a similar vein dedicated to one Stéphanie Nantas.

A Pantaloonery and a Puppet Show

It is clear from a number of letters of this period, especially those written to his brother, that Satie was "tired of being so desperately sad; everything I attempt with timidity," he confided in Conrad, "fails with a boldness never before imagined."[16] The extant notebooks for the period 1898–1905 seem to bear out this assertion, for they are littered with many dozens of incomplete sketches, false starts, and abandoned attempts at orchestration. However, in recent years a number of small pieces from the period have come to light and been published, and at least two comparatively large-scale works were completed, only to be mislaid by the composer, not to resurface until after his death when the stained and crumpled manuscripts were unearthed in a pile of debris found behind the piano in the mysterious rue Cauchy flat. One was a ballet called *Jack in the Box,* the other a marionette opera called *Geneviève de Brabant.*

For these two theater pieces Satie appropriated the sounds and the boisterous atmosphere of the circus and the music hall, thus simultaneously bidding farewell to the neo-Gothic world of Péladan's crumbling Rosicrucian dream and striking a blatant new note that would reverberate again and again in his music through to the closing pages of his dadaistic swan song, *Relâche. Jack in the Box,* a little pantomime on a scenario (since lost) by Jules Dépaquit, was conceived, Satie informs us, as a "pantaloonery" which, we are told, was his "way of making faces at the evil men who live in this world."[17] For this charming "*suite anglaise*" Satie composed three jigs—Prelude, Entr'acte, and Finale—in a stylized music-hall style, all three in a simple diatonic framework in a bright C major laced with seventh chords and odd harmonies which spice the jaunty tunes with piquant bitonal inflections and look ahead to the music of his disciple Darius Milhaud. Here we find in abundance the characteristic metric shifts, the surprising cadences, and the tendency for literal—though occasionally transposed—motivic repetition.

In 1922, while Satie was attempting a musical adaptation of Bernardin de Saint-Pierre's novel *Paul et Virginie,* Serge Diaghilev approached him about a ballet score to be written on a theme by the painter André Derain. The work was never realized, but in the spring of 1924 the Russian impresario again attempted to squeeze a ballet score out of the recalcitrant composer. This was to be called *Quadrille,* a theme suggested to Diaghilev by Chabrier's Wagnerian parody *Souvenirs de Munich,* with décor and costumes to be by Georges Braque. This too came to naught and in the end Diaghilev had to settle for the posthumous *Jack in the Box*. The rediscovered score, with orchestration by Milhaud, sets and costumes by Derain, and choreography by George Balanchine, was realized on 3 June 1926 at the Théâtre Sarah Bernhardt. In the Balanchine version, Satie's music accompanies the dancing of dolls from a nursery toy box, principally a colorfully garbed puppet, a Negress, and two ballerinas dressed half in black, half in white. The critical response was not generally encouraging. Louis Schneider, covering the concert for *Le Gaulois,* spoke for the majority of his confreres in considering *Jack in the Box* banal in the extreme,[18] while across the channel, where the program was repeated a month later at His Majesty's Theatre in London, the critic for the *Observer* dismissed it, with Satiean wit and malice, as "pert but hollow," a choice specimen of "the art of Vaudevillean taxidermy."[19] Even more damning was the notice in the *Morning Post,* in which the exasperated writer confessed his need "to be very rude about the compositions of Erik Satie, wafted into fame by an infinitesimal clique of Parisians. Suffice it to say that they seem to be imbecile and impotent."[20]

It is possible that the little marionette opera *Geneviève de Brabant* was conceived with the puppet theater of John Hewelt in mind. Hewelt—whose real name was Charles de Saint-Genois—developed a form of puppet theater that seems an early forerunner of the Muppet Show in that his plays included, in addition to the principal actors, a puppet orchestra and even puppet spectators. The connection with Satie and his circle is suggested by the fact that Hewelt's puppet plays often included impersonations of well-known music-hall personalities of the day, among them Yvette Guilbert, the English comedian Little Tich, and La Belle Otéro, one of the grandest of *les grandes horizontales,* who became a performer and actress of considerable notoriety. It seems reasonable to assume also that the composer and his librettist may have recalled the very popular puppet plays of Maurice Bouchor—*Tobie, Noël, ou le Mystère de la Nativité, La Légende de Sainte Cécile*—little dramas of a religious or mystical character much in the style of the medieval Mystery or Miracle play, which were performed from 1888 to 1893 by Henri Signoret's marionette troupe at the Petit Théâtre de la Galerie Vivienne. Throughout the last decades of the nineteenth century the marionette theater enjoyed a considerable vogue in Paris. A puppet theater preceded, and inadvertently gave birth to, the shadow plays at the Chat Noir. The early plays of Maeterlinck—*La Princesse Maleine* (1889), for example, which Satie once considered setting to music—were originally conceived as puppet plays, and an early version of Alfred Jarry's scatalogical *Ubu Roi* was originally privately performed with puppets before its turbulent public premiere at Lugné-Poë's Théâtre de l'Oeuvre in December 1896. A number of critics found the marionette theater aesthetically attractive, the stylized gestures and "divine awkwardness"[21] of the impersonal creatures of wood, cloth, and cardboard creating—not unlike the shadow theater—a sense of mythical distance entirely suited to the legendary and biblical subjects then so very much in fashion.

Satie's *Geneviève de Brabant* is not based on the semilegendary fifth-century patron saint of Paris, so splendidly commemorated by Puvis de Chavannes's frescoes in the Panthéon, but rather on the heroine of medieval legend, wife, it was said, of Siegfried of Treves, who falsely condemned her to death for alleged infidelity.[22] The legend, first recorded in the fifteenth century and popular since the seventeenth, has appeared in many guises, the subject of numerous ballads, novels, plays, and operas, most notably the drama by Ludwig Tieck on which Schumann's only opera *Genoveva* is based, and Offenbach's parodistic *Geneviève de Brabant* of 1859. It is interesting to note too that the legend became the subject of a popular *café-concert* song, dating from 1863, which entered the repertoires of a number of chansonniers of the period, so that when Contamine de Latour and Satie turned to it in the late 1890s they were extending a very popular Parisian tradition.

The legend has come down to us in the form of a *complainte* or tragic ballad called the *Canticle in Honor of Saint Geneviève,* which is printed as a frontispiece to the posthumously published score.[23] The story, as it appears in this version, tells of the noble and devout Geneviève, a countess of Brabant who is married in her eighteenth year to the Lord of the Palatinate. Soon thereafter the new husband is compelled to leave his now pregnant wife for the wars. In his absence the Palatine's chamberlain, Golo, attempts to seduce Geneviève and when he is rebuffed he falsely accuses her of adultery with her equerry and has her imprisoned. While in prison Geneviève gives birth to a beautiful baby boy, Bénoni.

Returning from the wars, the Palatine is intercepted in Strasbourg by the treacherous Golo who convinces his master of his wife's infidelity. Sorrowfully, he charges Golo with the task of killing Geneviève and the infant boy. Triumphantly Golo returns to the court, strips Geneviève of her patrician garments, and commands two underlings to escort her and the child to a desolate forest where they are to be put to death. Geneviève's only request is to be killed before her babe. Wary of murdering a woman of such high station and perhaps taking pity on the two innocents, Golo's men allow her to escape on the condition that she never return to the court. In the depths of the vast gloomy forest, mother and child, destitute, are sustained by the Good Lord who visits upon them a gentle doe who suckles the infant as her own.

Back in his castle, the Palatine grieves for his wife, unmoved by courtly games and diversions. One day while hunting in the forest he becomes separated from his companions while in pursuit of a doe, which he tracks to a grotto. Here he encounters a strange apparition in the form of a naked child standing next to a woman covered with hair. He questions her, hears her story, soon recognizes her as his wife, and, repentant and weeping with joy, praises the Lord for having restored to him his family. To the mournful lament of the birds and animals of the forest bidding her farewell, Geneviève returns home with her husband.

The wicked Golo is quickly brought to judgment, condemned to be flayed alive, and unceremoniously cast, piece by piece, into the town trash heap. Now more fervently pious than ever, Geneviève commits her life to the King of Kings, and one day soon after her reunion with the Palatine she surrenders her soul to Almighty God, to the great sorrow of husband and child, who mourn bitterly. A great heavenly light illumi-nates her funeral procession, as the poor and the rich and even the doe follow the remains of the saintly Geneviève to her tomb, where the poor doe, wishing to confirm the miracle through her own suffering, refuses all nourishment and soon follows her beloved companion to the grave.

As James Harding has pointed out, "there was much in this scenario to please Satie: an age remote from his own, simplicity of feeling and a gracious martyrdom."[24] From this picturesque allegory of trial and re-ward, Contamine de Latour fashioned a short three-act libretto consist-ing of three arias and three choruses (the first two identical in text and music), which Satie preceded with a prelude and interspersed with two entr'actes (both derived from the prelude), a hunting call, a cortege, and a little soldiers' march (also derived from the prelude), which appears, rondolike, four times in all. The music for this little morality play seems irreverent and incongruous, although the perky music-hall rhythms do reflect something of the mechanical movement of puppets. Certainly Sa-tie abhorred sentimentality, but if historical authenticity is sought, it should be recalled that medieval miracle plays—not unlike Shakespear-ean tragedy—often admitted a conspicuous element of comedy and slap-stick, occasionally to the point of running afoul of the ecclesiastical authorities. Satie's music—not unlike the more polished art of Ravel—has infinitely more surface charm than soulful depth, but a charm of such childlike innocence and candor as to disarm criticism. Despite its banality, the music is capable of enchanting the listener. Where more ambitious works have failed, Satie's naive popular tunes and diminutive wooden actors succeed in capturing, with that peculiar brand of ironic detachment he made all his own, something of the mythopoeic essence of the old legend.

It is entirely possible that further research may someday reveal preexisting tunes for much of *Geneviève de Brabant,* as for *Jack in the Box* and many other Satie scores. The choruses in particular have an overwhelming flavor of the cabaret and the music hall, Golo's aria and Geneviève's two arias only slightly less so. Much of the music seems to be a strange marriage of cabaret tune and "Rosicrucian" harmony, resulting at times in some rather odd and piquant effects. The opening motif of the prelude, for example—which also serves the four soldiers' marches and the two entr'actes—appears in a number of guises, often with a clearly bitonal effect:

Example 6. Satie: *Geneviève de Brabant* (1899), act 1, prelude

(a) Measures 1–4

(b) Measures 31–34

Then there are chromatic harmonic progressions that seem merely clumsy rather than expressive, such as this passage from Golo's aria where he fantasizes about the wealth and power he will enjoy in his master's absence:

Example 7. Satie: *Geneviève de Brabant* (1899), act 3, "Air de Golo," measures
24–30

Other Satiean earmarks are the asymmetrical phrasing and fluid, changing meters, especially evident in the three arias, and the "trick" cadences, familiar from the *Pièces froides* and to a lesser extent the
Gymnopédies and *Gnossiennes*. The closing measures of the cortege, for
example, reveal something of the cabaret musician's pawky humor as
Satie sets up a conventional cadential progression only to slip unexpectedly onto a flat submediant chord before the traditional resolution:

Example 8. Satie: *Geneviève de Brabant* (1899), act 3, "Cortege," measures
10–11

Shortly after Satie's death Roger Désormière made an orchestration
of *Geneviève de Brabant* in the "music-hall" style of the composer—with

rather prominent bass drum, snare drum, and cymbals—and in this colorful guise it was first performed on 17 May 1926 at the Théâtre des
Champs-Élysées as part of a Satie Festival organized by the Count
Étienne de Beaumont, one of Satie's wealthy patrons who, two years
previously, had commissioned the composer's penultimate ballet, *Mercure*. Décor for this production was designed by the Spanish cubist Manuel Angelo Ortiz. Two days after the performance the critic Henry
Malherbe, writing in the influential *Le Temps*, declared that he was absolutely charmed by the splendid spectacle of the puppets and the extraordinary, indeed unparalleled, simplicity of Satie's music.[25]

Pear-Shaped Pieces

A number of smaller pieces hidden away in Satie's notebooks have more
recently (1968–80) reached publication under the editorship of Robert
Caby: *Caresse* (ca. 1897), *Rêverie du pauvre, Petite ouverture à danser,
Petite musique de clown triste* (all tentatively dated 1900), and *The
Dreamy Fish* (ca. 1901). Even a cursory glance at this miscellany of little
piano pieces confirms that the composer was groping for a new direction
during these lean years, finding his main source of inspiration in the cabarets and music halls where he eked out a paltry living.

The little piece that Caby titled *Rêverie du pauvre* (along with the unpublished *Verset laïque et sompteux*[26] of the same year) reveal in their
unconventional homophony the lingering influence of the *Rose-Croix* fantasy, while *Caresse*, a tiny piece of thirty-two measures found among the
preliminary sketches for the *Pièces froides*, seems a strange marriage of
"Rosicrucian" harmonies with the wistful tunefulness of the "Airs à faire
fuir" and the "Danses de travers." As their titles suggest, the *Petite ouverture à danser* and the *Petite musique de clown triste* come to us straight
out of the milieu of the cabaret and the music hall, both pieces sounding
as though they might have begun life as sketches for Hyspa songs. Like
so much of Satie's music, the *Petite musique de clown triste* appears on
the surface utterly trivial. As a musico-poetic entity, however, it has a
deeper charm, a kind of Ivesian "substance" which allows it to transcend
the commonplace banalities of the popular idiom. We are asked to imagine a white-faced clown who hobbles into the arena and proceeds to play
a melancholy tune on the saxophone (later trumpet), its "wrong" notes
clashing rather pathetically with the "orchestra" which, mirroring the
clown's stumbling gait and inept musicianship, limps along in irregular
phrases in a brave attempt to follow his forlorn noodling:

Example 9. Satie: *Petite musique de clown triste* (1900), measures 6–17

  The most ambitious of these recently published scores—and the least
successful—is *The Dreamy Fish* (as Satie titled it in English), music intended to accompany a story of one Lord Cheminot, otherwise known to
us as Contamine de Latour. This piece—which Caby has edited in versions for solo piano and piano and orchestra—lives up to the strangeness
of its title. Whereas Satie's previous Contamine de Latour collaborations,
Uspud and *Geneviève de Brabant,* have, despite their unorthodoxy, a high
degree of stylistic unity—the former an extension of "Rosicrucian" homophony, the latter largely a stylization of music-hall gestures—*The
Dreamy Fish* is compounded of an unsettling mixture of two styles, curious and "illogical" harmonic progressions in the manner of *Uspud* appearing in stark juxtaposition with jig-trot music-hall tunes with oompah
accompaniment which seem to have strayed from certain pages of *Geneviève de Brabant* or from almost any page of *Jack in the Box.* As with
Uspud, the structure of *The Dreamy Fish* is diffuse almost to the point
of incoherence, the heterogeneous motivic ideas appearing and reap-
pearing in a seemingly random order, sometimes with no variation from
one appearance to the next, more often with subtle internal changes,
occasionally with transposition to different (and unexpected) tonal levels.
  One of Satie's most celebrated pieces, its peculiar title known to millions who have never heard the music, is the piano duet *Trois Morceaux
en forme de poire.* This delightful work, completed in September 1903, is
a kind of distillation of the cabaret style with which the composer was so
intensely preoccupied at the time, the material here being more thor-
oughly integrated into the musical structure than in *The Dreamy Fish,*

despite the fact that it is a compendium of bits and pieces, some of which date back more than a decade to 1890–91.

The story has long circulated that the quirky title was a characteristic Satiean response to a remark Debussy once directed to his friend concerning what he perceived to be a lack of form in Satie's music. A number of scholars, following Edward Lockspeiser's lead, have chosen to accept Henri Büsser's claim that the ironic title was intended, as early as 1890, as a slight not to Debussy but rather to Debussy's master Ernest Guiraud, whose composition class Satie may have audited for a brief period sometime during that year.[27] Büsser's version is suspect for a number of reasons. There is no trace of the title before its mention (as "*Two* Pieces in the Shape of a Pear") in a 1903 letter to Debussy.[28] Moreover, the only part of the work positively known to date from 1890 is the penultimate section, which is based on an orchestral sketch entitled "Danse." Of the remaining six movements four are known to be derived from music antedating 1890 and the remaining two would appear, from stylistic evidence, to have been composed no earlier than the turn of the century and probably date from 1903. To this evidence we can add two quite independent first-hand reports that support the thesis that Satie was indeed responding to Debussy's mild and no doubt friendly criticism. The critic Michel Calvocoressi, who met Satie through Ravel about 1905, claimed that Satie once told him that the title was in fact intended as a facetious commentary on Debussy's concern with formlessness,[29] a story reiterated many years later by the conductor Vladimir Golschmann who recollected playing four-hand piano music with Georges Auric and with the composer himself at the Golschmann home in Paris toward the end of World War I:

Once, after we had played *Morceaux en forme de poire*, I asked our hero, whom we called *mon bon Maître* why he gave such a title *Pieces in the Shape of a Pear* to this ravishing music. He answered with a twinkle in his eyes: "You do know that I visit Debussy quite often; I admire him immensely and he seems to think much of whatever talent I may have. Nevertheless, one day when I showed him a piece I had just composed he remarked, 'Satie, you never had two greater admirers than Ravel and myself; many of your early works had a great influence on our writing. . . . You have some kind of genius or you have genius, period. Now, as a true friend may I warn you that from time to time there is in your art a certain lack of form. . . .' All I did," added Satie, "was to write *Morceaux en forme de poire*. I brought them to Debussy who asked, 'Why such a title?' Why? Simply, *mon cher ami*, because you cannot criticize my *Pieces* in the shape of a pear. If they are *en forme de poire* they cannot be shapeless."[30]

Of course we still have only Satie's word that such a conversation actually took place and we must consider the possibility that the story—however delightfully Satiean—may be apocryphal.

Given Satie's penchant for mystification, it does not come as a surprise that *Three Pieces in the Shape of a Pear* should actually comprise seven pieces in all. As the work's subtitle promises, the three pear-shaped pieces are preceded by "A Manner of Commencement" and "A Prolongation of the Same" and succeeded by "A Little More" followed by a "Repetition." But even these titles are at odds with the music, considering that "A Prolongation of the Same" is entirely different music from the opening movement and that the final "Repetition" repeats nothing from before. Rather what we have are droll examples of characteristic Satiean wordplay. The second movement is a prolongation of the opening only in the sense that it prolongs the introduction to the first pear-shaped piece. Similarly, "Repetition" is an extension of "A Little More" in the sense that it is, in effect, more of "a little more."

It has been established that five of the seven sections of *Three Pieces in the Shape of a Pear* incorporate material from unpublished Satie sketches.[31] The composer himself indicated in the autograph score that the "Manière de Commencement" was based on a "Gnossienne" extracted from his incidental music to Péladan's *Le Fils des étoiles* of 1891, and indeed this movement, with its conspicuous augmented seconds and ringing nonharmonic grace notes, bears a marked resemblance to the third and the fourth *Gnossiennes,* which date from the same period. The second movement, "Prolongation du même," is based on a sprightly duple-meter tune derived from an uncompleted *café-concert* song, "Le Roi soleil de plomb," dating from the summer of 1903. Movements 3 and 5—the first and third of the pear-shaped pieces—have not been traced to preexisting material but would appear to date from 1903 and may in fact constitute the two original pear-shaped pieces mentioned in the letter to Debussy.

The fourth movement, a clear-cut ternary form, is again derived from music-hall material, its central A-flat major section making use of a lovely song called "Le Veuf" ("The Widower"), probably composed for Vincent Hyspa and dating from around the turn of the century. There exist a number of sketches for "Le Veuf" in two quite different settings, one in D major, the other in C major (later transposed to A-flat major). One of the untexted drafts of the latter version of "Le Veuf" was incorporated in its entirety—minus its three-bar introduction—into the A-flat major trio section of the second pear-shaped piece (from "De moitié" to letter A in the Salabert score). The fourteen measures of the song verse are quoted verbatim, the *prima* taking the soprano and alto voices, the *seconda* the tenor and bass.

The earliest music in the suite is found in the "En Plus," which utilizes material from the 1890 "Danse," possibly Satie's first attempt at composing an independent orchestral work. This piece, marked "Lent" and dated 5 December 1890, has come down to us complete in a fifteen-page manuscript scored for flute, oboe, clarinets (in B-flat and A), bassoon, timpani, and harp.[32] Again Satie has taken over his material virtually intact, in this case assigning the harp and timpani parts to the *seconda,* the remaining woodwind parts—excluding some harmonic doubling—to the *prima.* Considering its date of composition, it is not surprising that the "Danse" should have something of the flavor of the *Gymnopédies*—a thin, modally ambivalent melodic line sounding over a swaying chordal accompaniment:

Example 10a. Satie: "Danse" (1890) (Houghton Library, MS storage 159, Booklet no. 48, folios 1–2), measures 1–10

*The bracketed notes in measures 7–9 are crossed out in the manuscript. Here and elsewhere, all transposing parts are written at actual pitch.

Example 10b. Satie: *Trois Morceaux en forme de poire* (1903), 6. "En Plus," measures 1–10

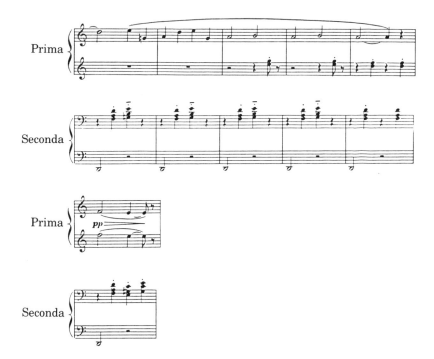

The closing "Redite" brings us back to the turn of the century. Among Satie's numerous abandoned works is a piece for large orchestra titled (both in French and English) *Le Boeuf Angora/The Angora Ox,* like *The Dreamy Fish* based on a tale of Contamine de Latour (alias Lord Cheminot). This curiously titled piece, scored for a very full orchestra (piccolo, two flutes, oboe, English horn, two clarinets in A, two bassoons, two horns, two trumpets in C, three trombones, tuba, timpani, tambourine, bass drum, and strings), consists of nine pages in full score, heavily marked with corrections and revisions. From the very last page of the draft score the composer salvaged a plaintive tune first given out in unison by muted trumpet and bassoon against a light pizzicato (except for the cellos) accompaniment in the strings. After four measures the melody is continued by the English horn against a soft (and now bowed, except for the double basses) string accompaniment with discreet harmonic filler from horns and first trumpet. Example 11 reveals that the trumpet / bassoon melody, its two halves reversed, is transferred intact to the *seconda* (measures 1–4), while the four-bar English horn continuation is stated, without variation, in the *prima* (measures 5–8):

Example 11a. Satie: *Le Boeuf Angora/The Angora Ox* (ca. 1900) (Bibliothèque
Nationale, Mus., MS 10.062), measures 66–73

Example 11b. Satie: *Trois Morceaux en forme de poire* (1903), 7. "Redite," measures 1–8

Appended to the manuscript—though not the published version—of the *Three Pieces in the Shape of a Pear* is a curious document couched in the stilted and ironic language familiar from the *Rose-Croix* period:

Recommendations
I find Myself at a prodigious turning-point in the History of My life. In this work, I express My appropriate and genuine astonishment. Believe Me, despite the predispositions. Do not fool with charms that are unknown to your ephemeral

understanding; keep your precious verbal bluster holy: God will forgive you, if He wishes, from the honorable center of the united Eternity, where with solemnity and conviction everything becomes known. The Determined One cannot freeze; the Passionate One obliterates himself; the Irascible One has no reason to exist. More I cannot promise, even though I have temporarily put Myself through a great deal of effort, against all precautions. Is that not everything? I tell Myself so.

ERIK SATIE
3 November 1903[33]

From these cryptic "Recommendations" we can deduce—if nothing else—that Satie recognized in his pear-shaped pieces an important juncture in his creative development. That he was well pleased with his latest invention we know from the less abstruse language of a letter to Debussy, written on 17 August 1903, in which he declared his pear-shaped pieces "to be better than everything which has been written up to now; he may be mistaken"—he continues in an ironical third person—"but it's no use telling him; he'd never believe it. . . ."[34] Indeed, the freshness and unpretentious charm of *Three Pieces in the Shape of a Pear* was not lost on a younger generation, especially that most Parisian of Satie's disciples, Francis Poulenc, whose youthful *Mouvements perpétuels* (1918) are inconceivable without the example of the master.

Satie appears to have had considerable difficulty following up on the success of his remarkable piano duet. The years 1904 and 1905 were rather barren for the composer. He continued to sketch and arrange cabaret songs, his close association with Vincent Hyspa persevering at least into 1905, a year highlighted in his creative life only by his collaboration with Jean Kolb and Maurice de Féraudy on an ill-fated operetta called *Pousse l'Amour*. Féraudy, a minor poet and playwright and an actor who distinguished himself at the Comédie-Française, failed to coax a completed score out of the unpredictable composer and *Pousse l'Amour* must be added to the lengthy list of aborted compositions dating from this period. Although reference has often been made to a performance of *Pousse l'Amour* at Monte Carlo in 1913 under a new title, *Coco chéri,* there is no evidence that any of Satie's music ever saw service. All that remains of his music for the operetta are a few draft sketches of which the following brief example provides some indication of the music's light and fluffy nature:

Example 12. Satie: "De Féraudy Valse" (1905) (Houghton Library, MS storage
159, Booklet no. 2, folio 17), measures 1–4

Schola Cantorum

In 1905, in his fortieth year, Satie made the remarkable and courageous
decision to enroll in the Schola Cantorum, that most austere and academic of institutions founded a decade earlier by the august and patrician
Vincent d'Indy to uphold the traditions of his revered master, César
Franck. In opposition to the Conservatoire, which d'Indy considered a
training ground for empty virtuosity, the official policy of the Schola Cantorum was to consider music an art, not merely a craft. Accordingly, a
broad range of historical study was required and students were introduced first-hand to a rich legacy of vocal music through the monthly concerts of the Chanteurs de Saint-Gervais, a choir founded by one of the
school's cofounders, Charles Bordes, initially for the express purpose of
performing early (pre–eighteenth-century) religious music, but eventually including the music of Bach, Gluck, Weber, Schumann, and even
Bordes's own French contemporaries. Although commonplace today,
such breadth of musical training and experience was unusual for the time.
Something of the impressive range of the curriculum can be gleaned from
d'Indy's *Cours de composition musicale,* an extensive survey of musical
forms and styles edited by Auguste Sérieyx from the composer's Schola
Cantorum lectures and published in three volumes between 1903 and
1933. Volume 1 is a historical survey of music theory—rhythm, melody,
notation, monody, harmony, expression, tonality (including a history of
harmonic theory from Zarlino to Riemann)—while the remaining volumes
offer a vast chronology of instrumental forms from fugue to symphonic
poem. (A fourth volume, dealing with dramatic forms—opera, song, can-
tata, oratorio—was edited by Guy de Lioncourt and published in 1950.)
Satie's major teachers at the Schola Cantorum were d'Indy, Sérieyx,

and Albert Roussel. The latter, along with Debussy, had tried to dissuade Satie from resuming his studies at his age, fearing that it would destroy a style already fully formed and unique. Roussel, a naval officer turned composer, who was three years Satie's junior, made the following observation about his industrious pupil:

> Satie was a professional musician. Those of his works that had already been printed clearly showed me that he had nothing to learn. I could not see what advantages he could derive from theoretical and academic studies. Nevertheless, he insisted. He became a very docile and assiduous student. He would punctually bring me the work I had assigned, carefully written out and adorned with notes in red ink. He was profoundly musical.[35]

Despite the initial reservations of his teachers and friends, Satie persisted and was graduated with first-class honors (*très bien*) in 1908 and presented with a Diploma in Counterpoint signed by d'Indy and Roussel.

Roussel's oft-quoted assessment of his pupil suggests that Satie was a full-fledged musician when he entered the Schola Cantorum in 1905. That the composer of the *Gymnopédies* and *Gnossiennes* was "profoundly musical" is beyond dispute; that he was woefully deficient in the craft of musical composition is blatantly revealed by his student exercise books, many of which have been preserved. They provide a startling record of the nature of his technical shortcomings, lending credence to Henri Büsser's observation that Satie was "very little gifted and toiled enormously to produce a simple counter-subject for a fugue, the sort of thing we were normally expected to produce on the spot,"[36] an incriminating revelation supported by René Peter, an intimate associate and biographer of Debussy, who claimed that "Satie, in music, knew just enough to jot down the ideas that came to him. But in order to harmonize them and dish them up, he had to go to Debussy, who helped him with ever ready patience and zeal. He would spend whole afternoons on Satie's rough sketches."[37] To these harsh assessments we can add the composer's own voice. His brother Conrad was one of the very few people to whom he ever opened up his heart, and when, a few years after his graduation from the Schola Cantorum, he confessed to Conrad that he sought formal musical instruction in 1905 because "I was tired of being reproached for an ignorance that I believed myself in truth to be guilty of, since competent people had pointed to it in my works,"[38] we can take it very much at face value.

The Paris and Harvard notebooks provide almost a monthly record of Satie's progress. Near the very beginning of his studies, in January 1905, he was writing out simple exercises in black and red ink using a variety of clefs. By early April he had progressed to three-part counterpoint of the first species, then four-part counterpoint of the first and second species. By October his exercises carry numerous corrections and comments (probably in Roussel's hand) chastising him for the commonplace sins of the student contrapuntist: parallel octaves, awkward tritone melodic intervals, unvarying rhythmic ideas, pseudohomophonic rather than true polyphonic textures. By November, however, Satie was able to demonstrate that counterpoint, at least of the first and second species, did not entirely defeat him, for the notebooks contain many counterpoint exercises that suggest the composer could sustain at least a two-part texture over a short period of time. The academic smoothness of example 13 suggests a degree of conscientiousness on Satie's part. Indeed, his teacher Roussel once observed:

. . . it seemed to me that his ironic smile signified "Oh, oh! So that's not allowed professor? Really? Well, that correction is just what I wanted. Here's some counterpoint without a wrinkle."
    But no, no irony at all; Satie brought me, with an utterly serious and convinced air, impeccable counterpoint exercises in an astonishing calligraphy, and his enthusiasm for Bach chorales would have set him apart even in an organ class.[39]

Example 13. Satie: "Counterpoint Exercise" from *Cahier de contrepoint No. 1 1905 (Novembre)* (Bibliothèque Nationale, Mus., MS 9638, p. 17)

*The notes in parentheses are lightly penciled in the manuscript.

By early 1906 Satie had progressed to florid counterpoint in up to five and six parts and was beginning to unravel the mysteries of fugue. For d'Indy he produced a series of formal analyses, among them analyses of a Palestrina motet—which he considered to be of immense religiosity—the seventh fugue from Bach's *Art of the Fugue,* and Ravel's charming *Noël des jouets,* a childlike vision of a toy Nativity scene complete with painted sheep, mechanical cattle, crinoline Virgin with enamelled eyes forever open, Christ Child of colored sugar, and silvery tinseled angels. Here is the artifice, the childlike purity, and the miniature mechanical world so beloved of the composer of *L'Enfant et les sortilèges,* a world of fantasy and make-believe also dear to the heart of Satie, who loved children and once mused upon the kind of music a one-year-old child would write—then proceeded to compose the *Enfantines.*

The one area of his studies that seemed to give Satie considerable difficulty was orchestration. The rather coarse orchestrations of the late ballets undoubtedly stem in part from his apparent inability to master this aspect of his craft. Again the notebooks give him away. As late as 1906 he was recording the compass of orchestral instruments and reminding himself of the peculiar qualities of each instrument. A perusal of his *Note d'un cours d'orchestration,*[40] which dates, surprisingly, from December 1909, a year and a half after his graduation from the Schola Cantorum, evokes a certain pity as one pictures the middle-aged composer still jotting down facts that would be common knowledge even for students on the most elementary levels of musical training. Indeed, it is difficult to imagine that Satie felt it necessary to note that there are "three families (strings, winds, percussion)." Or elsewhere: "Bassoon—very agile, like the flute—bass of the double reeds"; "trombone lacks agility," and so on. Perhaps the most amusing sections of the notebook are those concerned with the mixing of instrumental timbres: "In unison—flute and clarinet—bad"; "flute and trumpet blend very well" (but two pages later he declares this a bad combination); "English horn and flute—never" (but, he notes, English horn with clarinet or with French horn works well); "horn and trombone—useless"; "with three trumpets," he observes, "one can do everything"—although in a 1911 communication to Roland-Manuel, Satie declared that one should never have more than two trumpets, that three, according to d'Indy, meant the end of the world.[41]

Satie struggled with the craft of orchestration most of his creative life. As early as 1890 we find in addition to the draft score of "Danse" an attempted orchestration (for the same instrumental combination) of the first *Gnossienne* which, however, never got beyond two measures! Later we find orchestrated fragments of some of the music-hall songs and the unfinished *Angora Ox*. Most revealing are the series of frustrating attempts the composer made to orchestrate the "Airs à faire fuir" from the *Pièces froides*. One early attempt from around the turn of the century was ambitiously scored for flutes, English horn, clarinets, bassoons, two horns, trumpets, timpani, harp, and strings, but peters out after two pages. As late as 1913 Satie was still grimly determined to orchestrate these early pieces. For this final attempt he reduced his orchestral forces to English horn, clarinet, bassoons, and strings. But after a series of futile starts, he decided to add French horn, harp, and timpani. From this point on almost every page of the manuscript reveals changes of instrumentation and no less than nineteen fresh starts. The most sustained effort consists of a mere nine measures in full score arranged for flute, B-flat clarinets, two horns, timpani, harp, and strings, minus violas.

   Despite the damning evidence of these student notebooks, by 1916 the fifty-year-old composer seems to have attained sufficient confidence in his abilities to make an orchestral arrangement of another composer's work, "L'Aurore aux doigts de rose," the second of two *Pastels sonores* by Albert Verley. Verley, a chemical engineer by training, was a wealthy industrialist whose special interest in the manufacturing of perfumes strongly suggests that he may have been introduced to Satie through his brother Conrad. In addition to his scientific work, Verley was an amateur composer whom Satie, according to Vladimir Golschmann, actually took on as a pupil shortly after the premier of *Parade* in 1917.[42] Presumably Verley was known, or wished to be known, to Ravel, who received the dedication of "L'Aurore aux doigts de rose," and to Paul Dukas, to whom he dedicated a published extract from his ballet *Le Masque de la mort rouge*. He may also have been known to Edgard Varèse who, in a letter to Darius Milhaud written from New York in 1928, mentioned "a small score of Monsieur Verley orchestrated by Satie."[43] Perhaps it is significant, in view of his insecurity in matters of technique, that Satie chose a relatively obscure composer for his single exercise in arranging another person's music. The score in question, which Varèse (or Milhaud) deposited in the Bibliothèque Nationale, is an eleven-page manuscript scored for a very full orchestra consisting of piccolo, flutes, oboe, English horn, B-flat clarinets, bassoons, horns, two trombones and tuba, timpani, tambour de Basque, cymbals, harp, and strings. It remains unpublished, although an alternative version, also arranged by Satie, for piano four hands was published by Verley himself in 1916.

   It is curious that Satie, who was not known for his sustained efforts, should make these not entirely unskillful arrangements of another composer's music and then make no mention of the fact anywhere in his correspondence. Perhaps he undertook the task for purely pedagogical reasons and felt that only inferior music, music quite unknown to his colleagues, would best suit his purpose; or perhaps he was simply motivated by a more mundane yet time-honored consideration—that the wealthy Verley, flattered by the attention his music was receiving, was in a position to reward the impecunious composer quite handsomely for his services.

Fugues and Chorales

The music Satie composed during and shortly after his three-year period of study at the Schola Cantorum is the least known and, for the most part, least successful portion of his output. Its very existence, however, does prove that the composer was not nearly so "silent" during this little-known period of his career as was once thought. These works do, moreover, have a certain historical importance in that they can be seen as a kind of bridge between the earlier and later styles, culminating in the 1913–14 piano suites, which saw the full flowering of the composer's peculiar genius. All of the works in question—save the two piano duets *Aperçus désagréables* and *En Habit de cheval*—were published posthumously, most of them in 1968 in editions by Robert Caby.

The earliest of these, *Chanson médiévale* (Medieval Song), based on a poem by Catulle Mendès, a Parnassian poet and ardent Wagnerian whose *Rodrigue et Chimène* Debussy attempted to make into an opera early in his career, reveals the lingering influence of the Symbolist aesthetic, if indeed it was composed as late as 1906 as its editor claims. Written with bar lines and a key signature of four flats, the song is distinguished only in its tendency to linger around the dominant E-flat right through to the final cadence, and the occasional presence of the modal lowered leading-tone in the accompaniment.

The *Passacaille* and the *Prélude en tapisserie,* dating from July and October 1906, respectively, are equally undistinguished, the former, indeed, rather curiously titled, for it has none of the characteristics of a traditional passacaglia, despite the frequent repetition of its stately opening idea. The *Prélude en tapisserie* (Tapestry Prelude), like a number of works from this transitional period, is an awkward marriage of "Rosicrucian" harmony—chains of unresolved sevenths—and music-hall gestures, with neither the sustained mystery of the one nor the vulgar charm of the other.

The *Douze petits chorals* (Twelve Little Chorales) (ca. 1906–8) are quite literally a series of scraps from Satie's notebooks edited by Caby and published by Salabert in 1968. The editor has ignored the scholastic exercises in chorale harmonization hidden away in the composer's notebooks of the Schola Cantorum period in favor of thirteen (including nos. 6a and 6b) experimental exercises probably not intended for the critical eyes of d'Indy and Roussel. Not one of the chorales is entirely free of strange voice-leading or peculiar cadences or odd modulations. Occasionally the harmonic surprises seem willfully capricious and merely awkward: Choral no. 3, for example, with its sudden semitonal shift from an A-flat tonic chord to the mediant of F major. In other instances, the results are quite refreshing: the final E major triad of Choral no. 12, for example, seems entirely appropriate after the ambiguous chromaticism and augmented harmonies of the preceding phrases, despite the strong expectation, near the end, of a C major resolution.

A similar but more varied collection of sketches was published, also in 1968, under the title *Carnet d'Esquisses et de Croquis* (Notebook of Sketches and Rough Drafts). If these twenty miniatures have little intrinsic musical merit they do have a certain historical value, allowing us further glimpses of Satie's working habits and compositional activity during an interesting and little-explored transitional phase of his career. The sketches range chronologically from a wistful 1897 fragment ("Songerie vers 'Jack'") in the style of the "Airs à faire fuir" from the *Pièces froides* to a tiny "Air" from 1914. The majority of the pieces are short harmony and counterpoint exercises—many of them quite fluent and academically correct—almost certainly dating from the Schola Cantorum period. Two of the longer pieces, "Esquisses & Sketch Montmartrois," are written in a blatant cabaret style and date probably from around the turn of the century. The first of these, a delightful piece in a marked ragtime idiom subtitled "Petit Prélude de 'La Mort de Monsieur Mouche,'" deserves a place alongside "Tendrement" and "La Diva de l'Empire" as one of the composer's most successful music-hall confections. Equally charming is the "Petite Danse" which closes the collection, a gay bit of Satien whimsy that seems to have strayed from the *Sports et divertissements*.

Nine short pieces, published posthumously in 1968, were released in two sets, one under the prosaic title *Six Pièces de la période 1906–1913* (Six Pieces from the Period 1906–1913), the other with the more Satien title *Musiques intimes et secrètes* (Intimate and Secret Musics). None of the nine pieces is likely to find a regular place in the Satie canon, for they have neither the melodic freshness of the earlier *Gymnopédies* or *Pièces froides* nor the artless simplicity and musico-poetic whimsicality of the later sets. Some of the pieces are little more than rather dry counterpoint exercises—"Désespoir agréable" ("Pleasant Despair") from the first set, "Fâcheux exemple" ("Peevish Example") from the second—others, such as the "Prélude canin" ("Doggy Prelude") and "Effrontierie," both from the first set, contain some charming musical ideas but never seem to take flight. For once the composer's patented mosaic technique works against him. "Effronterie," for example, opens with a memorable phrase, which is stated four times in all only to be deflated on each appearance by the rather dull passage-work that follows. Occasionally the odd chromatic shifts capture something of the ironic poetry of the later pieces— the final cadence of "Froide songerie" ("Cold Musing") from the second set—but more often the music, with its wayward chromaticism and over-laden textures, sounds merely awkward and labored, giving some credence to Debussy's earlier warning that further academic training at Satie's age could undermine a style that was fresh and already fully formed.

Considerably more successful are the *Nouvelles Pièces froides* (New Cold Pieces) and the *Deux Rêveries nocturnes* (Two Nocturnal Reveries), both dating from 1910–12. The first two of the *Nouvelles Pièces froides,* "Sur un mur" ("On a Wall") and "Sur un arbre" ("On a Tree"), are in effect the same piece composed twice, by 1910 a well-established Satiean procedure. The same eight-bar theme is stated three times in each piece on the same three tonal levels, but with different harmonization and a change from a predominantly chordal texture ("Sur un mur") to a graceful arpeggiated accompaniment ("Sur un arbre"). With the third piece, "Sur un pont" ("On a Bridge"), the composer does not, as might be expected, complete a triptych, for the piece bears not the slightest resemblance to its companions, being more in the nature of yet another counterpoint exercise from the Schola period, with, to be sure, some rather characteristic harmonic twists, including the whimsical final cadence. The *Deux Rêveries nocturnes* sound like early studies for the more celebrated *Cinq Nocturnes* of 1919, especially the first, whose extended passages of parallel fifths would appear again in *Parade* and *Socrate* as well as the later *Nocturnes.*

Finally we come to the two piano duets, *Aperçus désagréables* (Unpleasant Glimpses) and *En Habit de cheval* (In Riding Habit), the latter also arranged by the composer for large orchestra. Here Satie seemed intent on putting his recently acquired contrapuntal skill to good use. *Aperçus désagréables* consisted initially of a "Choral" and a "Fugue," both composed in September 1908, shortly after his graduation from the Schola Cantorum, to which he added a melancholy "Pastorale" four years later, in October 1912, while *En Habit de cheval,* written between June and August 1911, is made up of two tiny chorales and two fugues, a "Fugue litanique" ("Litanical Fugue") and a "Fugue de papier" ("Paper Fugue"). The composer was pleased with both his inventions and released them for publication. "The beautiful and limpid *Aperçus désagréables,*" he wrote in 1913 for his publisher's catalog, ". . . are most elevated in style and show how the subtle composer is able to say:— 'Before I compose a piece, I walk round it several times, accompanied by myself.'"[44] As for *En Habit de cheval,* Satie told Roland-Manuel that his former teacher Roussel "found it all amusing" and approved of his "new way of making a fugue: especially the expositions."[45]

The first fugue in *En Habit de cheval,* the "Fugue litanique," is probably so-named because of its modal (Dorian) subject, which, however, is worked out in the traditional manner complete with three-voiced stretto in the final measures. The "Fugue de papier," on the other hand, begins with a Lydian inflected subject in the subdominant with a real answer at the fifth, which turns out to be the tonic C. Thus Satie has perpetrated one of his more subtle musical jokes by, as it were, standing the scholastic fugal exposition on its head, a kind of reversal of the traditional tonic-dominant axis admittedly more apparent to the eye than to the ear.

Though not among his more endearing creations, these post-Schola compositions do point the way to the lean, linear textures of the later piano works. With his newly acquired contrapuntal skills, Satie was able to purge his musical vocabulary of the abstruse "Rosicrucian" harmonic idiom which, by the turn of the century, had become a rather tiresome mannerism as well as a stylistic cul-de-sac.

6

Chapters Turned
Every Which Way

By 1910 Satie had gained a measure of local fame in Arcueil through his many community activities, which included membership in the Radical-Socialist committee, journalistic contributions to the local newspaper, *L'Avenir d'Arcueil-Cachan,* and active participation in the Patronage La-ïque d'Arcueil, a nonreligious charitable organization whose primary concern was the welfare of poor children. This latter association was particularly close to the composer's heart, and he spent many hours in the company of ragged street urchins, organizing outings for them to nearby points of interest, listening with great patience to their fascinating chatter, and enthralling them with his own fanciful yarns. So pleased were the citizens of Arcueil with their resident composer that they decorated him with the Palmes Académiques for his services to the community. A month later, on 7 August 1909, the mayor of Arcueil presided over a *vin d'honneur* in Satie's honor at which two of his cabaret songs—"Je te veux" and "Tendrement"—were performed by local amateurs to the enthusiastic acclaim of the assembled guests.

But despite this sudden flurry of social activity and local recognition, Satie remained on the fringe, buried in virtual anonymity in his remote Parisian suburb. During the twenty-seven years he lived in Arcueil's rue Cauchy no one, not even his closest friends, ever set foot in his small apartment. Only after his death in 1925 did Darius and Madeleine Milhaud, Roger Désormière, Jean Wiéner, and Robert Caby enter it, with some trepidation, in order to remove his effects. But by the beginning of the twentieth century's second decade there were indications that the

forty-five-year-old composer was about to emerge from his shadowy re-
treat and take his place in the vanguard of Parisian musical life.

Recognition

Debussy and Ravel, though at this time not well disposed toward one
another, were largely responsible for promoting Satie's career and bringing his works to the attention of a larger and more sophisticated audience
than he had ever known. On 16 January 1911, at a concert of the recently
formed (1910) Société Musicale Indépendante held at the Salle Gaveau,
Ravel himself played the second *Sarabande,* the Prelude to act 1 of *Le
Fils des étoiles* (which he later orchestrated), and the third *Gymnopédie.*
A program note paid tribute to the composer, now hailed as an explorer
and prophet whose early works, with their bold and astonishing harmonies, exercised a considerable influence on contemporary French music.[1]

Barely a month after the S.M.I. concert, Michel Calvocoressi, a
French-born writer and music critic of Greek extraction, echoed the sen-
timents of the anonymous writer for the *Guide du concert,* striking a
spark that would give rise to the Satie legend. In his review of the concert, Calvocoressi was unequivocal in his praise of Satie, claiming him as
an important forerunner of Debussy and Ravel. His early works, he
wrote, reveal "an extraordinary aural sensitivity, thanks to which a perfect artistic sensibility never ceases to preside over the elaboration of
the most bizarre sonorous rarities."[2]

On 25 March 1911, again at the Salle Gaveau, Debussy conducted his
orchestral versions of the two *Gymnopédies* at a concert of the Cercle
Musical devoted almost exclusively to his own works. As once before,
fourteen years previously, the enthusiastic reception of the *Gymnopédies*
in their lovely "impressionistic" orchestral dress reflected most favorably
on Debussy, causing the wounded Satie to register a complaint about his
old friend: "Why won't he allow me just a little corner of his shade? . . .
I don't want to take any of his sun."[3]

As a result of the exposure given his music by Ravel and Debussy in
the early months of 1911, Satie was taken up by the progressive press
and soon found himself something of a celebrity. Calvocoressi's sympathetic review was closely followed by Jules Écorcheville's article in the
Revue musicale S.I.M. which printed, along with La Rochefoucauld's portrait of the composer, the first *Sarabande,* excerpts from the *Trois Morceaux en forme de poire,* and the first of the *Danses gothiques.*[4] The

following month, in April 1911, Calvocoressi was back in print with a short article on Satie for *Musica*,[5] and by the end of the year the indefatigable critic had, in a manner of speaking, crossed the English Channel with an article in the *Musical Times* on "The Origin of To-Day's Musical Idiom" in which Satie figured prominently alongside Chopin, Liszt, Chabrier, Mussorgsky, and Debussy as one of the significant precursors of a bold new harmonic language.[6]

That same year saw the publication by Rouart-Lerolle of the *Sarabandes, Trois Morceaux en forme de poire,* and *En Habit de cheval,* and by 1912, the year in which the notorious "Memoirs of an Amnesiac" began to appear in the pages of the *Revue musicale S.I.M.,* Satie had acquired a considerable following among young musicians.

One of these, Roland-Manuel, a composer and critic who, at the urging of Satie, had studied counterpoint at the Schola Cantorum with Roussel and composition privately with Ravel, presented in June 1912 his orchestral version of the *Prélude de La Porte héroique du ciel* at a concert of the Société Musicale Indépendante. Satie's early works seem to have held a special interest for Roland-Manuel, for he also provided orchestrations of the second *Gymnopédie* and the first and last of the Preludes to *Le Fils des étoiles.* Though largely forgotten today as a composer, Roland-Manuel is still remembered for his perceptive studies of Ravel and Satie. Like Satie, he had a fascination for Gothic art, an interest that may have enhanced his neomedieval proclivities, for he continued to drink at the fountain of Symbolism long after the dream had begun to fade. *Pelléas et Mélisande* had been a major revelation to him, and he maintained an enthusiasm for Satie's *Rose-Croix* music that apparently went so far as to influence his sartorial habits and the furnishings of his apartment in the rue de Chazelles, where, "dressed in a gandurah, he would—by the light of a single taper—play *La Porte héroique du ciel* or, alternatively, read the poems of that mystical fop from Lyon, Sâr Péladan."[7]

In 1912, as a result of a referendum organized by the newspaper *Gil Blas,* more than four hundred friends and colleagues of the poet Paul Fort—editor of the literary review *Vers et prose,* in which some of Alfred Jarry's works first appeared, and founder (in 1890) of the Symbolist Théâtre d'Art—elected him "Prince of Poets." Taking their cue from their literary associates the young "Satieists" (who, the composer maintained, were "no more comical than the Wagnerians")[8] presented their hero as a candidate for the title "Prince of Musicians." In a letter to Roland-Manuel of 3 July 1912 Satie wrote in his characteristic beguiling manner:

. . . It's quite disgusting, my dear fellow. These dolts are completely ignorant. Écorcheville, who is guided by Vuillermoz refuses to pay any attention to what you told him about the P. of M. But don't let's give up, in Heaven's name; we can't do that. PS. Don't let's get upset about it; we must go into the question calmly; music needs a Prince and she shall have one, by God. Your old pal. E. S.[9]

Following Rouart-Lerolle's lead, the publishing firm of Demets requested some piano pieces from Satie and he responded by offering them the four *Préludes flasques (pour un chien),* which he completed in July 1912. But apparently Demets was not pleased with the *Flabby Preludes (for a Dog),* which were written, paradoxically, in the terse, angular style that would typify all the composer's post-Schola compositions, and in a moment of despair he wrote to Roland-Manuel on 8 August 1912: "I am going to destroy the *Préludes flasques,* and begin anew."[10] Failing to find a publisher for his *Flabby Preludes* Satie proceeded to compose three *Véritables préludes flasques (pour un chien),* and on 5 September 1912 he wrote once more to Roland-Manuel informing him that he had offered this "true" or "real flabby" version of his preludes to Debussy's publisher Durand. Nine days later, on 14 September, Satie reported to Roland-Manuel that Durand, fearing that his clients would not care to possess such a work, returned the manuscript "like a glove."[11] Finally, Demets agreed to publish the *Véritables préludes flasques* and, along with Rouart-Lerolle, asked for more.

On the 5 April 1913, at a concert of the Société Nationale in the Salle Pleyel, the distinguished Spanish pianist Ricardo Viñes, brilliant champion of contemporary French, Spanish, and Russian music, premiered Satie's *Véritables préludes flasques,* thus beginning an association that was to be of enormous benefit to Satie's career. As early as 1897 Viñes noted in his journal that he had seen extracts from the *Mass for the Poor,*[12] and although he actually met the composer three years later through Ravel, on 9 December 1900, he did not take up Satie's cause until now. Over the next few years he premiered a number of the composer's recent works in Paris, as well as introducing several of his early works—a *Sarabande,* a *Gymnopédie,* and a *Gnossienne*—to audiences in his native Spain and as far away as Buenos Aires. On 2 October 1912 Satie sent Viñes his *Pièces froides* accompanied by the following formal note: "Dear Monsieur Viñes—Here are the *Pièces froides.* Look them over, I beg you. When will I be able to see you? Amicably, Erik Satie."[13] By 1916 Viñes had become his "good old friend," his "delightful dear friend," and on 3 April 1916 he sent a *carte pneumatique* to his "good great friend":

. . . You are as good as bread. How can I thank you enough?
No: I'm too much of a duffer: I'll have to keep mum—mum-my.
Anyway—Please accept the thanks of an old nitwit who admires you as he is able.[14]

Satie had found an ideal interpreter in Viñes, a sensitive musician of prodigious technical ability, who, he wrote in reference to the pianist's premiere performance of the *Descriptions automatiques* at the Conservatoire in June of 1913, "played with an irresistibly droll air of secrecy."[15] That same year he dedicated "Chez le marchand d'or," the first of his *Vieux sequins et vieilles cuirasses,* to the great pianist. The admiration was clearly mutual, for Viñes, who was also a composer of slight pretension, left a touching tribute to the memory of his old friend in the form of a wistful *Threnody,* written two years after Satie's death, in 1927.

The floodgates of Satie's imagination were now opened, and in a burst of creative activity he composed the series of whimsical piano suites which, taken together, constitute a significant body of work in the repertoire of contemporary French piano music and which, more than any other of Satie's creations, remain the purist examples of his genius.

The Humoristic Piano Suites

1912   *Préludes flasques (pour un chien)*
         (Flabby Preludes [for a Dog])
         Véritables préludes flasques (pour un chien)
         (True Flabby Preludes [for a Dog])
1913   *Descriptions automatiques*
         (Automatic Descriptions)
         Embryons desséchés
         (Dried-up Embryos)
         Croquis et agaceries d'un gros bonhomme en bois
         (Sketches and Exasperations of a Big Wooden Fellow)
         Chapitres tournés en tous sens
         (Chapters Turned Every Which Way)
         Vieux sequins et vieilles cuirasses
         (Old Sequins and Armor)
         Enfantines
         (Children's Pieces)
           i. *Menus propos enfantins*
              (Childish Chatter)

    ii. *Enfantillages pittoresques*
       (Picturesque Childishness)
    iii. *Peccadilles importunes*
       (Tiresome Peccadilloes)
1914   *Sports et divertissements*
      (Sports and Diversions)
      Heures séculaires et instantanées
      (Age-old and Instantaneous Hours)
      Trois valses distinguées du précieux dégoûté
      (Three Distinguished Waltzes of a Disgusted Dandy)
1915   *Avant-dernières pensées*
      (Next-to-Last Thoughts)

In these twelve works, comprising sixty-one individual pieces in all, can be found in abundance the endearing qualities that have become virtually synonymous with Satie's name: wit, parody, irony, fantasy.

As early as 1897, in the *Pièces froides,* Satie had begun to reject the static chordal textures that typify most of his pre-1900 works. By 1912, the year that saw the severely contrapuntal *Préludes flasques,* the transformation was complete, Speaking of the change in Satie's style at this time, Charles Koechlin wrote, shortly before the composer's death:

Little by little, he gets rid of repetitions and redundancies. He prunes, throws out ballast, suppresses held notes, condenses, reduces the musical dialogue to a strict minimum (two parts, most often). . . . The air circulates, light and lively, in these quick pieces. At the same time, his language becomes bitonal; and when he uses only one tonality, some very unexpected harmonic relationships are created, in spite of an apparent simplicity.[16]

In the piano pieces of 1912–15 Satie was to make a virtue of brevity. And even though the emphasis had now shifted from the vertical to a linear texture, the timelessness, the "anti-teleological" aspect of the earlier music remains.

A perusal of the piano suites from the *Préludes flasques* of 1912 to the *Avant-dernières pensées* of 1915—excluding for the moment the somewhat atypical three sets of children's pieces—reveals a number of common denominators. All of the works in question—save the early *Préludes flasques*—are written in Satie's characteristic barless notation; they lack key signatures and, with the exception of "Sur une lanterne" from the *Descriptions automatiques* and "Chez le marchand d'or" from *Vieux se-*

quins et vieilles cuirasses, they lack time signatures. With the exception of the *Préludes flasques* and the *Sports et divertissements* they also reveal the composer's continuing trinitarian obsession, each suite containing three pieces (or, in the case of the *Enfantines,* three sets of three pieces).

The most beguiling and perhaps most controversial Satie mannerism—the droll and often nonsensical commentaries sprinkled liberally throughout the scores—is exploited in the suites of 1912–15 and carried to a new level of imaginative fancy. The short, cryptic phrases which began to appear sparingly as early as 1890 in the *Gnossiennes,* give way now to a veritable barrage of bizarre annotations and performance directions. By 1914, beginning with the *Heures séculaires et instantanées,* the verbal quips are replaced by virtually continuous monologues of a strange, frequently surrealistic nature. The fact that the composer prefaced this work with a "Warning" forbidding the text to be read aloud during performance has fed a certain amount of controversy. Most Satieans are inclined to take the composer at his word in this instance. A notable exception is the American critic Carl Van Vechten, who expressed the opinion as long ago as 1917 that Satie's comments, like the stage directions in a Bernard Shaw play, should be a vital component of the performance, that the audience should be allowed to share in the fun. He went on to suggest that the eccentric Russian-born pianist Vladimir de Pachmann, remembered not only for his sensitive performances of Chopin but also for his controversial habit of talking to his audiences while playing, would have made the ideal Satie interpreter. "Fancy de Pachmann," he wrote, "playing the delicate *Airs to make you run* from the *Cold Pieces,* saying at intervals, softly to his auditors . . . *En y regardent à deux fois . . . Se le dire . . . A plat . . . Blanc . . . Toujours . . . Passer . . . Pareillement . . . Du coin de la main. . . .*"[17] Van Vechten's is, to be sure, decidedly a minority view. Satie's intuition was right on this point. The ideal realization of a piece such as, say, the quintessentially Satiean *Sports et divertissements,* would be a private performance in intimate surroundings for a small group of connoisseurs gathered around the piano to delight simultaneously in the sounds, the drawings, the poems, and the composer's exquisite calligraphy. The fact that the score of *Sports et divertissements* was originally published in an oversize (almost seventeen inches square) loose-leaf format in the composer's autograph hand with illustrations by Charles Martin tends to substantiate such a claim.

If precedents for the composer's queer, whimsical titles are required they can readily be found in the keyboard works of Couperin, in Rossini's fanciful *Sins of My Old Age*—a collection of over 180 miscellaneous items for voices, chorus, piano, instrumental ensembles, and orchestra which appeared between 1857 and 1868 under such intriguing titles as "Harmless Prelude," "Little Bedroom Waltz," "Oh! The Green Peas"—and, closer to Satie's time, in the grotesqueries of the eccentric Charles-Henri-Valentin Alkan, the "Berlioz of the piano." Alkan, whose real name was Morhange, not only fancied strange titles for many of his enormously taxing piano works, but favored the kind of odd performance directions that Satie was to make peculiarly his own.

The 1912–15 piano suites represent the fulfillment of a creative ideal toward which Satie seems to have been moving almost from the beginning. In these whimsical miniatures we find a unique synthesis of elements—music, poetic fantasy, calligraphy—suspended in a delicate equilibrium. Like Connecticut's visionary transcendentalist, Charles Ives, Satie was deeply attached to a particular sonic environment, in his case, as we have seen, the breezy satirical world of the cabarets, circuses, and music halls of turn-of-the-century Montmartre. But whereas the American—his idealism rooted in a hard-headed Yankee Puritanism with its overtones of Emersonian individualism and Thoreauvian asceticism—incorporated jumbled fragments of his New England soundscape into musical structures of enormous complexity, the Frenchman, ever suspicious of the grandiose and the apocalyptic, placed his commonplace sonic fragments into musical structures of extreme simplicity, wherein each individual strand of experience stands out in bold relief. Nor should it be forgotten that apparitions of popular airs appear in numerous works of Debussy, beginning at least as early as 1880–83 with his setting of Vincent Hyspa's *La Belle au bois dormant,* which makes use of "Nous n'irons plus au bois," a children's song also quoted on one occasion by Satie and used again on three later occasions by Debussy: in the third of the 1894 *Images* for piano—which is virtually a set of variations on the tune—in "Jardins sous la pluie" from the *Estampes* (1903), and in "Rondes de printemps" from the orchestral *Images* of 1905–12.

Beginning with the *Descriptions automatiques* of 1913, Satie sprinkled his scores with tunes indigenous to his soundscape—children's songs, ragtime, folk songs, well-known airs from popular operettas, and, occasionally, themes from the "classics." Like Debussy in his use of the famous opening motif from the *Tristan* Prelude in the central section of "Golliwog's Cake-walk," Satie's quotations occasionally have a parodistic intent. Unlike Ives, however, he was not seeking anything nearly so grand as "transcendental unity," and neither of the French composers even remotely approached the free-association, "stream-of-conscious-ness" flow of the American's multilayered conceptions.

Satie, of course, would not have known of the existence of Ives as early as 1913, and likely not at all; nor does it seem that Debussy's music provided the direct stimulus for the piano suites.[18] Rather he was simply extending the commonplace practice of the Montmartrian chansonnier in using preexisting tunes in new—and often satirical—contexts. Most of the songbook collections of the period were printed entirely, or at least partially, without music, with an indication of the tune to be used for a particular chanson. Jules Jouy, for example, one of the Chat Noir regulars during Satie's tenure there, resorted to a number of the same tunes that later make an appearance in Satie's piano works, among them "Maman, les p'tits bateaux" and "La Carmagnole"; as well, we find numerous airs from the French opera and operetta repertoire—Boïeldieu's *La Dame blanche* and Planquette's *Les Cloches de Corneville,* for example.[19] Simi-larly, Léon Xanrof, in his collections of Chat Noir chansons,[20] appropri-ated well-known operatic airs, as did Satie's collaborator, Vincent Hyspa, whose "cover" composers included Offenbach and Massenet as well as fellow chansonniers such as Paul Delmet and Georges Tiercy.[21]

Geneviève de Brabant and *Jack in the Box* were the first of Satie's extended works to come directly out of the cabaret milieu, and, as we have seen, the *Three Pieces in the Shape of a Pear* was the first work to build at least partly on the same repertoire, although here the tunes were entirely his own.

Not unlike the majority of his French contemporaries Satie seemed to have had a strong need for extramusical stimuli in order to set his musical imagination in motion. And although both Debussy and Ravel occasionally made use of preexisting material for particular expressive purposes, Sa-tie's "found objects" seem to have been the actual stimuli that sparked a chain of events leading to the finished musico-poetic products.

Vieux sequins et vieilles cuirasses might be taken as a typical case in point. Unfortunately the surviving manuscripts do not point to a clear compositional modus operandi. However, we can speculate that the initial points of departure for these and most of the other piano works of 1913–14 were well-known French songs—children's ditties, political songs, op-eratic airs—that had a wide currency in France at the time and would have been familiar (as some of them still are) to several generations of French school children. Had Satie wished to locate a readily available printed source for most of the tunes he quotes, he would have had to look no further than the *Nouveaux Larousse illustré,*[22] the great French encyclopedia which, unlike most of its English-language equivalents, contains numerous entries for individual folk songs, popular airs, and operettas which include, in addition to historical backgrounds to the pieces, the texts as well as, in a good many cases, the printed music.

It is fairly obvious that the musico-poetic stimulus for the "Danse cuirassé" ("Armor-plated Dance") from *Old Sequins and Armor* was the song "La casquette du père Bugeaud" ("Father Bugeaud's Cap"), a military song that originated among the Zouaves, the companies of nineteenth-century Algerian infantry noted for their colorful uniforms of baggy trousers, open-fronted jackets, and tasseled caps or turbans. In the 1840s, during the French conquest of Algeria, Marshal Thomas-Robert Bugeaud, a veteran of the Napoleonic Wars, led his Zouave troops on a series of bloody campaigns against the Arabs that finally led to the defeat and capture of the Arab chief Abd-el-Kader in 1847 and the consolidation of the French empire in North Africa. According to the legend, the French camp was hit one night by a surprise attack, whereupon Bugeaud rushed from his tent to rally his men and repulse the enemy. When the struggle ended, he noticed that his victorious soldiers were staring at him with tittering amusement. Placing his hand on his head, the embarrassed Marshal discovered that, in the heat of the moment, he had fought the entire action without his large, visored officer's cap, his head adorned instead only by a simple cotton nightcap. "Go, look for my cap!" he cried, whereupon the troops began murmuring the refrain, "Have you seen the cap, the cap, have you seen the cap of father Bugeaud?" to a bugle tune known in the French army as "Aux champs (en marchant)." The Marshal was not offended. Several days later, when the word came to break camp, he commanded his bugler "to sound the *Casquette!*" The troops rode off singing a song that henceforth accompanied the Zouaves into battle and thus entered the annals of regimental folklore:

Example 1a. "La casquette du père Bugeaud" (from *Nouveaux Larousse illustré,* 2: 544)

Example 1b. "Aux champs (en marchant)" (from *Instruction du 18 juin 1912 sur les batteries et sonneries [commune à toutes les armes]*, p. 80)[23]

This is precisely the kind of story that would have delighted Satie. And no doubt the additional fact that the word "zouave"—in obvious reference to the odd uniforms of the Algerian infantry—eventually entered French slang in the sense of "playing the fool" (in dress or manners) would not have escaped him. Although it is likely that Satie, like most Frenchmen of his generation, would have been familiar with "La casquette du père Bugeaud," it is tempting to speculate that he turned to the *Nouveaux Larousse illustré* for background information on the song as well as for the text and music. We know that he was an inveterate reader, with a special fondness for anything that struck him as strange and exotic. It is in fact possible that it was a random encounter with the encyclopedia that suggested this and other tunes to him in the first place. Had he, then, located the entry for "La casquette du père Bugeaud," he could hardly have failed to notice the adjacent entries under "casque," which in French can refer either to a helmet or to a type of mollusk. Having previously dealt with mollusks in his *Dried-up Embryos,* the composer here seems to have been interested only in the military meaning of the word, and the article on helmets, lavishly illustrated with engravings of historical battle helmets from ancient Assyrian to contemporary colonial French, could only have served to reinforce the chain of associations that resulted in further military symbolism in the last piece of the set and contributed to the formulation of the suite's title.

The subtitle of "Danse cuirassé" ("Période grecque") may be an allusion to the Greek ancestry of its dedicatee, Michel Calvocoressi. The *Nouveaux Larousse illustré* prints only the opening period of the song, whereas most printed versions include, as an instrumental refrain, the B section of "Aux Champs (en marchant)" as well, which Satie also quotes in the "Danse cuirassé," making slight alterations to measures 2, 4, and 6 of the fanfare.

The first part of the suite's title is a reference to the first piece in the set, "Chez le marchand d'or" ("At the Gold Merchant's"), subtitled "Venise XIIIe siècle," a sequin being a gold coin first minted in Venice toward the end of the thirteenth century (ca. 1280) and maintained in use until the fall of the Venetian Republic five centuries later during the Napoleonic period. Here the musical symbolism is fairly obvious. The only identifiable preexistent tune found in the piece is the "Song of the Golden Calf" from act 2 of Gounod's *Faust,* in which Mephistopheles exhorts Wagner and the other students to worship the mighty Golden Calf, to submit, in other words, to the lure of gold, an obvious reference to the gold merchant's greedy passion for the shiny metal. As Satie's running verbal commentary informs us, he fondles his gold, smothers it in kisses, literally savors it by putting ten thousand gold francs into his mouth at one time, wallows in it, and rolls around in his coffer to the point where he feels stiff and sore all over from his exertion. Early in the piece when the merchant embraces an old sack full of coins Satie slyly introduces the opening motif of Mephistopheles's aria against a slithering chromatic accompaniment:

Example 2. Satie: "Chez le marchand d'or" from *Vieux sequins et vieilles cuirasses* (1913), line 5

Twice more the phrase is heard, the second time in the bass part over the verbal inscription "He takes a piece of gold and speaks to it in a low voice" (*à voix basse*), a veiled reference, perhaps, to Mephistopheles, one of the great *basso* roles in all opera. The last entrance of the Mephistophelian motif is accompanied in the score by the words "He is as happy as a king," but like many rich men before and since, he is, we can speculate, in clear danger of losing his soul, like the ambitious Faust of legend, the great German necromancer who sold his immortal soul to the Prince of Darkness.

In the last piece of the set, "La Défaite des Cimbres" ("The Defeat of the Cimbri"), Satie clearly reveals his extramusical sources in a short note he had printed in the score. We are asked to imagine a very old man who gives his little grandson a strange course in general history by telling him, each day, stories drawn from his vague memories, heroic tales of ancient battles involving legendary heroes such as the celebrated King Dagobert, the Duke of Marlborough, and the great Roman general Marius. Asleep in his tiny bed, the child has a dream (or rather, as the piece's subtitle informs us, a nightmare) in which he merges these historical figures into one formidable force which sets out to conquer Boïorix, king of the Cimbri, an ancient Teutonic people who invaded Gaul as far north as the Seine, waged war on Celtic tribes in the Danube valley, and penetrated the western borders of Italy until they were defeated in 102 B.C. at Aquae Sextiae (modern Aix-en-Provence) by the Romans under Gaius Marius and ultimately destroyed, along with their king, by the same forces the following year at a great battle on the Raudine Plain near Vercellae (modern Vercelli) in Piedmont, midway between Turin and Milan. As a result of this great victory over the barbarians, Marius was elected consul and hailed throughout the land as the "savior of the country."[24]

Once again we can speculate that this surrealistic fantasy was the offspring of two famous songs—"Le bon roi Dagobert" and "Malbrough s'en va-t-en guerre." And as before, Satie would not have had to go any further than the *Nouveaux Larousse illustré* to find both words and music as well as relevant historical background. Had he, in fact, troubled to look up "Cimbres" in the encyclopedia he could hardly have failed to notice the succeeding entry, "Cimbres, La Défaite des," the title of an 1833 painting by Alexandre-Gabriel Decamps, an artist noted particularly for his historical and religious subjects. Whether he learned of the painting in this fashion or had actually seen the work in the Louvre, which acquired it in 1903, it seems reasonably safe to assume that Satie borrowed the title of this somber painting commemorating the Roman victory at Aquae Sextiae, considered to be Decamps's masterpiece.[25]

"Le bon roi Dagobert" is a song of unknown provenance that became very popular after 1814 when its satirical couplets were directed at Napoleon and the disastrous Russian campaign. Suppressed by the authorities at the time, it gained a new level of popularity as a proroyalist song after Waterloo and the restoration of the hereditary Bourbon monarchy. Its hero is Dagobert I (ca. 602–39), a Merovingian king of the Franks, who is remembered not only for the magnificence of his court and for his personal love of comfort and luxury—he had in his short lifetime five wives and numerous concubines and ruled over his domains from a solid gold throne forged for him by his treasurer and trusted advisor, the goldsmith Saint Eloi—but also for his patronage of the arts and his protection of the Church, whose glory he celebrated by covering the land with religious monuments, among them numerous monasteries and the basilica of Saint-Denis, where he was interred in a splendidly ornate tomb.

Example 3. "Le bon roi Dagobert" (from *Nouveaux Larousse illustré* 3:490)

The subject of "Malbrough s'en va-t-en guerre" is John Churchill, first Duke of Marlborough, who distinguished himself during the War of the Spanish Succession (1701–14) as commander-in-chief of the combined armies of England and Holland with a brilliant series of victories over the armies of Louis XIV—Blenheim (1704), Ramillies (1706), Oudenaarde (1708), culminating in the battle of Malplaquet in September 1709. It is thought that the song dates from the time of Churchill's death in 1722, although there is an alternate theory that it came into existence thirteen years previously during the battle of Malplaquet when rumor swept the French lines that the English general had been killed. In any event it did not come into widespread popularity until the late eighteenth century (after 1781) when it reappeared in the form of a children's ditty, allegedly introduced to the court of Louis XVI and Marie-Antoinette by one Mme

Poitrine, nurse to the royal children. In the English-speaking world it is universally known as "For He's a Jolly Good Fellow":

Example 4. "Malbrough s'en va-t-en guerre" (from *Nouveaux Larousse illustré,* 5:868)

Common to both tunes is the bouncing iambic meter which Satie exploits at the very beginning of "La Défaite des Cimbres" with the incipit of "Le bon roi Dagobert" sounding in the bass. The opening motif of "Malbrough s'en va-t-en guerre" makes its first appearance as a "Portrait of Marius," and shortly thereafter the first two phrases of the song are sounded in the bass over triplet figurations in the right hand. Characteristically the tune fragments are heard each time on a different tonal level—C, B-flat, G—and occasionally the motifs undergo a process of distortion through small intervallic alterations which serves to reinforce the surrealistic nature of Satie's historical dreamscape.

"Boïorix, king of the Cimbri," is introduced with the last phrase of "Le bon roi Dagobert"—which is identical to the first phrase save for the tonic ending. In line 11 of the piece Satie introduces a phrase of ascending triplets with the verbal inscription "Les Dragons de Villars," a reference to Aimé Maillart's operetta of that name whose most famous aria, "Ne parle pas, Rose, je t'en supplie!," had figured in the first of his *Chapitres tournés en tous sens,* which he had completed just a few weeks previous to the composition of *Vieux sequins et vieilles cuirasses.* Here, however, there is no obvious musical connection with the operetta. The ghostly regiment of dragoons fleetingly passes through Satie's martial dreamscape, very softly, with a sweeping chromatic flourish in the bass dissonantly harmonized with conspicuous tritones and jarring major and minor seconds.

The final cryptic reference to "Le Sacre de Charles X (267[bis])," which is accompanied by one last grandiose statement of the opening phrase of "Le bon roi Dagobert," can only be assumed to be a veiled reference to the reactionary, ultraroyalist Comte d'Artois, crowned King of France as

Charles X in 1825—an association that may have been suggested to the composer by "Le bon roi Dagobert," considering its historical connection with the Bourbon restoration. In any event, the musical reference to the dissolute and by most accounts intellectually rather undernourished monarch takes on a deliciously satirical overtone in the context of the song's opening verse:

> The good king Dagobert
> Had his pants on inside out,
> The great Saint Eloi
> Said to him: O my king,
> Your Majesty
> Is badly trousered.
> It's true, replied the king,
> I'm going to put them on again right side out.

The satire is all the more pointed when we realize—as Satie quite probably did—that among the more extraordinary pieces of legislation passed by Charles's repressive government was a law making sacrilege a capital crime, a drastic measure to be sure but not a particularly unusual course of action for this last Bourbon king of France who, genuinely believing in the divine right of kings, could only view the Revolution as the work of the Devil. As for the parenthetical "267[bis]," whether it is a *Vexations*-like instruction inviting a marathon repetition of the final phrase or an arcane bit of Satiean numerology is anyone's guess!

To be sure, one need not be a student of French history nor recognize the musical quotations in order to understand and appreciate *Vieux sequins et vieilles cuirasses* or any other of Satie's piano works of this period. Like any music of quality, these pieces can be enjoyed on a more or less abstract plane. All music, however, has a semiological aspect, and to be aware of the musico-poetic symbiosis operating in Satie's music is to be brought more completely into the composer's imaginative world. In this sense Satie's music—as much as Ives's—will remain encapsulated by time and geography, for the internal symbolism no longer has the same weighted emotional ambience it surely once had.

Other pieces of the period reveal a similar compositional process. For example, in the little seascape "Sur un vaisseau" ("On a Ship") from the *Descriptions automatiques* Satie has the ship snigger (line 8) to the opening phrase of the children's song "Maman, les p'tits bateaux qui vont sur l'eau ont-ils des jambes?" ("Mama, the little boats that go on the water do they have legs?"). The second piece of the set, "Sur une lanterne" ("On a Streetlamp") is based on "La Carmagnole," a revolutionary song of unknown authorship that became enormously popular during the Terror as a traditional accompaniment to revolutionary activities, particularly executions. Satie's title, however, is quite probably a reference to an even more famous revolutionary song, "Ça ira!," whose refrain during the Terror became a rallying cry of the lynch mobs: "Ah! ça ira, ça ira, ça ira! Les aristrocrates à la lanterne" ("Ah! it will go! [i.e., succeed] Hang the aristocrats from the lamppost"). The *carmagnole* was a short coat of northern Italian origin introduced into France by immigrant Italian workmen from the district of Carmagnola in Piedmont. Along with black woolen trousers, a scarlet or tricolored vest, and a red hat it became a kind of official uniform of the insurgents after 1792, and about the same time the name was transferred to a round dance. So famous did the song become that French soldiers of the First Republic became known abroad as "les carmagnoles." The Madame Veto introduced in the first verse of the song is Marie-Antoinette, the haughty queen whose threat to slaughter the entire populace of Paris was neutralized by the revolutionary cannons:

Example 5. "La Carmagnole" (from *Nouveaux Larousse illustré*, 2: 509)

Satie borrowed only the opening phrase of the refrain, "Dansons la carmagnole." It is heard seven times in all, twice (in lines 3 and 13) in a slightly altered form. Each statement is heard on a different tonal level—

C, G, A, B, D, B-flat—ending on the dominant G, which, however, in the context is heard as a tonic, only to be negated by the closing dissonant ninth chord.

"Sur un casque" ("On a Helmet") has the piano imitating military drum tattoos and bugle calls. Its most overtly comic touch is its final cadence, a loud ostinato passage marked "Heavy as a sow" followed by an even louder (fortissimo) chord with heavy octaves in the bass, which Satie describes as "Light as an egg."

The titles of the *Embryons desséchés*—a work described in the manuscript by the composer as "absolutely incomprehensible, even to me"—suggests either a random encounter with an encyclopedia or a careful reading of Jules Verne, who indulged in such esoteric terminology in his detailed descriptions of marine life in *Twenty Thousand Leagues under the Sea* (1870), a book that very likely numbered Satie among its millions of readers.

It is interesting to compare Webster's definition of "holothuria"—"a Linnaean genus containing various rather wormlike aquatic animals . . . originally thought to be modified mollusks"—with Satie's fanciful lesson in ichthyology:

Ignorant people call it the "sea cucumber." The HOLOTHURIA usually clambers about on stones or rocks. Like a cat, this sea animal purrs; moreover, it spins a kind of moist silk. The action of the light seems to bother it. I once observed a Holothuria in the bay of Saint-Malo.

The only borrowed tune in this piece is "Mon rocher de Saint-Malo," a song composed by Loïsa Puget to words by her husband Gustave Lemoine. Puget's many songs, most of which date from the 1830s and 1840s, enjoyed an enormous vogue in their day, some of them—such as "Mon rocher de Saint-Malo"—retaining their popularity into the early years of this century. Appropriately, Satie quotes the song's opening phrase—"More than anything else I prefer my mother's home, my rock of Saint-Malo"—at "What a nice rock!" (lines 4–5) and at "It was a very nice rock! very sticky!" (line 17). "Holothuria" and its companion piece "Podolphthalma" are perhaps the most overtly comical pieces Satie ever wrote largely on account of their wildly parodistic final cadences. After the fluid and delicate two-part texture of these pieces, the sudden loud intrusion of obsessively repeated full-voice tonic chords ("Holothuria") or pompous, dramatically spaced tonic / dominant / tonic chords ("Podolphthalma") is quite hilarious. Here Satie's target would appear to be the

inflated closing perorations common to many works of the Romantic period—the closing pages of Beethoven's Fifth Symphony, for example, the
experience of which is forever altered in the light of Satie's joke. "Holothuria," moreover, has the distinction of containing Satie's most celebrated verbal quip, "like a nightingale with a toothache" (line 10), a phrase
that takes on an ironic twist when considered in the context of the previous phrase, "Life is so pleasant" (line 7).

Edriophthalma, the composer correctly informs us in the note to the
second piece, are "crustaceans with sessile eyes, that is to say without
stalks and immobile." But Satie brings us a deeper insight into the personality of these tiny marine animals by further noting that they are "by
nature of a very sad disposition" and prefer "to live in retirement from
the world, in holes pierced in the cliffs." Musically, "Edriophthalma" is a
parody of the third movement of Chopin's B-flat minor Piano Sonata,
perhaps the most famous funeral march in all musical literature. This
solemn threnody is suggested very near the beginning of the piece in the
dotted rhythm and descending tetrachord that accompanies the phrase
"How sad it is!" (line 1). Further insinuations of the theme follow, until
the lyrical D-flat major trio theme of the Chopin (here transposed to C
major) sings out as "Everyone is reduced to tears" (line 4). Characteristically, the parody operates on several levels simultaneously. The famous Chopin theme is identified in the score as "the celebrated mazurka
of SCHUBERT," a doubly curious statement considering that Schubert
wrote no mazurkas, celebrated or otherwise, and that, despite Chopin's
indelible association with the Polish dance form, the passage in question
bears not the slightest resemblance to the unmistakable mazurka
rhythm. Satie also tampers with the melody of the original, allowing it to
drop to the dominant G, thereby eliminating the expressive—and very
Chopinesque—rising seventh in the second measure. The original is further deflated through the substitution of a banal Alberti bass for Chopin's
elegantly spaced arpeggios:

Example 6a. Chopin. *Sonata no. 2 in B-flat Minor for Piano,* op. 35 (1839), 3.
Marche funèbre, measures 31–32

Example 6b. Satie: "d'Edriophthalma" from *Embryons desséchés* (1913), line 4

Ils se mettent tous à pleurer
(Citation de la célèbre mazurka de SCHUBERT)

Finally we are introduced to the stalk-eyed crustaceans, the podolph-thalma, "skillful and tireless hunters," the composer informs us, "found in every sea." Since these creatures are "very tasty and good to eat" we set off to hunt them. Here the musico-poetic symbolism is rather obscure. The first reference (beginning in lines 5 and 6) is to "The Orangutan Song" from act 3 of Edmond Audran's once enormously popular *La Mascotte* (1880), an operatic farrago of such endearing silliness as to appeal to Satie's highly refined sense of the absurd.

The operetta is set in fifteenth-century Italy during the reign of Lorenzo XVII, an impoverished Prince of Piombino. Learning of Bettina—the "mascot"—a beautiful farm girl who apparently brings good luck to her fortunate owner so long as she remains a virgin, Lorenzo proceeds to confiscate her from Rocco, a poor farmer who has just received her as a gift from his wealthy brother Antonio. Exercising his royal prerogative, Lorenzo offers Rocco in return the choice of a dungeon cell or a place in the palace as Lord Chamberlain, which latter situation, not surprisingly, he accepts. Unknown to Lorenzo, Bettina is in love with Pippo, a shepherd.

In the second act preparations are under way at the palace for the wedding of Lorenzo's daughter Fiametta to Fritellini, Prince of Pisa. Pippo arrives at the palace disguised as a dancer and secretly makes arrangements to fly with his willing Bettina, who has now been elevated to the rank of countess. Unfortunately the pair are discovered and sentenced to be hanged. Now we learn that the Princess Fiametta is also in love with Pippo, who, it seems, has been convinced by Lorenzo and Fritellini that Bettina has been unfaithful to him. Stimulated by revenge, Pippo falls easy prey to the seductive Fiametta. Their embrace is interrupted by Lorenzo who, far from being angry, sees a marriage between his daughter and the shepherd Pippo as a sure way to protect the virtue of his mascot, Bettina. Accordingly, Pippo is created Duke of Villa Rosa on the spot and offered a pension of fifty thousand crowns a year from the empty treasury of the destitute monarch. Learning of these developments, Bettina consents to marry Lorenzo, who intends it as a matter of form only, for the further protection of his mascot. The plans for the celebration of two royal weddings are disrupted when Bettina and Pippo decide once again to escape together, whereupon they leap from the castle window into the moat below and hence to freedom.

Act 3 opens in the neighboring Duchy of Pisa, whose Prince Fritellini is at war with Lorenzo. Beaten repeatedly in battle, the ill-fated Lorenzo is dethroned by his angry people and forced to flee with his daughter. Meanwhile Pippo and Bettina (now disguised as a man) reappear as soldiers in Fritellini's victorious army. With his talismanic mascot by his side, Pippo excels in battle and soon rises to the rank of captain. As a reward for his valiant services to the Prince he receives permission to marry his orderly, now revealed as his beloved Bettina. At this point Lorenzo, Fiametta, and Rocco appear at Fritellini's court in the disguise of wandering minstrels. Urged on by the soldiers, Fiametta is cajoled into singing "The Organgutan Song," a new chanson, we learn, whose satirical couplets lampoon none other than Fiametta's father, the deposed Lorenzo. Having no choice in the matter, and much to the chagrin of Lorenzo and Rocco, Fiametta launches into a song about a diabolical ape who once ruled Piombino. Seized by a sudden fit of colic, the ape raced off to the woods, where he routinely terrified pairs of young lovers, and, it seems, may have violated the young maid Zerlina. But the refrain assures us to tremble not, for they will capture him again. Separated from the operetta—with which it has really nothing much to do anyway!—"The Orangutan Song" became a great parlor favorite during the last decades of the last century:

Example 7. Audran: "Chanson de l'Orang-Outang" from *La Mascotte* (1880), act 3, refrain

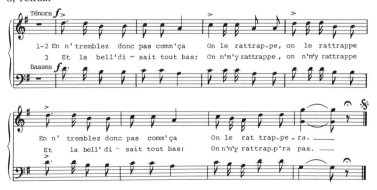

In the end youth and love triumph—as of course they always do in the world of operetta. Through her marriage to Pippo, Bettina automatically loses her power as a mascot. Happily, however, the charm will be transmitted to their progeny; hence all that is needed is a little time and a little patience.

This boisterous nonsense abounds in the kinds of zany non sequiturs, comic-book characters, and dramatic anarchy we recognize from Satie's own writing. In the context of such effervescent comedy, so dear to the composer's heart, his little drama *Le Piège de Méduse,* written in the same year as the *Embryons desséchés,* loses some—though not all—of its startling originality as a kind of Jarry-like prefiguration of Dada and the theater of the absurd.

Returning to "Podolphthalma," we can only surmise that Satie's intention was to advise us against trembling in the face of the fearsome stalk-eyed crustaceans. Perhaps, he suggests, the little creatures can be charmed into submission by a little shepherd girl, whose lovely pastoral melody ("Il était un' bergère") sounds in a clear, diatonic two-part texture before "the adviser" returns with his admonition to tremble not.

Croquis et agaceries d'un gros bonhomme en bois is unique in that its musical references are all derived from "classical" instrumental music, albeit pieces with an obvious programmatic element. The first piece, "Tyrolienne turque" ("Turkish Yodeling"), is a kind of Satiean homage to the Tirol and its most famous musical son. The piece is a clear-cut ternary form. Although the outer sections have not been traced to preexisting music, the tune that emerges at "Rather hot" (lines 3 and 4) has all the characteristics of a *tyrolienne* (or yodeling song). The middle section—beginning at "Very Turkish" (line 6)—is based on a fairly well disguised allusion to the third strain of Mozart's famous "Rondo alla turca" from the A major Piano Sonata, K. 331. Not only is the melody "stretched" out of shape by the repetition of certain notes, with the effect of changing the implied meter from duple to triple, it is undermined by dissonant chords which tend to pull it, as it were, out of harmonic focus.

The "Danse maigre" ("Meager Dance") does not appear to be based on borrowed material, although its title may have been intended as a pun on Cyril Scott's *Danse nègre* (1908), a once extremely popular trifle that Satie may have first encountered through Viñes, who was known to have included a number of Scott's works in his remarkably heterogeneous programs of contemporary music. Moreover, the subtitle of the "Danse maigre," "à la manière de ces messieurs" ("in the manner of these gentlemen"), would imply an awareness of Ravel's two pastiches *À la manière de . . .* Borodin and Chabrier, which appeared that same year, 1913.

The very title of the third piece, "Españaña," with its added syllable, suggests a parody of Chabrier's famous orchestral fantasia of 1883. The musical connection with *España* is revealed at the outset in the ostinato repetition of the rhythmic figure ♫ ♩ which figures so prominently in the orchestral work:

Example 8. Chabrier: *España* (1883), measures 61–64

Twice in "Españaña" Satie quotes the first two measures of Chabrier's motif exactly, once at "Plaza Clichy" (line 11) with dissonant bitonal harmonization, the second time at "Rue de Madrid" (line 13) with "normal" harmonziation—a sly dig, perhaps, at the venerable Paris Conservatoire which, in early 1911, moved into new quarters at No. 14, rue de Madrid:

Example 9. Satie: "Españaña" from *Croquis et agaceries d'un gros bonhomme en bois* (1913)

(a) Line 11

(b) Line 13

The other obvious points of correspondence with the Chabrier piece are the direct quotation (lines 9 and 10) of the big trombone tune that first appears at measures 218–26 of *España* and the final cadence which, unlike Satie's more usual indeterminate closing gestures, repeats the decisive authentic cadence of the original, even at the same pitch level.

Chapitres tournés en tous sens is aptly titled, considering that its three pieces—more so than is usually the case—have not the slightest programmatic (or musical) connection with one another. In turn we are introduced to a woman whose incessant, inane chatter exhausts her poor husband to the point of death; a man whose sole occupation seems to be hauling around very large (pumice) stones, much to the amazement of small children; and two prisoners, Jonah and Latude, who dream only of escape from their oppressive confinement.

In "Celle qui parle trop" ("She Who Talks Too Much"), the loquacious wife is represented by a rapid triplet patter that purrs along seamlessly in a (tonally) rather aimless fashion, mercifully stopping just short of the final cadence. The long-suffering husband shows his impatience at the very beginning with a few feeble dissonant interjections until, with a rapidly reiterated A (line 12), she commands him to listen to her. She proceeds to jabber aimlessly about mahogany hats, umbrellas made of bone, Mrs. Whats-her-name's marriage to a man as dry as a cuckoo, and the concierge's health. All the while, his isolation symbolized by a theme sounding in G major two octaves above the motorized triplets, the poor husband gives out the first phrase of the Romance, "Ne parle pas, Rose, je t'en supplie!" ("Don't talk, Rose, I beg you!") from act 1 of Aimé Maillart's 1856 operetta *Les Dragons de Villars*:

Example 10. Maillart: "Ne parle pas, Rose, je t'en supplie!" from *Les Dragons de Villars* (1856), act 1, measures 1–3

But all to no avail. The chatter grows louder and the husband, in yet another weary attempt to be heard, sounds his theme (now in C major) in octaves in the bass (lines 6 and 7). Again his theme is heard (line 10), this time in a slightly distorted shape, only to be cut short by yet another insistent "Listen to me now!" Yet again, now back in G major two octaves removed from the triplet figurations, the theme sounds, slowing very slightly at the end of the phrase. Suddenly the chattering triplets cease. Very slowly and very softly the husband's theme, dissonantly harmonized and chromatically distorted, sounds one last time. Utterly exhausted, he expires on an indeterminate chord, his theme fading on a forlorn minor third:

Example 11. Satie: "Celle qui parle trop" from *Chapitres tournés en tous sens* (1913), line 14

"Le Porteur de grosses pierres" ("The Hauler of Big Stones") is based upon an ironic use of the Finale of act 1 of Robert Planquette's operetta *Rip,* an amusing adaptation of a popular French stage version of Washington Irving's legendary tale of Rip Van Winkle, the man who slept for twenty years. One of the operetta's hit tunes was Rip's first-act air with choral refrain, "C'est un rien, un souffle, un rien" ("It's a trifle, a puff of air, a trifle"), which brings down the curtain on act 1:

Example 12. Planquette: "C'est un rien, un souffle, un rien" from *Rip* (1884), act 1, refrain

Satie quotes this phrase at the outset ("With a great deal of pain") changing only the little cadential melisma of the original to a more predictable arpeggiated figure. It is heard again—transposed from B-flat major to F major—at "In dragging his legs" (line 4), and one last time near the end (in G major) at "He feels the stone slipping from him: it's going to fall" (line 8)—and, with a crunching dissonance—which could be analyzed as superimposed augmented triads on D and E or, more accurately, as a whole-tone cluster spanning the augmented sixth D–B-sharp—"There it goes: it falls."

Finally we are introduced to Jonah and Latude in "Regrets des enfermés" ("Lament of the Confined"), the Old Testament prophet who displease God and the eighteenth-century French adventurer who displeased Louis XV—which amounts to the same thing. For thirty-five years Jean-Henri Masers de Latude was imprisoned in the Bastille and elsewhere for concocting a clumsy plot designed to ingratiate himself to Mme de Pompadour, the mistress of Louis XV. Secretly he sent her a box rigged to explode upon opening, and then arranged to inform her of a plot against her life before the fatal moment should arrive. Alas, the ruse was discovered. The royal mistress was not amused, and on 1 May 1749 the unfortunate Latude was incarcerated. Despite three attempts at escape he remained in custody until 1784. After the Revolution he was rehabilitated and awarded an indemnity from the heirs of Mme de Pompadour. He died in Paris on the first day of the year 1805, leaving behind a long account of his imprisonment which, some thirty years later, became the basis of a popular play coauthored by René-Charles Guilbert de Pixerécourt—"The Corneille of the Boulevards"—and Anicet Bourgeois.

Jonah and Latude, Satie informs us, though separated by many centuries, are seated in the shade, thinking. "I am the sailors' Latude," says Jonah, to which Latude replies: "I am the French Jonah." They seem to catch glimpses of the good old sun, and they dream only of escape—one from the dark seclusion of a whale's belly, the other from the musty confines of a royal dungeon—all this to repeated statements of the initial phrase of "Nous n'irons plus au bois" ("We will go no more to the woods"), a famous children's round dance used previously by several French composers of the period, notably Debussy.

Example 13. "Nous n'irons plus au bois"

Satie hints at the song at the outset in an ostinato figure based on the tune's first four notes, oddly harmonized with augmented fourths. In lines 3 and 4 we hear the entire opening phrase (with small adjustments to measures 2 and 3 of the melody) in the minor mode, followed immediately by a repetition of the four-note ostinato figure, transposed from C major to G major and now harmonized with perfect fourths. The remainder of the piece consists mainly of repetitions of the tune's opening phrase in varying dissonant and bitonal harmonizations and at varying tonal levels (C major, line 6; F major, line 8; D minor veering to C major, line 9; E-flat major, lines 12 and 13; G major, lines 16 and 17), interspersed with variants of the four-note motif. A particularly interesting statement (lines 12 and 13) contrapuntally combines the opening phrase (right hand) with a variant of the four-note motif (left hand):

Example 14. Satie: "Regrets des enfermés" from *Chapitres tournés en tous sens* (1913), lines 12 and 13

   The compositional process governing "Regrets des enfermés" is typical of the 1913 piano works in general. The borrowed tunes are remarkably similar: conjunct and diatonic, with a melodic range rarely exceeding an octave. Most of them, as we have seen, belong to the repertoire of French children's songs and all of them had a wide currency at the time— as indeed most of them still do, even to some extent outside the francophone world. Moreover, Satie makes little or no attempt to disguise his sources, the tunes for the most part being quoted exactly or with very minor alterations. Indeed, the pieces rely upon a ready recognition of the borrowed material for their sly musico-poetic humor to be fully savored.[26] Occasionally the humor takes the form of paradox—"The Orangutan Song," for example, counseling us not to fear the "hideous" stalk-eyed podolphthalma, or Rip's "It's a trifle, a puff of air, a trifle" accompanying the stone hauler as he staggers under the "enormous" weight of his gigantic pumice stone; in other instances it depends upon outright parody, as in the inflated closing perorations of "Holothuria" and "Podolphthalma" suddenly intruding on the composer's bald two-part texture.
   Typically a borrowed tune (or a characteristic fragment of one) is

stated clearly at or very near the beginning of a piece. What follows is usually a series of repetitions of the tune (or tunes) with little or no melodic variation but in various harmonic contexts and at varying tonal levels. The overall tonal framework of the pieces is usually defined either by a tonic / dominant or a tonic / tonic progression, although the final tonality is sometimes obscured through an unexpected twist in the cadence—the tone cluster at the end of "Le Porteur de grosses pierres," for example. Characteristically, short cells of music are juxtaposed, mosaiclike, in a seemingly haphazard fashion, negating any tendency toward a continuous narrative. Harmonies move about with abandon, the inherently tonal borrowed materials undermined by piquant and quirky harmonizations, often of a blatantly bitonal nature:

Example 15. Bitonality

(a) Satie: "Sur un casque" from *Descriptions automatiques* (1913), lines 1 and 2

(b) Satie: "La Défaite des Cimbres" from *Vieux sequins et vieilles cuirasses* (1913), line 9

There is in this music—as in all of Satie's music—a curiously objective and unatmospheric quality. The composer does not use chords for their rhetorical or coloristic possibilities but rather he delights in the unexpected relationships he can discover between them. Through a concept of form free from motivic development, a formal idea arrived at through the juxtaposition of bits and pieces of commonplace materials, Satie disallows the rhetorical element that results from the dramatic accumulation of related musical events. The sensuous element, too, is negated through the extreme bareness of the texture and the mechanistic rigidity of the rhythmic impulse.

Clearly all of Satie's piano music from this period explores the mysterious world of the child, reminding us of one of the composer's most celebrated aphorisms: "When I was young, people used to say to me: Wait until you're fifty, you'll see. I am fifty. I haven't seen anything."[27] Because he never allowed the child in himself to surrender to the man, Satie had an uncanny ability to see children other than as diminutive adults. As Wilfrid Mellers has suggested, he "saw in childhood an ideal of emotional sincerity which he looked for in vain in the adult world around him."[28] Also to the point is a perceptive comment by Satie's friend, the poet and critic René Chalupt, whose poem "Le Chapelier" he set to music in 1916. "The observation of the budding soul with an almost religious respect for its innocence, and the contemplation of its gradual awakening with a view of transforming it into artistic values," wrote Chalupt, "is an entirely modern inclination—possibly a symptom of decadence."[29] Certainly it seems that "children's music," as opposed to simple music for young pianists, is a relatively recent phenomenon, and, with the notable exceptions of Schumann and Mussorgsky, a peculiarly French preoccupation.

Though the majority of Satie's piano works appear technically simple on the surface, they require a fairly advanced technique for their proper realization. Notable exceptions are the nine children's pieces he composed in October 1913 collectively titled *Enfantines*. Here are a series of delightful "white-note" pieces in an extremely simple two-part texture wherein the musical material is stripped bare to the bone. In these little pieces Satie's verbal commentary is virtually continuous, resulting in a series of tiny sketches that offer sound moral advice while capturing to perfection the whimsical fantasy-world of the very young child:

"To Be Jealous of a Chum
Who Has a Big Head"

If you're jealous, you can't be happy.
I once knew a little boy who envied his
    parrot.
He would have liked to know his
    lessons like the parrot knew his.

"Eating His Bread and Jam"

You must get used to seeing a slice of
bread and jam without feeling the
need to swipe it.
It might give you a swollen head to filch
a friend's bread and jam.
I once had a dog who, in secret, used
to smoke all my cigars.
It gave him a tummy-ache.
That grieved his daddy very much.

Having borrowed frequently from the repertoire of children's songs, Satie repaid the debt by contributing a number of tunes of his own invention—simple, conjunct, diatonic, occasionally modal. The tiny pieces are mostly simple binary or ternary forms, with few odd harmonic surprises, and, for the most part, straightforward four-bar phrase structures. Aside from the whimsical texts, the chief Satiean mannerisms are the frequent ostinato figures and the abrupt transitions between phrases.

In 1972 Eschig published *Trois nouvelles enfantines* (Three New Children's Pieces), transcribed from manuscripts in the Bibliothèque Nationale by Nigel Wilkins. Here we meet an incorrigible little boy who laughs at his mother's scolding despite her threat to deprive him of jam, and a very pretty little girl who loves her doll and speaks sweetly to it. Separating naughty boy from pretty girl is a charming cradle song in a swaying 6/8 meter. All three pieces have the same bare two-part texture, the "white-note" diatonicism of C major breached only occasionally, notably in the first piece where slightly pungent diminished octaves in measures 2 and 18 and a sprinkling of tritones seems to underline the vexing behavior of the young scamp.

Leaving aside for the moment the remarkable *Sports et divertissements,* the group of piano pieces that began with the two sets of *Flabby Preludes* in 1912 is brought to a close with three additional strangely titled pieces: the *Heures séculaires et instantanées* and the *Trois valses distinguées du précieux dégoûté* of 1914 and the *Avant-dernières pensées* of 1915. Although preexistent tunes have not been discovered for any of these three sets of pieces, it seems probable, given the composer's well-established modus operandi, that borrowed music is utilized in at least some of them, although here the melodic material is on the whole relatively more chromatic, suggesting that Satie, having discovered an idiomatic approach to composition, was ready to fall back on his own musical resources.

Satie's extraordinary text for *Heures séculaires et instantanées* was written in June 1914, five years before the Romanian-born Tristan Tzara brought his Zurich-born Dada movement to Paris and began a series of fantastic "happenings" that were sometimes to amuse, more often to shock and scandalize, puzzled Parisians for the next half dozen years. Satie's text strongly prefigures the nonsensical banter and hallucinatory imagery that was to fill the pages of *Littérature*—from 1919 to 1924 the official organ of Dada—and which was later to become the special preoccupation of André Breton and his Surrealist colleagues, who broke with Tzara in 1924.

The work is dedicated to an Anglo-Norman figment of Satie's imagination, one Sir William Grant-Plumot—a relative, perhaps, of Samuel Pickwick, Esq., P.P.M.P.C—who seems to have been distinguished primarily by his "perpetual immobility":

To Sir William Grant-Plumot, I gratefully dedicate this work.
Up to now, two personalities have surprised me: Louis XI & Sir William—the first, by his weird sense of humor; the second, by his perpetual immobility. I am honored to pronounce, here, the names of Louis XI & of Sir William Grant-Plumot.

More about Sir William we cannot know. As for Louis XI, king of France from 1461 until his death in 1483, it is not difficult to comprehend Satie's fascination for this extraordinarily unattractive man—bald-headed, hooknosed, thick-lipped, rickety-legged—a man whose inordinate physical ugliness was compensated by his exceptional capacity for visionary statesmanship. Continuing the work of his father, Charles VII, Louis, with diplomatic cunning and intrigue as well as occasional force of arms, managed to forge the disparate fiefdoms of the land into a national monarchy, which endured, essentially intact, until the French Revolution. Satie would surely have taken notice of the fact that this eccentric monarch shunned the sumptuous attire of his exalted rank, preferring instead the simple and practical dress of the common folk—dark-colored wool cloak and breeches topped with a black hood or a battered old felt hat trimmed with little lead figurines of saints that he collected on his frequent pilgrimages; for Louis was also a pious man who lived in a pious age.

Precisely what constituted Louis's "weird sense of humor" in Satie's estimation is impossible to say: perhaps his odd sartorial habits, perhaps his gross indifference to courtly etiquette and protocol, perhaps his legendary cruelty, a popular (and somewhat exaggerated) image reinforced in the early nineteenth century by Sir Walter Scott's lurid "gothick" portrait of Louis in his Waverley novel *Quentin Durward.* How much Satie knew of the character and personality of this colorful monarch cannot be determined. However, a telling passage in one of the best modern studies of Louis XI cannot fail to perk up the ears of Satieans:

> He [Louis] was a connoisseur of irony, an indomitable actor, a comedian on a grand scale. Indeed, his career can be seen as a long comic poem, of which he is both author and protagonist. Like many other great comedians, he thoroughly appreciated his art; and like many other great comedians, he sometimes betrayed himself by his cleverness. But he always took his mission more seriously than he took himself.[30]

The text of *Heures séculaires et instantanées,* in three parts, follows:

"Venomous Obstacles"

This vast region of the globe has only one inhabitant: a negro. He is so bored he is ready to die of laughing. The shadows of the thousand-year-old trees indicate that it is 9:17 A.M. The toads are calling each other by their family names. In order to think better, the negro clasps his cerebellum in his right hand, with the fingers spread out. From a distance, he resembles a distinguished psychologist. He is captivated by four anonymous serpents, clinging to the tails of his uniform, which is rendered shapeless by a combination of sorrow and solitude. On the riverbank, an ancient mangrove tree slowly bathes its roots, which are revoltingly filthy. This is not the hour propitious to lovers.

"Morning Twilight (noon)"

The sun rose early and in a good mood. The temperature will be above average, since the weather is prehistoric and inclined to be stormy. The sun is high in the sky; he looks like a good chap. But don't let's trust him. Perhaps he's going to burn up the crops or deliver a mighty stroke: a sunstroke. Behind the shed, an ox is eating itself sick.

"Granitic Distractions"

The clock of the old abandoned village is also going to strike hard: to strike thirteen hours. An antediluvian rainstorm emerges from the clouds of dust; the great mocking trees are tugging at one another's branches, while the rough granite stones jostle one another about, and don't know where to put themselves so as to be a nuisance. Thirteen hours are about to strike, under the guise of: One o'clock in the afternoon. Alas! this isn't legal time.

Here is a surrealistic imagery worthy of Raymond Roussel, whose fantastical *Impressions of Africa* (1910) Satie may very well have read.

It seems likely that the *Trois Valses distinguées du précieux dégoûté* may have been intended as a gentle parody of Ravel's more celebrated *Valses nobles et sentimentales* of 1911. Indeed, given the dapper Ravel's well-known proclivity for natty dress, it is not unreasonable to assume that he may in fact be the "disgusted dandy" of the title. These charming waltzes provide further evidence of Satie's wide-ranging literary preferences. The epigrams that preface each of the three pieces are taken from La Bruyère, Cicero, and Cato. Jean de La Bruyère, France's master ironist, was an astute social critic who bared the foibles, vices, and hypocrisy of the Sun King's profoundly corrupt kingdom with a potent mixture of dead-pan humor, farcical exaggeration, and barbed wit. At the head of the first of the *Trois Valses,* "Sa Taille" ("His Waist"), Satie quotes from La Bruyère's *Characters* (1688) the eightieth maxim of chapter 8, "Of the Court":

Those who injure the reputation or the fortune of others, rather than miss the chance of a clever remark, deserve a degrading punishment. That has not been said before, and I venture to say it.

Of the 1,120 maxims or reflections in La Bruyère's book, this one is neither particularly perceptive nor entirely original. (Like a great deal else in the *Characters* it is indebted to the *Pensées* of La Bruyère's far more brilliant countryman Blaise Pascal.) Certainly it is a rather ironic remark in this context, considering that Satie himself was not above the occasional clever, catty, or downright rude gibe aimed at the reputation of others.

From La Bruyère the composer turned to Cicero's *De republica* and thence to Cato's *De agricultura,* or *De re rustica.* Cicero, we learn from the epigraph to the second waltz, "Son Binocle" ("His Spectacles"), declared modesty to be deeply rooted in the past, for ancient morals prohibited pubescent boys from appearing nude in the public baths, while to the third piece, "Ses Jambes" ("His Legs"), is appended Cato's rather commonplace counsel to the Roman landowner:

The first duty of the proprietor, upon arriving at his farm, must be to pay his respects to the household gods; then, on the same day, if he can spare the time, it is strongly recommended that he make a tour of his lands, that he learn the condition of his fields, and that, these tasks completed, he tackle those that are not.

Could Satie have known that Cato was something of an ascetic whose stringent regulations against luxury, particularly personal adornment, earned him the nickname "The Censor"? Quite probably. But to force a connection between La Bruyère and the Roman authors and the composer's whimsical monologue about a narcissistic dandy who pays himself lavish compliments on his entrancing waist, his beautiful silver spectacles with smoked gold lenses, and his fine flat legs, which dance only the best dances, is perhaps to miss the point, for the juxtaposition of unrelated imagery in the *Trois Valses* would seem to be a coy and deliberate attempt at mystification, resulting in what Rollo Myers quite aptly described as "a kind of surrealist *montage* of images on three separate entirely disconnected planes."[31]

In the last of his "humoristic" piano suites, *Avant-dernières pensées,* Satie paid tribute to three composers he greatly respected, offering an "Idylle" to Debussy, an "Aubade" to Paul Dukas, and a "Méditation" to his former teacher Roussel. In each of the three pieces the whimsical commentary remains, but there does not appear to be any allusion whatsoever either to popular tunes or to the musical styles of the three dedicatees. The structural principle in each piece is the same: an unvarying ostinato pattern—an Alberti bass for the "Idylle," an oscillating two-chord figure for the "Aubade," a reiterated triplet motif for the "Méditation"—against which are placed a series of quirky, cleanly chiseled phrases of a distinctly bitonal nature.

Sports and Diversions

If consideration of the *Sports et divertissements* has been left to last, it is because this delightful collection of twenty-one miniatures is not only Satie's most ambitious piano work but arguably his finest creative achievement, a superb marriage of style and idea, a crystallization of virtually everything that had preceded it, the purest distillation of an aesthetic ideal toward which he had been groping for a quarter century.

Apparently the publishing house of Lucien Vogel had commissioned Stravinsky to compose a work to accompany an album of sketches by the illustrator Charles Martin depicting various sports and entertainments. Stravinsky, fresh from his recent *succès de scandale* with the Ballets

Russes, refused on the grounds that the fee was too small. When similar terms were offered Satie, the beggarly composer is reported to have been insulted by what he considered too lavish an offer. Only when the publisher agreed to halve the fee did he settle down to compose a series of twenty miniatures, preceded by an "Unappetizing Chorale," which Vogel duly brought out in a deluxe limited edition that reproduced Satie's exquisite red and black notation along with Martin's drawings. In a Preface to the collection the composer explained his purpose:

> This publication is made up of two artistic elements: drawing, music. The drawing part is represented by strokes—strokes of wit; the musical part is depicted by dots—black dots [i.e., blackheads]. These two parts together—in a single volume—form a whole: an album. I advise the reader to leaf through the pages of this book with a kindly & smiling finger, for it is a work of fantasy. No more should be read into it.
>
> For the "Shriveled Up" and the "Stupified," I have written a serious & proper chorale. This chorale is a kind of bitter preamble, an austere & unfrivolous introduction.
>
> I have put into it all I know of Boredom. I dedicate this chorale to those who do not like me. I withdraw.

Once again Satie aimed his barbed wit at the scholasticism of the stuffy Academy. His tiny "Choral inappétissant" is to be played "hypocritically," in a "stern and surly" manner. So unappetizing is it, Satie tells us, that he composed it, on the morning of 15 May 1914, "on an empty stomach."

In his Preface the composer spoke of two artistic elements—drawing and music—modestly neglecting to mention a third, equally important, element, his inimitable verbal commentary, for each of the twenty miniatures, never more than four lines of music, is accompanied by a tiny poem in Satie's most delightful vein, surrealistic sketches which have been compared not without good reason to Japanese haiku:

"The Hunt"

> Do you hear the rabbit singing?
> What a voice!
> The nightingale is in its burrow.
> The owl is suckling her young.
> The Young wild boar is going to get married.
> As for me, I'm knocking down nuts with rifle shots.

"The Sleigh"

How cold it is!
Ladies, noses in your furs.
The sleigh flies along.
The landscape is very cold and doesn't know what to do with itself.

It should be obvious that an ideal performance of *Sports et divertisse-ments* would involve a mere handful of aficionados gathered around a piano in intimate surroundings to delight simultaneously in the music, the poetry, and the artwork—itself a three-tier system comprising Martin's full-page aquarelles, Satie's calligraphic notation, and the small ink sketches that adorn each title page.[32] As has been demonstrated, most of the "humoristic" piano pieces can be, and should be, approached as single musico-poetic entities with fairly obvious connections between quoted tunes and verbal commentary. In the *Sports et divertissements* the relationship between music and poetry, to which now is added a third element, drawing, is often quite subtle, even at times hermetic. But to perceive this fragile multidimensional texture is to savor the full flavor of these intriguing miniatures and experience them as the composer almost certainly intended.

In several of the pieces Satie indulges in a kind of *Augenmusik* wherein the musical score is an obvious graphic representation of the activity being depicted—the rocking accompanimental figure of "La Balançoire" ("The Swing" or "The Seesaw"), for example, or the plunging scalar passage in the third line of "Le Water-Chute":

Example 16. Satie: *Sports et divertissements* (1914)

(a) No. 2, "La Balançoire," line 1

(b) No. 16, "Le Water-Chute," line 3

Elsewhere the composer continues his practice of reflecting certain aspects of his verbal commentary in the music—the flourish of ascending fourths in "Le Golf," for example, as the Colonel's golf club flies to pieces, or, similarly, the ascending sweep of triplets ending in a bang, then a whimper, as the fireworks explode at the end of "Le Feu d'artifice":

Example 17. Satie: *Sports et divertissements* (1914)

(a) No. 11, "Le Golf," line 4

(b) No. 20, "Le Feu d'artifice," lines 3 and 4

Other musico-poetic correspondences are a little less obvious. "La Pêche" ("Fishing"), for example, opens with a soft ostinato pattern representing "the murmuring of the water in the riverbed." Soon a fish swims into view accompanied by a skittering bitonal flourish in the bass; seconds later the tiny figure is repeated, a ninth higher, as another fish swims by, followed by two concurrent flourishes in parallel fourths as two other fish momentarily appear. But the fish soon spot the angler and dart away home to the same flickering figures, their direction now reversed. The fisherman decides to pack it in and return home too, leaving only "the murmuring of the water in the riverbed," thus bringing to completion a perfect little arch form (A B C B A):

Example 18. Satie: *Sports et divertissements* (1914), no. 7, "La Pêche"

The subtlest level of intertextural relationship in the *Sports et divertissements* involves correspondence between the musical and the visual elements. The sweeping arpeggios of "Le Bain de mer" ("Sea Bathing"), for example, not only suggest (aurally and visually) the billowing waves of the ocean, the entire score itself is a graphic representation of the triangular drawing that accompanies it:

Example 19. Satie: *Sports et divertissements* (1914), no. 9, "Le Bain de mer"

Although *Sports et divertissements* does not make copious use of quoted material, there are a few recognizable snatches of familiar melody. In "Le Reveil de la Mariée" ("The Bride's Awakening"), for example, we hear a fortissimo version of the phrase ("Dormez-vous, dormez-vous?") from "Frère Jacques" near the beginning of the piece where it serves as a wakeup call for the bride, followed by a strident distortion of "Reveille" as she is commanded to get up. In "Les Courses" ("The Races") a slightly distorted version of the famous opening phrase of "La Marseillaise" is heard at the end of the race where it serves as an ironic accompaniment to "The Losers (with pointed noses and drooping ears)", while in "Le Flirt" there is an unmistakable allusion to the well-known children's song "Au clair de la lune," which sounds near the end in response to the words "Je voudrais être dans la lune" ("I would like to be in the moon"). One final curiosity is the rather startling prefiguration of Vincent Youmans's enormously popular "Tea for Two" from his 1923 musical *No, No, Nannette* at the beginning of "Le Golf."

Sports et divertissements is sui generis, the one work in which the variegated strands of Satie's artistic experience are unselfconsciously woven into a single fragile tapestry of sight and sound—a precarious union of Satie the musician, the poet, and the calligrapher. Here in abundance is the epigrammatic wit, irony, and fantasy that, taken together, have come to mean Satiean. At turns droll and amusing, serious and sardonic, this tiny *Gesamtkunstwerk* affords us as meaningful a glimpse of the composer's subconscious dreamworld as we are ever likely to get.

Things Seen to Right and Left (Without Glasses)

A miscellany of works, several of them published posthumously, helps to complete the picture while adding considerable interest to this remarkable "period of mystification and eccentricity" (Alfred Cortot's phrase). *Le Piège de Méduse* (Medusa's Trap), a twenty-five-minute "lyric comedy" with text by Satie and "dance music by the same gentleman," dates from February–March 1913, but (except for a private reading at Roland-Manuel's flat with the composer himself in the title role) was not performed until 1921 when the young actor Pierre Bertin produced it at the Théâtre Michel. The bizarre cast of this one-act farce includes the wealthy Baron Medusa, his arrogant and splendidly liveried servant Polycarpe, his "foster daughter" Frisette, her fiancé Astolfo, and Jonas, a giant stuffed monkey who unexpectedly breaks into dance from time to time between scenes of the drama. The mischievous Baron (like his creator) takes great delight in mystifying those around him, particularly the stunned Astolfo who is seeking Frisette's hand in marriage. Not unlike Satie's music, the dialogue of the play is compounded of short fragments that are more or less conceptually rational in isolation but decidedly surrealistic in context. The play abounds in non sequiturs, as the Baron continues a stream of inane chatter, much to the confusion of the dazed and disillusioned suitor. Finally, in order to test the loyalty, sincerity, and frankness of Astolfo ("I don't want an egoist for a son-in-law. . . . That would be dreadful") he springs his clumsy trap:

MEDUSA: Do you know how to dance on one eye? . . . on the left eye?

ASTOLFO: [*suffocating in his surprise*]: ? . . .

MEDUSA: [*behaving like a hypnotist. Harshly*]: I'm asking you if you know how to dance on one eye? . . . on the left eye? [*Sticks his forefinger in his right eye*] this one here?

ASTOLFO: [*in a strangled voice, his senses reeling*]: No.

MEDUSA: [*as if speaking to himself*]: Good: he's above board . . . [*His expression is one of great ecstasy*] Your answer pleases me greatly; you are an honest man, and don't beat about the bush.

ASTOLFO: Because I don't know how to dance on one eye?

MEDUSA: Good gracious, no![33]

The musical component of the drama, though in itself quite inconsequential, deliciously reinforces the atmosphere of uninhibited burlesque in the composer's most charming music-hall manner. For the seven tiny dance interludes he provided two quadrilles, a waltz, a mazurka, a polka, and a pair of perky two-steps, scored in a cheeky cabaret style for a small orchestra of clarinet, trumpet, trombone, violin, cello, and double bass, reinforced with a noisy percussion section consisting of bass drum, cymbals, side drum, triangle, and tambourine. Though of small intrinsic worth, *Le Piège de Méduse* has a certain historical value as an obvious precursor of the kind of zany antics Tristan Tzara and his Dada colleagues were to import to Paris some half dozen years later in the wake of—and largely in response to—the tragic debacle of a ruinous World War.

Also dating from 1913 is *Les Pantins dansent* (The Puppets are Dancing), a *poème dansé* delicately scored for flute, oboe, clarinet, bassoon, horn, trumpet, and strings. It was written in November for Valentine de Saint-Point, a dancer, poetess, and Futurist painter, who had intended to perform it the following month at a Métachorie festival. Lasting barely a minute and a half, the little piece (which also exists in a version for solo piano) has the flavor of a miniature march, its jerky staccato rhythms and wispy fragments of melody perfectly reflecting its title and, presumably, the poem it was intended to accompany.

Satie's only composition for violin and piano dates from January 1914. *Choses vues à droite et à gauche (sans lunettes)* (Things Seen to Right and Left [Without Glasses]), with its "Hypocritical Chorale," "Groping Fugue," and "Muscular Fantasy," is at once a throwback to the Schola Cantorum period and an amusing parody of the academic formalism to which he had been exposed by Roussel and d'Indy.

The little suite opens with a grave "Choral hypocrite" consisting of five two-bar phrases played very softly with the violin muted throughout. Double-stopped almost continuously, the violin plays a series of completely diatonic intervals, with a preponderance of open fourths and fifths, characteristically underpinned by slightly pungent harmonies in the piano, which tend to blur the C major tonal center the violin is intent on maintaining. "My Chorales equal those of Bach," the composer waggishly informs us in a postscript to the score, "with the difference that there are not so many of them and they are less pretentious."

The following "Fugue à tâtons" begins firmly in C major with a naive eight-bar subject in the piano (to be played with "a silly but suitable frankness") which continues ("cool as a cucumber") as the violin gives out the answer in the dominant. Episodic material follows, complete with spicy harmonization and a restatement of the subject in the submediant minor. Twice more the subject is heard, once in the subdominant, softly (and "winkingly") in the muted violin, the last time in the tonic, loudly ("starting off with a swoop") in the unmuted violin with a kind of stretto in the piano in the form of an inversion of the fugal subject, which brings the "groping fugue" to a grand conclusion with one of the composer's arcane cadences, ending on a resounding C major chord.

The concluding "Fantaisie musculaire" is a compendium of idiomatic violinistic techniques—pizzicato, harmonics, rapid arpeggiation, a double-stopped glissando—crowned with a grand cadenza whose very presence seems oddly out of place in a piece lasting less than a minute and a half. In turn the soloist is asked to play "enthusiastically," "sheepishly," and "coldly," and one passage of pianissimo sextuplets is somehow to sound "lacquered like a Chinaman." The unexpected warmth of the final vi–I cadence, played very softly and "very broadly" in piano and unmuted violin, is a typically Satiean *volte face,* standing as it does in stark opposition to the mechanical rigidity and dryness of this "cold" and "muscular fantasy."

Satie's last work of 1914, composed in November and December, was a set of *Trois Poèmes d'amour* (Three Love Poems) for baritone and piano. These tiny songs are unique in that they are settings of the composer's own peculiar poetry. In the three poems—"Ne suis que grain de sable" ("Am Only a Grain of Sand"), "Suis chauve de naissance" ("Am Bald from Birth"), "Ta parure est secrète" ("Your Attire is Discreet")— Satie forced upon himself an unvarying metric scheme of seven-syllable lines and a rigid rhyming scheme, giving rise to some rather odd poetic imagery bordering on the nonsensical:

> Suis chauve de naissance,
> Par pure bienséance.
> Je n'ai plus confiance
> En ma jeune vaillance.
> Pourquoi cette arrogance,
> De la si belle Hortense?

Très chauve de naissance,
Le suis par bienséance.

[Am bald from birth,
Out of sheer decency.
I have no more confidence
In my youthful ardor.
Why this arrogance,
From the beautiful Hortense?
Very bald from birth,
Am I out of decency.]

The *Trois Poèmes d'amour* are yet another example of Satie's penchant for composing one piece three times, for the songs bear a striking family resemblance. Each is a mere eight measures of conjunct, modally ambiguous melody animated by a single rhythmic pattern ♪♪♪♪♪♪♩ which appears consistently in every measure of each song. To be sure, the syllabic text setting and the modal, narrow-range melodies have something of the flavor of plainsong. However, Léon Guichard's claim (uncritically accepted by most later commentators) that the first song bears a striking resemblance to the Easter sequence *Victimae paschali laudes* is simply not borne out by the facts.[34]

Of greater importance in Satie's slender corpus of songs are the *Trois mélodies,* his only completed composition of 1916, composed between 14 April and 26 May. The first song, "La Statue de bronze" ("The Bronze Statue"), is a setting of a poem by Léon-Paul Fargue, a lovable eccentric whose poetry he would turn to again in 1923 for his last set of songs. Here we have a song about an ornamental bronze statue in the shape of a frog that sits in bored isolation under a bower—its mouth eternally open, poised to proclaim great things—dreaming of being with the others of its kind across the way perched around the rim of the rusty-red washing-place "blowing musical bubbles out of the soapy moonlight." Instead, it is doomed to suffer the indignity of passers-by tossing ten-franc coins, which usually miss the gaping mouth and fall harmlessly in a ring around the pedestal. And in the evening the insects crawl into the empty orifice to sleep.

The poem for the second song, "Daphénéo," was written by Mimie Godebska (M. God, as Satie called her), the beautiful seventeen-year-old daughter of Cipa and Ida Godebski, who, along with her younger brother Jean, had received the dedication of Ravel's delightful *Ma Mère l'Oye* eight years previously. Mimie's little poem is a charming conceit utterly dependent for its effect on the confusion of like-sounding words: "Tell me, Dapheneo, what is that tree whose fruit are crying birds? That tree, Chrysaline, is a bird tree [*un oisetier*]. Ah! . . . I thought that hazel trees [*les noisetiers*] yielded hazels nuts. Yes, Chrysaline, hazel trees yield hazel nuts, but bird trees yield birds that cry. Ah! . . ."

From the young Godebska's subtle word-play and surrealistic imagery to the topsy-turvy world of Lewis Carroll's Mad Hatter is but a step. In the final song, "Le Chapelier" ("The Hatter"), after *Alice in Wonderland,* René Chalupt tells of the Hatter's astonishment at learning that his watch is running three days slow, considering that he has always taken great care to grease it with only the finest quality butter. He has, however, gummed up the works with breadcrumbs, and even dipping the watch in a cup of tea will not make it go any faster. In June 1921 Satie told Louise Varèse that he adored *Alice in Wonderland* and thought it would make a splendid scenario for a ballet. After all, he told her, "he was the only Frenchman . . . who understood English humor (his mother had been English—or Scottish?) and the only composer whose music 'understood Alice.'"[35]

Whereas the first two of the *Trois mélodies* are recognizably Satian in their use of thumping music-hall rhythms and asymmetrical phrase structures ("La Statue de bronze") and juxtaposed ostinato patterns and whimsical cadences ("Daphénéo"), "Le Chapelier," marked "genre Gounod" in the score, is not so much a parody of Gounod's style as a pastiche of an old Provençal folk song, "Chanson de Magali," which the older composer appropriated in 1864 for his opera *Mireille,* a Mediterranean romance based on a long poem by the Provençal poet Frédéric Mistral.[36] Satie retained the repeated chordal accompaniment and, for the most part, the "proper" harmonization of the original, while foreshortening Gounod's flexible metric scheme (alternating measures of 9/8 and 6/8) into a single 12/8 meter. If there is a subtle element of parody in "Le Chapelier" it is most apparent in the last line of the first verse (measures 5–6) where the melody departs radically from the original, Gounod's arching melodic line and climactic high G being replaced by a plunging three-note sequential pattern harmonized with conspicuous parallel fifths in the left-hand accompaniment. Whether Satie was aware of the folk origin of Gounod's melody is not known. If he was, there is a certain irony in the fact that "Le Chapelier," his only excursion into Alice's wonderful (and very Satian) world, is an imitation of an imitation.

7

The Cock and the Harlequin

In the waning years of the nineteenth century, reinforcements for *ars gallica*'s struggle against Wagnerism arrived in Paris in the form of Rimsky-Korsakov's Russian Concerts, performed during the Paris Exhibition of 1889 in the huge hall of the Palais du Trocadéro. Included in two Saturday matinée concerts—22 and 29 June—were representative works of nearly every important nineteenth-century Russian composer. In addition to Glinka and Dargomizhsky, every member of "The Five" saw performance, as well as Liadov, Glazunov, and Tchaikovsky. Within a fortnight enthusiastic Parisian audiences were introduced to such staples of the Russian repertoire as Glinka's overture to *Russlan and Ludmilla,* Borodin's *In the Steppes of Central Asia* and *Polovtsian Dances,* and Rimsky-Korsakov's *Capriccio espagnole.* These fresh and exotic Slavic sounds were noticeably to affect the evolution of modern French music. The influence in particular of that great Russian "primitive," Modest Mussorgsky, on an entire generation of French composers, not the least of whom was Debussy, has been amply documented. This brief taste of the exotic in the fin de siècle was, however, only the advance guard, a raiding party as it were, and in the eyes of the concert-going public the Russian experience was soon overshadowed by the tremendous Wagnerian vogue, then at its peak in France. The main Russian force was not to arrive in the French capital until the spring of 1909. In late April of that year, an excited group of Russian artists gathered at the St. Petersburg station to begin a historic journey. In her biography of her famous husband, Romola Nijinsky has described that fateful day:

Finally, the great day of departure arrived, and when the troupe boarded the Paris-bound express the platform was full of well-wishers. Vaslav's mother came down to see him off. Many of the noblemen who had estates in France were accompanying the Ballet. The train left the St. Petersburg station with a flutter of waving hands behind, bearing unsuspected to the great audiences of the West the most powerful Russian invasion the modern world had known.[1]

Diaghilev and the Ballets Russes

On the evening of 19 May 1909 Serge Diaghilev's Russian Ballet opened for the first time at the Théâtre du Châtelet to the acclaim of the artistic elite of Paris. The opening program consisted of Nicolai Tcherepnin's *Le Pavillon d'Armide, Prince Igor,* with music from Borodin's opera, and *Le Festin,* a potpourri of Russian national dances using music from the works of Rimsky-Korsakov, Glinka, Tchaikovsky, Glazunov, and Mussorgsky. "Le Tout-Paris" showed up in a glittering array, and Diaghilev was assured at least a *succès de snobisme,* if not yet a *succès de scandale.* Among the many notables present in the old theater on that historic occasion were Maurice Ravel and the young Jean Cocteau. For the first time Parisian audiences were to witness an entire evening of ballet divorced from opera or spoken drama. The history of modern dance began with the opening curtain. To almost hysterical acclaim Diaghilev carried all of Paris before him. Thus began a series of historic performances that were to end only with the great impresario's death in 1929. His name became synonymous with modern ballet, and there was scarcely an artist living in Paris in the early decades of the century who was not swept into the dazzling orbit of the extraordinary Slav.

Serge Pavlovitch Diaghilev was a veritable renaissance man—art critic, musician, balletomane—and his influence on the development of the artistic avant-garde in the early twentieth century is inestimable. As a youth in Russia he was a brilliant student at the University of St. Petersburg, a student of composition for a time at the Conservatory under Rimsky-Korsakov, a skilled pianist, a tolerably good singer, and a connoisseur of modern art. His musical ambitions went so far as to result in fragments of an opera very much in the Mussorgsky manner, but Romola Nijinsky reports that Rimsky-Korsakov advised him: "Do whatever you want, Seroja, but promise me never to become a composer."[2]

From 1898 until 1904 he edited and largely financed a lavishly produced journal called *Mir Isstkustva* (The World of Art) which became a mirror of all that was chic and forward-looking in the European art world of those frenetic days before World War I. Diaghilev's magazine served as a kind of bridge between fin de siècle Symbolism and the Fauve art of the Ballets Russes. He was responsible, too, for acquainting Russia with Impressionist painting, and, as a sort of exchange, he organized, in 1906, an exhibition of Russian art at the Salon d'Automne in Paris. As a supplement to this activity his series of five Historical Concerts of 1907 introduced the young Scriabin and Rachmaninov in performances of their own works; and in 1908 he reached the high-water mark of his pre–Ballets Russes activities by presenting for the first time in Paris the incomparable Fedor Chaliapin in the title roles of *Boris Godunov* and *Ivan the Terrible.*

Although the great Nijinsky had many unflattering things to say about Diaghilev in his diary,[3] he once confided to his wife:

Among all the people I have ever known, Diaghileff, of course, meant the most to me. He was a genius, the greatest organizer, discoverer, and developer of talents, with the soul of an artist and a *grand seigneur,* the only man with universal talent that I could compare to Leonardo da Vinci.[4]

With uncanny precision Diaghilev anticipated the rapidly shifting artistic moods of his time, and almost miraculously his Ballets Russes held together for twenty years, representing during those two decades the vanguard of artistic activity, not only in France, but to a great extent in most of Europe and the Americas as well.

In order to finance his lavish productions Diaghilev needed wealthy patrons. Of the many well-connected Parisians whose purses the impresario relied on throughout his career, two remarkable women were to figure prominently in the life of Satie: Winaretta Singer, the enormously wealthy sewing machine heiress, who became the Princess Edmond de Polignac, and Misia Sert, who was to become the "patron saint" of the Russian Ballet and a lifelong friend of Diaghilev. The Belgian-born Misia (Marie) Godebska was the daughter of the Franco-Polish sculptor Cyprien Godebski who, after the death of Misia's mother, married Claire Natanson, aunt to the three Natanson brothers, cofounders of the influential *Revue blanche.* Misia's first husband, whom she married when she was fifteen, was Thadée Natanson, one of the brothers. Through him she was brought into close contact with a circle of artists around *La Revue blanche* which included such illustrious names as Debussy, Ravel, Mallarmé, Valéry, Renoir, Toulouse-Lautrec, Vuillard, Bonnard, and many others. In February 1904 Misia divorced Natanson to become, a year later, the fifth wife of Alfred Edwards, the wealthy owner of Europe's leading daily newspaper, *Le Matin*. At the time of her meeting with Diaghilev, Misia was already separated from Edwards and living with the Spanish-born painter and muralist José-Maria Sert whom she subsequently married, thus acquiring the name by which she is most widely known. Her step-brother and sister-in-law, Cipa and Ida Godebski, also figured prominently in the lives of many creative people in the early decades of the century; many of the piano works of Ravel and Satie were heard of a Sunday evening in the Godebski salon in the rue d'Athènes.

Having been enormously impressed with Diaghilev's production of *Boris Godunov,* Misia Sert, then Edwards, sought out the impresario in the spring of 1908; thus began a stormy relationship that was to endure for twenty years, despite the Russian's conspicuous misogyny. Jean Cocteau had met Misia several years previously at the home of the Rostand brothers, Maurice and Jean, and through her he effected a meeting with Diaghilev at her sumptuous apartment on the Quai Voltaire. Before long the witty, charming, gaminlike Cocteau had attached himself to the Ballets Russes, becoming, in the coy words of Frederick Brown, Diaghilev's "court jester" and "house pixy."[5] The mercurial Cocteau—poet, novelist, dramatist, filmmaker, caricaturist, critic—was soon to become a collaborator of Satie, and although the poet's brilliant career was in some measure indebted to the middle-aged composer from Arcueil (Satie was forty-eight years old when he met Cocteau in 1915), it is undeniable that he in turn was instrumental in paving the way for Satie's emergence into the limelight, thrusting him onto center stage through his myriad connections in the Paris art scene.

In the spring of 1915, Cocteau, in collaboration with the Cubist painter Albert Gleizes, decided to create a new, ultramodern production of Shakespeare's *A Midsummer Night's Dream;* it was to be presented in the Cirque Médrano, with appearances of the famous Fratellini clowns as Bottom, Flute, and Starveling, Cubist sets and costumes by Gleizes, and music by a French modern. Edgard Varèse was to be in charge of the orchestra, and Debussy, Stravinsky, Roussel, Ravel, and Florent Schmitt were at first considered for the musical score. Although the music, in Cocteau's words, was to be "a pot-pourri of everything we like,"[6] the only musical numbers mentioned in connection with the early rehearsals of the production were Satie's *Gymnopédies* (presumably Debussy's orchestral version) and the then new popular song *Tipperary,* jointly composed in 1912 by Harry J. Williams and the British music-hall entertainer Jack Judge.

Apparently Cocteau had been enchanted with a performance of Satie's *Three Pieces in the Shape of a Pear* that he had heard in April of 1915 at the Godebskis'; and he decided that Satie's musical collaboration was essential for the proper realization of his *Dream*. Accordingly, he arranged through Valentine Gross (later Hugo), whom he had met the previous year at the Opéra during a rehearsal of the Strauss-Diaghilev *Legend of Joseph*, to meet the solitary composer from Arcueil. Valentine, a talented Alsatian-born artist who became well known in Paris artistic circles in the early years of the Diaghilev ballet, was to become the third remarkable female patron of Satie. In addition to her considerable artistic talent, she possessed a solid musical background: her father was a composer and professor of music at Boulogne-sur-Mer. Her drawings and sketches of dancers executed during the rehearsals of *The Rite of Spring* were exhibited in the foyer of the Théâtre des Champs-Élysées on the night of the scandalous premiere of the Stravinsky ballet. Although Mme Cocteau had hoped for a match between the beautiful artist and her homosexual son, Valentine became the bride of the artist Jean Hugo (great-grandson of the famous poet) on 7 August 1919, with Cocteau and Satie as witnesses. Satie and Valentine had met in 1914 at the apartment of Roland-Manuel where, in the company of René Chalupt and the artist Roger de la Fresnaye, she witnessed the first performance of Satie's farcical drama, *Le Piège de Méduse,* with the composer himself playing the role of the eccentric Baron Medusa. Thus began an affectionate relationship between the aging composer and the beautiful young artist that was terminated only by Satie's death. In her own words she became, "little by little, his child, his friend, his sister."[7] From the time of that first meeting, Satie made weekly visits to Valentine's flat in the fashionable Quai Bourbon, where she held Wednesday salons; among the many guests were three people who also figured prominently in Satie's career: Ricardo Viñes, the poet Léon-Paul Fargue, and Georges Auric, youngest of *Les Six.*

The impecunious Satie had not forgotten that Valentine had been the force behind his commission to write the *Sports et divertissements,* for which he received the handsome sum of three thousand francs. Thus when Valentine wrote him in October 1915 that Cocteau desired a meeting, he replied: "Of course! I shall be delighted to see Cocteau—and you, needless to say. Your idea is charming, as your ideas always are. You are

one of the good ones."[8] In this way two remarkable creative figures were
brought together who in a very few years would astound Paris with their
famous "realistic ballet," *Parade.* Cocteau would remain Satie's greatest
champion.

On Monday, 18 October 1915, Cocteau, Satie, and the impresario Gabriel Astruc, the sponsor of the proposed spectacle, arrived at the home
of Valentine Gross to begin discussions of the projected *Dream.* Six
weeks later, on 29 November, a second meeting took place at the Gross
apartment. But for reasons that remain unclear, Cocteau's production of
the Shakespeare play failed to materialize; after several rehearsals at the
Cirque Médrano the whole enterprise collapsed. Nevertheless, on Satie's death, among the disorderly array of his papers was found, along
with the presumed lost *Geneviève de Brabant* and *Jack in the Box,* a score
for *Cinq Grimaces pour "Le Songe d'une nuit d'été"* (Five Grimaces for "A
Midsummer Night's Dream"), which was published posthumously in
1929, both in its original version for music-hall orchestra and in a piano
reduction by Darius Milhaud.

In some ways the *Five Grimaces* can be considered a preliminary
sketch for *Parade.* By 1914 Satie had fully realized a fusion of *café-concert*
and "serious" styles, and the *Grimaces* reveal many of the parodistic
traits of the 1913 piano suites. The five short numbers carry the following characteristic titles: 1. "Préambule" ("Preamble"), 2. "Coquecigrue"
("Fiddle-faddle"), 3. "Chasse" ("Chase"), 4. "Fanfaronnade" ("Bluster"),
and 5. "Pour sortir" ("For Exit"). The music recalls many of the familiar
earmarks of the composer's style as it developed in the first two decades
of the century. For example, the "wrong-note" harmonies (ex. la) which
were featured in numerous earlier works dating back at least to *Jack in
the Box* and *Geneviève de Brabant,* and, in a similar passage (ex. lb), the
passing polyharmonies resulting from arpeggiated triads of E-flat, D, C,
and B sounding over an ostinato bass consisting of an incomplete C major
triad:

Example 1a. Satie: "Préambule" from *Cinq Grimaces pour "Le Songe d'une nuit
d'été"* (1914), measures 1–4

Example 1b. Satie: "Fanfaronnade" from *Cinq Grimaces pour "Le Songe d'une nuit d'été"* (1914), measures 4–6

The modal ambiguity of some of the melodic lines was a characteristic feature of the Satie style as early as the *Trois Mélodies* and the *Ogives* of 1886, and what appear to be snatches of popular tunes in "Coquecigrue" and "Fanfaronnade" continue a precedent set as early as the late 1890s and brought to fruition in the 1913 piano suites. Finally, we might note a surprising echo of Satie's Rosicrucian world as filtered through two decades of Debussyan Impressionism as the *Dream* fades then vanishes in a gentle haze of seventh and eleventh chords:

Example 2. Satie: "Pour sortir" from *Cinq Grimaces pour "Le Songe d'une nuit d'été"* (1914), measures 49–52

Parade and the New Spirit

On a night in 1912, three years previous to his first meeting with Satie, Cocteau was involved in a conversation with Diaghilev that ultimately resulted in a significant landmark in the development of the avant-garde. Years later, Cocteau recalled the auspicious occasion:

> One night in 1912, I see us in the Place de la Concorde. Diaghilev is walking home after a performance, his thick underlip sagging, his eyes bleary as Portuguese oysters, his tiny hat perched on his enormous head. Ahead, Nijinsky is sulking, his evening clothes bulging over his muscles. I was at the absurd age when one thinks oneself a poet, and I sensed in Diaghilev a polite resistance. I questioned him about this, and he answered, "Astound me! I'll wait for you to astound me."[9]

It was to take Cocteau five years to obey Diaghilev's imperious command; but finally, "in 1917," he wrote, "the afternoon of the premier of *Parade,* I astounded him."[10]

As it had most concertgoers in 1913, Stravinsky's *Rite of Spring* hit Jean Cocteau like a thunderbolt, and from the night of the stormy premiere his overriding passion was to collaborate with the now famous man. Stravinsky's ballet had opened up a whole new world to the young poet and impressed upon him that rebellion was an indispensable component of the spirit of creation.

During the winter of 1913–14 Stravinsky was living in Switzerland, at Clarens on Lake Geneva, where he was in the process of completing his opera *The Nightingale.* Cocteau, perhaps in his frantic desire to share some future glory with the great composer, and at the same time astound Diaghilev, wrote to Stravinsky on 12 February 1914 concerning his ideas for a new ballet to be called *David,* a work that, despite its conventional biblical text (the story of David and Goliath in the *Book of Samuel*), was clearly a preliminary sketch for *Parade.*

At this stage of his career Cocteau seemed to specialize in stillborn productions, for *David* was never to progress beyond a few costume designs and a rather fragmentary scenario. Stravinsky had not shown a great deal of enthusiasm for the project and greatly resented the young poet's insistent wheedling behavior. Moreover, Diaghilev, who by now considered Stravinsky one of his private properties, had no small role to play in discouraging a liaison between his star composer and the upstart poet.

With Diaghilev's "Astound me!" still echoing in his brain, Cocteau now began to formulate plans for a new ballet, which would be built on the ruins of *David* and *A Midsummer Night's Dream.* In the autumn of 1915, when his dream of a collaboration with Stravinsky had begun to fade, the indefatigable poet, realizing the strength of her influence, decided to go through Misia Sert in an attempt to reach Diaghilev and interest him in a Satie-Cocteau project. In her memoirs Misia recalled that she had introduced Diaghilev to Satie as early as the summer of 1914 with the hope of fostering the impresario's interest in the neglected composer:

Diaghilev was in Paris at the moment, and I had been reproaching him for some time for not paying more attention to Erik Satie. He had ended by responding to my injunctions, and I brought them together in my house to give Serge the opportunity of hearing the music of the Arcueil hermit. Sitting at the piano, lean little Satie, his pince-nez precariously balancing on his nose, had just finished playing his *Morceaux en forme de poire* when an old friend of ours rushed in like a gust of wind, his beard on end. In one gasp, he told us about the Sarajevo murder and why war was logically inevitable. [11]

Two years after this important meeting between impresario and composer a series of events began to transpire that would directly result in a Cocteau-Satie-Diaghilev collaboration of great importance. In a communication to Pierre Reverdy's short-lived review *Nord-Sud,* Cocteau recorded his version of how *Parade* came into being:

> I first had the idea of it during a period of "leave" in April, 1915 [*sic*][12] (I was then in the Army), on hearing Satie play his *Morceaux en forme de poire* for four hands, with Viñes.
> A kind of telepathy inspired us simultaneously with a desire to collaborate. A week later I returned to the front, leaving with Satie a bundle of notes and sketches which were to provide him with the theme of the Chinaman, the little American girl and the acrobat (there was then only one acrobat). These indications were not in the least humorous. They emphasized, on the contrary, the prolongation of these characters on the other side of our showman's booth. The Chinaman could there torture missionaries, the little girl go down with the *Titanic,* and the acrobat win the confidence of the angels.
> Gradually there came to birth a score in which Satie seems to have discovered an unknown dimension, thanks to which one can listen simultaneously both to the "Parade" and the show going on inside. [13]

The "bundle of notes" of which Cocteau speaks may not have been humorous, but most certainly it was curious in the extreme, revealing the poet's mind in action, as half-digested scraps of ideas spewed forth from his fertile brain in an automatic, free association manner. The kaleidoscopic sketches at this stage read like the scenario of a surrealist movie, and it is not surprising that Satie (like Stravinsky before him) should have been somewhat mystified and uncertain as to Cocteau's true intentions. But Satie was intrigued, and on 25 April 1916 he wrote Cocteau: "Forgive me—sick—grippe. Impossible send word except by telepathy. All right for tomorrow. Valentine Gross tells me marvelous things. You are the *idea* man. Bravo!"[14] Anxious that everything should go smoothly with his unpredictable new collaborator, Cocteau queried Valentine Gross on 3 May: "Dear Valentine—a letter from Satie. 'Very marvelous,' he says. Does that mean enthusiasm, in his faun's language? Try to find out."[15]

Misia Sert, with her whimsical habit of interfering in the lives of artists, apparently had had no small part to play in the destruction of the Stravinsky-Cocteau collaboration on *David.* In order to secure her support for

their new effort—and through her the support of Diaghilev—both Cocteau and Satie wrote a series of sycophantic letters to her in the spring
of 1916, with the express purpose of convincing her that *Parade* had
been partly her inspiration, that it had, indeed, been initially conceived
in her presence (whereas in actual fact the first discussions of *Parade*
had taken place in the home of Valentine Gross in late 1915, close on the
heels of the abortive *David* project). In a letter to Misia requesting that
she be a patroness of a Granados-Satie concert on 30 May (the Spanish
pianist / composer Enrique Granados had died at sea a month previously,
his ship a victim of a German torpedo), Satie led her to believe that the
new ballet would be dedicated to her and that the idea for it had even
originated in her salon. Soon after his correspondence with Misia, the
composer wrote (on 8 June 1916) to Cocteau at Boulogne where the poet
was stationed with his ambulance corps, in order to assure him that he
was making good progress:

> For heaven's sake stop worrying, don't be nervous. I am at work. Let me do
> it my own way. I warn you, you won't see the thing until *October*. Not a note
> before that. I tell you so under oath. Will it be all right if I mention that you are
> the author of the scenario? I need to. Madame Edwards is all for the project. I
> told her that she would have to wait until October. I want to do a good job—very
> much so. You *must* trust me. If you come to Paris, let me know. Greetings to
> Valentine Gross and yourself.[16]

Shortly after he had witnessed Stravinsky's *Rite of Spring,* Cocteau,
in his constant and untiring search for artistic novelty, discovered and
became infatuated with Cubist painting. One result of this new interest
had been his meeting with Gleizes early in 1914 and the unsuccessful
attempt to launch the *Midsummer Night's Dream.* Now, two years later,
Cocteau sought an introduction to Pablo Picasso, the leader of the Cubist
movement, and in December 1915 the painter was brought by Edgard
Varèse to Cocteau's elegant apartment in the rue d'Anjou. Cocteau was
completely captivated by the volatile Spaniard, and soon after his first
meeting with him asked him to join forces with Satie and himself in the
production of *Parade.* On 11 August 1916 Cocteau wrote an enthusiastic
letter to Stravinsky in which Picasso's name is mentioned and in which
he revealed something of the flavor of the new ballet: "May it distill all
the involuntary emotion given off by circuses, music halls, carrousels,
public balls, factories, seaports, the movies, etc. etc."[17] Two weeks
later, on 24 August, a postcard, jointly signed by Cocteau and Satie, was
mailed to Valentine Gross with the following terse but important mes-

sage: "Picasso is doing *Parade* with us."[18] Cocteau was delighted. He now had as a collaborator the leader of the Cubist movement, then the most progressive—and therefore shocking—artistic trend on the Parisian art scene. Léonide Massine, Diaghilev's leading male dancer since the departure of Nijinsky, was to do the choreography.

Parade opened on 18 May 1917 at the Théâtre du Châtelet, under the direction of the Swiss conductor Ernest Ansermet, to a heterogeneous audience representative of the crosscurrents of Paris artistic life. Included in this motley group were Diaghilev's wealthy patrons, the Princesse de Polignac, Misia Sert, the Étienne de Beaumonts, numerous painters from Montmartre and Montparnasse who had come to see Picasso's Cubist sets and costumes; Satie's young disciples, among them Roland-Manuel, Auric, and Poulenc; and the poets Guillaume Apollinaire and E. E. Cummings.

On the day of the performance, an article by Cocteau appeared in the newspaper *Excelsior* in which the poet attempted to explain the meaning of the new ballet:

Our wish is that the public may consider *Parade* as a work which conceals poetry beneath the coarse outer skin of slapstick. Laughter is natural to Frenchmen: it is important to keep this in mind and not be afraid to laugh even at this most difficult time. Laughter is too Latin a weapon to be neglected. . . . It was appropriate . . . to do justice for the first time to the true meaning of "realism" in theatrical terms. What has hitherto been called "realistic art" is in a way a pleonastic art, especially in the theatre, where "realism" consists in admitting onto the stage real objects which lose their reality the moment they are placed in nonreal surroundings. The elements of *trompe-l'oeil* and *trompe-l'oreille* in *Parade* create reality—which alone has the power to move us, well disguised though it may be.[19]

In order to lend additional prestige to the undertaking, Apollinaire was invited to provide a program note, which turned out to be a kind of manifesto of *l'esprit nouveau* (the new spirit). Cocteau's term *ballet réaliste* was advanced one degree when Apollinaire in his note described *Parade* as *sur-réaliste,* thus coining a term that would in a short time lend itself to an important artistic movement.

Experimental ballet can be said to have originated with *Parade*.[20] It is a "realistic" ballet in the sense that it totally rejects not only the lavish sets but also the myth, legend, and fairy tale, as well as the traditional narrative perspective, that had been the staple of the genre from *Giselle* to *Swan Lake* and even, to a great extent, *The Rite of Spring*. *Parade* is a ballet of the Paris streets, incorporating in a kind of Cubist collage the music hall, ragtime, themes from American cinema, the circus, and variegated sound effects ranging from a steamboat whistle and sirens to pistol shots and a typewriter. It is, in short, a glorification of an ancient art—the circus—and a contemporary art—the then infant cinema—which, taken together, were the chief mythopoeic symbols of that perilous time of flux, decay, and resurrection. On another level it is a fusion of "low" art (the circus) with "high" art (the ballet), an uneasy alliance that had been a central tenet of the Satie aesthetic almost from the beginning.

The plot is simple. *Parade* is the story of a misunderstanding between the artists and the public—itself an implicit theme of the avant-garde.[21] In front of a fair-booth proscenium erected of a Sunday afternoon in a Paris street three Managers (or circus barkers) attempt to advertise their vaudeville by exhibiting excerpts from the show that is supposedly being enacted inside the theater (symbolized by Picasso's magnificent drop-curtain). The French Manager, a dehumanized walking cubistic sculpture, introduces his first act, a Chinese Prestidigitator, resplendently outfitted in a yellow, white, black, and red costume, who, with mechanical, puppetlike gestures, displays his conjuring prowess to the street crowd; he pulls an imaginary egg out of his pigtail, eats it and finds it again on the end of his shoe, pretends to spit fire, burns himself and stamps out the sparks.

His removal signals the American Manager, who appears encased in a huge ten-foot high cardboard skyscraper crowned with a top hat, a megaphone in one hand, a placard announcing PARADE in the other, and introduces the Little American Girl. She bounds onto the stage wearing a schoolgirl's navy blue sailor jacket, pleated white skirt, and knee stockings and cavorts like a character out of a silent film to ragtime music intermittently punctuated by the clacking of a typewriter, revolver shots, and the raucous blare of a ship's siren. Her routine is a kind of "cubistic" balletic stylization of film montage, a crazy counterpoint of seemingly unrelated images, a metaphorical amplification of the American experience as perceived through the eyes and ears of contemporary Europeans, whose mental image of America—then as now—was chiefly manufactured in Hollywood. She goes through the motions of a Western hoedown, shoots an arrow (like an Indian?), imitates the celebrated splayfooted Chaplinesque shuffle, pantomines a typist (American big business?) to the actual clacking of a typewriter in the pit orchestra, fires a pistol (cops and robbers?), rides an imaginary racehorse, and, finally, ends up on a steamboat, which, with forlorn blasts from its foghorn, appears to sink in stormy seas (like the *Titanic*?), leaving the Little American Girl stranded to bid a wistful farewell to the spectators. Still the audience fails to comprehend, whereupon a third Manager in the form of two dancers in an ungainly horse costume prances about the stage, the orchestra for the moment silent, followed by a pair of Acrobats in blue and white tights decorated with bold star shapes and spiral designs, who, to a lurching waltz-tune, dance a circus parody of a pas de deux. The crowd, still under the impression that it is seeing the *real* show rather than a preview, obdurately remains outside the theater. The performers return, urged on by the frustrated and by now enraged managers into a recapitulation of their respective acts in one last frantic but futile attempt to entice the spectators into the theater. In the end the Horse collapses in exhaustion, the Chinaman smiles his inscrutable smile, while the remaining performers droop in a posture of weary resignation to the strains of the lugubrious fugal theme that accompanied the curtain raising.

Like a Cubist painting, *Parade* achieves a different order of reality through the juxtaposition of common elements that are forced into uncommon relationships and perspectives. The many geometric planes and multiple dimensions of Cubism give rise to a confusion of connotative meanings. Through a process of analytic abstraction and pictorial distortion familiar forms are reduced to geometric shapes and interesting cubistic complexes. Lines and shapes transcend their indigenous forms, thereby becoming illusory objects that challenge the authenticity of other objects. There is a constant play between fact and falsity, opening a window onto a new reality arising out of contradiction and paradox.

As if to promote the ambiguity that is the essence of Cubism (and of Cocteau the poet) Cocteau designed a card to be flashed before the spectators just before the final curtain:

The drama
which
didn't
take place
for those people
who stayed outside
was
by
Jean Cocteau   Erik Satie   Pablo Picasso[22]

Satie's music, with its characteristic mosaic structure and its collage-like juxtaposition of familiar musical (and extramusical) elements, suited Cocteau's purpose admirably. Satie himself modestly described his contribution as "a background for certain noises which Cocteau considers indispensable in order to fix the atmosphere of his characters."[23] Four years before *Parade* the Italian visionary Luigi Russolo, one of the leaders of the Futurist movement, made an impassioned plea in his celebrated futurist manifesto for an "Art of Noises." In *Parade,* Russolo's ideas received their first large-scale application. Diaghilev, who was on good terms with the Futurist group and who had admired their "noise spectaculars," may have had some influence in the decision to introduce noise elements into the production. For Cocteau they were simply "bits of acoustical illusion" utilized "with the same object as the 'eye-deceivers'—newspapers, cornices, imitation wood-work, which the painters use."[24] Although Satie (encouraged by Picasso) had initially opposed the "aural collage" so important to Cocteau's conception, he grudgingly accepted some of the sound effects on the grounds that "we are dealing with a lovable maniac."[25] Eventually a compromise was reached, Cocteau's plan for speaking parts issuing from backstage through large stylized megaphones was jettisoned, the medley of sound effects was reduced to a few, and in subsequent performances even some of these were simulated by orchestral instruments. On a page of manuscript paper marked "Notes for the sound effects of 'Parade'" Satie made a list of the noise-makers that found their way into his score: clapper (or woodblock), revolver shots, a shrill siren and a deep siren, a typewriter, a lottery wheel, and, most curious of all, "squishy puddles" (*flaques sonores*), a sound effect usually realized by striking cymbals with sponge-tipped sticks.[26]

On the surface *Parade* would appear to be nothing more than comic entertainment. Yet, as Richard Axsom has pointed out, "a thin scrim of anxiety rests over the ballet from the beginning. *Parade* was tragicomedy of the highest order and its pathos was the creation of Cocteau."[27] The creation of pathos, however, was not Cocteau's alone. The air of pessimism and bitterness that pervades *Parade* is due in large measure to Satie's music. Its melodic banality and rhythmic rigidity, its wistful ragtime, its rude explosions of brass and harsh bitonal harmonies capture to perfection the metaphysic of the circus and the poetry of the streets.

The orchestra of *Parade* is the largest Satie ever employed. Of partic-

ular interest is the greatly augmented percussion section which includes—in addition to the noise-makers mentioned above—timpani, side
drum, bass drum, tarol (a shallow double-headed drum of Brazilian origin), tambourine, cymbals, triangle, tam-tam, xylophone, and bouteillophone (a series of fifteen tuned bottles suspended on a frame, which, it
would appear, was invented expressly for *Parade;* in some performances
it is replaced by a combination of celesta and glockenspiel or by a ma-
rimba). The remainder of the orchestra consists of a full complement of
woodwinds (including E-flat clarinet and English horn), a standard brass
section (with the addition of two cornets), a sixteen-foot pipe organ
drone, harp, and strings.

The melancholy mood of *Parade* is established at the outset in the
darkened theater with an eight-bar chorale, dissonantly harmonized and
darkly scored for low woodwinds, low brass, and low strings:

Example 3. Satie: *Parade* (1917), "Choral," measures 1–4

From the first three measures of the "Choral" (see bracketed passages
in ex. 3) Satie derives the motif that will dominate much of the opening
scene with the French Manager and the Chinese Prestidigitator. It is
introduced very softly in first violins and solo flute, the poignancy of its
repeated drooping semitonal figure (F–E) underscored by the sustained
dissonance in the second violins and the hollow cadence, gently reinforced by arpeggiated octaves in the harp:

Example 4. Satie: *Parade* (1917), "Choral," measures 9–12

The great red curtain of the Châtelet now parts to reveal Picasso's gigantic drop-curtain to the subdued strains of a fugal exposition (a Satiean bow to the Academy?) which is abruptly terminated by a descending passage of superimposed fifths (strings and harp) that functions as a bridge to the mechanical ostinato figure (marked in the manuscript "*ennuyeux*"—tedious," "boring") that introduces the French Manager.

In this opening scene (and indeed much of *Parade*) Satie transformed his characteristic mosaic technique into a sophisticated process not unlike that pioneered in Stravinsky's revolutionary *Rite of Spring*. The entire scene is constructed from shifting blocks of sound wherein momentum is maintained primarily through a process of metric displacement. Each block unit is built around a single melodic cell, strongly rooted on a tonal plane by means of an unvarying ostinato figure. These blocks are placed in stark juxtaposition to one another, although four- or eight-bar transition passages are employed to connect the major units.

The first part of the opening scene, for example, is made up of a symmetrical pattern of four units (12, 9, 12, and 9 measures, respectively), each utilizing the same melodic figure derived from the "Choral" (exs. 3 and 4). Variety is achieved through changing orchestration, shifting tonal planes, and—more subtly—a process of metric mutation. The following example illustrates the melodic interconnectedness of the four units (the parts have been transposed where necessary to simplify the example) and the vacillating metrical framework:

Example 5. Satie: *Parade* (1917), 1. "Prestidigitateur Chinois," units 1–4

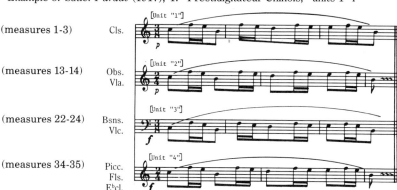

(measures 1-3)   Cls.

(measures 13-14)   Obs.
                        Vla.

(measures 22-24)   Bsns.
                        Vlc.

(measures 34-35)   Picc.
                        Fls.
                        E♭cl.
                        Cornet

An eight-bar transition (flutes, horn, and the rapid clicking of a roulette wheel) signals the entrance of the Chinese Prestidigitator, who begins his routine to the accompaniment of a stentorian brass theme—outlining the perfect fourth of the initial motif (ex 3)—reinforced by the beat of a side drum, the jangle of a tambourine, and dissonant nonharmonic grace notes in the upper strings and clarinets. (A decade later this brass motif would find a strong echo in "Mack the Knife" from Kurt Weill's *Three-penny Opera*.):

Example 6. Satie: *Parade* (1917), 1. "Prestidigitateur Chinois," measures 51–53

Trps.

Trbs.
I & II

The inscrutable Prestidigitator continues his routine to the accompaniment of mechanical ostinati—most of which are decidedly pentatonic (and therefore vaguely oriental) and clearly derived from the initial motif (ex. 3)—which unfold in regular four-bar units, shifting onto varying tonal planes with constantly changing orchestration spiced by the mysterious "squishy puddles." Soon the forceful brass theme (ex. 6) returns to signal the end of the Chinaman's act. To a flourish of drums, cymbals, tambourine, and a whirring roulette wheel he falls to his knees and bows to his uncomprehending audience as the curtains of the proscenium archway snap shut.

Without pause the American Manager introduces the Little American Girl who appears to a glitteringly bitonal ostinato figure derived from the falling second of the initial motif (ex. 3). After eight measures of this theme—its second half noisily augmented by tambourine, cymbals, and bass drum—a ragtime riff, somberly scored for clarinets, cornets, and tuba, instantly stamps "America" on the scene. To the persistent hollow ticking of a woodblock the music now swings into a two-step with a forceful pentatonic motif reinforced, upon repetition, by whole-tone flourishes in the upper strings and high woodwinds:

Example 7. Satie: *Parade* (1917), 2. "Petite fille Américaine," measures 21–24

This episode is abruptly cut short by a series of ascending augmented fourths (harp, violas, bassoons), a type of transitional figure (employed, in various configurations, several times in *Parade*) which, by the time of *Socrate* and the *Nocturnes* would become something of a Satie mannerism.

The episodes that follow introduce the most spectacular of the sound effects: the clacking typewriter and the revolver shots, the former heard against a suspenseful ostinato figure in clarinet and violins, the gunshots (six in all) against a quiet rocking figure in the strings (with horns and bassoons). Between the two episodes, Satie brings back briefly the ragtime riff and the pentatonic theme (ex. 7).

The central episode of the Little American Girl's scene is the "Steamboat Ragtime," which carries our heroine to near disaster as the ship sinks in a swirl of strings and winds preceded by mournful blasts of its foghorn.

By 1916 Satie had had considerable exposure to ragtime, having composed a number of works in the genre. The painter Gabriel Fournier recalled that Satie used to entertain his friends with ragtime performances, particularly the compositions of Jelly Roll Morton which he had discovered through Ernest Ansermet, who in 1916 had brought back from America recordings of the legendary jazzman.[28] Considering Satie's fondness for American vernacular music and his predilection for borrowed tunes, it may not be entirely fortuitous that the theme of the "Steamboat Ragtime" bears a striking resemblance to Irving Berlin's *That Mysterious Rag*, composed in 1911 within weeks of his world-famous *Alexander's Ragtime Band* and first heard publicly the following year in the Shubert Brothers's Broadway revue *The Passing Show of 1912:*

Example 8a. Satie: *Parade* (1917), 2. "Petite fille Américaine" ("Ragtime du Paquebot"), measures 74–79

Example 8b. Berlin: *That Mysterious Rag* (1911), chorus, measures 1–6

In the end the Little American Girl is stranded on a beach where we see her (according to Massine) building sand castles,[29] her isolation symbolized by a theme sounding high in flutes and piccolo, her childlike demeanor reflected by the ineffably sweet ostinato sounding softly below in harp and strings.

To the shimmering ostinato that introduced her, the Little American Girl fades from the scene, the spell of her wistful farewell suddenly broken by the awkward spectacle of Picasso's grotesque Horse, whose antics are all the more comic in the absence of the orchestra, an unexpected silence that appears puzzling even to the Horse as it hesitates, then invents a kind of clumsy soft-shoe shuffle of its own, its front and back ends not infrequently working at cross purposes.

The next major scene, featuring the two Acrobats, unfolds to a melancholy waltz-tune whose cool impersonality is underscored by icy glissandi on the bouteillophone and mechanical ostinati picked out in the brittle tones of the xylophone, the symmetry of its rigid foursquare structure set in bold relief by the periodic intrusion of short passages of asymmetrical phrasing which, in effect, keep the aerial artists slightly off-balance as they glide through their dangerous high-wire routine. The tension builds dramatically in the central episode of the scene as the harmonic movement suddenly freezes on a deep sixteen-foot organ pedal, a low octave E, sustained for fifteen measures against a rude ostinato in second violins and violas played out against a shrill pentatonic counterpoint in the flute's highest register. At the sixteenth measure the ostinato dramatically shifts upward a semitone—the piercing flute momentarily replaced by a rocking figure in harp and English horn—only to slip back onto the low E for nine more measures before the strings, reinforced by the glassy tones of the bouteillophone, resume a fragmentary waltz-tune that will lead back into a reprise of the opening material.

It is a wonderfully dramatic moment, superbly underscoring the inherent danger of the high-wire act as the Acrobats precariously walk a tightrope between safety and oblivion. The waltz sequence is brought to a close with a dramatic pause, followed by the return of the Managers's theme, obsessively reiterated in the full orchestra, with forceful percussion reinforced by the shrill wail of a siren, as the frenzied Managers make yet another desperate attempt to coerce the spectators into the booth.

The finale reunites the performers on stage where they frantically recapitulate their routines to the nervous acceleration of the music, crowned by one last frenetic statement of the Managers's dehumanized ostinato. It is cut short, unresolved, as the performers freeze in a final tableau, a tableau, in the words of one commentator, born of despair and rejection.[30] Very softly a version of the fugal theme heard near the beginning returns in the upper strings. They are joined by low strings, brass, and two woodwinds and slowly the curtain falls to a swelling C major chord, thus bringing the music full circle.

Like the grand illusion of the circus world itself, *Parade* is an elegant structure of mirrors within mirrors. Not only is the ballet framed by the music of the "Prélude du Rideau rouge" and the Managers's theme, which functions like a frame within a frame, each of the central episodes—the "Prestidigitateur Chinois," the "Petite fille Américaine," the "Acrobates"—is itself a mirror form, a series of ternary structures whose recapitulations reflect the opening episodes, in reverse order. In the perceptive words of Wilfrid Mellers, "the human beings are the circus performers, but what they do, or are made to do, bears only an illusory relationship to the dreams by which they live, which would seem to be dreams within a dream."[31]

Cocteau was no doubt secretly delighted that *Parade* was rather badly received, although his accounts of the "scandal" must be modified somewhat to conform to the truth. As the poet would have it, the major participants in *Parade* were physically attacked in a wild melee at the end of the performance by a vicious mob intent on nothing short of homicide. To the cries of "dirty Krauts" (*sales boches*), women armed with hatpins allegedly lunged at the authors, who saved themselves by finding refuge behind Apollinaire, whose army uniform and bandaged head commanded the respect of the attackers. It is reported that one of the less violent members of the audience indignantly declared to his wife: "If I had known it was going to be so stupid I'd have brought the children."[32] Paul Morand, a young diplomat-writer who was present at the premiere of *Parade,* has left what may be a slightly more balanced account of its reception:

Full house yesterday at the Châtelet, for *Parade.* Canvas scenery by Picasso, circusy, gracile music by Satie, half Rimsky[!], half dance-hall. The Managers . . . produced a ripple of surprise . . . Cocteau's pivotal idea—freeing dance from its conventions in favor of lifelike gestures—and his modern themes (the gunning of an automobile, photography, etc.), stylized in movement, seemed a little blurred. Lots of applause and a few jeers.[33]

If Cocteau did not quite succeed in obtaining the effect he desired at the first performance of *Parade,* namely a repetition of the *Rite* fiasco with which to astound Diaghilev, he did nonetheless succeed, with Satie's help, in creating something of a scandal in the wake of *Parade.* The critics attacked the new ballet with relentless enthusiasm. "The chief concern of the majority of writers," James Harding has humorously noted, "was to establish the exact degree of idiocy which *Parade* represented."[34] With scatalogical intensity the critic for *Le Courrier musical* dismissed *Parade* as "a dungy joke, a shitty trifle! [*plaisanterie stercoraire, amusement fécal!*]" and declared Satie's music to be "infinitely more stupid than ingenuous, more boring than droll, more senile and antiquated than audacious and innovative."[35] Another vicious attack came from the critic of *Le Carnet de la Semaine,* Jean Poueigh, who, under the pseudonym Octave Séré, charged Satie with incompetence and a complete lack of musical inventiveness, after having, the afternoon of the premier, personally assured the composer of his enthusiasm for the work. It was surely this blatant hypocrisy that moved Satie to respond; his reply was swift and not at all atypical in view of his general attitude toward critics. He sent Poueigh an open-faced card, written in his exquisite calligraphy, which read:

Sir and dear friend,
You are nothing but an asshole, and an unmusical asshole at
that.

Erik Satie[36]

Some weeks later Satie, in company with Cocteau, Léon-Paul Fargue,
Ricardo Viñes and a few other of his cronies, found himself in a court-
room facing a libel suit. During the stormy trial, which was punctuated
with cheers and jeers from Satie's claque, the composer of *Parade,* bow-
ler-hatted and gray-suited as always, heard himself and his colleagues
denounced as *boches* and cultural anarchists. In the end he was sentenced
to eight days confinement and a hundred francs damages. An appeal was
rejected at a second hearing on 27 November, whereupon the volatile
Cocteau, brandishing his cane at the prosecuting attorney, screamed,
"I'm going to smash his face in, the prick!"[37] a spontaneous act of threatened violence mixed with obscenity that cost the poet a beating at the
hands of the Paris constabulary. The spectacle finally came to an end
with a waiver of the damages against Satie, and his more influential
friends saw to it that he never saw the inside of a prison. Notwithstanding
Cocteau's assertion, in a letter to Misia Sert, that "Satie didn't take the
matter seriously,"[38] it would appear, from the evidence of the composer's
correspondence and notebooks, that the Poueigh affair caused him some
momentary anxiety but in the end no remorse.

Within a short time *Parade* became something of a cult object. Thanks
to Diaghilev's standing and a vitriolic press, Satie, who until now had
enjoyed not much more than a local reputation, became something of a
celebrity. On 6 June 1917, three weeks after *Parade'*s controversial premier, Blaise Cendrars, a Swiss-born poet and novelist who was early
associated with the Cubist movement, organized a concert at a Montparnasse studio in the rue Huyghens. Poems by Max Jacob, Apollinaire,
Cocteau, and Cendrars were recited, Satie played a duet version of *Parade* with a young pianist named Juliette Meerowitch, and three of the
composer's latest recruits, Georges Auric, Louis Durey, and Arthur Honegger performed their latest works. Inside six months another young
composer, Germaine Tailleferre, joined Satie at the Salle Huyghens,
where Cocteau dragged his friends to hear the new music and the new
poetry. Early in 1918 Francis Poulenc, released from the army, and Darius Milhaud, recently returned from Brazil, began to associate with *Les
Nouveaux Jeunes,* as Satie christened his young disciples, and *Les Six*

was born, with Satie as "spiritual father" and Cocteau as official spokesman.[39]

As chief apologist for *Les Nouveaux Jeunes,* Cocteau, with characteristic energy, burst into print with a lengthy declaration of the "new spirit," a seventy-four-page pamphlet, dedicated to Georges Auric, entitled *Le Coq et l'Arlequin* which appeared in the spring of 1918. As early as mid-1917 the poet had begun to develop the underlying theme of *The Cock and the Harlequin.* In his account of the collaboration of *Parade* in *Nord-Sud* he had praised Satie's orchestra for abjuring the vague and the indistinct. "It is," he wrote, "like an inspired village band. It will open a door to those young composers who are a little weary of fine impressionist polyphonies."[40]

In a word, *Le Coq et l'Arlequin* is a plea for a purely French music, free from the contamination of foreign elements. The Cock is the *coq gaulois,* standing in opposition to the Harlequin, who represents the impurities that have adulterated Gallic art. Cocteau's "manifesto" reflects the poet's scintillating and jocular speech. It sparkles with paradoxical aphorisms and witticisms that are flung at the reader in a breathless rapid staccato. The poet's main targets are Wagner and Germany, Debussy and Impressionism, and, somewhat surprisingly, Stravinsky and Russian music. The hero is Satie, who is the Cock incarnate, teaching "what, in our age, is the greatest audacity, simplicity."[41] The Cock, wrote Cocteau, "shuns the colossal. That is what I call *escaping from Germany.*"[42] Simplicity, not to be confused with poverty, is the chief virtue of French music. "A POET ALWAYS HAS TOO MANY WORDS IN HIS VOCABULARY, A PAINTER TOO MANY COLOURS ON HIS PALETTE, AND A MUSICIAN TOO MANY NOTES ON HIS KEYBOARD."[43] What is desired is a music stripped to the bone, a music of the café, the circus, and the music-hall, a music free from preoccupation with the sublime—in other words, a music such as Satie's. "Sick to death of flabbiness, fluidity, superfluity, frills, and all the modern sleight-of-hand . . . Satie voluntarily abstained, in order to . . . remain simple, clear and luminous."[44] If he is to cultivate the desired purity of line and clarity of design, the French composer, Cocteau warned, must not lose himself in the "Germano-Slav labyrinth."[45] This was Debussy's crime, for "Debussy played in French, but used the Russian pedal."[46] As for Stravinsky, he allowed himself to become corrupted by the theater. "I consider the 'Sacre du Printemps' a masterpiece," the poet wrote, "but I discern in the atmosphere created by its execution a religious complicity existing among the initiated, like the hypnotism of Bayreuth. Wagner wanted the theatre; Stravinsky," Cocteau observed with prophetic insight, "finds himself involved in it by circumstances. There is a difference."[47]

Cocteau asked for an everyday music, a music that one could live in like a house, and Satie gave it to him by inventing "furniture music." "Satie is the opposite of an improviser. His works might be said to have been completed beforehand, while he meticulously unpicks them, note by note. . . . Is this once more the music on which, as Nietzsche said, 'the spirit dances,' as compared with the music 'in which the spirit swims'?"[48]

Cocteau, like his hero Satie, thrived on scandal, and there has been a tendency among some critics to take *Le Coq et l'Arlequin* too seriously, granting it more attention than it deserves. But to doubt, as David Bancroft does, that Cocteau's little treatise had any real affect on *Les Six,* to doubt even the existence of a Cocteau-Satie school, however short-lived, is to overshoot the mark. "If *Le Coq et l'Arlequin* has a value today," Bancroft wrote, "it is not to be found in its statement of musical aesthetics, nor in its plea for a French, French music. . . . "[49] The members of *Les Six* themselves refute Bancroft's assertion. Auric and Poulenc had been in tune with Cocteau's ideals from the beginning and are, indeed, usually considered the most purely "Parisian" of *Les Six.* Louis Durey noted that "Cocteau's remarks, expressed with such originality and pungency, sometimes anticipated our own experiments and sometimes came after them—they were almost always in harmony with our work."[50] Even Arthur Honegger, the member least attuned to the ideals of Cocteau and *Les Six,* admitted that "it is true that around 1920 Cocteau gave the signal for music in the trenchant style . . . [and] served as a guide to many young folk. He stood for the general sense of a reaction against the prewar aesthetic."[51] And clearly the composer was echoing Cocteau when he told an American audience in 1929 that "music above all must please, and moreover, must be a national language; no complications, no studied elegance, only simple melodies, diatonics of harmony according to the rules, in a word compositions following the classical model!"[52]

With its music-hall vulgarity and its mythologization of urban folklore, *Parade* dealt a mortal blow to the aesthetic of Impressionism. Stravinsky, who had witnessed the revival of *Parade* in 1920, recorded in his autobiography that "the performance gave me an impression of freshness and real originality. *Parade* confirmed me still further in my conviction of Satie's merit in the part he had played in French music by opposing to the vagueness of a decrepit impressionism a language precise and firm, stripped of all pictorial embellishments."[53] Even though Stravinsky claimed not to have seen a performance of *Parade* until 1920, by his own admission he was familiar with the score long before, and one wonders if it was entirely fortuitous that his own forays into the American vernacular—the "Ragtime" from *A Soldier's Tale, Ragtime for Eleven Instruments,* and *Piano-Rag Music*—all happened to appear within a year or two of the *Parade* premiere in 1917. In 1919 Darius Milhaud recorded his colorful memories of Brazilian popular music in his jaunty *Boeuf sur le toit* (on a scenario by Cocteau), which premiered in February 1920. The following year Cocteau unveiled his surrealist fantasy *Les Mariés de la Tour Eiffel,* with breezy music by *Les Six* (minus Durey); on the same program appeared Auric's fox-trot for two pianos, *Adieu, New-York!,* and the list could be greatly extended. But perhaps the most touching tribute to the "new spirit" was Henri Sauguet's little ballet *Les Forains* (The Traveling Players), a poignant tale of itinerant circus performers that begins with a *parade* but, unlike its obvious model, allows us into the theater to see the show: a little girl doing stunts with a chair, a sad clown, Siamese twin sisters, a conjuror, and a life-size dancing doll. Sauguet goes so far as to quote (as a kind of unifying leitmotiv symbolizing the arrival and departure of the raggle-taggle band of players to and from their shabby little stage) the low brass motif that appears with hypnotic insistence in *Parade* during the Chinese conjuror's routine. Not surprisingly *Les Forains,* completed in 1945 near the end of another devastating war, is dedicated to the memory of Erik Satie.

8

Socrate

The scandal of *Parade* had served to thrust Satie into the mainstream of Parisian artistic life. The hermit of Arcueil found himself in the most fashionable salons of the great city, feted by the rich and adored by the young, who continued to look upon him as their "master." For a brief period he enjoyed the novel sensation of receiving what to him must have seemed astronomical sums for his compositions. His attitude toward money was very simple—it was meant, of course, to be spent, and the sooner the better. As he confided in a letter to his brother: "If the dead vanish fast, money, which is no more stupid than anything else, vanishes as fast as they do; and it's a pleasure to see it go, straight ahead, with never a glance behind and proud as a peacock for all that."[1] Accordingly, the composer immediately invested his royalties (still meager by normal standards) in three relatively new vices—great quantities of shirt collars, umbrellas, and handkerchiefs—and one old vice, the one that would eventually kill him—alcohol.

Bureaucratic Sonatina

During the messy aftermath of *Parade,* in the summer of 1917, Satie completed his *Sonatine bureaucratique,* an extraordinarily clever parody of a Clementi sonatina that predates Stravinsky's neoclassical *Pulcinella* by two years. The idea of using Clementi's music as source material may have been suggested to Satie by Massine's ballet *The Good-Humored Ladies*, an adaptation of a Goldoni play with music by Vincenzo Tommasini derived from Scarlatti piano sonatas, which opened, under Diaghilev's careful supervision, on 12 April 1917, shortly before the premiere of *Parade*.

Satie's model is the *Sonatina in C Major*, op. 36, no. 1, one of the most popular of Clementi's numerous sonatas and sonatinas, known to generations of young pianists. The *Bureaucratic Sonatina* is modeled very closely on the Clementi work, assuming its general structure and incorporating verbatim some of its melodic material.

Satie provides a broad hint of his musical source in the satirical verbal commentary, which outlines a "typical" day in the life of a bureaucrat. We meet him in the morning merrily making his way to his office, pleasantly daydreaming en route about his fair and most elegant lady love and about the cherished tools of his trade—his penholder, his green oversleeves, and his chinese skullcap. Arriving at his office, he rushes up the stairs like a whirlwind, happily sinks into his armchair, and immediately proceeds to reflect upon the likelihood of a promotion or a raise in salary which would enable him to acquire the new apartment he has had his eye on for some time. Still dreaming of promotion, he hums an old Peruvian air he once collected from a deaf-mute in Lower Brittany. Nearby a piano plays Clementi (literally), a vivacious tune which, for some inscrutable reason, strikes him as sad, very sad indeed; nonetheless he (not the piano) dares to waltz to it. He benevolently questions himself, the cold Peruvian air goes to his head again, the piano continues playing Clementi. Alas! the bureaucrat has reached the end of another "hard" day at his dear office, and in a flurry of sprightly triplets he reluctantly dashes off.

In the outer movements of the *Sonatine bureaucratique* Satie expanded the modest proportions of Clementi's *Allegro* and *Vivace* by means of the repetition of certain phrases, the introduction of new, nonanalogous melodic material, and the extension of cadential figures. Although the broad (tonic-dominant) tonal framework of Clementi's three movements remains unaltered, Satie manages to inject liberal doses of his own inimitable brand of humor into the music, largely through a process of harmonic distortion whereby the simple progressions of the original are twisted into odd and unpredictable shapes. The second half of Clementi's *Allegro*, for example, begins in the parallel minor mode, in preparation for the return to the principal theme and the tonic C major:

Example 1a. Clementi: *Sonatina in C major,* op. 36, no. 1 (1797), 1. *Allegro,* measures 16–19

Cm: V$_2^4$ i^6 vii°   i   V

The analogous measures of the *Sonatine bureaucratique* copy Clementi exactly for two measures (less a beat), before veering off in an "illogical" retrograde progression which, we can speculate, is a witty reflection of the bureaucrat's frame of mind, as his thoughts are derailed by pleasant images of his fair lady:

Example 1b. Satie: *Sonatine bureaucratique* (1917), 1. *Allegro,* measures 24–27

A: V$_2^4$ i^6 V$_2^4$ I^6 vii$_2^o$ vii^6 V   IV   ♮ III
                                            V   CM:I

Socrate: A Symphonic Drama

With hindsight we can see that *Parade* is far from being the frivolous bit of Dadaistic antiart claimed by its most vociferous critics in 1917. If the majority of Satie's contemporaries could not recognize the pathos beneath the crude exterior of the ballet, there would be little such confusion of ends and means with his next major work, a setting of three Socratic dialogues, plans for which were afoot several months before *Parade* reached the stage of the Châtelet. The earliest reference to the *Life of Socrates,* as it was initially called, is contained in a letter of 6 January

1917 to Valentine Gross in which Satie confessed that he was in a "dither" over the possibility of "mucking up" a work he felt must be "as white and pure as Antiquity."[2] Fear of failure notwithstanding, the composition of *Socrate* seems to have progressed smoothly, for less than two weeks later the composer wrote again to Valentine in a mood of excitement bordering on the ecstatic:

January 18, 1917,
. . . What am I doing? I'm working on the *Life of Socrates*. I have found a very attractive translation: one by Victor Cousin. Plato is a perfect collaborator, very gentle and never importunate. It's like a dream! I am swimming in happiness. At last! I am free, free as the air, free as the water; free as the wild sheep. Long live Plato! Long live Victor Cousin! I am free! really free! What happiness! . . .[3]

In a letter of 16 August to Madame Fernand Dreyfus, the mother of his protégé Roland-Manuel, he claimed that *Socrate* was well under way, that it would in fact be ready by October.[4] Several weeks later, on 4 October, Satie, as always desperate for money ("I am in a most critical situation: without a *sou*"), begged his publisher Rouart to accept two new works for publication: *Socrate,* which he was writing for the Princesse de Polignac, and three farces after Tabarin—a seventeenth-century clown—for Jacques Copeau, actor, producer, and director of the experimental Théâtre du Vieux-Colombier.[5] The Satie-Copeau collaboration never reached fruition; *Socrate,* on the other hand, would become one of the composer's most discussed works and a landmark in the evolution of the neoclassical aesthetic in the 1920s.

The Princesse Edmond de Polignac, friend and patron of Fauré, Ravel, Stravinsky, and many others, has described how the commission for *Socrate* came about:

I was very anxious to know Satie, and I intended to ask him to write music for the Death of Socrates in Plato's *Phaedo*. I asked Jeanne Bathori to bring him to dinner one evening. He was then a man of about 52, neither tall nor short, very thin, with a short beard. He invariably wore pince-nez, through which one saw his kindly but rather mischievous pale blue eyes, always ready to twinkle as some humorous thought crossed his mind. . . .

At the time when I met Satie I had been learning a little Greek and was becoming more and more enthusiastic as I managed to read the tragedies of Euripides or the Dialogues of Plato in the original text. Satie was equally enthusiastic, so he decided to write music for the *Death of Socrates,* and after much thought suggested that the scene should be set in a small salon in the Empire Style in which, in armchairs, Madame de Wendel and Argyropoulo who knew Greek perfectly, and I myself, would read in turns the glorious words of Plato. At first this seemed an excellent idea, and we spent many evenings talking it over, but in the end Satie decided to give up the idea of the Empire Salon and to have no scenery at all, and he wrote an oratorio [*sic*] for a woman's voice and a small orchestra. There is no doubt that this is his masterpiece, and nothing could be more moving than this music written for the beautiful words of Plato. When he had finished it he sent me the score, which is now [1945] in Paris in my collection of musical manuscripts. Jeanne Bathori sang *Socrates* for the first time in my music room accompanied by the ethereal music of Satie.[6]

That the first performance of *Socrate* took place for a private gathering in the music room of the Polignac mansion near Versailles as the Princesse claims seems likely considering that the work had been, after all, her commission. A number of commentators, however, taking their cue from Valentine Hugo,[7] have suggested that the first reading occurred on 24 June 1918, at the home of Jane Bathori, despite the fact that Bathori herself, in her recollections of the period, made mention only of a performance in her home at the beginning of January 1919, and then only of the first part of *Socrate,* with the composer again at the piano and Cocteau, Roland-Manuel, Valentine Gross, and the Count Étienne de Beaumont among the invited guests. Although Bathori claimed that "all were delighted and astonished"[8] on this occasion, it would appear that at least one member of the small but discerning audience was somewhat disenchanted with Satie's latest work, for we find the composer writing a number of letters to Roland-Manuel at this time in which he expressed his disappointment over his former disciple's failure to accept a work "of a totally different conception from the sort of thing that appeals to you."[9] Here were the first signs of a rupture in the friendship between the two composers which would become quite complete shortly before Satie's death. Soon thereafter, however, Roland-Manuel must have experienced a change of heart, for his review of the first public performance of *Socrate* in February 1920 for *L'Éclair,* a newspaper for which he had become a critic the previous fall, was most favorable. "All the emotion of the admirable text," he wrote on this occasion, "was expressed with nobility, discretion, and the most perfect purity."[10]

On 21 March 1919 *Socrate* received another private performance, this time at La Maison des Amis des Livres, Adrienne Monnier's famous Left Bank bookshop in the rue de l'Odéon, for an assortment of distinguished guests, among them the poets Paul Claudel, André Gide, Francis

Jammes, and Jean Cocteau, who introduced the work. The singer on this occasion was Suzanne Balguerie, with the composer once again presiding at the piano. It would appear that Jacques Doucet—a rich couturier whose collection of manuscripts, letters, and rare editions form the nucleus of the library now bearing his name—had also figured among the guests on that auspicious occasion, for on 24 March, three days after the performance in the rue de l'Odéon, Satie sent Doucet a flattering letter thanking him profusely for honoring the reading of *Socrate* by his presence.[11]

Socrate did not receive its first public performance until 1920, first on 14 February at a concert of the Société Nationale with Jane Bathori and Suzanne Balguerie assisted by André Salomon at the piano, then on 7 June during a Satie Festival at the Salle Erard, with soprano Marya Freund and full orchestra under the direction of Félix Delgrange.

As was almost always the case with a Satie premiere, *Socrate* received a remarkably mixed reception at the hands of the critics, many of whom no doubt had expected another Satie "joke" and were, not surprisingly, puzzled by the apparent seriousness of the music. Jean Marnold, powerful critic for the *Mercure de France,* saw *Socrate* as a "total nullity," a string of relentlessly reiterated phrases, all too reminiscent of *Boris* and *Pelléas,* serving as an insipid background to a text by Victor Cousin "intoned in the manner of a drawing-room conversation."[12] The Paris correspondent of the London *Observer,* who had attended a revival of *Socrate* in the spring of 1921 at the Salle des Agriculteurs in the rue d'Athènes, reported that he had never heard anything so lamentable. His eye-witness account shows him to have been completely out of sympathy with the composer's austere portrait of Socrates:

The work is of interminable length. M. Satie seemed to be playing practically the same phrase all the time, except when he tried to brighten the monotonous proceedings by thumping out some inconsequential discords. I was sorry for the singer [Marya Freund], who had to rush through the dialogues of Plato in a dreary recitative, without variety, without tunefulness, without punctuation, or declamatory emphasis, in what the French call her "voix de tête." Her performance was a great physical feat. Everybody seemed bored, and wondered when it would all finish; but so afraid have we grown of being accused of lack of understanding that there was plenty of applause and very few hisses and unfriendly cries.[13]

One notable exception to British antipathy and incomprehension was Leigh Henry, a perceptive free-lance critic and editor of the progressive little review *Fanfare,* who had championed Satie as early as 1914 when he was all but unknown outside a small circle of devoted Parisian friends. Writing in *The Musical Standard,* Henry praised "the purity of conception" and the "clarity, directness and simplicity" of *Socrate,* concluding his article with a glowing assessment that stands as a worthy testament for all those—by no means a small minority—who see in *Socrate* at least a touch of genius:

> Some may find this—as early Egyptian and Greek sculpture—bald, its reticence unsympathetic, its passionlessness inhuman. But those who realize the psychological tensity of terribly level and resigned speech, of simple gestures, of calm recognition and acceptance of the ordinariness of things portentous to romantic temperaments, will recognise in "Socrate" something of the spirit of its namesake subject, and of that lofty tragic insight which gave the world the drama of Aeschylus and Sophocles.[14]

Of course Satie did not lack for champions on the Continent, some of them the most distinguished critics and composers of the day. Cocteau remained loyal, *Les Six* rallied once again around "the good master," the Belgian critic Paul Collaer considered *Socrate* one of the most significant works in all modern music,[15] while for Charles Koechlin it was an altogether new and original creation, "a synthesis of Socratic Hellenism."[16] Even the great Stravinsky, despite some criticism of what he considered the "clumsy" orchestration and the "boring" metrical regularity, felt that the music of Socrates' death was "touching and dignifying in a unique way."[17]

Why Satie should have turned to Plato after the Coctelian conceit of *Parade* seems on the surface mildly puzzling. The most likely explanation of the composer's choice of topic makes of him a kind of latter-day Socrates, mysteriously imparting dangerous advice to the young in the shadowy recesses of Parisian cafés. Indeed it seems reasonable to assume that Satie saw in his own ascetic existence a reflection of the martyred life of the Greek sage. Some uncanny resemblances between the philosopher and the composer tend to support this view, although the extent to which Satie knew the details of Socrates's life is open to speculation. Had he troubled to read the account of Socrates's defense in Plato's *Apology,* he would have noted, no doubt with wry satisfaction, that the great philosopher was brought before the Athenian court on two serious charges: failure to worship the officially recognized gods of state, and—perhaps of even graver import in the eyes of the ancient guardians of the status quo—corruption of the minds of the young.

It is instructive to note certain details of the life of Socrates, as related by the great Platonic scholar Alfred Edward Taylor in his illuminating study of the man and his thought. Two passages in particular cannot fail to perk up the ears of Satieans. "From his earliest days," Taylor wrote, "Socrates must have been something of what we call an 'oddity,' both physically and mentally. . . . In his manhood he used to wear the same single garment winter and summer, and habitually went barefoot, even, according to Plato, in the rigours of a winter campaign."[18] Naturally, Taylor further noted, the wider public thought of him as "an amusing eccentric, a combination of pedant, paradox-monger, free-thinker, and necromancer. . . ."[19]

Socrate, "symphonic drama in three parts with voice," is scored for an orchestra of modest proportions consisting of flute, oboe, English horn, clarinet, bassoon, horn, trumpet, harp, timpani, and strings. Although most modern performances of *Socrate* employ four singers for the parts of Socrates, Alcibiades, Phaedrus, and Phaedo (which are, in fact, layed out on separate staves in the orchestral score), it seems, from the evidence of the early performances (and the work's subtitle), that the composer may have intended one singer to take all the parts. It is also reasonably clear that Satie intended the soprano voice, despite the fact that the characters are all male. Although the orchestral score is unclear on this point, simply placing all the vocal parts in the treble clef which, of course, does not rule out the possibility of the tenor voice or voices, there can be no denying that the cool "white" sound of the soprano voice more readily enhances the remote "antique" flavor of *Socrate,* and indeed most modern performances wisely adhere to a tradition that began in the composer's own lifetime with Jane Bathori, Suzanne Balguerie, and Marya Freund.

That *Socrate* is a deadly serious work is beyond dispute; that it marks a fundamental change in the composer's musical style is less clear, for the structural principles governing the earlier *Parade* are essentially the same as those that govern *Socrate,* despite the fact that the extramusical basis has radically shifted from the circus and the fairground to a Frenchman's vision of Greek antiquity, a vision—pure, abstract, remote—that persists in the modern Western consciousness. If *Socrate* can lay claim to the status of masterpiece, it is because in this work—as in the *Sports et divertissements*—there is a congenial mating of style and idea. There is in *Socrate* an aloofness and emotional neutrality all the more poignant in its cool objectivity, "a kind of divine *ennui,*"[20] to borrow Eric Salzman's felicitous phrase. The American composer and ardent Stravinskyan Arthur Berger is surely right in assigning *Socrate* a privileged place as a historical document of considerable importance:

In 1919 . . . "Socrate" was already abreast of Stravinsky's vital contemporary move to reinstate classical principles. The defiantly casual structural procedures of "Socrate" are far indeed from classical form or development. But musical texture had been scrubbed clean of romantic unctuousness and growth and of impressionistic whipped cream. In this pristine state it was ready for the fulfilment that Stravinsky ultimately brought about by embracing with it a wider area of musical resources.[21]

What Berger fails to mention, however, is that Satie had reached that "pristine state" at least as early as 1888—shortly before Stravinsky's sixth birthday—in a much earlier evocation of ancient Greece, the remarkable *Gymnopédies*.

From Plato's *Dialogues,* in Victor Cousin's rather dry and precise translation, Satie chose Alcibiades's eulogy of Socrates at the banquet, a casual conversation between Socrates and Phaedrus on the banks of the river Ilissus, and Phaedo's touching account of the philosopher's calm and tragic death.

In the first part of *Socrate,* "Portrait of Socrates," the drunken Alcibiades, with what at first seems like questionable propriety, compares his master to the satyrs Silenus and Marsyas—Silenus, constant companion of the young Dionysus and father of the satyrs, often depicted as a plump and jovial (and generally drunken) old man; and Marsyas, flute-playing satyr, who bewitched mankind with his beautiful music, until he made the fatal mistake of challenging Apollo to a musical contest, an imprudent act that resulted in his being flayed alive by the Muses, his hide made into leather bottles. But Alcibiades makes no mention of these unsavory things. Rather he compares his master's eloquence to the magical sound of Marsyas's flute, marveling at an oratorical gift of such staggering power as to bring tears to the eyes and quicken the heartbeat more strongly than the wild orgiastic dancing of the Corybantes.

The second part, "The Banks of the Ilissus," is an idyllic interlude picturing Socrates and Phaedrus in conversation under the shade of a lofty plane tree by the riverside, a restful place of cool fragrant breezes and the summery sound of singing cicadas. As master and disciple gaze into the sparkling clear waters of the Ilissus they are reminded of the legend of Boreas, god of the North Wind, who, it was said, carried off the naiad Orithyia.

The crowning movement of *Socrate* is "The Death of Socrates" as related by his devoted pupil Phaedo, who had been with him to the end. Phaedo and a number of other faithful friends and disciples—but not Plato, who was ill at the time—arrive at the prison on the day of the execution. In one of the most beautiful passages in European prose literature, the doomed philosopher calmly speaks to his tearful disciples of his belief in the immortality of the soul, of its liberation from the fears and desires of the body and, thus purified and enlightened, its union with the gods in a better, freer world. In his last recorded words Socrates asks Crito not to forget to offer, as was the custom, a rooster to Asclepius, the god of healing, for in his mind Socrates was not dying but rather entering into an unseen world where the soul shares in the eternity of Truth, Goodness, and Beauty. Thus was the end of "the wisest and most just of all men."

The subtitle *drame symphonique* is something of a misnomer, for *Socrate* is certainly not dramatic in the conventional sense and hardly symphonic. It is less a setting of Plato's words than a musicalization of their meaning, for the music is devoid of rhetoric and sentimentality. Through a calm and simple narrative the timeless drama unfolds with cold, imperturbable tragedy. The dynamic level only occasionally rises above mezzo forte, the rhythms, almost without exception, are derived from combinations of only two note values (quarters and eighths), frequent ostinato figures support a supple, undulating vocal line that moves conjunctly and syllabically in a conversational manner, the accompanying harmonies are made up of mildly dissonant chords, with a preponderance of parallel fourths and triads, even the orchestration is cool, monochrome, "neutral," the instruments sounding mostly in their middle registers, the brass serving mainly to reinforce and sustain the many pedals in the work, the harp discreetly doubling other parts or providing little ostinato figures of its own, the sole percussion, the timpani, silent most of the time, the woodwinds used sparingly, unobtrusively, and en masse only once—in the final two measures, where they are instructed to play sweetly and softly.

The major structural device in all three movements of *Socrate* is Satie's favorite cellular "mosaic" technique, first employed in a relatively large-scale work as early as *Uspud*. "The Death of Socrates" is by far the longest of the three movements and perhaps the most moving music Satie ever wrote. It incorporates about a dozen distinctive motivic ideas whose rhythmic and melodic shapes are maintained against varying harmonizations and shifting tonal planes. After their initial statements the motivic cells are juxtaposed in seemingly random patterns of two-, four-, or six-bar units. There is, however, a perceptible musico-dramatic form based on repetition of the ascending tetrachord (motif "A") with which the movement opens:

Example 2. Satie: *Socrate* (1918), 3. "Mort de Socrate," motif "A," measures 1–4

This four-note figure, softly oscillating between minor triads on E and A, will gradually and inexorably come to dominate the movement, insinuating itself into the listener's imagination as a kind of musico-poetic symbol of the serene and stoic death of the great philosopher. After this initial statement the motif is rarely heard, until about the midpoint of the dialogue (and the movement) where there occurs an exact repetition of the opening music as Socrates calmly bids farewell to his tearful jailor, who had become genuinely fond of his courageous and gentle prisoner. From this point on, the "Socrates" motif begins to weave itself more and more into the music in varying guises: as an ostinato figure in the violas over a countermelody first in oboe then English horn (ex. 3a); in block chords in the strings and brass (ex. 3b); as parallel triads in upper strings and English horn (ex. 3c); as a dialogue between woodwind and strings (ex. 3d); as a series of root-position triads in low strings and horn (ex. 3e):

Example 3. Satie: *Socrate* (1918), 3. "Mort de Socrate"

(a) Measures 162–65

(b) Measures 170–73

(c) Measures 176–79

(d) Measures 180–83

(e) Measures 184–87

Other motifs follow—all of them, however, based on a four-note figure—
until the dramatic moment when Socrates, having drunk the poison, replies in the negative when asked if he feels any sensation in his feet and
legs. Gradually the flesh grows cold and stiff. Softly the ascending tetrachord returns in the high strings, this time against a brief countermelody
in oboe then English horn:

Example 4. Satie: *Socrate* (1918), 3. "Mort de Socrate," measures 258–60

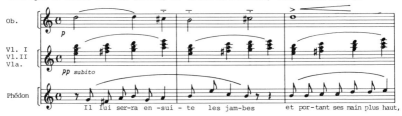

From here to the extended coda the tetrachord figure is never absent,
remaining fixed on the tonal plane defined by the oscillating minor triads
on E and A. The strings maintain the ostinato with discreet doubling by
one woodwind or another. At Socrates's last words—"Crito, we owe a
rooster to Asclepius; don't forget to settle this debt . . . "—the motif,
softly played by pizzicato strings doubled by harp, suddenly reverses
direction, descends the scale from E to G, then rises a tone to settle on
a hollow open fifth (A–E). At this point—marked "Funèbre" in the orchestral, though not the piano / vocal, score—the four-note figure has
been reduced to a single repeated chord. Against the soft tread of the
empty fifth in low strings reinforced by low woodwinds and brass, the
voice of Phaedo recites on a monotone low E, rising a fourth to the A
only at phrase ends, thus reinforcing the tonality—A—that had been implicit from the very beginning of the movement: "A little while afterwards
he made a convulsive movement; the attendant uncovered him completely: his features were set. Crito closed his mouth and eyes. . . . "

Then, a chillingly effective moment as the pulsating fifth quietly shifts upward a whole-tone to an open B–F-sharp: "Thus was the end, Echecrates, of our friend. . . ." The voice pauses momentarily and the orchestral drone unobtrusively slips back to the original pitches: ". . . the wisest and most just of all men." For the briefest of moments the tragedy has resolved onto that hollow fifth (A–E), until, without warning, the music moves, as it were, out of time, sinks onto an unexpected tritone (E-sharp–B), which "resolves" onto the perfect fourth (F-sharp–B), on which pale and remote interval the music slowly fades into silence. It is a haunting moment of ineffable sweetness that lingers in the memory like one of those friezelike, pastel-colored Puvis de Chavannes murals so greatly admired by the composer:

Example 5. Satie *Socrate* (1918), 3. "Mort de Socrate," measures 286–94

The linear transparency of Satie's small orchestra seems entirely appropriate, contributing in large measure to the clarity and directness of style for which the composer constantly strove. "Impressionism," he recorded in one of his sketchbooks for *Socrate,* "is the art of Imprecision; today the tendency is toward Precision."[22] As usual Satie builds with a mere handful of musical materials which are placed in odd relationships, arbitrarily transposed, subtly varied, but rarely extended or developed. In *Socrate* there is an admirable simplicity and a quiet dignity which finds an echo in certain pages of Stravinsky's "white" music of the 1920s. As Pierre Boulez once noted: "*Socrate* dates from 1918, that is to say, ten years before *Apollon Musagète.*"[23]

For many listeners there is also a deploring metrical regularity, a monochrome flatness, a dryness and lifelessness in *Socrate,* a total absence of warmth and humanity. This psychological vacuity may, however, be *Socrate*'s strength. In no other work has the composer so completely removed his own personality. In this sense, all of Satie's works are contained in *Socrate.* The ancient Greek text is furnished with a timeless musical frame untainted by preciosity. As the American composer Ned Rorem so aptly put it, "the music is not 'ahead' of its time, but rather (and of what other work can this be said?) outside of time, allowing the old, old dialogues of Plato to sound so always new."[24]

Furniture Music

Socrate was an experiment never to be repeated, although the five *Nocturnes* for solo piano, composed between August and November 1919, are closely related to *Socrate* in style and spirit. Here, in a highly condensed form, is the same purity of line and spiritual solitude. Gone are the parodies of children's songs, the facetiousness and explicit irony, the coarse humor of the music hall, the whimsical performance directions and surrealistic commentary. Restored are key signatures, bar lines, and time signatures. Like the early *Sarabandes, Gymnopédies,* and *Gnossiennes,* the *Nocturnes* seem to be one piece viewed from slightly different angles. Common to all of them is a simple ternary (A B A) structure, a flowing 12/8 meter, and a lilting, graceful melodic line of exceptional beauty underpinned by an austere harmonic vocabulary characterized by a preponderance of bare parallel fourths and fifths. There is something of Fauré in these haunting miniatures—the same undulating arpeggiated left-hand configurations, the same metric and tonal elasticity, the same gentle lyricism and classical restraint. They remain among Satie's most effective piano works, a very pure distillation of the pathos of the composer's lonely existence.

Barely had the ink dried on the manuscripts of the five *Nocturnes* than Satie reverted to his familiar *café-concert* idiom with two curious suites for small music-hall orchestra (also arranged for piano four hands), the *Trois petites pièces montées* of 1919 and *La Belle Excentrique,* completed the following year. The *Trois petites pièces montées* (Three Little Stuffed Pieces) are based on episodes from the marvelous lives of the giant Gargantua and his son Pantagruel, as recorded by France's master satirist François Rabelais. The little suite opens with a "Rêverie" ("De l'Enfance de Pantagruel") recalling the bizarre childhood of Pantagruel who, according to Rabelais, was so gigantic and gluttonous as a babe that he required at each meal the milk of 4,600 cows. Once, we are told, when nursing a cow—for he never had any other wet-nurses—he nearly succeeded in devouring the unfortunate creature, udders, belly, and all, until the bellowing animal was rescued from the ravenous infant by her attendants. Having depicted Pantagruel's childhood, Satie turned in the third movement ("Jeux de Gargantua"), a little polka, to the equally bizarre games that his father played in his youth. Rabelais lists 215 mostly nonsensical card games and board games enjoyed by the young Gargantua—among the more quintessentially Rabelaisian, Fat-arse, Shit-in-his-beard, and The Salvo of Farts—the playing of which, understandably, made him very thirsty and very sleepy. The title of the brassy middle movement, "Marche de Cocagne," would appear to be a reference to the fabulous country of medieval French legend where the gutters run with wine and roast pigs prance through the streets ready for the carver's knife alluded to by Rabelais in his depiction of a utopian country with mountains of butter, rivers of milk, and hot pies shooting out of the rich soil like mushrooms. The *Trois petites pièces montées* were premiered on 21 February 1920, Vladimir Golschmann conducting, at the Comédie des Champs-Élysées, the small second-floor theater of the Théâtre des Champs-Élysées, for a select group of invited guests. Public performances followed within a few days. This was the first of two "*Spectacles Concerts*" organized by Cocteau, with the financial backing of the Count Étienne de Beaumont, to promote the work of his young collaborators. On the same program were Poulenc's very Satiean *Cocardes,* settings of three poems by Cocteau, Auric's *Adieu, New York!,* and the delightfully zany Milhaud-Cocteau *Le Boeuf sur le toit,* also making its first appearance.

La Belle Excentrique (The Eccentric Belle), a little suite of four brief numbers—"Grand Ritornello," "Franco-Lunar March," "Waltz of the Mysterious Kiss in the Eye," "High-Society Cancan"—continues in much the same vein. This little buffoonery was confected, in collaboration with Cocteau, for the dancer Élisabeth (Élise) Toulemon, known as Caryathis. A colorful, flamboyant beauty, whose stormy relationship with the novelist Marcel Jouhandeau gave him much to write about, Caryathis, under Cocteau's careful guidance, developed a choreographic conception of *La Belle Excentrique* that most critics have construed as a genial parody of music-hall routines. It opened in June 1921 at the Théâtre du Colisée, Vladimir Golschmann conducting, in a program that included music by Granados and Ravel as well as all the members of *Les Six.* A month later it was repeated at Paul Poiret's little theater, L'Oasis, with Satie himself conducting the orchestra.

Whereas much of the humor in Satie's music depends on an ironic interplay of familiar quoted tunes allied with whimsical verbal commentary, the humor of *La Belle Excentrique* and the *Trois petites pièces montées* is very much on the surface. These two diminutive suites for music-hall orchestra are perhaps the most inherently comic pieces Satie ever wrote. In the Rabelaisian suite, Satie exploits the comic possibilities of his little orchestra of flute, oboe, clarinet, bassoon, horn, two trumpets, trombone, bass drum, cymbal, tarol, and strings. The bassoon, in particular, earns its reputation as the clown of the orchestra as it lugubriously rumbles along in unison with the double basses against a muted string background in Pantagruel's "Reverie," or, in the final "Polka," plays a coy cat-and-mouse game with the clarinet, which is abruptly terminated by a powerful descending tetrachord blatted out by the trombone in its deepest register before the suite is brought to a raucous close by the full orchestra, reinforced by a resounding thump on the bass drum complete with cymbal crash and the dry rattle of the tarol.

La Belle Excentrique is equally comic, with its jaunty ragtime rhythms, syncopated waltz tunes, and high-spirited cancan galop, all decked out in the coarse colors of the music-hall orchestra, complete with oompah bass, offbeat snare drum riffs, and tinny cymbal crashes. That this "Fantaisie Sérieuse," as it is ironically subtitled, is a deliberate reversion to Satie's turn-of-the century music-hall manner is clear from the opening "Grande Ritournelle," which is based on a sketch for a *café-concert* song, dating from around 1900, with words by Contamine de Latour and the intriguing title "Légende Californienne."[25]

One of Satie's most interesting experiments followed the premiere of the *Trois petites pièces montées* by two weeks. On 8 March 1920 the actor Pierre Bertin organized a concert at the Galerie Barbazange in the rue du Faubourg St.-Honoré, an art gallery owned by the eminent dressmaker Paul Poiret. The featured work of the evening was a three-act play, *Ruffian toujours, truand jamais,* by Max Jacob, a Breton Jew who, after a dramatic conversion to Catholicism shortly before World War I, divided most of his time over the next twenty years or so between the pleasures of Paris and a monk's cell in the Benedictine monastery at Saint-Benoît-sur-Loire, ending his days in 1944 in a Nazi concentration camp at Drancy to the northeast of Paris. Between the acts of Jacob's play, Satie, in collaboration with Darius Milhaud, presented a new discovery: *musique d'ameublement,* furniture or furnishing music.

Satie himself seems to have coined the term. The painter Fernand Léger, who often accompanied Satie on his long walks across Paris to and from his suburban lodgings in Arcueil, recalled a luncheon meeting with the composer and some friends during which the resident orchestra became so boisterously loud that the diners were obliged to vacate the premises, whereupon Satie turned to Léger and said:

You know, there's a need to create furniture music, that is to say, music that would be a part of the surrounding noises and that would take them into account. I see it as melodious, as masking the clatter of knives and forks without drowning it completely, without imposing itself. It would fill up the awkward silences that occasionally descend on guests. It would spare them the usual banalities. Moreover, it would neutralize the street noises that indiscreetly force themselves into the picture.[26]

The composer further explained his intentions in a note to Cocteau in which he explained that furniture music was designed, unlike art, to satisfy useful needs, filling much the same role in our daily lives as light and heat and other such comforts. "Furniture music for law offices, banks, etc.," he proclaimed. "No marriage ceremony complete without furniture music. . . . Don't enter a house which does not have furniture music."[27] Satie had officially invented Muzak in 1920. Unofficially it might be said that it was invented in 1887 with the *Sarabandes,* or even the *Ogives* of 1886 or the *café-concert* music of the turn of the century, for in a very real sense all the composer's music might be considered "furniture music," even *Socrate,* for in a small notebook where Satie copied Victor Cousin's words we find the following revealing but rather cryptic tables:

The Banquet—"Musique d'ameublement" —For an assembly-hall.	Frame (dance) Tapestry (the Banquet, subject) Frame (dance, reprise)
Phèdre—"Musique d'ameublement" —For a lobby.	Colonnade (dance) Bas-relief (marble, subject) Colonnade (dance, reprise)
Phédon—"Musique d'ameublement" —For a shop window.	Casket (pig-down, dance) Cameo (Asian Agate—Phédon, subject) Casket (dance, reprise)[28]

At the Galerie Barbazange, which on that March evening in 1920 housed an exhibition of children's drawings called "Les Belles Promesses," Satie and Milhaud stationed three clarinets, a trombone, and a piano around the hall and provided them with fragments of well-known pieces such as Saint-Saëns's *Danse macabre* and Thomas's *Mignon,* together with simple ostinato patterns repeated endlessly while Satie circulated through the audience exhorting people to talk, walk about, drink, to carry on as if nothing was happening. But lifelong habits are not easily broken and, contrary to the expectations of Satie and Milhaud, the audience insisted on remaining in the hall during the intermissions to listen in silence to the music, despite Satie's shouted pleas to "Go on talking! Walk about! Don't listen!"[29] The score, recently discovered in the possession of the daughter of the music's dedicatee, the pianist Marcelle Meyer, is in two parts, the titles of which, "Chez un Bistrot" and "Un Salon," are explained by the stage settings for the first and second acts of the Jacob play, a tavern and a drawing-room, respectively.

Although this was Satie's only public experiment with *musique d'ameublement* he did produce several more examples of the genre for private use. For Mrs. Eugene Meyer, wife of the owner of the *Washington Post,* who had requested a Satie autograph through Milhaud, he provided *Tenture de cabinet préfectoral* (Wall Hanging for a Prefectural Office). This little musical tapestry consists of a mere twelve measures of music in E minor scored for a tiny orchestra of piccolo, clarinet, bassoon, horn, trumpet, cymbal, snare drum, bass drum, and strings with instructions to be repeated as often as desired. In the only recording of the piece (Erato STU 71336), conductor Marius Constant has opted for a total of seventeen statements of the tiny piece, whose asymmetrical phrase structure (4 + 6 + 2) and droll instrumentation make a curious effect. With characteristic irony, Satie described his dry little piece in a letter to Milhaud as "decorative and sumptuous in appearance—meant to appeal visually,"[30] leading one to wonder if he intended the manuscript to be framed and displayed on the wall of the Meyers's Crescent Place study in Washington, D.C.

Even tinier are *Tapisserie en fer forgé* (Forged Iron Tapestry), a mere four measures of music in a swaying 6/8 meter scored for flute, clarinet, trumpet, and strings and designed to be played in the vestibule of a house during the arrival of guests, and *Carrelage phonique* (Phonic Floor Tiles), for flute, clarinet, and strings, intended, as the composer noted in the manuscript,[31] to complement either a luncheon engagement or a marriage proposal, or, it seems reasonable to assume, a combination of the two. Satie's concept of furniture music seems to have reached so far into a world of fantasy that he composed, for two trumpets, a curious *Sonnerie pour réveiller le bon gros Roi des Singes (lequel ne dort toujours que d'un oeil)* (Fanfare for Waking Up the Big Fat King of the Monkeys [Who Always Sleeps with One Eye Open]), which, appropriately enough, first appeared in the inaugural issue (1 October 1921) of Leigh Henry's magazine *Fanfare.*

In the *Cinéma* ("Entr'acte symphonique") from *Relâche,* the principle of *musique d'ameublement* was applied, with great success, to the musical accompaniment of a René Clair film. Satie not only invented furniture music, in *Relâche* he demonstrated a serious application for his idea as well. What he would have thought of the "environmental" music of Max Neuhaus or the "ambient" music of Brian Eno—who recognizes the French composer as a strong influence—we can only imagine. The less discriminating applications of *musique d'ameublement* are only too much in evidence in the contemporary urban soundscape and need hardly be cataloged.

In June of 1920 Satie completed his *Premier Menuet,* which, despite the implication that a second and perhaps a third piece would follow, was to be his last work for piano. Like the *Nocturnes* it is a reversion to an abstract neoclassical mode of expression, without, however, the melodic freshness of the earlier pieces. The little ternary work is unified through frequent repetition of a four-note figure, first stated as A C D B, which may be a subtle musical translation of key letters in the dedication: "À Claude DuBosq." If indeed this is the case, Satie's *Premier Menuet* would join numerous similarly constructed pieces by French composers—Ravel's *Menuet sur le nom d'Haydn* (1909) and the later *Berceuse sur le nom de Gabriel Fauré* (1922), for example, as well as works by Debussy, Dukas, Honegger, Poulenc, and Jacques Ibert.

Satie's last completed compositions of 1920, appearing at one-month intervals between September and December, were the *Quatre petites mélodies.* "Élégie," the first of the four songs, is a setting of a Lamartine poem and is dedicated "to the memory of Claude Debussy, in remembrance of an admiring and sweet friendship of thirty years." It first appeared in print in December 1920 in a special Debussy memorial issue of *La Revue musicale,* along with musical tributes by Dukas, Ravel, Roussel, Bartók, Stravinsky, and four other composers. It is a forlorn little song. The poet questions the value of valleys, palaces or cottages, the charm of rivers, rocks, and forests in the face of the loss of a single cherished friend, which makes everything seem so empty and barren. The voice freely declaims Lamartine's elegiac verse over a sparse chordal accompaniment which, despite its chromaticism and unorthodox harmonic movement, heads awkwardly but surely toward a C major / minor tonal center. Through a strange final cadence, however—a modally ambiguous second-inversion leading-tone triad slipping onto a kind of augmented Neapolitan sixth—the implied tonal goal remains elusive, suspended in limbo:

Example 6. Satie: *Quatre petites mélodies* (1920), 1. "Élégie," measures 10–12

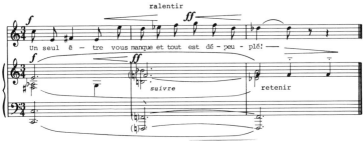

A mere twelve measures of music, the entire song has an unsettling tonal disorientation that surely reflects the composer's acute sense of loss.

The remaining three songs of the set, though not without harmonic and melodic quirks of their own, are a reversion to the composer's more popular vein. "Danseuse," a poem by Cocteau, concerns a ballerina whose delicate stance *sur pointe* with arms gracefully encircling her head is rather unflatteringly compared to the posture of a crab. The third song is a droll setting of an anonymous eighteenth-century drinking song, with more than a tinge, we might note, of autobiographical significance:

> It is my treasure, it is my jewel,
> The pretty opening through which
> my strength is renewed . . .
> Yes, I am mad, mad, mad,
> About the opening of my bottle.

Dare we read into the fact that this rather straightforward little song in a clear D major ends on a bleak D minor chord?

Perhaps the most successful of the four songs is the last, "Adieu," a setting of a poem by Raymond Radiguet, that precocious youth whose genius burned brightly for a very brief time in the early 1920s with two remarkable novels—*The Devil in the Flesh* and *Count d'Orgel's Ball*—until, his body ravaged by alcohol, he was claimed by typhoid in his twentieth year. This little song of farewell is set to a haunting waltz-tune that seems to drift in from the past, like the ghost of a carrousel.

What was to have been Satie's next work was never completed, despite the composer's claim to the contrary. In September 1920 he made a few rough sketches for *Paul et Virginie,* an operetta by Radiguet and

Cocteau based on the famous story by Bernardin de Saint-Pierre. It was, Satie publicly announced in Cocteau's broadsheet *Le Coq,* to be his farewell to musical composition.[32] A year later he still claimed, in a letter to Poulenc, to be hard at work on *Paul et Virginie.* And then we hear no more. All that is left to us now is to speculate that this sentimental eighteenth-century tale of lost innocence in Arcadia would have sadly disillusioned the composer, who all his lonely life tried desperately to cling, against impossible odds, to a nostalgic dream world of lost childhood.

9

The Late Ballets

The last five years of Satie's life were full of hectic activity. The composer was now something of a celebrity, known not only for his eccentric musical works but also for his equally eccentric journalistic efforts, which, after a six-year hiatus, had begun to appear again in such odd places as *Le Pilhaou-Thibaou,* a special illustrated supplement of Picabia's *391,* Marcel Raval's *Feuilles libres, Le Coeur à barbe,* which, in true Dada fashion, managed to last only one issue, and even the chic American magazine *Vanity Fair.* As if to reinforce his connection with his newfound Dada friends, Satie perpetrated his own Dadaist act by joining, in 1921, the Arcueil Soviet of the Communist Party. The composer was certainly not a political creature in the ordinary sense. He despised jingoism in any form and was too much of an anarchist at heart to submit to any doctrinal viewpoint, religious or political. Rather, as his first biographer Templier observed, "he loved to go to those smoky meetings, where he would savor the assorted militant loudmouths. Moreover, he adored the little scandals that he caused among his wealthy friends when he spoke of his involvement in the Soviet of Arcueil."[1] Such a mischievous attitude is, of course, entirely in character. As if to confirm Templier's observation, Darius Milhaud reported that Satie once asked to be introduced to a Belgian cabinet minister's wife in the following curious manner: "Erik Satie of the Arcueil Soviet greets her, his belly to the ground."[2] This droll anecdote dates from the year 1921. In April of that year the composer, who loathed traveling, preferring to remain in the shadows of his familiar Parisian haunts, was persuaded, largely through the efforts of the actor and theatrical producer Pierre Bertin, to journey to Belgium to attend performances of *Socrate* in Ghent and Brussels and participate in two important events in the Belgian capital, a conference honoring *Les Six,* followed by a festival of his own music. On 11 April, at the first concert of music by *Les Six,* he paid homage to his young disciples, declaring, in his usual ironic vein, that these young people (Honegger excepted) were dangerous influences and that strong action would be required to protect innocent people from such subversive music.[3]

Not long after his return to Paris, Satie's farcical *Medusa's Trap* finally received its first public performance, on 24 May, at Bertin's "Théâtre Bouffe" in the Théâtre Michel, rue des Mathurins, with Bertin himself, conspicuously made up to look like Satie, in the title role of the eccentric Baron. Although greatly displeased by this impertinent impersonation, Satie was delighted with Milhaud's expert conducting of his seven "Monkey" Dances. That same year a deluxe edition of the play, with Satie's music and wood engravings by Georges Braque, was published by Éditions de la Galerie Simon. There could no longer be any doubt that Satie was ripe for adoption by the Dadaists, who by the early 1920s had become a dominant force in Parisian artistic life.

The Dada Congress

It is now generally accepted that Dada was a movement of artistic revolt born of the cataclysmic events of a ruinous World War. It was in large part a reaction on the part of young European intellectuals to what they perceived to be the complete bankruptcy of a social order whose hallowed traditions seemed nothing more than an elaborate facade. Not unlike a later generation's response to the agony of Vietnam, the Dadaists saw a world turned upside down, with obscene paradoxes the order of the day. Accordingly, they collectively decided that if the bourgeois power brokers who controlled the destinies of great nations were deemed to be sane, then sanity was not a condition greatly to be prized.

The Paris Dadaists, led by men such as Tristan Tzara, André Breton, Louis Aragon, Philippe Soupault, and Francis Picabia, became the anarchist terrorists of art and culture, finding joy and meaning in nihilistic and scandalous acts designed to undermine the cultural and moral assumptions of the age. For a brief period they held center stage with a series of savage assaults on bourgeois complacency, their chief weapons a potent and cynical mixture of laughter and ridicule. As Soupault put it:

We simply wanted to create scandals—why should I not admit, in the end, that we loved scandal with passion. Anyway, it was a reason for existence. (And how many are there?) Perhaps the time we chose was unfortunate; but we were not looking for success. We wanted only to create sensations. And that gave us a rare joy. But the public also behaved scandalously. It tried to understand us, in vain. What madness![4]

Since Dada was never a clearly defined movement, but rather a more or less spontaneous gathering of artistic anarchists, it was inevitable that there would be breaks within the ranks. André Breton emerged as one of the more dogmatic members of the Paris group, and in the early part of 1922 he called for a Dada Congress with the express purpose of giving direction and organization to the movement. Breton's chief rival for the leadership was Tzara, who insisted that Dada be kept pure and spontaneous at all costs and free from the kind of official organization that would be sure to destroy it. The battle lines were clearly drawn. Breton and Tzara began to attack each other in the pages of *Comoedia,*[5] Breton becoming more assertive and apparently serious with each exchange. Finally, on 14 February 1922, a communiqué signed by Paul Éluard, Georges Ribemont-Dessaignes, Erik Satie, and Tristan Tzara was sent to *Comoedia* inviting Breton to a meeting at the Closerie des Lilas to discuss the idea of the congress. At 8:30 on the evening of 17 February 1922, what became known in Paris as the Breton "trial" began in the upstairs banquet room of the old café. Virtually all of artistic Paris was in attendance—Picasso, Matisse, Brancusi, Cocteau of course, along with his young friend Radiguet, and about a hundred others had come to participate in the spectacle. Hiding behind his goatee and his gold-rimmed pince-nez, Satie presided as "judge" over a stormy session that saw the supporters of Breton and Tzara exchange passionate insults and absurd charges. After the boisterous meeting was adjourned, a group of Dadaists, among them Satie, repaired to another café to draw up the terms of Breton's "defeat." As Matthew Josephson reported in his memoir of the period, "Satie busied himself, in consultation with the others, in writing the terms of the majority resolution condemning Breton, which was to be handed to the press; he kept gurgling into his beard with amusement, as he selected some especially pompous phrases in the style in which André Breton delighted."[6]

Five Bottle Imps and a Trip to Monte Carlo

Save for the tiny *Fanfare for the Big Fat King of the Monkeys,* the catalog of Satie's musical compositions is conspicuously blank for the years 1921 and 1922. Work may have continued on *Paul et Virginie* and it appears that there were plans around this time for a ballet to be called *The Birth of Venus* with décor by André Derain, yet another of Satie's close artistic friends, whose only collaboration with the composer would be the posthumous *Jack in the Box*. Temporarily sidetracked from musical composition through his involvement with the Dadaists, who had discovered one of the very few composers in all of Paris outrageous enough to belong in their irreverent company, Satie devoted a good part of 1921 and nearly all of the following year penning articles for the Dadaist press, giving the occasional public "lecture," and attending performances of his music, which by now were quite frequent, barely a month passing when at least one of his works was not being played somewhere in the French capital.

Near the beginning of January 1923 Darius Milhaud presented to Satie several young musicians who had openly expressed their admiration for him. His fervent belief in youth and what he perceived to be the "moral" necessity of constant renewal in art unshakable to the end, the composer warmly embraced his new disciples. Thus was born the short-lived School of Arcueil, headed by Henri Sauguet and including Roger Désormière, Maxime Jacob, and Henri Cliquet-Pleyel. Sauguet, a pupil of Joseph Cantaloube and Charles Koechlin, has earned a certain reputation for his elegant and charming music, particularly his one-act comic opera *Le Plumet du colonel* (1924), his ballet *La Chatte,* written for Diaghilev in 1927, and *Les Forains,* his touching tribute to the composer of *Parade.* Of the remaining members of the School of Arcueil, Désormière is best remembered as a distinguished conductor (he became principal musical director of the Ballets Russes in 1925), Jacob—like his namesake the poet Max Jacob—was a Jewish convert to Catholicism who ended his days in the Benedictine abbey of En-Calcat in the south of France where, as Dom Clément, he played the organ and continued to compose in a variety of genres until his death in 1977, while Cliquet-Pleyel has lapsed into almost complete obscurity, despite his rather large catalog of works, principally chamber music and film scores.

By 1923 *Les Six,* by Satie's own admission, had ceased to exist, and the composer now pinned his hopes on his latest recruits, whom he introduced to the public on 14 June 1923 in a *causerie* presented at the Collège de France in a program organized by the Cercle Internationale des Étudiants des Nations Alliées et Amies de la France.[7] That same fall Satie contributed an article to *Les Feuilles libres* in which he made a spirited plea for the public defense of these young musicians against critical attack, for to place one's trust in the young is, he declared, "something that is always absolutely essential."[8]

In addition to the tiny *Tenture de cabinet préfectoral,* composed on 28 March shortly after his return to Paris, Satie's only other original compositions of 1923 were the *Ludions* (Bottle Imps), settings of five poems by his old friend Léon-Paul Fargue, whose "Statue de Bronze" he had set in 1916. This bohemian "Poet of Paris" had much in common with Satie, loving nothing so much as to wander the streets of his beloved Paris, recording his impressions with wit, irony, tenderness, and quiet humor. Just as Satie cultivated a loving response to the homely and commonplace sounds of his Parisian environment—the music hall, the circus, the songs of children and the cabaret—so Fargue absorbed into his poetry the simple sights and sounds of the great city. "I have a taste for everything," the poet once told a young woman during an interview. "The least little thing, the humblest, reflects the light. It has its own little story, its own little smell, which it may be amusing, or pathetic, to discover and then to reveal. . . ."[9]

In Satie, Fargue found a sympathetic collaborator capable of transforming the tender irony of his poetry into a whimsical musical expression true to the poet's childlike vision, a vision all the more pure considering that one of the *Ludions,* "Air du Rat" ("Rat's Tune"), was written in 1886 by the ten-year-old Fargue for his pet white rat. Satie has captured something of the artless naivety of this poem in a singsong pentatonic melody with a prominent augmented fifth (G–D-sharp), which circles around a simple oompah accompaniment rocking uneasily between an obsessively reiterated augmented tonic chord and its submediant—a third-inversion seventh chord that tends to function as a kind of weakened dominant because of the strong root movement between D and G. The second song, "Spleen," mirrors to perfection the poet's poignant image of "an old garden where an ocean of ill-feeling sits on a forlorn bench with rain-filled eyes," a mood of tender nostalgia shattered the next instant as the poet pines, not for some pure and ennobling image of womanhood, but for "a cute but worthless blonde in this cabaret of Nothingness which is our life," an ironic shift captured in the music by a modulation from the opening E-flat major to C minor and thence to a resounding C major cadence in the piano, ever so slightly darkened by the single flatted seventh in the voice part.

Two of the remaining songs, "La Grenouille américaine" ("The American Frog") and "Chanson du Chat" ("Cat's Song"), are straight out of the music hall, with only a few odd harmonic twists to hint at their authorship, while the fourth song, "Air du Poète" ("Poet's Tune"), a mere ten bars of music, is a gloomy little song built around a static one-bar chordal figure that serves as the sole support for the vocal line, a pentatonic melody of utter simplicity which persistently folds back upon itself within the narrow confines of a perfect fifth (F–C), before coming to rest on the tonic F.

The *Ludions* were completed in May 1923 and first performed some six months later, on 21 December, in a concert of Satie's music at the Salle des Agriculteurs, with the composer himself accompanying Jane Bathori. It may have been this performance or a later private performance of the songs that led to a rupture of the friendship between Fargue and Satie. Apparently the poet, who very much liked Satie's settings of his poems, took great offense when some master of ceremonies unwittingly announced the *Ludions* as Satie's creations, omitting any reference to the authorship of the poetry, an unintentional faux pas that sent Fargue into a blind rage and resulted in a series of insulting letters addressed to the innocent composer from the irate poet, hand-delivered notes of such scurrilous invective as to be worthy of the Master of Arcueil himself. The last of them, according to Sylvia Beach, "too outrageous to repeat, failed to get anything but a laugh from Satie, a mild, philosophical-minded man, the composer, after all, of *Socrate;* and I think that was the last shot fired."[10]

At the suggestion of Stravinsky, Diaghilev, in his endless search for new ideas, decided to refurbish three comic operas by Gounod—*Le Médecin malgré lui, Philémon et Baucis,* and *La Colombe*—for presentation in Monte Carlo for the Ballets Russes's 1923–24 winter season. Wishing to have the spoken dialogue of Gounod's little operas set to music, the impresario, in the summer of 1923, commissioned Satie, Auric, and Poulenc to provide recitatives. *Le Médecin malgré lui* (The Doctor in Spite of Himself) was assigned to Satie. Gounod's 1858 opera is a nearly word-for-word setting of Molière's farcical tale of a woodcutter who, tricked into masquerading as a medical doctor, becomes embroiled in the convoluted courtship of his wealthy neighbors, with predictably hilarious results. Although precisely the kind of sparkling nonsense that so delighted Satie, his work on the recitatives proceeded at a snail's pace, occupying him on and off for most of the second half of 1923. By late September—"working like a worker at work (a rare thing),"[11] as he told Milhaud—he had finally finished act 2. Feeling, perhaps, the guilt of the confirmed procrastinator, five weeks later, on 3 November, he informed Sybil Harris that he had in fact finished the third (and final) act of *Le Médecin malgré lui,* adding a note to the effect that Gounod's heirs were bringing a lawsuit against Diaghilev for alleged "harm done to the memory of their august relation,"[12] a most serious charge, which set Satie to pondering whether he might have to sell his jewels and furs to cover his share of the damages. That the composer was stretching the truth concerning his progress we know from a letter of 14 December addressed to Diaghilev in which he informed the impresario that the third act was almost finished (up to no. 9 in the score) and that he was very pleased with the results: "Pretty, plump, elegant, delicate, superior, exquisite, varied, melancholy, extra . . . etc., . . . such is this, my work, fruit of my diurnal, even my nocturnal (but rarely), vigils."[13]

Sometime shortly before Christmas, Satie must have completed his assignment, for *Le Médecin malgré lui* opened at the Casino in Monte Carlo on 5 January 1924, with sets and costumes by Alexandre Benois and dance interludes choreographed by Bronislava Nijinska and danced by Serge Lifar, a young dancer (and later choreographer) from Kiev who had just recently joined the company and who one day would become one of Diaghilev's most important early biographers. Although the performance went well, *Le Médecin malgré lui* was overshadowed by the premiere the following day of Poulenc's delightful *Les Biches,* which turned out to be the biggest hit of the 1924 season and the young composer's first great success.

As we learn from Poulenc, Satie seems to have been well pleased with the production of *Le Médecin malgré lui.*[14] Unfortunately, however, the Monte Carlo sojourn was marred in the days to come by the presence there of one of the composer's longstanding enemies, the critic Louis Laloy, a great champion of Debussy and Impressionism, who over the years had attacked Satie and his followers in the pages of *Comoedia* at every opportunity. The recent works of Poulenc and Auric, however, especially *Les Biches* and Auric's *Les Fâcheux,* which had also premiered that season, on 19 January, had found favor with Laloy. Consequently a conciliation took place between the critic and the two young composers who, along with Cocteau, were frequently seen in his company in Monte Carlo. This act of treachery infuriated Satie, who saw the new alliance in terms of a complete and deliberate betrayal of the ideals for which he had fought so long and hard. Accordingly, he broke immediately with all three of his friends. Screaming maniacal insults at them, he boarded the night train for Paris and disappeared into the great city, never to become reconciled with his young disciples. As a parting shot he contributed a characteristic piece to the *Paris-Journal* in which he attacked Laloy with uninhibited malevolence and accused his erstwhile friends of selling out. The composer was as intransigent in human affairs as he was in artistic matters, and when Poulenc and Auric, as he claimed, began writing "lollipop" music, forgiveness was impossible. "How were things musically? . . . Hm! . . . Monte Carlo? . . . Superbly sugary. . . . Lots of syrupy things . . . buckets of musical lemonade . . . Yes . . . *Les Biches,* . . . *Les Fâcheux,* . . . Gounod. . . . Glimpsed the horrible Laloy (more ghastly than ever) . . . How awful! . . . A real mole, with his shortsightedness; but more malicious than a Monkey . . . Yes . . . ."[15]

Mercure

A few months after his return from Monte Carlo, Satie made a second trip to Belgium, in company with Milhaud, where he gave talks in Brussels and Antwerp. On 15 March he appeared in Brussels where he spoke to an audience of artists, critics, and students on "The Musical Spirit." After taking his usual swipe at the critics—". . .they know all things! . . . (*At least, . . . I suppose so*) . . ."[16]—the composer went on to announce to his audience that he was giving up, just for this occasion, his habitual irony, and, true to his word, he concluded his address in dead seriousness with a moving summary of his artistic credo:

The exercise of an Art requires us to live in a state of complete self-denial . . .
       . . . It was not to be funny that I spoke to you, . . . just now, . . . about sacrifice . . .
       Music requires a great deal from those who wish to serve her . . . That is what I wanted to convey to you . . .
       A true musician must be subjugated to his Art; . . . he must put himself above human misery; . . . he must draw his courage from within himself, . . . within himself alone.[17]

Satie's lecture was followed by performances of several songs and piano pieces, among them the *Trois Valses distinguées du précieux dégoûté,* which in the opinion of one Belgian critic seemed to be a musical portrait of the composer himself.[18]
       The following week, on 21 March, Satie repeated his talk in Antwerp

at the Cercle artistique et littéraire français and again participated in a program of his works, which included performances of the *Véritables préludes flasques,* the *Trois Morceaux en forme de poire,* and the piano-duet version of *Parade.* The aging hermit of Arcueil ended his colorful career in a manner befitting a born Dadaist. Whereas *Parade* hid behind a thin veil of seriousness (largely owing to Cocteau, who theorized about everything), Satie's last two ballets, *Mercure,* written for the Count Étienne de Beaumont, and *Relâche,* created in collaboration with that prince of Dada rebels, Francis Picabia, were conceived in a spirit of pure farce.

Mercure, subtitled "plastic poses in three tableaux," brought together Picasso, Massine, and Satie (but not Cocteau) for the second, and last, time. It opened on 15 June 1924 at the Théâtre de la Cigale in Montmartre as one of the Soirées de Paris, a series of benefit concerts for war widows and Russian refugees organized by the wealthy balletomane Count Étienne de Beaumont. The three tableaux of the ballet, for which Massine created the choreography, were designed to reveal the multiple personalities of the mythological Mercury: messenger of the gods, god of commerce, eloquence, travel, and patron deity of tricksters and thieves. *Mercure,* as the composer explained in an interview with the young critic Pierre de Massot, is a divertissement, a purely decorative work devoid of plot. The sole function of the music is to provide a sonic backdrop for Picasso's plastic poses.[19]

The prevailing atmosphere of *Mercure* is light and frivolous. The music-hall atmosphere is intentionally enhanced by a skillful use of clichés designed to highlight Mercury's preposterous adventures. It is the least known of Satie's late ballet scores largely because of the "furnishing" quality of the music, which, like much successful film music, refuses to take on a life of its own. In *Mercure* the principle of *musique d'ameublement* was applied for the first time to a relatively large-scale stage work. The ballet has nothing approaching a logical sequence of dramatic events. Rather *Mercure* is a farcical romp through Greek and Roman mythology, a farrago of ludicrous scenes depicting such things as a "Dance of Tenderness" between Apollo and Venus, the sudden appearance of Mercury with the "Signs of the Zodiac," the killing and subsequent magical restoration of Apollo by Mercury, a "Dance of the Graces" followed by the "Bath of the Graces," "Mercury's Flight" with the stolen pearls of the three Graces and his pursuit by the angry Cerberus, the terrible canine guardian of the entrance to Hades, a party thrown by Bacchus, the Roman Dionysus, at which Mercury entertains the guests with a "Letter

Polka" and a "New Dance," and, finally, the abduction of Proserpine by
Pluto with the aid of Chaos.

After the first performance of *Mercure,* René Chalupt reported that
the ballet was poorly received, even by Satie's best friends.[20] Serge
Leonidovich Grigoriev, who had served as Diaghilev's regisseur for
twenty years and who in that time had witnessed many strange and wonderful things, felt that *Mercure* was, quite simply, "utterly nonsensical."[21]
Apparently the critic for the London *Observer* was inclined to the same
view, for his droll description of the ballet's revival in England some three
years later has captured something of the frivolous atmosphere of Picasso's décor, Massine's choreography, and Satie's banal musical clichés:

> It began with a picture called "Night." This suggested an anthropomorphic
> powder-puff transfixed by hairpins to a square but sparsely-curranted, bun.
> There followed a dolorous love-dance between Venus and Apollyon, as rigorous
> in pose as it was abortive; slow processions of Ugly-wugglies contrived from
> cardboard and expanding metal; "The Bath of the Graces," suggestive of life on
> a submerged houseboat as lived by three Edwardian barmaids with hypertrophied
> period busts; a sharp encounter with Cerberus, and other celestial and infernal
> pranks whose pagan character defies brief description.
>
> Through this series of plastic poses flew Mercury, a vivid figure in white tunic
> and scarlet cloak, enthusiastically danced by Massine. The whole was accompa-
> nied by music to suit, dominated by a grumbling tuba.[22]

In 1924 the line was clearly drawn between the Surrealists and the
Dadaists. The evening of the second performance of *Mercure* was
marred by a group of Surrealists, led by Breton and Aragon, who booed
Satie (while cheering Picasso) with such persistence that the curtain had
to be lowered in the middle of the show, a hostile act that prompted
Francis Picabia to write a letter to the Paris press in defense of Satie:

> I have received from Paris a letter [from Pierre de Massot] in which I am told
> that the other evening at the Cigale Erik Satie triumphed before all the musicians
> who witnessed *Mercure.* But I am also told, and this is astonishing, that two
> pseudo-Dadaists present at the performance, Louis Aragon and André Breton,
> have got up a demonstration against the composer of *Parade.* Why? . . . Louis
> Aragon and André Breton have often told me that they understand absolutely
> nothing about music. What then does this blackmail mean? What is the meaning
> of this sudden bewildering admiration for Picasso? For the cries of "Down with
> Satie" were doubled with those of "Long live Picasso. . . ."
>
> As for Satie, if they accuse him of being old simply because he is sixty years

of age [*sic*], they betray, for poets, the mentality of wine and cheese merchants who judge art exclusively by the number of years. Erik Satie, sirs, is younger than you are. What he has to say is shrewd and amusing. . . . He loves life quite simply, dares to drink, and dares to compose his own music without wondering if it will please or displease the right or the left.[23]

Relâche

Satie not only anticipated Dada by a decade or more, he was instrumental in providing the short-lived movement with one of its most glorious spasms. *Relâche* (No Performance), a supremely Dadaist free-for-all, was the Master of Arcueil's parting snub at the old world he entered (and left) very young. By 1924, the year that saw the publication of André Breton's first *Surrealist Manifesto,* the force of Dadaism was nearly spent. It had begun to take itself seriously, becoming more politically conscious, with the result that it soon underwent a transformation into something more systematic and constructive—though still combative and provocative—and reemerged as Surrealism.

The poet and novelist Blaise Cendrars, fresh from his successful collaboration with Milhaud and Léger on *La Création du monde,* brought together Francis Picabia and Rolf de Maré, founder and director of the Ballets Suédois, with an idea for a new ballet originally to be called *Après dîner* (After Dinner).[24] Although Picabia eventually substituted his own scenario for Cendrars's, he and de Maré did agree with the poet that Satie was the obvious choice for the music. The composer was in congenial company. The ingredients for the making of a scandal were already in place: Cendrars, a colorful eccentric of Swiss background whose biography reads like the script of a Surrealist movie; Picabia, a gregarious Cuban-French poet, painter, and unrepentent prankster, and de Maré, a wealthy Swede whose Ballets Suédois became, for a brief period in the early 1920s, a strong rival of Diaghilev's Ballets Russes, moving to the forefront of the modern movement by introducing during its brief five-year existence some two dozen ballets representative of the very latest artistic trends.

Satie was delighted with Picabia's plans for *Relâche* and celebrated the confirmation of the agreement with de Maré with numerous glasses of plum brandy, exclaiming all the while to Picabia: "Ah, old chap! It's chic! It's going to be wonderful!"[25] In choosing to call the new ballet *Relâche—* the term used to denote "no performance," "theater closed," or "closed for the summer"—Picabia wished to signal a complete break with convention, a resolute slamming of the door on tradition. As for his part, Satie was highly pleased with the title chosen for what would be his last work, for, as he waggishly explained to his friends, it had always been his great ambition to have a work of his running simultaneously—during the summer months—at theaters all over Paris.[26]

It was Picabia's idea to include a film in *Relâche* to be shown briefly at the beginning after the overture and during the interval between the two acts of the ballet. For this purpose he hired René Clair, a young film critic who had had some experience in the medium. The tiny *Entr'acte* that resulted, for which Satie provided the musical score, became one of the most admired examples of early film art, an inspiration for countless Surrealist films that followed in its wake, and today something of a classic of the early experimental film.

Entr'acte is an anarchistic and outrageously funny film. It makes use of unusual camera angles, rapid juxtaposition of fast and slow motion, and nonlinear sequences to create an effect not unlike Satie's music. The film begins with amorphous images of expanding and contracting dots of light that soon fade into a series of long shots of Paris rooftops and chimneys seen from various crazy angles. Abruptly the film cuts to an image of three little dolls in the form of balloons with painted faces—one male, two female. Between shots of their deflated and reinflated heads the viewer is transported to a stage where he observes, from below through a sheet of glass, a dancing ballerina, her skirt billowing out and closing up again like the petals of some exotic flower filmed with time-lapse photography. Images of sunlight sparkling through treetops seen from directly below are followed by disembodied boxing gloves—white on a black background—throwing rapid punches at each other.

The battling gloves are juxtaposed with night shots of Parisian streets, with the city lights moving in and out of focus. A man's hair is seen from above. Wooden matches, appearing from left and right, are superimposed on the hair, which bursts into flame. Images of colonnaded buildings dissolve to reveal Man Ray and Marcel Duchamp engaged in a game of chess on the roof of the Théâtre des Champs-Élysées. The game is washed away by a shower of sunlit water. The camera follows a paper boat sailing in the sky over the rooftops. The ballerina (Inge Friis) reappears, still seen from below. Now the camera closes in on her thighs, then her legs, before slowly tilting upward to reveal her face—a face with a false black beard, moustache, and pince-nez.

Jean Börlin, the Ballets Suédois's principal male dancer and choreographer, appears in Tirolean hunter's garb armed with a double-barreled shotgun and attempts to shoot a large egg bobbing up and down on a jet of water. The bobbing egg multiplies then becomes one again, much to the annoyance of the nervous hunter. Finally he shoots and the egg shatters in a swirl of smoke and water, out of which emerges a pigeon, which flies off, only to return and perch on the hunter's feathered hat. A man (Picabia), silhouetted against the sky on a rooftop, aims a rifle at the bird, but it is the hunter's head that fills his sight, with the image of an amusement park target superimposed on it, the bull's-eye centered on the mouth. The rifleman fires and the hunter plummets to his death from the roof of the theater.

The second part of *Entr'acte* unfolds in a more linear—though no less zany—sequence of events. It is a mock funeral procession for the unfortunate hunter, complete with camel-drawn hearse decorated with a heart-shaped monogram made up of the initials F. P[icabia] and E. S[atie] and with paper streamers, hams, and wreaths in the form of circular loaves of bread. The mourners, the majority of them men in dark suits and top hats, some wearing wreaths around their necks, form a procession behind the hearse, which lumbers off, slowly gathers speed, and eventually breaks into an absurd gallop, with the motley entourage leaping after it in a dreamlike slow motion. Gaining speed all the while, the procession moves through traffic and into the Luna Park, Paris's vast amusement park, with a model of the Eiffel Tower in its center and a huge roller coaster winding through its grounds.

At this point the camel, unnoticed by the procession, breaks loose from the hearse, which, nevertheless, continues to move rapidly past fairground stalls and down tree-lined avenues, much to the consternation of the astonished driver. The frenzied mourners doggedly jog after it in hot pursuit, among them a seemingly legless cripple on a trolley, who, at one point in his determination to keep up, abandons his vehicle and dashes after the procession on a perfectly sound pair of long legs.

As the momentum increases, the camera races through a dizzying series of images—flashing trees, racing cyclists, crazily tilted landscapes—topped by a meteoric ride on the Luna Park roller coaster. The speeding hearse, now a blur of movement, finally comes to rest in an open field. The coffin falls to the ground; the pursuing mourners reappear in small groups and gather around it in animated discussion. Slowly the coffin lid opens, much to the amazement of the onlookers, and out leaps Börlin, the "deceased," now dressed as a magician. Grinning mischievously at his pursuers, he waves his wand at them causing them one by one to disappear. Standing alone now in the deserted field, he points the wand at himself and fades from the picture. The word *FIN* appears against a white paper backdrop, which, however, is suddenly rent as Börlin burst through in slow motion. He is knocked to the ground and given a violent kick in the head by an angry Rolf de Maré, whereupon the film reverses itself, propelling him back through the torn screen, which heals itself with the reappearance of *FIN,* followed by the final credits.

As for the ballet itself, it virtually defies description. From what can be reconstructed from contemporary eyewitness accounts and the extant scenario,[27] we know that the spectacle began, after the brief overture, with the lowering of a movie screen on which were projected images of Satie and Picabia leaping in slow motion on the roof of the Théâtre des Champs-Élysées admiring a huge field gun which, after some deliberation, they gleefully fired—not surprisingly—directly at the audience. As the screen exploded into blackness the curtain rose to reveal a glittering backdrop consisting solely of metallic disks, 370 in all, ranged row upon row in a series of three recessed arches, looking like so many shiny cymbals or large silver breasts complete with electric lightbulb nipples, all lit to a dazzling brilliance.

A fashionably dressed woman (Edith Bonsdorff) in spangled hip-waisted dress and matching turban sauntered onto the stage from her place in the audience, coolly examined the décor, sat down, smoked a cigarette while listening to the pit orchestra, then danced briefly, in silence, a "Dance without Music." She was joined by a man (Jean Börlin) in formal evening dress, who made his entrance gliding across the stage in a motorized wheelchair. Stirred by the woman's beauty, he soon found the use of his legs, abandoned his paraplegic's chair, and joined her in a "Dance of the Revolving Door." Eight men, similarly dressed in tails and top hats, one by one left their seats in the auditorium and joined the man and the woman on stage. As they circled around the woman, she stripped down to a pair of rose-colored silk tights. The men backed away from her. Balloons exploded. A general dance ensued bringing the first act to a close with the woman raised high in the air at center stage by her escorts.

After the novel entr'acte the main curtain rose on the second act to reveal a drop curtain, designed by Picabia, on which appeared amidst numerous squiggly lines, circles, and arrows, the names of the principal authors along with a series of cheeky slogans, among the more provocative, "Erik Satie is the greatest musician in the world," and among the more insulting, "Those who are dissatisfied are authorized to piss off," a sensible and appropriate directive, in the opinion of one critic, which everyone would do well to obey.[28] As powerful spotlights swept the audience Börlin and the eight men in evening dress returned and once again surrounded the woman, still dressed in silk tights but now with a wreath of orange blossoms in her hair. While she redressed herself the men proceeded to divest themselves of their evening clothes until stripped down to top hats and spotted silk tights. One by one the men returned to their seats in the auditorium to reclaim their overcoats, leaving the woman to collect their evening clothes, which, in a "Dance of the Wheelbarrow," she gathered and dumped unceremoniously in a heap in a corner of the stage. The woman then approached the front of the stage, removed her bridal wreath and threw it to one of the male dancers in the audience, who carried it to a box seat near the front of the auditorium and placed it on the head of the popular singer (and friend of Picabia) Marthe Chenal, thus symbolically crowning her as the most beautiful spectator in the house. This done, the woman slowly wandered off the stage and took her seat in the audience. Finally, the stage set vanished behind a white drop curtain, before which a young woman appeared dancing and miming the words to the closing music, "La Queue du chien" ("The Dog's Tail").

Throughout the entire ballet a man dressed as a fireman, the distinguished ribbon of the Legion of Honor prominently displayed on his tunic, wandered aimlessly in and around the dancers chain-smoking and routinely emptying a pail of water back and forth from one bucket to another—a rather obvious symbol of officialdom standing by to extinguish the fires indiscriminately ignited by Picabia and his dangerous coterie of cultural arsonists.

In a letter to Milhaud of 10 August 1924 Satie included a musical extract from the "Rentrée de la Femme" from act 2 of *Relâche* to which he added the words "ballet obcène" [*sic*].[29] Certainly Picabia was not above exploiting obscenity in his scatological slogans, and the ballet did include scenes of stylized striptease, but what appeared to be most shocking to the first-night audience (and to the critics) was the music itself, for *Relâche* is a compendium of derisory and bawdy songs, the words of which would have been familiar to anyone, as one disgruntled critic pointed out, who had done military service.[30] True to form, Satie based much of his music on preexistent tunes, among the identifiable ones, "Le Marchand de navet," "As-tu vu la cantinière?," "R'tire tes pieds, r'tire tes pieds, tu n'vois que tu m'ennuies?" and "Le Père Dupanloup," a vulgar army barracks song sung to the tune of the children's song "Cadet Rousselle."[31]

It is clear from the scenario that the second act of *Relâche* mirrors much of the action of the first: the woman enters the stage from the audience, dances briefly by herself, and is joined by the man in the "Dance of the Revolving Door"; they in turn are joined by the eight men in evening dress who dance while the woman strips to flesh-colored tights; she dances again by herself; finale of act 1. In the second act much of this action is repeated and reversed: the men in evening dress now reappear first, followed by the woman, who proceeds to redress herself while the men now undress; she dances again with the man, followed by the departure of her escorts, who return to their places in the audience; after the "Dance of the Wheelbarrow" the woman performs her "Dance of the Coronet," then reclaims her seat in the audience, thus bringing the action full circle.

Here we have a musico-dramatic symmetry not unlike that found in *Parade,* for much of the music of the eleven numbers of act 1 is recycled for the eleven numbers of act 2, while certain musical motifs reappear throughout the score in varying guises and transpositions. For example, the music for the "Entrée de la Femme" in act 1 is recycled for her return ("Rentrée de la Femme") in act 2 and appears a third time near the end of the ballet when she reclaims her seat in the audience ("La Femme rejoint son fauteuil"):

Example 1. Satie: *Relâche* (1924)

(a) Act 1, no. 4 ("Entrée de la Femme"), measures 1–2

(b) Act 2, no. 14 ("Rentrée de la Femme"), measures 1–2

(c) Act 2, No. 21 ("La Femme rejoint son fauteuil"), measures 1–2

Similarly, the music of the "Entrée des Hommes" in act 1 reappears, newly harmonized, for the "Rentrée des Hommes" in act 2:

Example 2. Satie: *Relâche* (1924)

(a) Act 1, no. 8 ("Entrée des Hommes"), measures 2–3

(b) Act 2, no. 13 ("Rentrée des Hommes"), measures 5–6

And again, the men undress in act 2 ("Les Hommes se dévêtissent") to musical material recycled from the finale of act 1:

Example 3. Satie: *Relâche* (1924)

(a) Act 1, no. 11 ("Final"), measures 9–11

(b) Act 2, no. 15 ("Les Hommes se dévêtissent"), measures 1–3

A number of other musical themes reappear from time to time within each act and between acts, resulting in a pattern of interlocking motifs that lend unity to the score. Motifs from the "Ouverture" (no. 1)—based on the student song "Le Marchand de navet" ("The Turnip Vendor")—show up in "Musique" (no. 5) and "Entrée de l'Homme" (no. 6) in act 1 and again in "Le Danseur dépose la Couronne sur la tête d'une spectatrice" (no. 20) in act 2. The main theme of "Projection" (no. 2) is used again in the "Danse des Hommes" (no. 9) of act 1 and yet again in the finale, "La Queue du Chien" (no. 22) of act 2. Some of the waltz music for the "Danse de la Porte tournante" (no. 7) of act 1 is used again in the "Danse de la Couronne" (no. 19) of act 2. And in act 2 the nine men reclaim their places in the audience (no. 17) to the same military tattoo (the French army version of "Reveille") as opened the act (no. 12).

Only one number, the "Danse de la Brouette" (no. 18), bears absolutely no motivic relationship to any other music of the ballet, nor would it appear to have its roots in popular music like its companion pieces. It stands entirely alone, a serene melody in a limping 5/4 meter given out in the upper strings in parallel thirds, with occasional woodwind doubling, and dry punctuation on first and third beats of the measure by low strings, brass, and bassoon. It is a lovely, luminously scored passage, redolent of the neoclassical Stravinsky, which seems somehow misplaced in the context of the surrounding waltz tunes and jaunty two-steps. Charming as some of the music for *Relâche* is, Satie's most important contribution to the ballet was the music he provided for Clair's intermission feature. The scandal of *Relâche* and the poverty of much of the music has tended to obscure the fact that Satie was one of the first composers to possess an instinctive understanding of what many critics to this day deem to be the proper function of film music. Applying his principle of *musique d'ameublement,* he composed a kind of neutral rhythmic counterpoint to the visual action. Divorced from the film the music is practically meaningless, refusing to take on a musical identity of its own, but as film music it fulfills its function admirably. For once Satie's inability (or refusal) to develop and extend his musical material worked entirely to his advantage. At no point does the music obtrude on the screen images and create a logic of its own. It is entirely self-effacing, objective, devoid of sentimentality, and perfectly wedded to the rhythm of the action, for *Entr'acte* is above all else a playful manipulation of the temporal element, like music itself an elaborate counterpoint of flowing and colliding gestures.

Satie's music for *Entr'acte,* scored in a "music-hall" fashion for flute, oboe, clarinet in A, bassoon, two horns, two trumpets, trombone, strings, and a percussion section consisting of tarol, cymbals, tam-tam, triangle, tambourine, woodblock, and bass drum, is constructed entirely of a series of mostly four- and eight-measure ostinato patterns mechanically repeated and juxtaposed with neither marked variation nor smooth transition from one unit to the next. Like the film, Satie's music has no narrative continuity, for each sound-block is tonally stationary and often tonally ambiguous. As in *Relâche* there is a wholesale translocation of themes and motifs. The initial gesture in particular, a one-measure dotted sixteenth-note figure rigidly repeated eight times, accompanies not only the film's opening sequences—"Chimneys, exploding balloons," "Boxing gloves and matches"—but is used again for the hunter's episodes, later when the cortege sets out in slow motion, and yet again near the end of the film when Börlin bursts through the screen.

In only two episodes does the composer come close to an expressive response to the screen imagery. In the scene featuring the dancing ballerina he introduces a short phrase in waltz time that very nearly is allowed to blossom into a graceful tune before being nipped in the bud and reduced to a series of repeated motivic fragments. And at the beginning of the funeral, as the mourners assemble, he alludes to Chopin's ubiqui-

tous Funeral March—long a staple of the silent cinema for such scenes—
with its solemn dotted rhythm alone sufficient to conjure up the famous
melody. A lugubrious horn melody of Satie's own invention and the
mournful resonance of the tam-tam sounding against the slow, measured
tread of the strings and low woodwind create an appropriately sepulchral
mood, which, of course, is comically contradicted by the images of Clair's
ludicrous mock funeral.[32]

Satie's last public appearance was on the stage of the Théâtre des
Champs-Élysées where *Relâche* survived a dozen performances before
"*relâche*" was inscribed on the theater bills and marquees in earnest. At
the end of each performance Satie and Picabia put-putted across the
stage in Börlin's five-horsepower motor-scooter chair, gleefully waving
to the jeering and cheering crowd they had so magnificently ridiculed.
That the composer was conscious of once again running ahead of the
pack, quite aware from the beginning of the shock value of his latest
creation, we know from a letter of 21 October 1924 to Marcel Raval,
director of *Les Feuilles libres* where several of his last writings appeared.
"It is in *Relâche,*" he wrote, "that the signal for departure will be given.
Picabia cracks the egg, and we move forward, leaving behind us the
Cocteaus and other blinkered dolts."[33] Satie and his collaborators were
no doubt well prepared for a virulent critical response to *Relâche*. And
they were not to be disappointed, for the ballet unleashed a storm of
protest, reminiscent of the heady days of *Parade*. Roland-Manuel penned
a farewell to his old mentor rather bluntly entitled "Adieu à Satie," thus
setting the tone for a flood of adverse criticism. In his opinion the spirit
of Dada had fed Satie's incoercible appetite for sly buffoonery and had
tragically undermined the graceful whimsy of the earlier piano works.
The result was *Relâche,* a vulgar work of unimaginable boredom and distressing silliness.[34]

Perceptive readers of *Le Journal littéraire* six weeks before the premiere of the ballet would have been better prepared for the fiasco at the
Théâtre des Champs-Élysées on 4 December.[35] In a rare interview, Satie
outlined briefly the surrealist scenario of *Relâche* and explained that he
intended the music to be lively and colorful, that he had in fact composed,
"for the 'chic set,' amusing and pornographic (*sic*) music."[36] Additional
bait, if any were needed, was provided by Picabia in a mock interview
with the director of the Ballet Suédois, who asked him to explain the
scenario of the ballet prior to the opening performance a week away;
Picabia's characteristically supercilious reply: "*Relâche?* Music by Erik
Satie . . . explain what to you my dear Rolf de Maré? Do you take me

for Einstein?"[37] Good Dadaist that he was, Picabia fervently believed that life, after all, was far more important than art. *"Relâche,"* he declared in his breezy program note, "is life, life as I love it; life without tomorrow, life today, everything for today, nothing for yesterday, nothing for tomorrow."[38]

Forewarned or not, the Parisian press descended upon the composer and his Dada colleagues with a vengeance. All the major critics were in attendance—André Messager for *Le Figaro,* Henry Malherbe for *Le Temps,* Émile Vuillermoz for *Excelsior,* Jean Gandry-Rety for *Comoedia,* Robert Dezarnaux for *La Liberté,* Fernand Le Borne for *Le Petit Parisien,* Paul Dambly for *Le Petit Journal,* even Louis Schneider representing the *New York Herald.* Although there was considerable praise in some quarters for Clair's pioneering film,[39] Satie's music suffered almost universal condemnation, the general opinion being that the score was so poor and simple that it was beneath contempt.

Only months before his death it appeared that the godfather of *Les Six* and *L'École d'Arcueil* was about to disappear beneath a mountain of negative publicity. The "official" attitude toward the composer was perhaps best summarized by Georges Jean-Aubry in a scathing article that appeared several months before Satie's death.[40] Less than a decade earlier Jean-Aubry had paid homage to Satie in his *Musique française d'aujourd'hui* (1916); and, in the same year, writing for an English journal in advance of a proposed Satie visit to Great Britain, the French critic wrote of the "genuine musicality" of the composer, and concluded that "behind his apparent lack of respect for music, lurks a sincere love of it, such as one sometimes fails to find in the depths of the soul of certain master builders of works of large dimensions, for whom music is nothing more than scientific boredom."[41] But exposure to the late ballets had radically altered Jean-Aubry's view, and, after witnessing the scandal of *Relâche,* the disgruntled critic was compelled to write:

. . . "Relâche" has at last opened the eyes, or rather the ears, of those who would neither see nor listen and who persisted in maintaining that Satie was a master. Disillusioned, and having decided to remain no longer among those of whom the proverb says, "none so deaf as those who will not hear," they were forced to confess, while listening to "Relâche," that they were, in fact, listening to nothing.[42]

Writing in the vituperative vein of one who has just discovered that he has been duped, Jean-Aubry went on to denounce *Parade,* and even *Soc-*

rate—perhaps Satie's chief claim to immortality—which he dismissed as a pretentious piece wherein poverty and boredom are in open conflict. His bitter conclusion is a judicious marriage of poetic imagery and invective tinged with regret, as he saw in the composer "an old actor who, because he has once played the part of Napoleon and been applauded by provincials, imagines himself to be really the great captain, but who, looking in a mirror, sees only an old man abandoned in the melancholy twilight of a deserted café."[43]

Shortly after the premiere of *Relâche,* Satie's health began to decline rapidly, his liver ravaged by some four decades of indiscriminate drinking in the bars of Montmartre and Montparnasse. Still, he continued for a time to make the daily journey from Arceuil to Paris, where he would dine with friends. Alarmed by his haggard appearance and his increasingly morose behavior, his closest friends, led by the faithful Milhauds, Darius and Madeleine, arranged lodging for him in town, first at the Grand Hôtel on the Place de l'Opéra and later, when a room became available, at the Hôtel Istria in Montparnasse, then a kind of unofficial headquarters of Left Bank bohemianism, where Picabia and his entourage had set up court during the production of *Relâche.* Satie's condition steadily worsened, the cirrhosis of the liver now complicated with pleurisy, and, through the influence of Étienne de Beaumont, a private room was obtained for the ailing composer at the Hôpital Saint-Joseph in the rue Pierre-Larousse.

For the next six months the Milhauds visited Satie nearly every day. Among the other faithful visitors were Constantin Brancusi, the Romanian sculptor with whom the composer had become very close during the last four or five years of his life; Valentine Hugo, who on one occasion brought him some lovely handkerchiefs he had fancied; the young musicians Jean Wiéner, Roger Désormière, and Robert Caby; the critic Yves Dautun; Sybil Harris; and Jacques Maritain, who once brought with him a priest whom Satie, his ready wit undiminished to the end, described the following day to his friends as "looking like a Modigliani, black on a blue background."[44] When Francis Poulenc heard of his older mentor's illness he begged to be allowed to see him. But Satie refused, saying: "No, no, I would rather not see him; they said good-bye to me, and now that I am ill, I prefer to take them at their word. One must stick to one's guns to the last."[45] On Wednesday 1 July the composer slipped into a coma; about eight o'clock that same evening he died.

The funeral took place five days later, on the morning of the 6th, at the charming fifteenth-century church in Arcueil, where the composer had lived the last twenty-seven years of his life in poverty. In addition to a delegation of friends and neighbors from the town, led by the mayor, many of Satie's colleagues and disciples came to bid farewell to their old friend and master. *Les Six* (minus Durey) were in attendance, as were Maxime Jacob and Henri Sauguet, Jean Cocteau and his mother, Paulette Darty, Ricardo Viñes, Valentine Hugo and her husband Jean, Pierre Bertin, the conductor Vladimir Golschmann, Jacques Maritain, René Clair, his former teacher from the Schola Cantorum Albert Roussel, even his publishers Rouart-Lerolle and Lucien Vogel were represented. The simple pine coffin was profusely covered with flowers, including a wreath of roses from the Ballets Suédois and another of hydrangea from Les Amis du Vieil Arcueil. After the simple church service, the cortege wound its way through the streets of the town, passed under the lofty arches of the ancient Roman aqueduct—still a striking feature of the Arcueil landscape—and thus proceeded to the local cemetery, nestled on the side of a hill. Here a young priest recited a final prayer for the dead, holy water was sprinkled over the grave, and Satie was laid to rest in the poor working-class suburb he had served well, with love and humility. His tomb, partly designed by Brancusi, is a plain granite marker with ERIK SATIE engraved on the transverse beam of a large stone cross.

There was scarcely a Parisian newspaper that did not carry an obituary of Satie within the week. And, as some measure of his international stature, obituary notices—in some instances substantial articles—appeared as far away as New York and Buenos Aires, as well as in the English, Dutch, and Belgian press. Even a Czech newspaper, *Lidové Novimy,* reported the death of Erik Satie.

The distinguished musicologist Henri Prunières, founder and first editor of *La Revue musicale,* echoed the opinion of many of his colleagues by suggesting that Satie's rediscovery in the postwar period, thrusting him abruptly into the limelight, was detrimental to his art. The composer on several occasions experienced the frustration of seeing his innovations taken up by younger more talented composers who quickly outgrew their need of him. Consequently, Prunières contended, he became jealous of the success of composers whom he had supported, and his former modesty, dignity, and charm were gradually displaced by an intense bitterness and irascibility that barely managed to hide under the surface of an increasingly caustic wit. As Prunières bluntly put it: "His success killed him."[46]

The composer had been dead only a fortnight when the British critic and editor Eric Blom, in a harsh notice for the *Musical News and Herald,* wrote of France's "original but ineffectual musician" with the apparent intention of closing the Satie case once and for all:

Independent critics at no time cherished any illusion about the fertility of Satie's work. He mildly amused them once or twice by his humorous pieces and by the pathetically comic false position into which he had been thrust by a few of the people who are ever eager for innovation, whatever its quality may be. But his last few years deserved unalloyed pity. One was sorry for him as for a preposterous eccentric who has been robbed of his belief in the reality of his attitudes, whom life has left high and dry on an arid sandbank once mistaken by him for a fruitful island. It was said of Satie by some manipulator of *clichés* that he was born before his time; all one can say now, with the sorrowful indulgence one owes to the departed, is that he unhappily died too late to leave a world of unwholesome flattery without bitterness.[47]

Thus many of Satie's cronies, perhaps under some pressure from the critics, began to desert him and his ideals, some, like Roland-Manuel, with considerable fanfare, the greater number silently, although those closest to him—Milhaud, Sauguet, Désormière, Caby—remained faithful to the end. Significantly, despite his periodic difficulties with the implacable composer, Georges Auric, speaking perhaps for all *Les Six,* was genuinely moved by his death, and he had the courage to conclude his front-page obituary for *Les Nouvelles littéraires* with a simple, touching, and prophetic statement: "I will never regret having heeded the lesson of Satie. The years pass—and the misunderstandings."[48]

The Parisians did not wait long to honor their eccentric citizen. A festival to raise money for Satie's tomb opened at the Théâtre des Champs-Élysées on what would have been the composer's sixtieth birthday, 17 May 1926. That June the Ballets Russes revived *Parade,* and the long lost *Jack in the Box* and *Geneviève de Brabant* received their posthumous premieres. Throughout 1927 and 1928 Satie's music continued to appear on Parisian programs with fair frequency—an occasional song or piano piece, culminating in a revival of *Mercure,* mounted by Diaghilev on 2 June 1927 at the Théâtre Sarah Bernhardt. On 30 June 1929 Satie's friends commemorated the fourth anniversary of his death with the unveiling of a plaque on the side of his house in the rue Cauchy, followed by a concert of his music in the Arcueil town hall. Among the performers were Maxime Jacob and Robert Caby in the four-hand piano version of *Parade;* Paulette Darty singing several of the *café-concert* songs she had

introduced a quarter century before; Ricardo Viñes playing a *Gymnopédie*, a *Gnossienne*, and the *Croquis et agaceries d'un gros bonhomme en
bois*, as well as his own *Thrénodie*, composed in memory of his old friend;
and finally, and perhaps most appropriately, Marya Freund, with the assistance of Milhaud at the piano, performing the poignant final movement
of *Socrate*.

On 25 June 1950 a number of Satie's old friends gathered once again
in Arcueil to commemorate the twenty-fifth anniversary of his death.
Roger Désormière conducted a small orchestra in several works, Caby,
Sauguet, and Wiéner performed a few piano pieces, while memorial
speeches were delivered by Caby and the composer's first biographer
Pierre-Daniel Templier. Sixteen years later, on the centenary of his
birth, the Arcueillais honored their fellow townsman in a more definitive
fashion by renaming a park after him in which stands a bust of the composer, gazing—benignly one would like to think—at the little children at
play.

During the cerebral, "post-dodecaphonic" 1950s Satie's stock, not surprisingly, fell dramatically, especially outside of France. Interestingly,
however, two American musicians were chiefly responsible for keeping
the Satiean spirit alive. Suspicious from the beginning of Germanic rhetoric as well as the seductive powers of Debussyan Impressionism, both
Virgil Thomson and John Cage found in Satie an antidote to the deadening
weight of tradition; they discovered in him a music quiet, precise, and
direct, a music fresh and new-born, devoid of rhetoric and a preoccupation with the sublime. For Thomson the great Austro-German tradition
had by 1925 simply lost contact and was hopelessly out of tune with the
times. In the members of the Second Viennese School he saw a curious
and unsatisfying blend of old and new, a group of composers vainly attempting to prolong an exhausted tradition by flaying the corpses of Wagner and Mahler, urging them, zombielike, into a world of hallucination
and nightmare. Austro-German music was, Thomson felt, still burdened
with too many layers of post-Romantic fat, whereas French music was
free to be modern because "there was," in his view, "no pressure for it
to be anything else, no weighted emotional ambience."[49]

For John Cage, who discovered Satie shortly after World War II, the
French composer is, as he once quipped, not only relevant but indispensable. "To be interested in Satie," he wrote in 1958, "one must be dis-
interested to begin with, accept that a sound is a sound and a man is a
man, give up illusions about ideas of order, expressions of sentiment,
and all the rest of our inherited aesthetic claptrap."[50] For Cage the

French composer's career was an elaborate attempt to tear down not just the walls of tradition and convention, but all the barriers that separate art from life:

> When life is lived, there is nothing in it but the present, the "now-moment."
> . . . Art when it is art as Satie lived it and made it is not separate from life. . . .
> Satie . . . never lived in an ivory tower, nor does any artist of his quality ever
> need to: for there is nothing in life from which he separates himself.[51]

To the very end of his solitary existence Satie continued, in his quixotic fashion, to beat down the barriers of convention with an undiminished taste for adventure and a self-destructive impulse unique in the annals of modern music. On several occasions after his "rediscovery" at the hands of Debussy and Ravel after 1910, the way was open to the composer to withdraw from the fray, had he been willing to accept the role of leader, prophet, and indeed pundit. But the idea of becoming even a *petit maître* was alien to the Satie aesthetic, even though the rejection of such a role meant his own certain destruction.

Satie was a born iconoclast. It is evident that from his earliest years he was uninterested in (and probably incapable of) mastering the traditional forms of musical expression. As a consequence, he created his own psychological island, developing nearly everything out of himself, even to the point of devising his own parodistic "church." There is an overwhelming tendency on the part of many critics to conclude that Satie was somehow forced into his role as musical humorist through his inability to compose music in the accepted elitist sense. But once again we must remind ourselves that his art was rooted not in the The Great Tradition, French or German, but rather in fin de siècle popular music; one can best arrive at an appreciation of his muse by tracing a line from Chabrier to Picabia by way of the Chat Noir and a host of lesser luminaries of the caliber of Dynam-Victor Fumet, Alphonse Allais, and Vincent Hyspa.

Clearly Satie was never a part of, nor chose to become a part of, the musical Establishment. "Forced, nervous laughter takes place," Cage has noted, "when someone is trying to impress somebody for purposes of getting somewhere."[52] Satie was singularly free of such self-interest and one must conclude with Cage that the Master of Arcueil was free to laugh or weep as he chose. "He knew in his loneliness and in his courage," the

American wrote, "where his center was: in himself and in his nature of loving music."[53]

For those utterly encapsulated by the gods of haute culture, Satie remains a source of puzzlement, mild amusement, or exasperation. To such critics the irreverent, clownish posture of Satie is anathema, and if a few of them happen to be sympathetic toward him, they are forced inevitably into the role of apologist. For Satie the sportive taste for action, the sheer joy of dynamism, of confrontation and rejection, was his very lifeblood. It is in one sense a nihilistic impulse, but the passion for destruction is also a creative passion, an uncompromising acceptance of no stage of experience as final. The creative act itself, elevated to the status of a first principle, becomes pervasive and omnipotent when life is approached in a celebratory manner. Art, in this light, becomes nothing more nor less than a ritualistic and symbolic expression of the fullness of life here and now, which we are invited to embrace, in a spirit of humility and submission.

In *Clea,* the final volume of his *Alexandria Quartet,* Lawrence Durrell has the ironic Pursewarden say: "Like all young men I set out to be a genius, but mercifully laughter intervened." It is a lovely aphorism which, at first blush, would appear to be a fitting epitaph for the Master of Arcueil, until we realize that the laughter was there from the beginning and the genius, unsummoned, appeared of its own accord. So we are left with the more prosaic testimonials of two former disciples, Roland-Manuel and Louis Durey. Reminiscing shortly before the Satie memorial concert at Arcueil in June 1929, Roland-Manuel, putting aside the disillusionment he had felt in later years, declared:

. . . I admired him, and still admire him deeply, because he was one of those rare spirits whom no magic can blind, and who immediately see in a new aesthetic its latent weakness, the germ of decay whose presence imitators do not suspect, but which sooner or later will assert itself. Satie was against Wagner in 1885, against Debussy in 1905, against Ravel during the war, against the "Six" just before his death. This is altogether admirable.[54]

And the retiring Durey, least renowned of *Les Six* who early on severed his ties with the group and disappeared to the south of France, nonetheless maintained a touching loyalty to his old mentor. "We should cherish an affectionate sympathy for Erik Satie," he wrote in 1930, "mystic or

Bohemian, for what he brought that was new to music: a clear judgment, a horror of hackneyed ways, love of discovery and of risk, the relief of good humor and systematic rejection of all that was heavy and tiresome. It was," Durey concluded with Gallic elegance, "a stone of small dimensions which was his contribution to the edifice, but one of very pure whiteness and brilliance."[55]

Notes and References

PREFACE

All translations are the author's unless otherwise indicated.

1. Or perhaps Schoenberg and Satie are not so dissimilar. In the early 1900s cabaret shows in the Parisian style became very popular in Germany, and, in 1901, while Satie was eking out a living as a pianist / composer / arranger in various Montmartre establishments, Schoenberg was performing a similar service as musical director and resident composer for a Berlin cabaret called the Überbrettl. Despite the Austrian's far loftier artistic aims—he was then working on his monumental *Gurrelieder*—he turned out a series of popular cabaret songs for his employer.

2. "Pas de casernes," *Le Coq*, no. 2 (June 1920); Nigel Wilkins, ed. and trans., *The Writings of Erik Satie* (London: Eulenburg, 1980), 84.

3. Rollo Myers, "The Strange Case of Erik Satie," *Musical Times* 86 (1945):201.

4. Rosette Renshaw, "Erik Satie (1866–1925)," *La Nouvelle revue canadienne* 1 (1951):77.

5. Peter Dickinson, "Erik Satie (1866–1925)," *Music Review* 28 (1967):146.

6. The bulk of Satie's published writings appeared originally in a variety of obscure "little reviews" between 1912 and 1924, and although portions of his literary output have been reprinted in a number of publications over the past thirty years, the first complete scholarly edition of Satie's writings (published and unpublished) is that of Ornella Volta, ed., *Erik Satie: Écrits* (Paris: Éditions Champ Libre, 1977; rev. ed. 1981), the first of a planned three volumes that eventually will include the composer's correspondence and the texts and poems that accompany many of his musical scores.

Although restricted primarily to the published material, Nigel Wilkins's 1980 edition of Satie's writings, cited above, is of inestimable value to the English reader, bringing together in excellent translation (much of it for the first time) the best of Satie's subtle and idiomatic prose. In addition, Wilkins has published extensive selections from Satie's correspondence; see "The Writings of Erik Satie: Miscellaneous Fragments," *Music and Letters* 56 (1975):288–307; "Erik Satie's Letters to Milhaud and Others," *Musical Quarterly* 66 (1980):404–28; and "Erik Satie's Letters," *Canadian University Music Review*, no. 2 (1981):207–27.

7. Lothar Klein, "Twentieth Century Analysis: Essays in Miniature," *Music Educators Journal* 53 (1966):25–26.

CHAPTER 1

1. Roger Shattuck, *The Banquet Years,* rev. ed. (New York: Vintage Books, 1968), 4.

2. Philippe Jullian, *Dreamers of Decadence: Symbolist Painters of the 1890s,* trans. Robert Baldick (New York: Praeger Publishers, 1971), 66.

3. Romain Rolland, *Musicians of To-Day,* trans. Mary Blaiklock (London: Kegan Paul, Trench, Trubner, 1915), 253.

4. Frederick Brown, *An Impersonation of Angels: A Biography of Jean Cocteau* (New York: Viking Press, 1968), 8.

5. It is not known precisely when the baptismal spelling was changed from "Eric" to "Erik," although it should be noted that the Paris Conservatoire register for the year 1879 records the future composer as "Erik Satie." Moreover, his first extant composition, the tiny *Allegro* of 1884, is signed "Erik Satie."

6. George Auriol, "Erik Satie: The Velvet Gentleman," *La Revue musicale* 5 (1924):209.

7. Quoted in Pierre-Daniel Templier, *Erik Satie,* trans. Elena L. French and David S. French (Cambridge, Mass.: MIT Press, 1969), 7–8.

8. "L'Origine d'instruction," *Les Feuilles libres,* no. 27 (June / July 1922):204; Wilkins, ed. and trans., *The Writings of Erik Satie,* 95.

9. Shattuck, *The Banquet Years,* 116–17.

10. Joanna Richardson, *The Bohemians: La Vie de Bohème in Paris 1830–1914* (London: Macmillan, 1969), 141.

11. Templier, *Erik Satie,* 25.

12. Constant Lambert, *Music Ho! A Study of Music in Decline,* 3d ed. (London: Faber & Faber, 1966), 172.

13. Quoted in Francis Poulenc, *Emmanuel Chabrier,* trans. Cynthia Jolly (London: Dennis Dobson, 1981), 54.

14. Two ballads, "L'Île heureuse" and "Toutes les fleurs," complete the set.

15. Rollo Myers, *Emmanuel Chabrier and His Circle* (London: J. M. Dent & Sons, 1969), 91–92.

16. Émile Vuillermoz, *Gabriel Fauré,* trans. Kenneth Schapin (Philadelphia: Chilton, 1969), 68–69.

17. "Cahiers d'un mammifère," *L'Esprit nouveau,* no. 7 (April 1921):833; Wilkins, ed. and trans., *The Writings of Erik Satie,* 68.

18. Quoted in Joseph Desaymard, *Emmanuel Chabrier d'après ses lettres* (Paris: Fernand Roches, 1934), 118.

CHAPTER 2

1. Satie's unusual manner of dating the manuscript—"Honfleur le 9 7bre 84"—has misled some sources into dating the sketch 9 July 1884; clearly "7bre" is an abbreviated version of "sept'bre."

2. The rhythmic accents are such that the piece would have been better barred in simple duple meter (6 + 6 + 6).

3. A full-color reproduction of the original is reproduced in Ornella Volta, *L'Ymagier d'Erik Satie* (Paris: Éditions Van de Velde, 1979), 101.

4. See Marius Richard, "Une controverse musicale: Claude Debussy et Erik Satie," *La Liberté*, 13 January 1932, 2.

5. The Société Lyre et Palette was founded in 1914 by the expatriot Swiss artist Émile Lejeune to raise money for his indigent artistic friends. During the war years Lejeune's large studio in Montparnasse at no. 6, rue Huyghens became an important center of experimental artistic activity. Here fashionable Parisians could witness exhibitions of paintings by Picasso and other rising stars, poetry readings by Cocteau, Apollinaire, Blaise Cendrars, and Max Jacob, and musical performances of works by Satie and those of his young disciples soon to be known as *Les Six*.

6. Roland-Manuel, *Erik Satie* (Paris, 1916), 3.

7. Henri Collet, "Erik Satie," *L'Esprit nouveau* 2 (1916):149.

8. See W. Wright Roberts, "The Problem of Satie," *Music and Letters* 4 (1923):314.

9. "Suddenly the heavens opened and the damned fell / Hurtling and colliding in a gigantic whirlwind; / And when they were alone in the sunless night, / They discovered they were completely black. Then they blasphemed." ("Damnation")

10. Alfred Cortot, "Le Cas Erik Satie," *La Revue musicale* 19 (1938):253.

11. Quoted in Paul Collaer, *A History of Modern Music,* trans. Salley Abeles (Cleveland: World Publishing, 1961), 204.

12. Abraham Skulsky, "Erik Satie," *Musical America* 70 (15 November 1950):5.

13. In 1983 Angel Records reported that the first album of pianist Aldo Ciccolini's six-record survey of the piano music of Satie—the volume containing the popular *Gymnopédies* and *Gnossiennes*—was the sixth best-selling recording in their classical catalog, and that, altogether, Ciccolini's Satie recordings have sold well over a quarter of a million copies, making Satie the best-selling twentieth-century composer on Angel Records.

14. Lillian B. Lawler, *The Dance in Ancient Greece* (London: Adam & Charles Black, 1964), 108.

15. See Grete Wehmeyer, *Erik Satie* (Regensburg: Gustav Bosse Verlag, 1974), 26.

16. "Obliquely piercing the darkness a blazing torrent / was flowing in waves of gold over the polished tiles, / Where amber specks reflecting in the fire, / Mingled their sarabande with the gymnopedia."

17. See Lambert, *Music Ho! A Study of Music in Decline,* 119.

18. Quoted in Templier, *Erik Satie,* 12.

19. Ibid.

20. See Jean Roy, "Erik Satie," in *Musique française* ("Présences contemporaines") (Paris: Nouvelles Éditions Debresse, 1962), 32. The American critic

Carl Van Vechten has suggested another influence on the *Gnossiennes,* the Greek chorus at Saint-Julien-le-Pauvre, where Satie is known to have spent many hours listening to the organ and the chanting of the priests. (See Carl Van Vechten, *Interpreters and Interpretations* [New York: Knopf, 1917], 262.)

21. On the back of page two of the autograph manuscript of the fifth *Gnossienne* appears a four-bar sketch for a *Chanson hongroise.* Its date of composition is probably the same as that of the fifth *Gnossienne,* that is, July 1889. A transcription of the sketch is printed in Wehmeyer, *Erik Satie,* 32. In view of the general style of the *Chanson hongroise* it would appear that Satie made little distinction between the Hungarian and the Romanian folk music he undoubtedly heard at the 1889 Exposition.

CHAPTER 3

1. Guy de Maupassant, "The Mask," in Roger Colet, trans., *Selected Short Stories* (Harmondsworth, Middlesex: Penguin Books, 1971), 345.

2. See Jean Barreyre, *La Chanson française depuis le second empire* (Paris: Flammes et Fumées, 1963), 3.

3. Raymond Rudorff, *The* Belle Epoque: *Paris in the Nineties* (New York: Saturday Review Press, 1973), 76–77.

4. "I'm writin' to you from prison, / My poor Polyte, / I don't know who dragged me here yesterday, / For a check-up; / It's one of those diseases you can't see / Right away, / So today they threw me in the jug, / At Saint-Lazare! / But while I'm stuck in here, my sweetie, / What're you gonna do? / I can't send you a damn thing, / It's really rotten, / Everybody here's totally busted, / Money's really scarce; / Takes three months just to scrape up a few coins, / At Saint-Lazare! / I hate to see you like this, flat broke, / It worries me! . . . / You might pull a dirty job, / And that really frightens me. / You're too proud to bum / A few cigar butts, / While I'm stuck in here, / At Saint-Lazare! / Go and find 'la grand'Nana', / Tell her that I beg her / To cough up some dough for me, which I'll pay back / When I get out. / But I sure don't want you foolin' around with her, / While I'm languishin' in here / Takin' my medecines, / At Saint-Lazare! / And most of all, my darlin', don't drink too much, / You know what booze does to you, / When you get a bit tipsy / You screw up and get into trouble; / If you're picked up, some night, / In a brawl, / There'll be nobody to come and see me / At Saint-Lazare! / I close my letter with an embrace, / Farewell, my man, / Even though you aren't a very affectionate sort, / Ah! I adore you / And worship you like I used to worship the good Lord, as I did my daddy, / When I was a little girl, / And would go to communion, / At Saint'-Marguerite."

For revealing eyewitness accounts of Bruant performances see W. C. Morrow, *Bohemian Paris of To-Day* (London: Chatto & Windus, 1899), 285–95; and Arthur Symons, "A Visit to Aristide Bruant: 1892," in *Parisian Nights* (London: The Beaumont Press, 1926), 10–13.

5. Symons, "At the 'Chat Noir': 1892," in *Parisian Nights,* 21.

6. J. P. Contamine de Latour, "Erik Satie intime: Souvenirs de jeunesse," *Comoedia,* 3 August 1925, 2. Even though the composition of the *Gymnopédies* was still several months off, Satie, Contamine de Latour reports, had already dreamed up the unusual title, taking great pleasure in the strangeness of the word.

7. Ibid.

8. Lawrence & Elisabeth Hanson, *Verlaine: Prince of Poets* (London: Chatto & Windus, 1958), 79. Sivry, it should be noted, avoided mention of his "aristocratic" origins for good reason, for it seems that the family's elevated social standing was purely a figment of his snobbish mother's imagination. (See Marcel Dietschy, "The Family and Childhood of Debussy, *Musical Quarterly* 46 [1960]:312.)

9. See Stanislas Fumet, "Eironeia," in *La Poésie à travers les arts* (Paris: Alsatia, 1954), 128–29; this chapter originally appeared in the special Satie number of *La Revue musicale* 214 (1952):19–22.

10. Ibid., 130.

11. Laurence Davies, *César Franck and his Circle* (London: Barrie & Jenkins, 1970), 271.

12. Fumet, "Eironeia," 130.

13. The precise date of compositon of *Les Enlisements d'en haut* is open to question. Although the piano score in the Bibliothèque Nationale (B.N., Mus., Vm^{12} 10401) carries the date 1897, this may indicate not the year of composition but more likely the date of publication or the date of acquisition by the library, since that date is stamped in ink on the title page of the publication and therefore would appear to have been added later. The problem is further compounded, however, by the critic José Bruyr, who in a 1946 newspaper article on Fumet dates the work 1889, thus making it posterior to the *Sarabandes* and *Gymnopédies* and contemporaneous with the fifth *Gnossienne.* Nonetheless, Bruyr also makes the claim that Fumet was a precursor of Satie, a statement that may well have been influenced by the editor of his paper, Stanislas Fumet. (See José Bruyr, "Le Compositeur le moins souvent joué," *Temps Présent,* 25 October 1946, 5.)

14. Stanislas Fumet, "Le Musicien mal entendu," in *La Poésie à travers les arts,* 138. This essay, written in collaboration with Raphaël Fumet, dates from 1949.

15. Davies, *César Franck,* 274–75.

16. Fred E. Goldbeck, "Fumet, Dynam-Victor," in *Grove's Dictionary of Music and Musicians,* 5th ed., vol. 3, Eric Blom, ed. (London: Macmillan, 1954), 524.

17. Quoted in James Harding, *Sacha Guitry: The Last Boulevardier* (London: Methuen, 1968), 40.

18. Shattuck, *The Banquet Years*, 22.

19. Harding, *Sacha Guitry*, 39.

20. Full-color reproductions of Allais's seven submissions to the Expositions des Arts Incohérents—the remaining four canvases are, respectively, blue, green, yellow, and red—as well as the complete score of the *Funeral March* are printed in Alphonse Allais, *Oeuvres posthumes*, vol. 2, François Caradec and Pascal Pia, eds. (Paris: La Table Ronde, 1966), 376–81.

21. See "L'Intelligence et la musicalité chez les animaux" ("Mémoires d'un amnésique"), *Revue musicale S.I.M.* 10 (Fcburary 1914):69; Nigel Wilkins, ed. and trans., *The Writings of Erik Satie* (London: Eulenburg, 1980), 61; see also "La Musique & les animaux," in Ornella Volta, ed., *Erik Satie: Écrits*, rev. ed. (Paris: Éditions Champ Libre, 1981), 73–77.

22. See "Ce que je suis" ("Mémoires d'un amnésique"), *Revue musicale S.I.M.* 8 (April 1912):69; Wilkins, ed. and trans., *The Writings of Erik Satie*, 58.

23. Alphonse Allais, "The Imprudential Assurance Company," in Miles Kington, trans., *The World of Alphonse Allais* (London: Chatto & Windus, 1976), 55–56.

24. Allais, "Lighthouses," in *World of Alphonse Allais*, 31.

25. Allais, "Personal Column," in *World of Alphonse Allais*, 132–33.

26. "Éloge des critiques," *Action: Cahiers de philosophie et d'art*, no. 8 (August 1921):8–9; Wilkins, ed. and trans., *The Writings of Erik Satie*, 86.

27. See Anatole Jakovsky, *Alphonse Allais: "Le Tueur à gags"* (Paris: Les Quatres Jeudis, 1955), 162.

28. Colette, *My Apprenticeships*, trans. Helen Beauclerk (London: Secker & Warburg, 1957), 39–40.

29. Sisley Huddleston, *Bohemian Literary and Social Life in Paris* (London: George G. Harrap, 1928), 59.

CHAPTER 4

1. Quoted in Jullian, *Dreamers of Decadence: Symbolist Painters of the 1890s*, 260.

2. Alfred Edward Carter, *The Idea of Decadence in French Literature, 1830–1900* (Toronto: University of Toronto Press, 1958), 22.

3. Ibid., 104.

4. George Ross Ridge, *The Hero in French Decadent Literature* (Athens: University of Georgia Press, 1961), 81–82.

5. Quoted in Édouard Bertholet, *La Pensée et les secrets du Sâr Joséphin*

Péladan, Vol. 1: *Péladan Grand Maître de l'Ordre de la Rose-Croix du Temple et du Graal, son oeuvre occulte, philosophique et spiritualiste* (Lausanne: Éditions Rosicruciennes, 1952), 13.

6. See Rudorff, *The* Belle Epoque: *Paris in the Nineties,* 187–88; see also Robert Pincus-Witten, *Occult Symbolism in France: Joséphin Péladan and the Salons de la Rose-Croix* (New York & London: Garland Publishing, 1976), 78–84 passim.

7. Quoted in Jullian, *Dreamers of Decadence,* 71.

8. Rudhyar D. Chennevière, "Erik Satie and the Music of Irony," *Musical Quarterly* 5 (1919):470–71.

9. Quoted in Pincus-Witten, *Occult Symbolism in France,* 211.

10. This interesting exception can be explained by the fact that the French painter Nicolas Poussin (1594–1665) would appear to be a figure of some importance in the history of Rosicrucianism. He seems to have been privy to an ancient "underground stream" of highly explosive knowledge possibly relating to the circumstances surrounding the death of Jesus Christ. The key document is his painting *The Shepherds of Arcadia* (ca. 1640–42), a depiction of four shepherds standing and kneeling around a tomb set in a mountainous landscape until recently thought to be wholly imaginary but now assumed to be an actual site near the village of Rennes-le-Château in southeastern France. The tomb's inscription, ET IN ARCADIA EGO ("And in Arcadia I"), is thought to be an anagram of I TEGO ARCANA DEI ("Begone! I conceal the secrets of God"). (See Michael Baigent, Richard Leigh, and Henry Lincoln, *The Holy Blood and the Holy Grail* [London: Jonathan Cape, 1982], 33–40, 143–44, 187–90 passim.)

11. See Pincus-Witten, *Occult Symbolism in France,* 215.

12. It seems highly likely that Bihn Grallon was in reality Erik Satie. Péladan's novel *Le Panthée,* the tenth installment of *La Décadence latine,* appeared in 1892, the year of the first Rosicrucian Salon, with a frontispiece by the Belgian Symbolist painter Fernand Khnopff and a reproduction of a musical "Leitmotif du Panthée" by Satie. Interestingly, the central character of the novel is an impoverished composer called Bihn. Roy Howat has speculated that the character Bihn may be a composite of Satie and Debussy, although Satie would seem the more likely candidate given his obvious state of poverty at the time, especially as compared to Debussy who at no time in his life could be said to have been truly impoverished. Moreover, we note that the program for Péladan's first Rosicrucian Salon refers to Bihn Grallon as "our chapelmaster." (See Roy Howat, *Debussy in Proportion: A Musical Analysis* [Cambridge: Cambridge University Press, 1983], 170–71.) On the strength of this circumstantial evidence it seems reasonable to conclude also that the *Marche antique pour la Rose-Croix* is actually the untitled, conspicuously marchlike work dating from early 1891 that Robert Caby called the *Première pensée Rose + Croix.*

13. Wilfrid H. Mellers, "Erik Satie and the 'Problem' of Contemporary Music," *Music and Letters* 23 (1942):212.

14. See Leonard B. Meyer, *Music, the Arts, and Ideas: Patterns and Pre-*

dictions in Twentieth-Century Culture (Chicago: University of Chicago Press, 1967), 72.

15. "Swaddling bands of all sons / Mantle of all fathers / Cloth stained with the blood of a people / Hail to the Flag! / Your staff is the mainmast of the ship of state / Your staff is the pillar that supports the people / If you falter, if you fall, disgraced, the people die / Hail to the Flag! / Sail swollen by all breasts / Proud standard / Spread wing of throbbing multitudes / You carry in your flight the destiny of a race! / Noble symbol / Collective ideal / Hail to the Flag!"

16. Contamine de Latour, *Comoedia,* 3 August 1925, 2.

17. See Howat, *Debussy in Proportion,* 33–34.

18. On the opening night of the Auberge du Clou shadow theater in 1892, two plays were performed, *La Styliste* by Henri de Weindel, and *Un Noël* by Vincent Hyspa, both with scenery by Miguel Utrillo and the latter with music by Satie. No trace of either production remains. It seems probable, as Steven Whiting has suggested, that an original score for *Un Noël* never existed, that Satie simply recycled one of his recently completed works for the occasion, such as the *Gnossiennes.* (See Steven M. Whiting, "Erik Satie and Parisian Musical Entertainment, 1888 to 1909" [Master's thesis, University of Illinois, 1984], 68.)

19. See Robert Orledge, *Debussy and the Theatre* (Cambridge: Cambridge University Press, 1982), 124, 355 n.39.

20. This inscription appears on a copy of Debussy's *Cinq Poèmes de Baudelaire* (1887–89) presented by the composer to Satie on 27 October 1892.

21. Patrick Gowers, "Satie's Rose-Croix Music (1891–1895)," *Proceedings of the Royal Musical Association* 92 (1965 / 66):10.

22. ["Open Letter to the Editor of *Gil Blas*"], *Gil Blas,* 16 August 1892, 3; Nigel Wilkins, ed. and trans., *The Writings of Erik Satie* (London: Eulenburg, 1980), 150.

23. This document, in its original black and red, is reproduced in Volta, *L'Ymagier d'Erik Satie,* 98.

24. See Templier, *Erik Satie,* Plate 36; and Volta, ed., *Erik Satie: Écrits,* 179; see also the Glossary in Volta, *Erik Satie: Écrits,* 331, for definitions of Satie's archaic ecclesiastical terminology.

25. "Épître de Erik Satie—Première aux Artistes catholiques et à tous les Chrétiens," *Le Coeur* 1, nos. 6 & 7 (September / October 1893), 11; Wilkins, ed. and trans., *The Writings of Erik Satie,* 36.

26. "Commune qui mundi nefas," in Wilkins, ed. and trans., *The Writings of Erik Satie,* 39.

27. Wilson Lyle, "Erik Satie and Rosicrucianism," *Music Review* 42 (1981):242.

28. "Intende votis supplicum," in Wilkins, ed. and trans., *The Writings of Erik Satie,* 40–41.

29. Colette, *My Apprenticeships,* 74.

30. Ibid., 76.

31. Ibid., 77.

32. "Suprématiales," *Cartulaire de l'Église Métropolitaine d'Art de Jésus Conducteur,* no. 1—63 (May 1895), 1; Wilkins, ed. and trans., *The Writings of Erik Satie,* 44.

33. Ibid.

34. Quoted in Nigel Wilkins, "Erik Satie's Letters," *Canadian University Music Review,* no. 2 (1981):209.

35. ["Open Letter to Camille Saint-Saëns"], *Le Ménestrel,* 10 June 1894, 183; Wilkins, ed. and trans., *The Writings of Erik Satie,* 151.

36. Victor-Émile Michelet, *Les Compagnons de la hiérophanie: Souvenirs du mouvement hermétiste à la fin du XIXe siècle* (Paris: Dorbon-Aîné, 1937), 76.

37. "Mes trois candidatures" ("Mémoires d'un amnésique"), *Revue musicale S.I.M.* 8 (November 1912):70; Wilkins, ed. and trans., *The Writings of Erik Satie,* 59.

38. Quoted in John Storm, *The Valadon Drama: The Life of Suzanne Valadon* (New York: E. P. Dutton, 1958), 104.

39. Ibid., 105.

40. Ibid.

41. Quoted in Wilkins, "Erik Satie's Letters," 207–8.

42. Quoted in Storm, *The Valadon Drama,* 107.

43. See Contamine de Latour, "Erik Satie intime," *Comoedia,* 6 August 1925, 2.

44. Both these documents are printed, in part in facsimile and in whole in translation, in Wilkins, ed. and trans., *The Writings of Erik Satie,* 130–35.

45. James Harding, *Erik Satie* (London: Secker & Warburg, 1975), 57–58.

46. Contamine de Latour, *Comoedia,* 3 August 1925, 2.

47. Orledge, *Debussy and the Theatre,* 47.

48. See Gavin Bryars, "'Vexations' and its Performers," *Contact: A Journal of Contemporary Music,* no. 26 (Spring 1983):15–16.

49. Certainly this is the view of two of Satie's most intimate friends and disciples. Henri Sauguet considered "Vexations" a joke and claimed that Satie himself did not take it seriously, while Darius Milhaud felt that the composer would not have approved of a literal interpretation of his score, that his essential *pudeur,* or modesty, would not have allowed it. (See John Cage, Roger Shattuck, and Alan Gillmor, "Erik Satie: A Conversation," *Contact: A Journal of Contemporary Music,* no. 25 [Autumn 1982]:24.)

50. See Bryars, "'Vexations' and its Performers," 12.

51. The opening of the "Kyrie," notated in halved note values, appears in one of Satie's notebooks (ca. 1895) under the title *Grande Messe de l'Église Métropolitaine d'Art.* It is reproduced in facsimile in Wilkins, ed. and trans., *The Writings of Erik Satie,* 43.

52. Conrad Satie, "Erik Satie," *Le Coeur* 2, no. 10 (June 1895):2.

53. Jacques Maritain and Jean Cocteau, *Art and Faith: Letters between*

Jacques Maritain and Jean Cocteau, trans. John Coleman (New York: The Philosophical Library, 1948), 23.

54. Ibid., 85.

55. Francis Jourdain, *Né en 76* (Paris: Les Éditions du Pavillon, 1951), 244.

CHAPTER 5

1. Steven M. Whiting, "Erik Satie and Parisian Musical Entertainment, 1888 to 1909" (Master's thesis, University of Illinois, 1984) is a thorough and detailed study of the period. Whiting's is the first comprehensive examination of the Houghton Library (Harvard University) collection of Satie manuscripts. After Satie's death in 1925, Darius Milhaud came into possession of a large quantity of the composer's sketches and music notebooks. Most of this material was deposited in the Bibliothèque Nationale in 1939, the remainder brought to the United States by Milhaud the following year. Eventually the bulk of Milhaud's Satie material was sold to Mrs. Robert Woods Bliss, philanthropist and art patroness, whose estate, Dumbarton Oaks, was left in 1940 to Harvard University, becoming the Dumbarton Oaks Research Library. After the death of Mrs. Bliss in 1969, the Satie collection was transferred from Washington, D.C., to Cambridge, Mass., and—in July 1973—deposited in Harvard's Houghton Library. The collection is particularly rich in material dating from the period ca. 1892–ca. 1906.

2. An 1892 Grass-Mick sketch of Satie reading a newspaper on the terrace of the Auberge du Clou is reproduced in Mariel Oberthur, *Cafés and Cabarets of Montmartre,* trans. Sheila Azoulai (Layton, Utah: Gibbs M. Smith, 1984), 70. The Grass-Mick sketch reproduced in Volta, *L'Ymagier d'Erik Satie,* 8–9, commemorates the October morning in 1897 when Satie and Henry Pacory helped Grass-Mick transport his wordly possessions from his family home to new lodgings at no. 67, rue Lepic in Montmartre.

3. Augustin Grass-Mick, "Le Souvenir d'Erik Satie," *Arts: Beaux-Arts, Littérature, Spectacles,* 4 August 1950, 1, 7.

4. Huddleston, *Bohemian Literary and Social Life in Paris,* 68.

5. "Trois lettres d'Erik Satie à Claude Debussy (1903)," *Revue de musicologie* 48 (1962):74; reprinted in part in translation in Nigel Wilkins, "Erik Satie's Letters," *Canadian University Music Review,* no. 2 (1981):208.

6. Wilkins, "Erik Satie's Letters," 208–9.

7. Quoted in Templier, *Erik Satie,* 22.

8. Ibid., 25.

9. The French pianist Maurice Dumesnil, who was known to Satie, seems to be alone in stating that the composer may at this time have supplemented his meager income by playing the organ in various small suburban churches. (See

"Erik Satie: The Mischievous Man of French Music," *Etude* 60 [December 1942]:816.)

10. In 1900, Dominique Bonnaud revived several of the Chat Noir shadow plays at a cabaret called the Quat-z-Arts. Shortly afterwards he moved to the Boîte à Fursy, then, in 1904, to his own Lune Rousse in the boulevard de Clichy, where he again directed a shadow theater, which continued on the premises even after the Lune Rousse relocated and was replaced by a cabaret known as the Chaumière. There is at least circumstantial evidence that Satie may have performed as an accompanist at some or all of these establishments. (See, for example, Virgil Thomson, "In the Theater," *Modern Music* 14[1937]:102; and Whiting, "Erik Satie and Parisian Musical Entertainment," 91–92, 104–6; see also Denis Bordat and Francis Boucrat, *Les Théâtres d'ombres: Histoire et techniques* [Paris: L'Arche, 1956], 168–69.)

11. See Théophile Briant, "Erik Satie et Vincent Hyspa," *Le Goéland,* 22 April 1937, 2. Briant states that Satie and Hyspa met when they were both twenty-one years of age (in 1887), although he places the meeting at the Auberge du Clou.

12. Adrien Vély, "Spectacles Divers—Soirée Parisienne—Au Tréteau de Tabarin," *Le Gaulois,* 3 October 1898, 3.

13. These figures were compiled by Whiting ("Erik Satie and Parisian Musical Entertainment," 198–202) who has argued that those songs appearing in the notebooks in several draft stages are probably original compositions whereas those appearing only as fair copies are probably not. (Moreover, Whiting has traced at least twenty songs in this latter category to printed song collections—e.g., Hyspa's *Chansons d'humour* [1903]—where they are attributed to other sources.) Considering that additional cabaret song sketches can be found in the large collections of Satie manuscripts held by the Bibliothèque Nationale and the Bibliothèque du Conservatoire, it is clear that the handful of published items represents only a fraction of the "popular" material, indicating that Satie's involvement—as pianist *and* composer—with the world of Parisian light entertainment was much more extensive than hitherto generally recognized.

14. Excerpts from four unpublished cabaret songs attributed to Satie, two of them—"Imperial-Oxford" (ca. 1900–5) and "Allons-y Chochotte" (ca. 1905–6)—in ragtime rhythm, are printed in Wilkins, ed. and trans., *The Writings of Erik Satie,* 152–55. The incipits of a large number of other songs—waltzes, two-steps, cakewalks—from the Houghton manuscripts are transcribed in Whiting, "Erik Satie and Parisian Musical Entertainment," Appendix 3, 223–65.

15. See Templier, *Erik Satie,* Plate 65.

16. Quoted in Wilkins, "Erik Satie's Letters," 211; a more complete version of this letter—which dates from about 1900—is quoted in Templier, *Erik Satie,* 24–25. There is in this same letter more than a hint of envy as Satie goes on to note that his brother's career, luckily for him, is unfolding in a quite different manner from his own. "You shall have a horse and a big carriage, open in the

summer, closed in the winter. And you shall go to and fro just like the fortunate people." Conrad, whom Satie for his own inscrutable reasons often referred to as "Monsieur Pouillot" ("Mr. Willow-Warbler"), was by this time gaining recognition in the field of chemistry and in 1904 would coauthor (with Paul Jeancard) a short treatise on the chemistry of perfumes.

17. Quoted in Templier, *Erik Satie*, 24.

18. See Louis Schneider, "Le 'Gaulois' au théâtre—Les Premières," *Le Gaulois*, 6 June 1926, 5.

19. H. H. [Horace Horsnell], "The Russian Ballet—'Parade' and 'Jack in the Box,'" *Observer*, 11 July 1926, 13.

20. F. T. [Francis Toye], "A Satie Festival: Music Without Merit, but Dancing Excellent," *Morning Post*, 6 July 1926, 7.

21. Anatole France, "Hrotswitha aux Marionnettes," in *La Vie littéraire* (troisième série), *Oeuvres complètes*, vol. 15, no. 2, Jacques Suffel, ed. (Paris: Calmann-Lévy, 1968), 28.

22. It would appear that the legend of Geneviève de Brabant may be based on the history of Marie de Brabant, wife of Louis II, Duke of Bavaria and Palatine of the Rhine, who was accused—falsely it seems—by her husband of infidelity, tried and found guilty, and, in 1256, beheaded.

23. Of the two recorded performances of *Geneviève de Brabant* (Musicdisc 30 RC 676 and Arabesque 8053-L), the latter employs a male voice to narrate the *Canticle* after the Prelude, as well as, in the appropriate places, the stage directions printed in the piano / vocal score (Universal-Edition, no. 9386 [1930]). Although there is no evidence that Satie and Contamine de Latour intended this, the effect is charming, reinforcing the fabulous element of the old tale and the theatrical ambience of the puppet stage.

24. James Harding, *Erik Satie* (London: Secker & Warburg, 1975), 85.

25. See Henry Malherbe, "Chronique Musicale," *Le Temps*, 19 May 1926, 3.

26. This short piece, dated 5 August 1900 and signed with the "Parcener's" double cross, is reproduced in facsimile in Volta, *L'Ymagier d'Erik Satie*, 40.

27. See Edward Lockspeiser, *Debussy: His Life and Mind*, vol. 1 (London: Cassell, 1962–65), 146–47.

28. See "Trois lettres d'Erik Satie à Claude Debussy (1903)," 73; reprinted in part in translation in Wilkins, "Erik Satie's Letters," 214. The title is a characteristic bit of Satiean wordplay, for "poire" was current Parisian slang for "head" in the sense of "stupid head" or "fool." It is tempting to speculate that the title may at the same time have been a conscious or unconscious recollection of the virulently antibourgeois and conspicuously pear-shaped Père Ubu from Jarry's notorious 1896 play.

29. See Michel D. Calvocoressi, "Erik Satie: A Few Recollections and Remarks," *Monthly Musical Record* 55 (January 1925):6.

30. Vladimir Golschmann, "Golschmann Remembers Erik Satie," *High Fidelity / Musical America* 22 (August 1972):MA–11.

31. See Patrick Gowers, "Erik Satie: His Studies, Notebooks and Critics," vol. 1 (Ph.D. diss., University of Cambridge, 1966), 118–46; see also Grete Wehmeyer, *Erik Satie* (Regensburg: Gustav Bosse Verlag, 1974), 166–67.

32. Satie may have intended two flutes, for in measures 7–9 (and at analogous places later in the piece) he added a second part to the flute line a third below. In measures 9–10 (and again at several other analogous places) he added a staff above the flute line to which he assigned the cadential measure of the oboe melody. It is not clear whether this was intended as an additional woodwind part (or parts) or, as is more likely the case, simply as a sketch intended for later insertion in the flute (or oboe) part. In any event, the notes on the added staff—as well as the second flute line—do end up in the piano duet version.

33. *Trois Morceaux en forme de poire,* autograph score (Archives de l'Opéra, Nouveau Fonds, Rés. 218), 30.

34. "Trois lettres d'Erik Satie à Claude Debussy (1903)," 73; Wilkins, "Erik Satie's Letters," 214.

35. Quoted in Templier, *Erik Satie,* 27.

36. Henri Büsser, *De Pelléas aux Indes Galantes* (Paris: Fayard, 1955), 49; quoted in Lockspeiser, *Debussy: His Life and Mind,* I:146.

37. René Peter, *Claude Debussy: Vues prises de son intimité* (Paris: Gallimard, 1931), 69–70; quoted in Michel D. Calvocoressi, "Concerning Erik Satie," *Musical Mirror and Fanfare* 1 (n.s.) (April 1933):208.

38. Quoted in Templier, *Erik Satie,* 32.

39. Albert Roussel, "À propos d'un récent festival," *Le Gaulois,* 12 June 1926, 3; quoted in Shattuck, *The Banquet Years,* 134.

40. Bibliothèque Nationale, Mus., Ms. 9651. It would appear, from the evidence of this notebook, that Satie enrolled in a formal course in orchestration the year following his graduation from the Schola Cantorum.

41. See Wilkins, "Erik Satie's Letters," 216.

42. See Golschmann, "Golschmann Remembers Erik Satie," MA–12. It would appear that Verley may have made some sort of arrangement to study with Satie before 1917 since the first of the *Pastels sonores,* "Cloches dans la vallée," published privately in 1916, is inscribed "to my master and friend Erik Satie."

43. Letter from Varèse to Milhaud, 22 April 1928 (Bibliothèque Nationale, Mus., Ms. 10.034).

44. Agence Musicale E. Demets (*Bulletin des Éditions Musicales,* December 1913, 42); quoted in Wilkins, ed. and trans., *The Writings of Erik Satie,* 79.

45. Quoted in Wilkins, "Erik Satie's Letters," 215.

CHAPTER 6

1. See "Notes sur les concerts: La S.M.I.," *Le Guide du concert* 2 (14 January 1911): 156–57. An excerpt from this program note is quoted in Templier, *Erik Satie*, 32–33.

2. Michel D. Calvocoressi, "Aux concerts," *Comoedia illustré* 3 (15 February 1911):305. Not all the critics, however, were as enamored of Satie's daring harmonies as Calvocoressi. Marcel Orban, reviewing Ravel's performances of the Satie pieces for *Le Courier musical,* quipped: "a great deal of harmony, and very little music." (Marcel Orban, "La Quinzaine: Société Musicale Indépendante," *Le Courrier musical* 14 [1 February 1911]:100.)

Whereas the direct musical influence of Satie on Debussy is tenuous and difficult to document, owing in large part to Debussy's conspicuous silence on the subject, Ravel freely acknowledged his indebtedness to the man he was pleased to call "a clumsy but talented explorer." (Quoted in Roland-Manuel, *Maurice Ravel*, trans. Cynthia Jolly [New York: Dover, 1972], 21.) In particular Ravel singled out his early *Ballade de la reine morte d'aimer* (ca. 1893), to which might be added the Verlaine song *Un grand sommeil noir* (1895), the early Mallarmé song *Sainte* (1896), and *Si morne!* (1898), a setting of a poem by the Belgian Symbolist Émile Verhaeren. All four of these early songs, composed around the time of Ravel's first meeting with Satie in Montmartre at the Nouvelle Athènes, are strongly reminiscent of the *Sarabandes* and the *Rose-Croix* works. Concerning a Satiean influence on the later works, it was Roland-Manuel who first referred to "Conversations of Beauty and the Beast" from *Mother Goose* (1908) as "that delightful fourth *Gymnopédie*" (Roland-Manuel, *Maurice Ravel*, 21), a kinship Ravel himself acknowledged when he inscribed a copy of the score "to Erik Satie, grandpapa of the *Conversations* and other works, with the affectionate compliments of a disciple." As for Satie himself, we can assume he was not exaggerating when he wrote to his brother concerning Ravel in January 1911: "He assures me—every time I meet him—that he owes me a great deal. . . ." (Quoted in Nigel Wilkins, "Erik Satie's Letters," *Canadian University Music Review,* no. 2 [1981]:212.) See also Maurice Ravel, "Contemporary Music," *Rice Institute Pamphlet* 15 (April 1928):131–45; and Arbie Orenstein, *Ravel: Man and Musician* (New York: Columbia University Press, 1975).

3. Quoted in Rollo H. Myers, *Erik Satie* (New York: Dover, 1968), 43. It is interesting to note that the first American performance of the Satie / Debussy *Gymnopédies* was given in Boston as early as 4 January 1905 at a concert of the Orchestral Club under the direction of Georges Longy.

4. See Jules Écorcheville, "Erik Satie," *Revue musicale S.I.M.* 7 (15 March 1911):29–40.

5. See Michel D. Calvocoressi, "M. Erik Satie," *Musica* 10 (April 1911):65–66.

6. See Michel D. Calvocoressi, "The Origin of To-Day's Musical Idiom," *Musical Times* 52 (1 December 1911):776–78.

7. Brown, *An Impersonation of Angels: A Biography of Jean Cocteau,* 123.

8. Quoted in Templier, *Erik Satie,* 34.

9. Quoted in Myers, *Erik Satie,* 43.

10. Quoted in François Lesure, ed., *Erik Satie: Catalogue des manuscrits dans la Bibliothèque Nationale* (Paris: Bibliothèque Nationale, Département de la Musique, 1966), 24.

11. Quoted in Wilkins, "Erik Satie's Letters," 217.

12. The Journal of Ricardo Viñes (14 May 1897). I am indebted to Professor Elaine Brody for information concerning Viñes's journal. Since the *Mass for the Poor* did not reach publication until 1929, Viñes must have seen the excerpts from the work printed in Jules Bois's *Le Coeur* in June 1895.

13. Bibliothèque Nationale (L.a. Satie (E.) 2 [B.N. Acq. 4481]).

14. Bibliothèque Nationale (L.a. Satie (E.) 8 [B.N. Acq. 4481]); Wilkins, "Erik Satie's Letters," 224.

15. Quoted in Wilkins, ed. and trans., *The Writings of Erik Satie,* 79.

16. Charles Koechlin, "Erik Satie," *La Revue musicale* 5 (1924):196.

17. Carl Van Vechten, *Interpreters and Interpretations* (New York: Knopf, 1917), 264. Such an approach has occasionally been put into practice, generally with unsatisfactory results. A 1970 recording of the *Embryons desséchés* in an orchestral version by Friedrich Cerha (Candide CE 31018) has a female voice reciting Satie's running commentary over the music. A more acceptable though still less than ideal solution has been to project slides of a score such as *Sports et divertissements* onto a large screen to coincide with the performance.

18. It is in fact quite possible that the influence went the other way. One of Debussy's most "Satiean" works is *La Boîte à joujoux,* a "ballet for children" intended originally for marionettes and completed near the end of 1913. Debussy's charming make-believe world of dancing dolls is a veritable compendium of familiar tunes—children's ditties, folk songs, military tattoos, popular operatic airs—some dozen tunes in all, among them several that found their way into Satie's music the very same year. Like Satie's piano suites, the score of *La Boîte à joujoux* carries a fairly continuous verbal commentary, printed over the appropriate music, outlining the action of the ballet. Moreover, Debussy's quotations bear the same musico-poetic relationship to the drama as Satie's to his fanciful programs, though with less of the latter's ironic detachment and delicious sense of the absurd. Although Debussy had discussed the scenario of the ballet with its author, André Hellé, as early as February 1913, he did not begin work on the score until the beginning of the summer, by which time Satie's *Descriptions automatiques*—the first of the suites to make liberal use of quoted material—had been completed and even performed at the Conservatoire by Ricardo Viñes. *La Boîte à joujoux,* its orchestration completed by André Caplet, had to wait until

December 1919 for its first public performance, although the piano score was published by Durand in 1913.

19. See Jules Jouy, *Les Chansons de l'année* (Paris: Bourbier et Lamoureux, 1888).

20. See, for example, Léon Xanrof, *Chansons sans-gêne* (Paris: Ondet, 1890).

21. See Vincent Hyspa, *Chansons d'humour* (Paris: Enoch, 1903).

22. *Nouveaux Larousse illustré: Dictionnaire universel encyclopédique,* Claude Augé, ed. (Paris: Libraire Larousse, 1898–1904). The more extensive *Grand Dictionnaire universel du XIXᵉ siècle,* Pierre Larousse, ed. (Paris, 1866–79) contains many of the same musical entries, but with fewer examples of printed music.

Almost all the songs Satie quotes in the 1913–14 piano pieces belong to the repertoire of French children's songs. Even such songs as "La casquette du père Bugeaud," "Le bon roi Dagobert," and "Malbrough s'en va-t-en guerre," which he borrowed, were firmly entrenched in the repertoire of children's songs by the end of the nineteenth century. Among other printed sources of this material that Satie may have consulted are several collections made in the 1880s by the composer and archivist Jean-Baptiste Weckerlin: *Chansons de France pour les petits Français* (Paris: Plon-Nourrit, 1884), *Chansons et rondes enfantines* (Paris: Garnier, 1885), *Nouvelles chansons et rondes enfantines* (Paris: Garnier, 1886), and *Chansons et rondes enfantines des provinces de la France* (Paris: Garnier, 1889), charmingly illustrated editions with piano accompaniments by the author. To these we might add a similar collection arranged by the composer / organist Charles-Marie Widor: *Vieilles chansons et rondes pour les petits enfants* (Paris: Plon-Nourrit, 1883). These collections alone contain every children's song Satie is known to have borrowed.

An immediate precedent for the wholesale quotation of children's songs in a series of piano pieces is *La Nursery,* five suites composed by Désiré-Émile Inghelbrecht and published between 1905 and 1911. Considering Inghelbrecht's close association with Debussy and his circle—he conducted the first concert performance of *Le Martyre de Saint-Sébastien* in 1912—it is probable that Satie was aware of *La Nursery,* each of whose thirty pieces is based on a children's song, among them several that later appear in his own piano works.

23. Ministère de la défense, *Instruction du 18 juin 1912 sur les batteries et sonneries (commune à toutes les armes)* (Paris: Charles Lavauzelle, 1958).

24. These are the historical facts. In his note to the score, however, Satie has the dreaming child, his head a jumble of historical facts, confuse time and geography by placing the defeat of the Cimbri at Mons-en-Puelle (now Mons-en-Pévèle), in reality a village in northern France near the Belgian border where, in 1304, the French under Philip the Fair recorded a decisive victory over the Flemings. This surrealistic transmogrification of history mirrors the actual process of subconscious dream activity wherein time becomes suspended in a phantasmagoria of shifting memory fragments. Here we can speculate that the memory of

Mons-en-Puelle was triggered by the dreamer's awareness of the fact that Marlborough's 1709 victory at Malplaquet took place not far to the east, about ten miles south of the Belgian city of Mons.

25. A color reproduction of *The Defeat of the Cimbri* can be found in Pierre Miquel, *Le Paysage français au XIXe siècle, 1824–1874: L'École de la nature*, vol. 2 (Maurs-la-Jolie: Éditions de la Martinelle, 1975), 169.

26. Given the consistency of Satie's practice in this matter, the tendency of some writers to identify "influences" where the musical connections are rather tenuous is highly suspect. See, for example, Léon Guichard, "À propos d'Erik Satie: Notules incohérentes," *Recherches et travaux (Université de Grenoble, Unité d'Enseignement et de Recherches des Lettres)*, Bulletin no. 7 (March 1973):63–80.

27. *Le Coq*, no. 1 (May 1920); Wilkins, ed. and trans., *The Writings of Erik Satie*, 84.

28. Wilfrid H. Mellers, "Erik Satie and the 'Problem' of Contemporary Music," *Music and Letters* 23 (1942):216.

29. René Chalupt, "Children's Music," *Chesterian* 1 (1919-20):45.

30. Paul Murray Kendall, *Louis XI* (New York: Norton, 1971), 29.

31. Myers, *Erik Satie*, 83.

32. There are five published verisons of *Sports et divertissements:* In 1923 Lucien Vogel brought out a deluxe (and now rare) limited edition of 900 copies in two versions: 1) nos. 1–225 include, with facsimiles of the music (black on red staves), all twenty of Martin's full-page copperplate engravings (colored by Jules Saudé), as well as small ink sketches decorating the title page of each piece; 2) the remaining 675 copies are identical except that they include only one-full-page colored drawing as a frontispiece: 3) the 1964 Salabert edition, which retains the music in facsimile (minus the original red staves) and the black-and-white half-title pages preceding the individual pieces but eliminates Martin's aquarelles and reduces the size (15⁷⁄₁₆ × 17⅛) of the original by approximately half; 4) the 1975 Salabert edition in regular notation with English translations of Satie's texts by Virgil Thomson, but minus Martin's illustrations; 5) the 1982 Dover reprint of (1) also in smaller format (8¹³⁄₁₆ × 11¹³⁄₁₆) with black-and-white reproductions (and one color reproduction on the front cover) and English translations of Satie's texts, but minus the red staves and the half-title pages.

33. *Le Piège de Méduse* (1913), scene 9; Wilkins, ed. and trans., *The Writings of Erik Satie*, 146.

34. See Léon Guichard, "Erik Satie et la musique grégorienne," *La Revue musicale* 17 (1936):334–35; and Guichard, "À propos d'Erik Satie: Notules incohérentes," 65–67.

35. Louise Varèse, *Varèse: A Looking-Glass Diary*, vol. 1: 1883–1928 (New York: Norton, 1972), 161.

36. The song appears in act 2, scene 3 of *Mireille*, where it is sung as a duet by Vincent and Mireille. Some thirty years later Jules Massenet incorporated the same folk song into his *Sapho* (1897), where it is sung, in the original

dialect, near the end of the second act by the beautiful artists' model "Sapho" (Fanny Legrand) to her Provençal lover Jean Gaussin.

CHAPTER 7

1. Romola Nijinsky, *Nijinsky* (London: Victor Gollancz, 1933), 81.
2. Ibid., 66.
3. See Vaslav Nijinsky, *The Diary of Vaslav Nijinsky,* Romola Nijinsky, ed. (New York: Simon & Schuster, 1936).
4. Quoted in Nijinsky, *Nijinsky,* 76.
5. Brown, *An Impersonation of Angels: A Biography of Jean Cocteau,* 87, 88.
6. Ibid., 125.
7. Valentine Hugo, "Le Socrate que j'ai connu," *La Revue musicale* 214 (1952):140.
8. Quoted in Francis Steegmuller, *Cocteau: A Biography* (Boston: Little, Brown and Company, 1970), 135.
9. Ibid., 82.
10. Ibid., 190.
11. Misia Sert, *Two or Three Muses: The Memoirs of Misia Sert,* trans. Moura Budberg (London: Museum Press, 1953), 139–40.
12. Cocteau is telescoping events here; he did hear Satie's *Three Pieces in the Shape of a Pear* as early as 1915, but the army furlough of which he speaks took place in 1916. In his recollections of the genesis of *Parade,* Cocteau often confused, perhaps deliberately, the abandoned *David* and the later *Parade,* often speaking of the two ballets as though they were one and the same.
13. Jean Cocteau, "La Collaboration de 'Parade,'" *Nord-Sud: Revue littéraire,* nos. 4–5 (June / July 1917):29; reprinted in Jean Cocteau, *A Call to Order,* trans. Rollo H. Myers (London: Faber and Gwyer, 1926), 50–51.
14. Quoted in Arthur Gold and Robert Fizdale, *Misia: The Life of Misia Sert* (New York: Knopf, 1980), 186.
15. Quoted in Steegmuller, *Cocteau,* 151.
16. Ibid., 154.
17. Ibid., 162.
18. Ibid., 165.
19. Jean Cocteau, "Avant 'Parade,'" *Excelsior,* 18 May 1917, 5; quoted in Steegmuller, Cocteau, 183–84.
20. The most extensive scholarly treatments of *Parade* are Richard H. Axsom, *"Parade": Cubism as Theater* (New York: Garland Publishing, 1979), which focuses primarily on Picasso's contribution; Conrad DeBold, "'Parade' and 'Le Spectacle intérieur': The Role of Jean Cocteau in an Avant-Garde Ballet"

(Ph.D. diss., Emory University, 1982), which, as its title reveals, focuses primarily on Cocteau's contribution; and Jacinthe Harbec, "'Parade': Les Influences cubistes sur la composition musicale d'Erik Satie" (Master's thesis, McGill University, 1987), which is an analysis of Satie's musical score from a Cubist perspective.

21. The French word *"parade,"* an English-speaking audience should understand, can mean, according to *Larousse,* "a burlesque scene played outside a sideshow booth to entice spectators inside."

22. Quoted in Brown, *An Impersonation of Angels,* 144.

23. Quoted in Cocteau, *A Call to Order,* 54.

24. Ibid.

25. Quoted in Boris Kochno, *Diaghilev and the Ballets Russes,* trans. Adrienne Foulke (New York: Harper & Row, 1970), 120.

26. Bibliothèque Nationale [Mus., Ms. 9077(5)]. The "Notes" also list three sounds that do not appear in the published score: an electric bell, a dynamo, and a steam whistle (although the deep siren is clearly intended to suggest the sound of a ship's horn and is so used in the score).

27. Axsom, *"Parade": Cubism as Theater,* 63.

28. See Gabriel Fournier, "Erik Satie et son époque," *La Revue musicale* 214 (1952):130.

29. See Léonide Massine, *My Life in Ballet* (London: Macmillan, 1968), 104.

30. See DeBold, "'Parade' and 'Le Spectacle intérieur,'" 174.

31. Wilfrid Mellers, *Caliban Reborn: Renewal in Twentieth-Century Music* (New York: Harper & Row, 1967), 80.

32. Quoted in Steegmuller, *Cocteau,* 186–87.

33. Paul Morand, *Journal d'un attaché d'ambassade 1916–17* (Paris: La Table Ronde, 1948), 266; quoted in Brown, *An Impersonation of Angels,* 152.

34. James Harding, *The Ox on the Roof: Scenes from Musical Life in Paris in the Twenties* (London: Macdonald, 1972), 38.

35. Jean d'Udine, "Couleurs, mouvements et sons: Les Ballets Russes, en 1917," *Le Courrier musical* 19 (June 1917):239.

36. Quoted in Fournier, "Erik Satie et son époque," 130. Raissa Maritain, who knew Satie toward the end of his life, recalled that Poueigh had received a whole series of postcards, "unscrupulously composed in terms of revolting obscenity," sent daily by Satie as a punishment for his sin. (See Raissa Maritain, "A Handful of Musicians," *Commonweal* 39 [October 1943]:34.)

37. Quoted in Brown, *An Impersonation of Angels,* 153.

38. Quoted in Steegmuller, *Cocteau,* 187–88.

39. The appellation "Les Six" did not appear until 16 January 1920 when the critic Henri Collet, writing in *Comoedia,* spoke of "Les Cinq Russes, Les Six Français et Erik Satie."

40. Cocteau, *A Call to Order,* 54.

41. Jean Cocteau, *Cock and Harlequin,* trans. Rollo H. Myers (London: The Egoist Press, 1921), 20.

42. Ibid., 3.

43. Ibid., 11.

44. Ibid., 26

45. Ibid., 22.

46. Ibid., 35.

47. Ibid., 36.

48. Ibid., 20.

49. David Bancroft, "Two Pleas for a French, French Music," *Music and Letters* 48 (1967):254.

50. Quoted in Steegmuller, *Cocteau,* 207.

51. Arthur Honegger, *I am a Composer,* trans. Wilson O. Clough in collaboration with Allan Arthur Willman (London: Faber and Faber, 1966), 104, 116.

52. Arthur Honegger, "Modern Music," *Rice Institute Pamphlet* 16 (July 1929):124.

53. Igor Stravinsky, *Chronicle of My Life* (London: Victor Gollancz, 1936), 154.

CHAPTER 8

1. Quoted in Templier, *Erik Satie,* 42.

2. Quoted in Nigel Wilkins, "Erik Satie's Letters to Milhaud and Others," *Musical Quarterly* 66 (1980):410.

3. Ibid.

4. Ibid., 407–8.

5. See François Lesure, ed., *Erik Satie: Catalogue des manuscrits dans la Bibliothèque Nationale* (Paris: Bibliothèque Nationale, Département de la Musique, 1966), 37.

6. Princesse Edmond de Polignac, "Memoirs," *Horizon* 12 (August 1945):137-38.

7. See Valentine Hugo, "Le Socrate que j'ai connu," *La Revue musicale* 214 (1952):143.

8. Jane Bathori, "Les Musiciens que j'ai connus," trans. Felix Aprahamian, *Recorded Sound* 15 (1964):239.

9. Quoted in Wilkins, "Erik Satie's Letters to Milhaud and Others," 410; see also Nigel Wilkins, "Erik Satie's Letters," *Canadian University Music Review,* no. 2 (1981):220–21.

10. Roland-Manuel, "La Quinzaine musicale: Le 'Socrate' de M. Erik Satie—Concerts Pasdeloup et Lamoureux," *L'Éclair,* 23 February 1920, 3.

11. See Wilkins, "Erik Satie's Letters to Milhaud and Others," 411.

12. Jean Marnold, "Revue de la quinzaine," *Mercure de France* 139 (1920):786.

13. "Paris Week by Week: Erik Satie," *Observer,* 8 May 1921, 7.

14. Leigh Henry, "'Socrate' and the New Asceticism," *Musical Standard,* 23 April 1921, 146.

15. See Paul Collaer, "Socrate," *Action: Cahiers de philosophie et d'art,* no. 10 (November 1921):32.

16. Charles Koechlin, "Erik Satie," *La Revue musicale* 5 (1924):205.

17. Igor Stravinsky and Robert Craft, *Conversations with Igor Stravinsky* (London: Faber and Faber, 1959), 68.

18. Alfred Edward Taylor, *Socrates* (Boston: The Beacon Press, 1951), 43–44.

19. Ibid., 94.

20. E. S. [Eric Salzman], "Satie: *Socrate,*" *Stereo Review* 24 (June 1970): 90.

21. Arthur Berger, "Mainly 'Socrate,'" *Saturday Review* 35 (30 August 1952):50.

22. Erik Satie, *Esquisses pour "Socrate"* [B.N., Mus., Ms. 9611].

23. Pierre Boulez, "Chien flasque," *La Revue musicale* 214 (1952):154.

24. Ned Rorem, *Critical Affairs: A Composer's Journal* (New York: George Braziller, 1970), 118.

25. An excerpt from "Légende Californienne" is printed in Wilkins, ed. and trans., *The Writings of Erik Satie,* 155.

26. Quoted in Fernand Léger, "Satie inconnu," *La Revue musicale* 214 (1952):137.

27. "Texte d'Erik Satie," *Empreintes,* nos. 7–8 (May / June / July 1950):98; quoted in Shattuck, *The Banquet Years,* 169.

28. Quoted in Templier, *Erik Satie,* 46.

29. See Darius Milhaud, *Notes without Music,* trans. Donald Evans (New York: Knopf, 1953), 123.

30. Quoted in Wilkins, "Erik Satie's Letters to Milhaud and Others," 425. In her autobiography, Mrs. Meyer recorded a flattering tribute to Satie: "Satie's peculiar genius, his sense of the ridiculous, his staunch independence in art as in life, his extreme poverty due largely to a fierce and defensive pride, his loving and lovable nature, can still make my heart ache with the fervent wish that our sad contemporary world could produce more artists of Satie's integrity." (Agnes E. Meyer, *Out of These Roots: The Autobiography of an American Woman* [Boston: Little, Brown, 1953], 82.)

31. The autograph score of *Carrelage phonique,* first printed in facsimile in John Cage, *Notations* (New York: Something Else Press, 1969), carries a note in the composer's hand: "Peut se jouer à un lunch ou à un contrat de mariage." The published score (Salabert 1975), however, has eliminated the second part of Satie's instructions, thereby limiting *Carrelage phonique* to lunchtime performances.

32. See *Le Coq,* no. 4 (November 1920).

CHAPTER 9

1. Templier, *Erik Satie,* 72–73.
2. Quoted in Shattuck, *The Banquet Years,* 181.
3. See "Les Six," *Les Feuilles libres* 4 (February 1922):42–45; Wilkins, ed. and trans., *The Writings of Erik Satie,* 91–92. Satie's exclusion of Honegger is an ironic reference to the fact that he alone of *Les Six* was at this time, as Satie put it, "finding any favour in the opinion of the musicographers, calligraphers and other graphologists—generally called Critics."
4. Quoted in Matthew Josephson, *Life Among the Surrealists* (New York: Holt, Rinehart and Winston, 1962), 115.
5. These exchanges are reprinted in "À Propos du Congrès de Paris," *Les Feuilles libres* 4 (April / May 1922): 154–56.
6. Josephson, *Life Among the Surrealists,* 150. Satie must have relished the opportunity to wreak revenge on Breton, whose journal *Littérature,* the previous year had published a "statistical" survey to determine the present value of famous personalities, living and dead. A panel of judges, including Breton, Aragon, Éluard, Soupault, and Ribemont-Dessaignes, devised a three-tier rating system with 20 representing the highest level of approval, − 25 the greatest aversion, and 0 complete indifference. Predictably the judges gave themselves very high ratings, along with such kindred spirits as Alfred Jarry, Charlie Chaplin, and Marcel Duchamp. Satie rated a rather low 2.72, which put him below Bach (5.09) but slightly ahead of Stravinsky and Proust, who both registered a flat 0.00. Satie's highest score, 15, came from the writer Pierre Drieu La Rochelle, his lowest, a harsh − 25, from Paul Éluard; but the greatest insult was a completely indifferent 0 dealt him by André Breton. For the record, the lowest rating was given to the Symbolist poet Henri de Régnier (− 22.90), closely followed by Anatole France and Marshal Foch (tied at − 18.00), and the Unknown Soldier (− 15.63). (See *Littérature,* no. 18 [March 1921]:1–7.)
7. See Volta, ed., *Erik Satie: Écrits,* 97–98.
8. "Parlons à voix basse," *Les Feuilles libres* 5 (September / October 1923):185; Wilkins, ed. and trans., *The Writings of Erik Satie,* 99.
9. Quoted in André Beucler, *The Last of the Bohemians: Twenty Years with Léon-Paul Fargue* (New York: William Sloane, 1954), 21.
10. Sylvia Beach, *Shakespeare and Company* (New York: Harcourt, Brace, 1956), 154.
11. Quoted in Darius Milhaud, *Notes without Music,* trans. Donald Evans (New York: Knopf, 1953), 156.
12. Quoted in Nigel Wilkins, "Erik Satie's Letters to Milhaud and Others," *Musical Quarterly* 66 (July 1980):414. Sybil Harris was the wife of the American ambassador to France and a patroness of the arts whose Montparnasse apartment in the rue Delambre habitually received numerous progressive artists of the postwar period. It was through her that Satie was commissioned to contribute articles on Stravinsky and Debussy to *Vanity Fair.* Both of these articles were

completed but for some reason only the Stravinsky article appeared in print during Satie's lifetime. (See Wilkins, ed. and trans., *The Writings of Erik Satie,* 102–10.)

13. Quoted in Kochno, *Diaghilev and the Ballets Russes,* 240–43.

14. See Harding, *The Ox on the Roof: Scenes from Musical Life in Paris in the Twenties,* 150.

15. "Les Ballets Russes à Monte-Carlo (Souvenirs de voyage)," *Paris-Journal,* 15 February 1924, 1; Wilkins, ed. and trans., *The Writings of Erik Satie,* 111.

16. "L'Esprit musical," *Sélection: Chronique de la vie artistique et littéraire* 3 (April 1924):79; Wilkins, ed. and trans., *The Writings of Erik Satie,* 112.

17. Ibid., 113.

18. See Élisabeth Bénard-Sesboüé, "Erik Satie chez les belges," *Renaissance politique, littéraire, artistique,* 19 April 1924, 14.

19. See Pierre de Massot, "Vingt cinq minutes avec Erik Satie," *Paris-Journal,* 30 May 1924, 2.

20. See René Chalupt, "Paris Letter," *Chesterian* 6 (October 1924):24.

21. Serge Leonidovich Grigoriev, *The Diaghilev Ballet, 1909–1929,* trans. Vera Bowen (London: Constable, 1953), 238.

22. H. H. [Horace Horsnell], "'Mercury,'" *Observer,* 17 July 1927, 15.

23. Francis Picabia, "Erik Satie," *Paris-Journal,* 27 June 1924, 1; reprinted in Francis Picabia, *Écrits: 1921–1953 et posthumes,* Olivier Revault d'Allonnes and Dominique Bouissou, eds. (Paris: Pierre Belfond, 1978), 145–47.

24. The scenario of *Après dîner* is published in Michel Sanouillet, *Francis Picabia et "391,"* vol. 2 (Paris: Eric Losfeld, 1966), 255–56.

25. Quoted in Germaine Everling, *L'Anneau de saturne* (Paris: Fayard, 1970), 154.

26. See George Antheil, *Bad Boy of Music* (Garden City, N. Y.: Doubleday, Doran & Co., 1945), 135.

27. Picabia's scenario for *Relâche* is printed in Sanouillet, *Francis Picabia et "391,"* 2: 256–57; in *Francis Picabia: Portrait de l'Auteur par lui-même* (Paris: Centre National d'Art et de Culture Georges Pompidou—Musée National d'Art Modern, 1976), 126; and in Picabia, *Écrits: 1921–1953 et posthumes,* 155–56. A comparison of Picabia's *Relâche* with Cendrars's *Après dîner* reveals a number of points of resemblance between the two scenarios.

28. See Émile Vuillermoz, "Les Théâtres: Ballets suédois," *Excelsior,* 6 December 1924, 5.

29. See Volta, *L'Ymagier d'Erik Satie,* 85, 116.

30. See Louis Schneider, "Music in Paris," *New York Herald* [Paris], 6 December 1924, 4.

31. This is the complete list of the borrowed material given by W. Mayr, who presumably received his information from the composer himself. (See Mayr, "Entretien avec Erik Satie," *Le Journal littéraire,* no. 24 [4 October 1924]:11.) The words of "Le Père Dupanloup" can be found in *Chansons de Salles de Garde*

(Amsterdam: Éditions du Scorpion, 1936), 281–82. I have been unable to locate printed sources (words or music) for the remaining three songs.

Grete Wehmeyer's case for the citation of the children's song "Savez-vous planter des Choux?" ("Do You Know How to Plant Cabbages?") (see Wehmeyer, *Erik Satie* [Regensburg: Gustav Bosse Verlag, 1974], 273–74) is suspect, not only because a children's song would be entirely out of place in an "obscene ballet," but also in the light of Satie's practice in all previous instances of musical quotation of presenting his borrowed material straightforwardly—at least initially—with little or no melodic (though not necessarily harmonic) disguise, and, moreover, of relating it to a broader musico-poetic theme. But more to the point, the tune Wehmeyer cites bears only a superficial resemblance to the music of the "Entrée de l'Homme" from act 1 of *Relâche*. Moreover, the tune she cites is radically different from all versions of "Savez-vous planter des choux?" that I have seen.

Similarly, Léon Guichard's claim for the quotation of "Flagrant délit," a fin de siècle cabaret song attributed to the chansonnier Léon Xanrof (see Guichard, "À propos d'Erik Satie: Notules incohérentes," *Recherches et travaux (Université de Grenoble, Unité d'Enseignement et de Recherches des Lettres),* Bulletin no. 7 [March 1973]:71) is doubtful despite the song's risqué story of a husband who catches his unfaithful wife flagrante delicto and the fact that the music of the "Entrée des Hommes" in act 1 and the "Rentrée des Hommes" in act 2 of the ballet bears some resemblance to the song. (The words and music of "Flagrant délit" can be found in Léon Xanrof, *Chansons sans-gêne* [Paris: Ondet, 1890], 80–82.)

32. The most detailed analyses of the music of *Entr'acte* are Douglas W. Gallez, "Satie's *Entr'acte:* A Model of Film Music," *Cinema Journal* 16 (Fall 1976):36–50; and Martin Marks, "The Well-Furnished Film: Satie's Score for *Entr'acte," Canadian University Music Review,* no. 4 (1983):245–77.

33. Quoted in Jean Roy, "Tout autour d'une lettre: Erik Satie," *Journal musical français: Musica-Disques,* no. 174 (November 1968):45.

34. See Roland-Manuel, "Adieu à Satie," *Revue Pleyel,* no. 15 (December 1924):21–22.

35. *Relâche* lived up to its name, for there is still some confusion concerning the precise date of the premiere. Scheduled to receive "Le Tout Paris" on Thursday , 27 November, the Théâtre des Champs-Élysées remained resolutely closed to the elegant crowd of anxious first-nighters, ostensibly owing to the indisposition of Jean Börlin. It was at first generally assumed that Picabia had perpetrated one of his grandest Dada jokes. However, two days later an explanation for the cancellation was printed in *Comoedia,* followed by a short explanatory note by Picabia entitled "Pourquoi 'Relâche' a fait relâche," which appeared in the same newspaper on 2 December, two days before the rescheduled opening.

36. The editorial (*sic*) is in the original. Mayr, "Entretien avec Erik Satie," 11.

37. Rolf de Maré, "À propos de 'Relâche,'" *Comoedia*, 27 November 1924, 2.

38. Francis Picabia, "Programme de 'Relâche,'" *La Danse* (November / December 1924); reprinted in Picabia, *Écrits: 1921–1953 et posthumes*, 166.

39. See, for example, Robert Desnos, "Cinéma: *Entr'acte* par Francis Picabia, mise en scène de René Clair," *Le Journal littéraire*, no. 34 (13 December 1924):15; Desnos does not hesitate to nominate *Entr'acte* as "the most beautiful film of the year."

40. Georges Jean-Aubry, "The End of a Legend," *Chesterian* (1924–25):191–93.

41. Georges Jean-Aubry, "Erik Satie: A Musical Humorist," *Music Student* 9 (December 1916):136. The proposed visit to Great Britain never materialized. Satie was to have appeared in performances of his own music at the War Emergency Concerts in Steinway Hall on 7 December 1916, and from London he was to have travelled to Newcastle and Edinburgh, where on 12 December he was scheduled to appear with Jean-Aubry in a lecture-recital at the Oak Hall. In a letter of 6 November 1916 to Jean-Aubry the composer explained that his work on *Parade* made it imperative for him to remain at home. This, combined with his general distaste for lengthy absences from Paris, would seem sufficient reason for Satie to decline an opportunity to visit his maternal homeland. One wonders, however, if a deeper reason was not his great antipathy to Jean-Aubry, for, on 14 November, just one week after sending his regrets to the critic, he described him to Roland-Manuel, in his most pointed Rabelaisian vein, as "a twat. . . . Close up," he added for good measure, "he even looks like an arse." (Quoted in Gavin Bryars, "Satie and the British," *Contact: A Journal of Contemporary Music*, no. 25 [Autumn 1982]:5.)

42. Jean-Aubry, "The End of a Legend," 191.

43. Ibid., 193.

44. Quoted in Darius Milhaud, "Les Derniers jours d'Erik Satie," *Le Figaro littéraire*, 23 April 1949, 5; reprinted in Milhaud, *Notes without Music*, 175.

45. Quoted in ibid., 176.

46. Henri Prunières, "The Failure of Success," *Musical Digest* 8 (28 July 1925):5.

47. Erik Blom, "Erik Satie (1866–1925)," *Musical News and Herald* 69 (18 July 1925):53.

48. Georges Auric, "Erik Satie," *Les Nouvelles littéraires*, 11 July 1925, 1.

49. Virgil Thomson, *Virgil Thomson* (New York: Knopf, 1966), 119.

50. John Cage, "On Erik Satie," *Art News Annual* 27 (1958):81; reprinted in John Cage, *Silence* (Middletown, Conn.: Wesleyan University Press, 1961), 82.

51. John Cage, "More Satie," *Musical America* 71 (1 April 1951):26; reprinted in Richard Kostelanetz, ed., *John Cage* (New York: Praeger, 1970), 93.

52. John Cage, "Satie Controversy," *Musical America* 70 (15 December 1950):12; reprinted in Kostelanetz, ed., *John Cage,* 89.

53. Ibid. For more extended discussions of the Satie-Cage relationship see Michael Nyman, "Cage and Satie," *Musical Times* 114 (December 1973):1227–29; Alan Gillmor, "Satie, Cage, and the New Asceticism," *Contact: A Journal of Contemporary Music,* no. 25 (Autumn 1982):15–20; and John Cage, Roger Shattuck, and Alan Gillmor, "Erik Satie: A Conversation," *Contact: A Journal of Contemporary Music,* no. 25 (Autumn 1982):21-26.

54. Quoted in Lucien Chevaillier, "Un entretien avec . . . Roland Manuel," *Le Guide du concert et du disque* 15 (24 and 31 May 1929):952.

55. Louis Durey, "Erik Satie," *Arts* 17 (1930):164–65.

Bibliography

PRIMARY SOURCES

Writings

Satie's published writings appeared originally in a variety of journals and "little reviews," many of them obscure and difficult to obtain. Five very small volumes of selected writings, edited by Pierre Aelberts, were published by Éditions Dynamo in Liège between 1950 and 1954, and excerpts have appeared elsewhere in books and journals. Ornella Volta's three-volume edition of the writings (including the texts and poems accompanying musical works) and the correspondence promises to be complete. For English translations of the published writings (excluding the texts and poems accompanying musical works) see Wilkins, *The Writings of Erik Satie,* 1980. For a complete list of the published writings consult Volta, *Erik Satie: Écrits,* rev. ed., 1981, 339–58.

Johnson, Ronald, trans. *Sports and Divertissements.* Dunsyre: Wild Hawthorn Press, 1979.

Volta, Ornella, ed. *Erik Satie.* Paris: Éditions Seghers-Humour, 1979.

———. *Erik Satie: Écrits.* Paris: Éditions Champ Libre, 1977; rev. ed., 1981.

———. *Indications de jeu* (in preparation).

Wilkins, Nigel, ed. and trans. *The Writings of Erik Satie.* London: Eulenburg, 1980.

———. "The Writings of Erik Satie: Miscellaneous Fragments." *Music and Letters* 56 (1975):288–307.

Winkfield, Trevor, trans. *Erik Satie: Dried Embryos.* London: Aloes Books, 1972.

Letters

Lockspeiser, Edward. *The Literary Clef: An Anthology of Letters and Writings by French Composers.* London: John Calder, 1958.

Oui: Lettres d'Erik Satie adressées à Pierre de Massot. Alès: Éditions Pab, 1960.

"Trois lettres d'Erik Satie à Claude Debussy (1903)." *Revue de musicologie* 48 (1962):71–74.

Volta, Ornella, ed. *Correspondance* (in preparation).

Wilkins, Nigel. "Erik Satie's Letters." *Canadian University Music Review,* no. 2 (1981):207–27.

――――. "Erik Satie's Letters to Milhaud and Others." *Musical Quarterly,* 66 (1980):404–28.

Iconography
Volta, Ornella, ed. *L'Ymagier d'Erik Satie.* Paris: Éditions Van de Velde, 1979.

Miscellaneous
Bélicha, Roland. "Chronologie Satiste ou Photocopies d'un original." *La Revue musicale* 312 (1978):7–63.

Lesure, François, ed. *Erik Satie: Catalogue des manuscrits dans la Bibliothèque Nationale.* Paris: Bibliothèque Nationale, Département de la Musique, 1966.

SECONDARY SOURCES

Books
Antheil, George. *Bad Boy of Music.* Garden City, N.Y.: Doubleday, Doran & Co. 1945.

Appignanesi, Lisa. *The Cabaret.* London: Studio Vista, 1975.

Astruc, Gabriel. *Le Pavillon des fantômes.* Paris: Grasset, 1929.

Austin, William W. *Music in the 20th Century: From Debussy through Stravinsky.* New York: W. W. Norton, 1966.

Axsom, Richard H. *"Parade": Cubism as Theater.* New York: Garland Publishing, 1979.

Les Ballets Suédois dans l'art contemporain. Paris: Éditions du Trianon, 1931.

Barbier, Jean-Joël. *Au piano avec Erik Satie.* Paris: Éditions Sequin-Vagabondage, 1987.

Barreyre, Jean. *La Chanson française depuis le second empire.* Paris: Flammes et Fumées, 1963.

Bayard, Jean-Émile. *Montmartre, Past and Present.* Translated by Ralph Anningson and Tudor Davis. New York: Brentano, 1926.

Beach, Sylvia. *Shakespeare and Company.* New York: Harcourt, Brace, 1956.

Beaumont, Cyril W. *Complete Book of Ballets: A Guide to the Principal Ballets of the Nineteenth and Twentieth Centuries.* London: Putnam, 1937; rev. ed., 1949.

――――. *Puppets and Puppetry.* London: The Studio, 1958.

Béhar, Henri. *Étude sur le théâtre dada et surréaliste.* Paris: Gallimard, 1967.

Bercy, Anne de, and Armand Ziwès. *À Montmartre . . . le soir: Cabarets et chansonniers d'hier.* Paris: Grasset, 1951.

Bercy, Léon de. *Montmartre et ses chansons: Poètes et chansonniers.* Paris: H. Daragon, 1902.

Bertholet, Édouard. *La Pensée et les secrets du Sâr Joséphin Péladan.* 4 vols. Lausanne: Éditions rosicruciennes, 1952–59.

Bertin, Pierre. *Le Théâtre et(est) ma vie.* Paris: Le Bélier, 1971.

Beucler, André. *The Last of the Bohemians: Twenty Years with Léon-Paul Fargue.* New York: William Sloane, 1954.

Blackham, Olive. *Shadow Puppets.* London: Barrie & Rockliff, 1960.

Bochner, Jay. *Blaise Cendrars: Discovery and Re-creation.* Toronto: University of Toronto Press, 1978.

Bois, Jules. *Les Petites religions de Paris.* Paris: Léon Chailley, 1894.

Bordat, Denis, and Francis Boucrat. *Les Théâtres d'ombres: Histoire et techniques.* Paris: L'Arche, 1956.

Boschot, Adolphe. *La Musique et la vie.* Paris: Plon, 1931.

Bredel, Marc. *Erik Satie.* Paris: Éditions Mazarine, 1982.

Brody, Elaine. *Paris: The Musical Kaleidoscope 1870–1925.* New York: George Braziller, 1987.

Brown, Frederick. *An Impersonation of Angels: A Biography of Jean Cocteau.* New York: Viking Press, 1968.

Bruyr, José. *L'Écran des musiciens.* Paris: Les Cahiers de France, 1930.

Büsser, Henri. *De Pelléas aux Indes Galantes.* Paris: Fayard, 1955.

Cabanne, Pierre. *Pablo Picasso: His Life and Times.* Translated by Harold J. Salemson. New York: William Morrow, 1977.

Cage, John. *Notations.* New York: Something Else Press, 1969.

———. *Silence.* Middletown, Conn.: Wesleyan University Press, 1961.

Calvocoressi, Michel D. *Musician's Gallery: Music and Ballet in Paris and London.* London: Faber & Faber, 1933.

Camfield, William A. *Francis Picabia: His Art, Life and Times.* Princeton: Princeton University Press, 1979.

Carco, Francis. *La Belle époque au temps du Bruant.* Paris: Gallimard, 1954.

———. *From Montmartre to the Latin Quarter.* Translated by Madeleine Boyd. London: Cayme Press, 1929.

Carter, Alfred. *The Idea of Decadence in French Literature, 1830–1900.* Toronto: University of Toronto Press, 1958.

Cendrars, Blaise. *Blaise Cendrars vous parle.* Paris: Éditions Denoël, 1965.

Centenaire du Cabaret du Chat Noir. Paris: Musée de Montmartre, 1981.

Charles, Jacques. *Caf' conc'.* Paris: Flammarion, 1966.

Charpentier, Octave. *À travers Montmartre.* Paris: Éditions d'Art du Croquis, 1921.

Clair, René. *À Nous la liberté and Entr'acte.* Translated by Richard Jacques and Nicola Hayden. New York: Simon & Schuster, 1970.

————. *Cinema Yesterday and Today*. Translated by Stanley Appelbaum and edited by R. C. Dale. New York: Dover, 1972.

Cocteau, Jean. *A Call to Order*. Translated by Rollo H. Myers. London: Faber & Gwyer, 1926.

————. *Cock and Harlequin*. Translated by Rollo H. Myers. London: The Egoist Press, 1921.

————. *Erik Satie*. Liège: Éditions Dynamo, 1957.

————. *The Journals of Jean Cocteau*. Edited and translated with an introduction by Wallace Fowlie. Bloomington: Indiana University Press, 1964.

————. *My Contemporaries*. Translated by Margaret Crosland. London: Peter Owen, 1967.

————. *Professional Secrets: An Autobiography of Jean Cocteau Drawn from his Lifetime Writings by Robert Phelps*. Translated by Richard Howard. New York: Farrar, Straus & Giroux, 1970.

Coeuroy, André. *La Musique française moderne*. Paris: Libraire Delagrave, 1922.

————. *Panorama de la musique contemporaine*. Revised edition. Paris: Éditions Kra, 1930.

Collaer, Paul. *A History of Modern Music*. Translated by Sally Abeles. Cleveland: World Publishing Co., 1961.

Cooper, Douglas. *Picasso: Theatre*. New York: Abrams, 1968.

Cooper, Martin. *French Music: From the Death of Berlioz to the Death of Fauré*. London: Oxford University Press, 1951.

Corazzol, Adriana Guarnieri. *Erik Satie tra ricerca e provocazione*. Venice: Marsilio Editori, 1979.

Corinne, Henry. *Musiciens d'Île de France*. Sceaux: Musée de l'Île de France, 1973.

Cortot, Alfred. *La Musique française de piano*. 3 vols. Paris: Presses Universitaires de France, 1948.

Crespelle, Jean-Paul. *La Folle époque*. Paris: Libraire Hachette, 1968.

————. *Montparnasse vivant*. Paris: Libraire Hachette, 1962.

Crosland, Margaret, ed. *Cocteau's World: An Anthology of Writings by Jean Cocteau*. Translated by Margaret Crosland. New York: Dodd, Mead & Company, 1972.

————. *Jean Cocteau: A Biography*. London: Peter Nevill, 1955.

Dantinne, Émile. *L'oeuvre et la pensée de Péladan*. Brussels: Office de Publicité, 1948.

Davies, Laurence. *César Franck and His Circle*. London: Barrie & Jenkins, 1970.

————. *The Gallic Muse*. New York: A. S. Barnes, 1967.

————. *Paths to Modern Music: Aspects of Music from Wagner to the Present Day*. London: Barrie & Jenkins, 1971.

Demuth, Norman. *Musical Trends in the 20th Century*. London: Rockliff, 1952.

Desaymard, Joseph. *Emmanuel Chabrier d'après ses lettres: l'homme et l'oeuvre.* Paris: Fernand Roches, 1934.

Desnos, Robert. *Cinéma.* Paris: Gallimard, 1966.

Dietschy, Marcel. *La Passion de Claude Debussy.* Neuchâtel: Éditions de la Baconnière, 1962.

Donnay, Maurice. *Autour du Chat Noir.* Paris: Grasset, 1926.

———. *Des souvenirs.* Paris: Fayard, 1933.

Donnay, Maurice, Dominique Bonnaud, and Vincent Hyspa. *L'Esprit montmartrois.* Paris: Ullman, 1938.

Doret, Gustave. *Temps et contretemps: Souvenirs d'un musicien.* Fribourg: Éditions de la Librairie de l'Université, 1942.

Dorgelès, Roland. *Au beau temps de la Butte.* Paris: Albin Michel, 1963.

———. *Bouquet de Bohème.* Paris: Albin Michel, 1947.

Dumesnil, René. *L'Aube du XXᵉ siècle.* Vol. 4 of *Histoire de la musique des origines à nos jours* by Jules Combarieu and René Dumesnil. Paris: Libraire Armand Colin, 1958.

———. *La Musique contemporaine en France.* 2 vols. Paris: Libraire Armand Colin, 1930.

———. *La Musique en France entre les deux guerres, 1919–1939.* Geneva: Éditions du Milieu du monde, 1946.

———. *Portraits de musiciens français.* Paris: Plon, 1938.

———. *La Première moitié du XXᵉ siècle.* Vol. 5 of *Histoire de la musique des origines à nos jours* by Jules Combarieu and René Dumesnil. Paris: Libraire Armand Colin, 1960.

Erik Satie à Montmartre. Paris: Musée de Montmartre, December 1982–April 1983.

Erismann, Guy. *Histoire de la chanson.* Paris: Pierre Waleffe, 1967.

Everling, Germaine. *L'Anneau de saturne.* Paris: Fayard, 1970.

Feschotte, Jacques. *Histoire du music-hall.* Paris: Presses Universitaires de France, 1965.

Fields, Armond. *George Auriol.* Layton, Utah: Gibbs M. Smith, 1985.

———. *Henri Rivière.* Salt Lake City: Gibbs M. Smith, 1983.

Fosca, François [pseud. of Georges de Traz]. *Histoire des cafés de Paris.* Paris: Firmin-Didot, 1934.

Fowlie, Wallace. *Jean Cocteau: The History of a Poet's Age.* Bloomington: Indiana University Press, 1966.

Francis Picabia: Portrait de l'Auteur par lui-même. Paris: Centre National d'Art et de Culture Georges Pompidou—Musée National d'Art Modern, 1976.

Fréjaville, Gustave. *Au music-hall.* Paris: Éditions du Monde nouveau, 1923.

Frère, Jean-Claude. *Vie et mystères des Rose + Croix.* Paris: Maison Mame, 1973.

Fumet, Stanislas. *La Poésie à travers les arts.* Paris: Alsatia, 1954.

Fursy, Henri. *Mon petit bonhomme de chemin: Souvenirs de Montmartre et d'ail-

leurs. Paris: L. Querelle, 1928.

Gold, Arthur and Robert Fizdale. *Misia: The Life of Misia Sert*. New York: Knopf, 1980.

Gosling, Nigel. *Paris 1900–1914: The Miraculous Years*. London: Weidenfeld and Nicolson, 1978.

Graf, Max. *Modern Music: Composers and Music of Our Time*. Translated by Beatrice R. Maier. New York: Philosophical Library, 1946.

Grigoriev, Serge Leonidovich. *The Diaghilev Ballet, 1909–1929*. Translated and edited by Vera Bowen. London: Constable, 1953.

Guilbert, Yvette. *La Chanson de ma vie (Mes Mémoires)*. Paris: Grasset, 1927.

Hägar, Bengt. *Modern Swedish Ballet*. London: Victoria and Albert Museum, 1970.

Harding, James. *Erik Satie*. London: Secker & Warburg, 1975.

———. *The Ox on the Roof: Scenes from Musical Life in Paris in the Twenties*. London: Macdonald, 1972.

———. *Sacha Guitry: The Last Boulevardier*. London: Methuen, 1968.

Hartog, Howard, ed. *European Music in the Twentieth Century*. London: Routledge & Kegan Paul, 1957.

Hedges, Inez. *Languages of Revolt: Dada and Surrealist Literature and Film*. Durham, N.C.: Duke University Press, 1983.

Hell, Henri. *Francis Poulenc*. Translated by Edward Lockspeiser. London: John Calder, 1959.

Herbert, Michel. *Chanson à Montmartre*. Paris: La Table Ronde, 1962.

Hill, Edward Burlingame. *Modern French Music*. Boston: Houghton & Mifflin, 1924.

Honegger, Arthur. *I am a Composer*. Translated by Wilson O. Clough in collaboration with Allan Arthur Willman. London: Faber and Faber, 1966.

Howat, Roy. *Debussy in Proportion: A Musical Analysis*. Cambridge: Cambridge University Press, 1983.

Huddleston, Sisley. *Bohemian Literary and Social Life in Paris*. London: George G. Harrap, 1928.

Hugnet, Georges. *L'Aventure Dada (1916–1922)*. Revised edition. Paris: Seghers, 1971.

Hyspa, Vincent. *Chansons d'humour*. Paris: Enoch, 1903.

Indy, Vincent d'. *La Schola Cantorum: son histoire depuis sa fondation jusqu'en 1925*. Paris: Bloud & Gay, 1927.

Jankélévitch, Vladimir. *Le Nocturne: Fauré, Chopin et la nuit, Satie et le matin*. Paris: Albin Michel, 1957.

Jakovsky, Anatole. *Alphonse Allais: "Le Tueur à gags."* Paris: Les Quatres Jeudis, 1955.

Jean-Aubry, Georges. *French Music of Today*. Translated by Edwin Evans. London: K. Paul, Trench & Trubner, 1919.

———. *An Introduction to French Music*. Translated by Percy Scholes. London: C. Palmer & Hayward, 1917.

Jean Cocteau and the French Scene. New York: Abbeville Press, 1984.

Jeanne, Paul. *Les Théâtres d'ombres à Montmartre.* Paris: Les Presses modernes du Palais-Royal, 1937.

Josephson, Matthew. *Life Among the Surrealists.* New York: Holt, Rinehart and Winston, 1962.

Jourdain, Francis. *Né en 76.* Paris: Les Éditions du Pavillon, 1951.

Jourdan-Morhange, Hélène. *Mes amis musiciens.* Paris: Les Éditeurs Française Réunis, 1955.

Jouy, Jules. *Les Chansons de l'année.* Paris: Bourbier et Lamoureux, 1888.

Jullian, Philippe. *Dreamers of Decadence: Symbolist Painters of the 1890s.* Translated by Robert Baldick. New York: Praeger, 1971.

———. *Montmartre.* Translated by Anne Carter. Oxford: Phaidon, 1977.

Kington, Miles, ed. *The World of Alphonse Allais.* London: Chatto & Windus, 1976.

Kochno, Boris. *Diaghilev and the Ballets Russes.* Translated by Adrienne Foulke. New York: Harper & Row, 1970.

Kostelanetz, Richard, ed. *John Cage.* New York: Praeger, 1970.

Kovács, Steven. *From Enchantment to Rage: The Story of Surrealist Cinema.* London and Toronto: Associated University Presses, 1980.

Lajoinie, Vincent. *Erik Satie.* Lausanne: Éditions l'Age d'Homme, 1985.

Laloy, Louis. *La Musique retrouvée, 1902–1927.* Paris: Libraire Plon, 1928.

Lambert, Constant. *Music Ho!: A Study of Music in Decline.* 3d ed. London: Faber & Faber, 1966.

Landormy, Paul. *La Musique française après Debussy.* Paris: Gallimard, 1943.

———. *La Musique française de Franck à Debussy.* Paris: Gallimard, 1943.

Landowski, Wanda Alice L. *Histoire de la musique moderne (1900 à 1940).* Paris: Aubier, Éditions Montaigne, 1941.

Lifar, Serge. *A History of Russian Ballet from its Origins to the Present Day.* Translated by Arnold Haskell. London: Hutchinson, 1954.

———. *Serge Diaghilev: His Life, His Work, His Legend.* London: Putnam, 1940.

Lockspeiser, Edward. *Debussy.* Rev. ed. London: J. M. Dent, 1951.

———. *Debussy: His Life and Mind.* 2 vols. London: Cassell, 1962–65.

Macdonald, Nesta. *Diaghilev Observed: By Critics in England and the United States 1911–1929.* New York: Dance Horizons, 1975.

Maritain, Jacques, and Cocteau, Jean. *Art and Faith: Letters between Jacques Maritain and Jean Cocteau.* Translated by John Coleman. New York: The Philosophical Library, 1948.

Marks, Elaine. *Colette.* New Brunswick, N. J.: Rutgers University Press, 1960.

Massine, Léonide. *My Life in Ballet.* London: Macmillan, 1968.

Massot, Pierre de. *Francis Picabia.* Paris: Seghers, 1966.

McGerr, Celia. *René Clair.* Boston: Twayne, 1980.

McPharlin, Paul. *Repertory of Marionette Plays.* New York: Viking Press, 1929.

Mellers, Wilfrid H. *Caliban Reborn: Renewal in Twentieth-Century Music.* New York: Harper & Row, 1967.

———. *Studies in Contemporary Music.* London: Dennis Dobson, 1947.

Mellow, James R. *Charmed Circle: Gertrude Stein & Company.* New York: Praeger, 1974.

Metzger, Heinz-Klaus, and Riehn, Rainer, eds. *Erik Satie. Musik-Konzepte,* no. 11. Munich, 1980.

Michelet, Victor-Émile. *Les Compagnons de la hiérophanie: Souvenirs du mouvement hermétiste à la fin du XIXᵉ siècle.* Paris: Dorbon-Aîné, 1937.

Milhaud, Darius. *Études.* Paris: Éditions Claude Aveline, 1927.

———. *Ma vie heureuse.* Paris: Belfond, 1973.

———. *Notes sur la musique: Essais et chroniques.* Paris: Flammarion, 1982.

———. *Notes without Music: An Autobiography.* Translated by Donald Evans. New York: Knopf, 1953.

Mitchell, Yvonne. *Colette: A Taste for Life.* London: Weidenfeld and Nicolson, 1975.

Mitry, Jean. *Le Cinéma expérimental: Histoire et perspectives.* Paris: Seghers, 1974.

———. *René Clair.* Paris: Éditions Universitaires, 1960.

Monnier, Adrienne. *The Very Rich Hours of Adrienne Monnier.* Translated by Richard McDougall. New York: Charles Scribner's Sons, 1976.

Montloin, Pierre, and Bayard, Jean-Pierre. *Les Rose-Croix.* Paris: Grasset, 1971.

Montorgueil, Georges. *Le Vieux Montmartre.* Paris: Hachette, 1925.

Morand, Paul. *Journal d'un attaché d'ambassade 1916–17.* Paris: La Table Ronde, 1948.

Morrow, William Chambers. *Bohemian Paris of To-Day.* London: Chatto & Windus, 1899.

Myers, Rollo H. *Emmanuel Chabrier and His Circle.* London: Dent, 1969.

———. *Erik Satie.* London: Dennis Dobson, 1948; New York: Dover, 1969.

———. *Erik Satie: Son temps et ses amis.* Paris: Éditions Richard-Masse, 1952.

———. *Modern French Music: Its Evolution and Cultural Background from 1900 to the Present Day.* Oxford: Basil Blackwell, 1971.

———. *Modern Music. Its Aims and Tendencies.* London: K. Paul, Trench & Trubner, 1923.

———. *Music in the Modern World.* London: E. J. Arnold, 1939.

———, ed. *Twentieth-Century Music: A Symposium.* London: John Calder, 1960.

Nabokov, Nicolas. *Old Friends and New Music.* Boston: Little, Brown, 1951.

Nadeau, Maurice. *The History of Surrealism.* Translated by Richard Howard. New York: Macmillan, 1965.

Newman, Ernest. *A Musical Motley.* London: John Lane, 1920.

Nijinsky, Romola. *Nijinsky.* London: Victor Gollancz, 1933.

Nijinsky, Vaslav. *The Diary of Vaslav Nijinsky.* Edited by Romola Nijinsky. New York: Simon and Schuster, 1936.

Oberthur, Mariel. *Cafés and Cabarets of Montmartre*. Translated by Sheila Azoulai. Layton, Utah: Gibbs M. Smith, 1984.

O'Brien, Patrick. *Pablo Ruiz Picasso: A Biography*. London: William Collins, 1976.

Orenstein, Arbie. *Ravel: Man and Musician*. New York: Columbia University Press, 1975.

Orledge, Robert. *Debussy and the Theatre*. Cambridge: Cambridge University Press, 1982.

Ouellette, Fernand. *Edgard Varèse*. Translated by Derek Coltman. New York: Viking Press, 1968.

Oxenhandler, Neal. *Scandal and Parade: The Theater of Jean Cocteau*. New Brunswick, N.J.: Rutgers University Press, 1957.

Penrose, Roland. *Picasso: His Life and Work*. London: Victor Gollancz, 1958.

Peter, René. *Claude Debussy: Vues prises son intimité*. Paris: Gallimard, 1931.

Picabia, Francis. *Écrits: 1921–1953 et posthumes*. Edited by Olivier Revault d'Allonnes and Dominique Bouisson. Paris: Pierre Belfond, 1978.

Pincus-Witten, Robert. *Occult Symbolism in France: Joséphin Péladan and the Salons de la Rose-Croix*. New York and London: Garland Publishing, 1976.

Poulenc, Francis. *Emmanuel Chabrier*. Translated by Cynthia Jolly. London: Dennis Dobson, 1981.

———. *My Friends and Myself*. Translated by James Harding. London: Dennis Dobson, 1978.

Ray, Man. *Self-Portrait*. Boston: Little, Brown, 1963.

Rey, Anne. *Erik Satie*. Paris: Éditions de Seuil, 1974.

Richardson, Joanna. *The Bohemians: La Vie de Bohème in Paris 1830–1914*. London: Macmillan, 1969.

———. *Colette*. London: Methuen, 1983.

Richter, Hans. *Dada: Art and Anti-Art*. New York: McGraw-Hill, 1965.

Ridge, George Ross. *The Hero in French Decadent Literature*. Athens: University of Georgia Press, 1961.

Ries, Frank W. D. *The Dance Theatre of Jean Cocteau*. Ann Arbor, Michigan: UMI Research Press, 1986.

Rischbieter, Henning, ed. *Art and the Stage in the 20th Century*. Translated by Michael Bullock. Greenwich, Conn.: New York: Graphic Society, 1968.

Rochas, Milès. *Chroniques musicales*. Neuchâtel: L. A. Monnier, 1958.

Rohozinski, Ladislas, ed. *Cinquante ans de musique française, de 1874 à 1925*. 2 vols. Paris: Libraire de France, 1925.

Roland-Manuel [Roland-Alexis Manuel Lévy]. *Erik Satie* ("Causerie faite à la Société Lyre et Palette"). Paris, 1916.

———. *Maurice Ravel*. Translated by Cynthia Jolly. London: Dennis Dobson, 1947; New York: Dover, 1972.

———, ed. *Histoire de la musique*. 2 vols. *Encyclopédie de la Pléiade*. Paris: Gallimard, 1960–63.

Rolland, Romain. *Musicians of To-Day*. Translated by Mary Blaiklock. London:

Kegan Paul, Trench, Trubner, 1915; Freeport, N.Y.: Books for Libraries Press, 1969.

Rorem, Ned. *Critical Affairs: A Composer's Journal*. New York: George Braziller, 1970.

———. *The Paris Diary of Ned Rorem*. New York: George Braziller, 1966.

Rosenfeld, Paul. *Musical Chronicle (1917–1923)*. New York: Harcourt & Brace, 1923.

———. *Musical Impressions: Selections from Paul Rosenfeld's Criticism*. Edited with an Introduction by Herbert A. Leibowitz. New York: Hill and Wang, 1969.

Rostand, Claude. *French Music Today*. Translated by Henry Marx. New York: Merlin Press, 1955.

Roy, Jean. *Musique française* ("Présence contemporaines"). Paris: Nouvelles Éditions Debresse, 1962.

Rudorff, Raymond. *The Belle Epoque: Paris in the Nineties*. New York: Saturday Review Press, 1973.

Sachs, Maurice. *The Decade of Illusion, 1918–1928*. Translated by Gwladys Matthews Sachs. New York: Knopf, 1933.

———. *Au temps du Boeuf sur le Toit*. Paris: Éditions de la Nouvelle Revue Critique, 1939.

Salazar, Adolfo. *Music in Our Time*. Translated by Isabel Pope. New York: W. W. Norton, 1946.

Samazeuilh, Gustave. *Musiciens de mon temps*. Paris: Marcel Daubin, 1947.

Samson, Jim. *Music in Transition: A Study of Tonal Expansion and Atonality 1900–1920*. London: Dent, 1977.

Samuel, Claude. *Panorama de la musique contemporaine*. Paris: Gallimard, 1962.

Sanouillet, Michel. *Dada à Paris*. Paris: Jean-Jacques Pauvert, 1965.

———. *Francis Picabia et "391."* 2 vols. Paris: Eric Losfeld, 1966.

———. *Picabia*. Paris: Éditions du Temps, 1964.

Sarde, Michèle. *Colette: Free and Fettered*. Translated by Richard Miller. New York: William Morrow, 1980.

Schub, Louise Rypko. *Léon-Paul Fargue*. Geneva: Libraire Droz, 1973.

Segel, Harold B. *Turn-of-the-Century Cabaret*. New York: Columbia University Press, 1987.

Séré, Octave [pseud. of Jean Poueigh]. *Musiciens français d'aujourd'hui*. 8th ed. Paris: Mercure de France, 1921.

Sert, Misia. *Two or Three Muses: The Memoirs of Misia Sert*. Translated by Moura Budberg. London: Museum Press, 1953.

Shattuck, Roger. *The Banquet Years: The Origins of the Avant-Garde in France 1885 to World War I*. Rev. ed. New York: Vintage Books, 1968.

Shead, Richard. *Music in the 1920s*. London: Gerald Duckworth, 1976.

Sprigge, Elizabeth, and Kihm, Jean-Jacques. *Jean Cocteau: The Man and The Mirror*. London: Victor Gollancz, 1968.

Steegmuller, Francis. *Cocteau: A Biography*. Boston: Little, Brown, 1970.

Storm, John. *The Valadon Drama: The Life of Suzanne Valadon*. New York: E. P. Dutton, 1958.

Stravinsky, Igor. *Chronicle of My Life*. London: Victor Gollancz, 1936.

Stravinsky, Igor, and Craft, Robert. *Conversations with Igor Stravinsky*. London: Faber and Faber, 1959.

———. *Dialogues and a Diary*. London: Faber and Faber, 1961.

Stuckenschmidt, Hans-Heinz. *Twentieth-Century Music*. Translated by Richard Deveson. London: Weidenfeld and Nicolson, 1969.

Swan, Alfred J. *Music, 1900–1930*. New York: W. W. Norton, 1929.

Symons, Arthur. *Parisian Nights*. London: Beaumont Press, 1926.

Templier, Pierre-Daniel. *Erik Satie.* Paris: Les Éditions Rieder, 1932; Éditions d'Aujourd'hui, 1978. Translated by Elena L. French and David S. French. Cambridge, Mass.: MIT Press, 1969; New York: Dover, 1980.

Thiher, Allen. *The Cinematic Muse*. Columbia and London: University of Missouri Press, 1979.

Thompson, Oscar. *Debussy: Man and Artist*. New York: Tudor Publishing Co., 1940.

Thomson, Virgil. *The Musical Scene*. New York: Knopf, 1947.

———. *Music Right and Left*. New York: Henry Holt, 1951.

———. *Music Reviewed: 1940–1954*. New York: Random House, 1967.

———. *Virgil Thomson*. New York: Knopf, 1966.

———. *A Virgil Thomson Reader*. With an Introduction by John Rockwell. New York: E. P. Dutton, 1984.

Tiersot, Julien. *Un demi-siècle de musique française: Entre les deux guerres, 1870–1917*. Paris: Libraire Félix Alcan, 1918.

Valbel, Horace. *Les Chansonniers et les Cabarets Artistiques*. Paris: E. Dentu, 1895.

Vallas, Léon. *Claude Debussy: His Life and Works*. Translated by Maire and Grace O'Brien. London: Oxford University Press, 1933.

Van Vechten, Carl. *Excavations*. New York: Knopf, 1926.

———. *Interpreters and Interpretations*. New York: Knopf, 1917.

Varèse, Louise, *Varèse: A Looking-Glass Diary*. Vol. 1: 1883–1928. New York: W. W. Norton, 1972.

Verkauf, Willy, ed. *Dada: Monograph of a Movement*. London: Alec Tiranti Ltd., 1957.

Vuillermoz, Émile. *Musiques d'aujourd'hui*. Paris: G. Crès, 1923.

Weckerlin, Jean-Baptiste. *Chansons de France pour les petits Français*. Paris: Plon-Nourrit, 1884.

———. *Chansons et rondes enfantines*. Paris: Garnier, 1885.

———. *Chansons et rondes enfantines des provinces de la France*. Paris: Garnier, 1889.

———. *Nouvelles chansons et rondes enfantines*. Paris: Garnier, 1886.

Wehmeyer, Grete. *Erik Satie.* Regensburg: Gustav Bosse Verlag, 1974.
Whanslaw, Harry William. *Shadow Play.* Redhill, Surrey: Wells Gardner, Darton, 1950.
Whittall, Arnold. *Music Since the First World War.* London: Dent, 1977.
Widor, Charles-Marie. *Vieilles chansons et rondes pour les petits enfants.* Paris: Plon-Nourrit, 1883.
Wissant, André de. *Théâtres d'ombres.* 2 vols. Paris: Nouvelles Éditions Debresse, 1969.
Wolff, Pierre. *La Musique contemporaine.* Paris: Fernand Nathan, 1954.
Xanrof, Léon. *Chansons sans-gêne.* Paris: Ondet, 1890.
Yates, Peter. *Twentieth Century Music.* New York: Pantheon Books, 1967.

Theses and Dissertations

Baskerville, David Ross. "Jazz Influence on Art Music to Mid-Century." Ph.D. diss., University of California at Los Angeles, 1965.
Berthe, Mireille. "*Parade*: Ballet cubiste." Mémoire de Maîtrise, Université de Strasbourg, 1979.
Blickhan, Charles T. "Erik Satie: Musique d'ameublement." D.M.A. thesis, University of Illinois, 1976.
Bobbitt, Richard B. "The Harmonic Idiom in the Works of 'Les Six.'" Ph.D. diss., Boston University, 1963.
Braunlich, Helmut. "Satire in Music—1900 to 1920." Ph.D. diss., The Catholic University of America, 1966.
Cailleux, Françoise. "Erik Satie et l'aphorisme." Mémoire de Maîtrise, Université de Paris-Sorbonne, 1985.
Campiotti, Giuseppina. "Erik Satie nella cultura del suo tempo." Tesi di Laurea in Lettere, Università Cattolica del Sacro Cuore (Milan), 1973.
Clanet, Bernard. "Essai sur une personnalité particulière: Erik Satie." Mémoire, Faculté de Médecine (Certificat d'Études Spéciales de Psychiatrie), Université de Caen, 1985.
Debold, Conrad. "'Parade' and 'Le Spectacle intérieur': The Role of Jean Cocteau in an Avant-Garde Ballet." Ph.D. diss., Emory University, 1982.
Fleuriel, Marie-Claude. "L'oeuvre de piano d'Erik Satie." Mémoire de Maîtrise, Université de Paris-Sorbonne, 1978.
Gérard, Yves. "Introduction à l'oeuvre d'Erik Satie." Mémoire du Prix d'Esthètique, Conservatiore Nationale Supérieur de Musique, Paris, 1958.
Gillmor, Alan M. "Erik Satie and the Concept of the Avant-Garde." Ph.D. diss., University of Toronto, 1972.
Gowers, Patrick. "Erik Satie: His Studies, Notebooks and Critics." 2 vols. Ph.D. diss., University of Cambridge, 1966.
Greer, Thomas Henry. "Music and its Relation to Futurism, Cubism, Dadaism, and Surrealism, 1905 to 1950." Ph.D. diss., North Texas State University, 1969.

Harbec, Jacinthe. "'Parade': Les Influences cubistes sur la composition musicale d'Erik Satie." Master's thesis, McGill University, 1987.

Hill, Barbara Ferrell. "Characteristics of the Music of Erik Satie that Suggest the Id." D.M.A. thesis, University of Colorado, 1966.

Koon, Margery A. "Aspects of Harmonic Structure in Piano Works of Erik Satie." D.M.A. thesis, University of Wisconsin, 1974.

Mills, Kathleen Jane. "Erik Satie: An Enigmatic Composer." Master's thesis, Smith College, 1967.

Perloff, Nancy. "Art and the Everyday: The Impact of Parisian Popular Entertainment on Satie, Milhaud, Poulenc, and Auric." Ph.D. diss., University of Michigan, 1986.

Privitera, Massimo. "Erik Satie: Produzione e Riproduzione." Tesi di Laurea, Università di Bologna, 1981.

Rey, Anne. "Dada et le pré-surréalisme dans l'oeuvre d'Erik Satie." Diplôme d'Études Supérieures, Université de Paris, 1967.

Rosenbaum, Earl. "Erik Satie: *Parade*." Master's thesis, California State University, Fullerton, 1974.

Sasser, William Gray. "Erik Satie: A Study of Mutations in His Style." Master's thesis, University of North Carolina, 1949.

Schnöll, Alois. "Erik Satie, Genie oder Scharlatan? Ammerkungen zu den Klavierstücken mit Stories." M.A. diss., Hochschule für Musik und darstellende Kunst, Salzburg, 1982.

Trickey, Samuel Miller. "Les Six." Ph.D. diss., North Texas State College, 1955.

Whiting, Steven Moore. "Erik Satie and Parisian Musical Entertainment, 1888 to 1909." Master's thesis, University of Illinois, 1984.

Encyclopedia Entries

Gowers, Patrick, and Wilkins, Nigel. "Satie, Erik" in *The New Grove Dictionary of Music and Musicians*, ed. Stanley Sadie, Vol. 16, 515–20. London: Macmillan, 1980.

Roy, Jean. "Satie, Erik" in *Die Musik in Geschichte und Gegenwart*, ed. Friedrich Blume, Vol. 11, 1428–31. Kassel: Bärenreiter, 1963.

Magazine/Journal Articles

Ahlstrom, David. "Furnishing Music: An Analysis of Mass Media Music in Terms of Music Systems." *Arts in Society* 12, no. 2 (1975):249–56.

Andrée, Maurice. "Les Concerts: Mme Olénine d'Alheim." *Le Courrier musical* 23 (August / September 1921):230.

———. "Les Concerts: M. Ricardo Viñes." *Le Courrier musical* 23 (1 June 1921):181.

L'Approdo Musicale, nos. 19–20, 1965 (special issue, "Il Gruppo dei Sei").

"À propos du congrès de Paris." *Les Feuilles libres,* no. 26 (April / May 1922):154–56.

Arnaud, Noël. "Rétrobiographie ombilicale d'Erik Satie." *Cahiers dada surréalisme: Association internationale pour l'étude de dada et du surréalisme,* no. 2 (1968):40–54.

Auric, Georges. "Bibliographie." *Le Courrier musical* 19 (1 March 1917):129–30.

———. "Concerts divers, récitals et conférences: M. Pierre Lucas et Mme Jourdan-Morhange." *Le Courrier musical* 19 (July / August 1917):291.

———. "Découverte de Satie." *La Revue musicale* 214 (June 1952):119–24.

———. "Erik Satie: Musicien humoriste." *Revue française de musique* 12 (10 December 1913):138–42.

———. "Jean Cocteau et la musique." *Empreintes,* nos. 7–8 (May / June / July 1950):100–1.

———. "La leçon d'Erik Satie." *La Revue musicale* 6 (August 1925):98–99.

———. "Une oeuvre nouvelle de Satie." *Littérature,* no. 2 (April 1919):23–24.

———. "Théâtre des Champs-Élysées—Les ballets russes: à propos de *Parade.*" *La Nouvelle revue française* 16 (1921):224–27.

Auriol, George. "Erik Satie: The Velvet Gentleman." *La Revue musicale* 5 (March 1924):208–16.

Austin, William. "Satie before and after Cocteau." *Musical Quarterly* 48 (1962):216–33.

Baker, Robb. "Joffrey's 'Parade': A Controversial Collaboration—56 Years Later." *Dance Magazine* 47, no. 3 (March 1973):40–43.

Bancroft, David. "Two Pleas for a French, French Music." *Music and Letters* 48 (1967):109–19; 251-58.

Bathille, Pierre. "Aspect littéraire d'Erik Satie." *La Nouvelle revue critique* 17 (February 1933):73–80.

Bathori, Jane. "Les Musiciens que j'ai connu." *Recorded Sound* 15 (1964):238–45.

———. "Le Socrate d'Erik Satie." *Journal musical français: Musica-Disques,* no. 191 (April 1970):14–15.

Bauer, Marion. "The Composer's Plight: An Interview with Arthur Honegger." *Modern Music* 1 (June 1924):22–24.

Beaumont, Le Comte Étienne de. "The Soirées de Paris." *Little Review* 11 (1925–26):55–57.

Bell, Clive. "The New Ballet." *New Republic* 5 (30 July 1919):414–16.

Berger, Arthur. "Mainly 'Socrate.'" *Saturday Review* 35 (30 August 1952):50–51.

Bertelin, Albert. "Les Concerts: Société Nationale." *Le Courrier musical* 22 (1 March 1920):84–85.

———. "L'Évolution de la musique contemporaine." *Le Courrier musical* 15 (1 and 15 August 1912):445–49; 15 (1 October 1912):502–6; 15 (1 October 1912):529–37.

Bertin, Pierre. "Comment j'ai connu Erik Satie." *La Revue musicale* 214 (June 1952):73–75.

———. "Erik Satie et Le Groupe des Six." *Les Annales: revue mensuelle de lettres françaises* 58, no. 4 (February 1951):49–60.

Bertrand, Paul. "La Semaine musicale." *Le Ménestrel* 86 (12 December 1924):518–19.

Beylie, Claude. "Entr'acte: Le film sans maître." *Cinéma* 69, no. 133 (February 1969):115–117.

Blackmur, Richard P. "Erik Satie—Three Men in a Tub." *Phonograph Monthly Review* 4, no. 10 (July 1930):351.

Blom, Eric. "Erik Satie (1866–1925): 'An Original But Ineffectual Musician.'" *Musical News and Herald* 69 (18 July 1925):52–53.

Boulanger, Nadia. "Modern French Music." *Rice Institute Pamphlet* 13 (April 1926):113–52.

Boulez, Pierre. "Chien flasque." *La Revue musicale* 214 (June 1952):153–54.

Brody, Elaine. "Viñes in Paris: New Light on Twentieth-Century Performance Practice." In *A Musical Offering: Essays in Honor of Martin Bernstein,* edited by Edward H. Clinkscale and Claire Brook. New York: Pendragon Press, 1977, 45–62.

Bruyère, André. "À Honfleur, au siècle dernier: Ce Maître-de-Chapelle et ce petit Satie." *Bulletin des Amis du Musée de Honfleur* (1970):15–26.

Bryars, Gavin, "Berners, Rousseau, Satie." *Studio International* 192 (November / December 1976):308–18.

———. "Satie and the British." *Contact: A Journal of Contemporary Music,* no. 25 (Autumn 1982):4–14.

———. "'Vexations' and its Performers." *Contact: A Journal of Contemporary Music,* no. 26 (Spring 1983):12–20.

Caby, Robert. "Erik Satie." *Orbes,* no. 3 (Spring 1932):31–34.

———. "Erik Satie à sa vraie place." *La Revue musicale* 214 (June 1952):27–32.

———. "Quelques émouvants aspects de la musique d'Erik Satie." *Montparnasse: Bi-mensuel de littérature et d'art* 22 (January 1929):4–5.

Cage, John. "The Beginning of a Connection between Satie and Thoreau." *Musik-Konzepte,* no. 11 (January 1980):37.

———. "Brief über die Uraufführung von *Vexations.*" *Musik-Konzepte,* no. 11 (January 1980):47.

———. "More Satie." *Musical America* 71 (1 April 1951):26.

———. "On Erik Satie." *Art News Annual* 27 (1958):74–81.

———. "Satie Controversy." *Musical America* 70 (15 December 1950):12.

Cage, John, Roger Shattuck, and Alan Gillmor. "Erik Satie: A Conversation." *Contact: A Journal of Contemporary Music,* no. 25 (Autumn 1982):21–26.

Calvocoressi, Michel D. "A Point for Satie's Biographers." *Musical Times* 78 (July 1937):622.

———. "Aux concerts." *Comoedia illustré* 3, no. 10 (15 February 1911):305–6; 5, no. 14 (20 April 1913):668.

——. "Concerning Erik Satie." *Musical Mirror and Fanfare* (April 1933):208–9.

——. "Erik Satie: A Few Recollections and Remarks." *Monthly Musical Record* 55 (1 January 1925):6–7.

——. "M. Erik Satie." *Musica* 10 (April 1911):65–66.

——. "Milhaud on Satie." *Dominant* 2, no. 1 (February 1929):23–26.

——. "More about Satie." *Musical Times* 65 (May 1924):423.

——. "Musical Events of the Month." *Le Courier musical* 14 (15 February 1911):146–47.

——. "The Origin of To-Day's Musical Idiom." *Musical Times* 52 (December 1911):776–78.

Cannon, Stephen. "Erik Satie." *HiFi / Stereo Review* 19 (October 1967):98–101.

Carol-Bérard. "Les Concerts: Concerts Jean Wiéner." *Le Courrier musical* 25 (15 February 1923):69.

Carroll, Noël. "Entr'acte, Paris and Dada." *Millennium Film Journal* 1, no. 1 (Winter 1977):5–11.

Cate, Phillip Dennis. "Empathy with the Humanity of the Streets." *Art News* 76, no. 3 (March 1977):56–59.

Chalupt, René. "Children in Music." *Chesterian* 1 (1919–20):45–47, 72–75.

——. "Paris Letter." *Chesterian* 1 (1919–20):119–20, 2 (1920–21):279–80, 470–71; 4 (1922–23):148–49; 6 (1924–25):23–25, 196–97; 7 (1925–26):58–59, 132–33; 8 (1926–27):24–25.

——. "Quelques souvenirs sur Erik Satie." *La Revue musicale* 214 (June 1952):39–46.

Cheiner, Sophie. "Erik Satie (1866–1925) y su Influencia en la obra de Ravel." *Heterofonia* 13, no. 68 (1980):29–31.

Chennevière, Georges. "Concerts: Société Nationale." *Le Monde musical* 25 (15 April 1913):120.

Chennevière, Rudhyar D. "Erik Satie and the Music of Irony." *Musical Quarterly* 5 (1919):469–78.

Chevaillier, Lucien. "Un entretien avec . . . Roland-Manuel." *Guide du concert et du disque* 15 (24 and 31 May 1929):951–53.

Cingria, Charles-Albert. "Le M'Sieur d'Arcueil." In *Oeuvres complètes.* Lausanne: Éditions l'Age d'Homme, 1968–69, 9:287–98.

Clair, René. "Picabia, Satie et la première d'*Entr'acte.*" *L'Avant-Scène,* no. 86 (November 1968):5–7.

Cocteau, Jean. "La Collaboration de 'Parade.'" *Nord-Sud: Revue littéraire,* nos. 4–5. (June / July 1917):29–31.

——. "Eric Satie." *Action: Cahiers de philosophie et d'art,* no. 2 (March 1920):15–21.

——. "Erik Satie." *Fanfare* 1, no. 2 (15 October 1921):21–25.

——. "L'exemple d'Erik Satie." *La Revue musicale* 6 (August 1925):97–98.

——. "Fragments d'une conférence sur Erik Satie (1920)." *La Revue musicale* 5 (March 1924):217–23.

———. "Parade: Ballet Réaliste." *Vanity Fair* 5 (September 1917):37, 106.

———. "Picasso." *Les Feuilles libres* 5, no. 34 (November / December 1923):217–32.

———. "Ravel et nous." *La Revue musicale* 19 (December 1938):396–97.

———. "Satie." *La Revue musicale* 214 (June 1952):17–18.

———. "Zwei meiner Mitarbeiter." *Anbruch: Monatsschrift für moderne Musik* 12 (April / May 1930):146–47.

Coeuroy, André. "The Cure by Literature." *Modern Music* 2 (April 1925):3–6.

———. "The Esthetics of Contemporary Music." *Musical Quarterly* 15 (1929):246–67.

———. "Fauré-Caplet-Satie." *Musikblätter des Anbruch: Monatsschrift für moderne Musik* 7 (August / September 1925):430–31.

———. "La fin des Six et de Satie." *La Revue générale: perspectives européennes des sciences humaines* 6–7 (June / July 1974):1–25.

———. "French Gains and Losses." *Modern Music* 3 (November / December 1925):35–37.

———. "Further Aspects of Contemporary Music." *Musical Quarterly* 15 (1929):547–73.

———. "Le Groupe des Six." *La Revue générale: perspectives européennes des sciences humaines* 5 (May 1974):1–27.

———. "La Musique et les Lettres: Hommages littéraires à Erik Satie." *La Revue musicale* 5 (March 1924):283–84.

———. "Les Revues et la Presse: Le double visage d'Erik Satie." *La Revue musicale* 5 (March 1924):284–85.

———. "Satie (Erik Leslie)." *Larousse mensuel*, no. 225 (November 1925):962–63.

Collaer, Paul. "Erik Satie: 'Mercure'—'Relâche.'" *Sélection: Chronique de la vie artistique et littéraire* 4, no. 4 (January 1925):304–6.

———. "L'Influence d'Erik Satie." *Sélection: Chronique de la vie artistique et littéraire* 3, no. 6 (April 1924):82–85.

———. "'Socrate.'" *Action: Cahiers de philosophie et d'art*, no. 10 (November 1921):29–32.

Collet, Henri. "Erik Satie." *L'Esprit nouveau* 2 (1916):145–58.

"The Comic Spirit as Realized in the Music of Erik Satie." *Current Opinion* 61 (October 1916):245.

Cooper, Martin. "Pierrot of Paris." *Opera News* 30 (7 May 1966):6–7.

Cortot, Alfred. "Le cas Erik Satie." *La Revue musicale* 19 (April / May 1938):248–72.

Cox, David. "Erik Satie: Inspired Eccentric." *Listener* 64, no. 1646 (13 October 1960):657.

———. "Peculiar Homage to Socrates." *Listener* 64 no. 1708 (21 December 1961):1089.

Csampai, Attila, and Holland, Dietmar. "Der Skandal Satie." *Hi Fi Stereophonie* 15 (November 1976):1257–62.

Dale, R. C. "René Clair's *Entr'acte,* or Motion Victorious." *Wide Angle* 2, no. 2 (1978):38–43.

Damon, S. Foster. "American Influence on Modern French Music." *Dial* 65 (15 August 1918):93–95.

Danckert, Werner. "Der Klassizismus Erik Saties und seiner geistesgeschichtliche Stellung." *Zeitschrift für Musikwissenschaft* 12 (1929):105–14.

Desnos, Robert. "Cinéma: *Entr'acte* par Francis Picabia, mise en scène de René Clair." *Le Journal littéraire,* no. 34 (13 December 1924):15.

Dewey, Stoddard. "Novel Music in Paris." *Nation* 104 (28 June 1917):769.

Dickinson, Peter. "Erik Satie (1866–1925)." *Music Review* 28 (1967):139–46.

————. "Transformations of Erik Satie." In *Twenty British Composers,* edited by Peter Dickinson. London: J. & W. Chester, 1975, 47–49.

Dietschy, Marcel. "The Family and Childhood of Debussy." *Musical Quarterly* 46 (1960):301–14.

Dinwiddie, John. "Mewantemooseicday: John Cage in Davis, 1969." *Source: Music of the Avant-Garde* 4, no. 1 (January 1970):21–26.

Dumesnil, Maurice. "Erik Satie: The Mischievous Man of French Music." *Etude* 60 (December 1942):816, 849, 855.

Durey, Louis. "Erik Satie." *Arts* 17 (1930):162–65.

Écorcheville, Jules. "Erik Satie." *Revue musicale S.I.M.* 7 (15 March 1911):29–40.

Emié, Louis. "Éloge d'Erik Satie." *Les Feuilles libres* 3, no. 5 (October 1921):267–71.

Engel, Carl. "Views and Reviews." *Musical Quarterly* 8 (1922):622–25.

"*Entr'acte.*" *L'Avant-Scène,* no. 86 (November 1968):9–18.

"*Entr'acte*: trois opinions de 1924." *L'Avant-Scène,* no. 86 (November 1968):7.

"Erik Satie e Claude Debussy." *Musica d'oggi* 6 (April / May 1924):133.

"Erik Satie: Introduction." *Musicalia: International Music Review* 1 (1970):2–3.

"Erik Satie: Nota biografica." *Bollettino bibliografico musicale* 3 (August / September 1928):1–8.

Filenko, G. "'Parad' Satie" ["Satie's 'Parade'"]. *Sovetskaia Muzyka* 30 (1966):110–13.

Fisher, Fred. "Erik Satie's Piano Music: A Centenary Survey." *Clavier* 5 (October 1966):14–19.

————. "Weightless Atmospheric Disclosures in the Shape of a Music Rack." *Clavier* 5 (October 1966):25–27.

Fournier, Gabriel. "Erik Satie et son époque." *La Revue musicale* 214 (June 1952):129–35.

Frankenstein, Alfred. "The Music of Erik Satie: Cold Pieces that Aren't Cold, and Other Delightful Things." *High Fidelity* 18 (July 1966):71.

Frèrebeau, Mariel. "What is Montmartre? Nothing! What should it be? Everything!" *Art News* 76 (March 1977):60–62.

Fumet, Stanislas. "Eironeia." *La Revue musicale* 214 (June 1952):19–22.

Gallez, Douglas W. "Satie's *Entr'acte*: A Model of Film Music." *Cinema Journal* 16, no. 1 (Fall 1976):36–50.

Gatti, Guido M. "Il 'Socrate' di Erik Satie." *Musica d'oggi* 2 (November 1920):299–301; reprinted in German as "'Sokrates' von Erik Satie." *Musikblätter des Anbruch: Monatsschrift für moderne Musik* 3 (February 1921):75–77.

Giddins, Gary. "Vienna Jazz Satie Style." *Village Voice* 29, no. 45 (6 November 1984):82, 85.

Gillmor, Alan M. "Erik Satie and the Concept of the Avant-Garde." *Musical Quarterly* 69 (1983):104–19.

———. "Satie, Cage, and the New Asceticism." *Contact: A Journal of Contemporary Music*, no. 25 (Autumn 1982):15–20.

Gilman, Lawrence. "Monsieur Satie and Mr. Carpenter." *North American Review* 215 (May 1922):692–97.

Godebska, Marie [Misia Sert]. "A 'Spectacle-Concert' in Paris." *Chesterian* 1 (1919–20):165–67.

Goléa, Antoine. "Erik Satie." *Neue Zeitschrift für Musik* 127 (November 1966):418–23.

Golschmann, Vladimir. "Golschmann Remembers Erik Satie." *High Fidelity / Musical America* 22 (August 1972): MA 11–12; 32.

Goodfriend, James. "Satie." *Stereo Review* 44 (June 1980):124.

Gowers, Patrick. "Satie's Rose Croix Music (1891–1895)." *Proceedings of the Royal Musical Association* 92 (1965–66):1–25.

Guichard, Léon. "À propos d'Erik Satie: Notules incohérentes." *Recherches et travaux (Université de Grenoble, Unité d'Enseignement et de Recherches des Lettres)*, Bulletin no. 7 (March 1973):63–80.

———. "Erik Satie (1866–1925)." *Médecine de France* 179 (1967):38–40, 48.

———. "Erik Satie et la musique grégorienne." *La Revue musicale* 17 (November 1936):334–35.

———. "Prélude à l'Oeuvre d'Erik Satie." *Le Point: Revue artistique et littéraire* 3, no. 14 (April 1938):83–85.

Harrington, Charles. "Erik Satie: The Piano Music." *American Record Guide* 35 (October 1968):110–17.

———. "From Philips, Satie by Evelyne Crochet." *American Record Guide* 35 (October 1968):117–18.

Harrison, Max. "Satie: Disquiet and Dislocation." *Composer*, no. 38 (Winter 1970–71):27–28.

Helm, Everett. "Erik Satie zum 100. Geburtstag." *Österreichische Musikzeitschrift* 21 (1966):239–42.

———. "Das Leben von Erik Satie: Eine wahre Tragödie in kinematographischen Szenen." *Antares* 1, no. 7 (1953):53–59.

———. "The Man with the Mask." *High Fidelity* 13 (December 1963):54–56; 119.

————. "Satie—Still a Fascinating Enigma." *Musical America* 78 (February 1958):27–28, 166.

Henderson, Robert. "Erik Satie." *Musical Times* 107 (December 1966):1076.

Henderson, W. J. "The Gods of Modern Music." *American Mercury* 2 (July 1924):335–39.

————. "The Revolutionary Art of Paris." *Independent* 110 (3 February 1923):102–4.

Henry, Leigh. "'Contemporaries:' Erik Satie." *Musical Opinion* 43 (March 1920):459–60.

————. "Erik Satie and 'L'Esprit Gaulois' in Music." *Musical Standard* 14 (2 August 1919):28–29; 14 (16 August 1919):45–46.

————. "Erik Satie and the Ironic Spirit." *Egoist* 1 (1 July 1914):252–54.

————. "Erik Satie: A Tribute." *Musical Standard* 26 (25 July 1925):23.

————. "The Fantaisiste Spirit in Modern French Music." *Egoist* 3 (1 January 1916):3–4; 3 (1 March 1916):43–46.

————. "'Parade' at the Empire." *Musical Standard* 14 (6 December 1919):181.

————. "'Socrate' and the New Asceticism." *Musical Standard* 16 (23 April 1921):146.

Hesford, Bryan. "The Performance and Problems of Erik Satie's 'Messe des Pauvres.'" *Musical Opinion* 89 (June 1966):533.

————. "Towards Understanding Erik Satie's 'Messe des Pauvres.'" *Musical Opinion* 105 (March 1982):201–7.

Higgins, Dick, "Boredom and Danger." *Source: Music of the Avant-Garde* 3, no. 1 (January 1969):14–17.

Hijman, Julius. "Satie's dood en wederrdood." *Caecilia en de Musiek* 92, nos. 10–11 (August / September 1935):406–8.

Hill, Edward Burlingame. "Musical Boston in the Gay Nineties." *Etude* 67 (1949):229, 264–65.

Hinton, James, Jr. "In One Ear: The Day of an Artist." *High Fidelity* 4 (March 1954):47–48.

Hirsbrunner, Theo. "Erik Saties revolutionäre Tendenzen." *Melos: Neue Zeitschrift für Musik* 4 (January / February 1978):19–21.

————. "Erik Satie und Willy." *Schweizerische Musikzeitung/Revue musicale suisse* 112, no. 5 (September / October 1972):265–69.

Holland, Philip. "*Relâche* Revisted." *Ballet News* 2, no. 5 (November 1980):26–30.

Honegger, Arthur. "Modern Music." *Rice Institute Pamphlet* 16 (1929):123–31.

Hopkins, Bill. "Satie's Century." *Music and Musicians* 14 (July 1966):49.

Howe, Martin. "Erik Satie and his Ballets." *Ballet* 5, no. 8. (August / September 1948):25–39, 53–54; 6, no. 1 (October 1948):25–30.

Hugo, Valentine. "Le Socrate que j'ai connu." *La Revue musicale* 214 (June 1952):139–45.

Imbert, Maurice. "Erik Satie." *Le Courrier musical* 27 (15 July / 1 August 1925):423.

"Is Satie's Music Satirical or Merely Silly?" *Current Opinion* 68 (February 1920):198–99.

Jachimecki, Zdzislaw. "Erik Satie." *Muzyka: Miesiecznik Ilustrowany* 4, no. 3 (March 1927):114–18; 4, no. 5 (May 1927):216–18.

Jacob, Dom Clément. "Erik Satie et le chant grégorien." *La Revue musicale* 214 (June 1952):85–94.

Jacob, Maxime. "L'exemple d'Erik Satie." *Vigile* 2 (1930):123–35.

"James Cuomo Still World Champ on 'Vexations' as Australian Collapses." *School Musician* 41, no. 9 (May 1970):12.

Jean-Aubry, Georges. "The End of a Legend." *Chesterian* 6 (1924–25):191–93.

———. "Erik Satie: A Musical Humorist." *Music Student* 9 (December 1916):135–36.

Jeanneret, Albert. "'Parade.'" *L'Esprit nouveau* 4 (1918):449–52.

———. "'Socrate.'" *L'Esprit nouveau* 9 (1923):989–95.

Jungheinrich, Hans-Klaus. "Der ganze Satie fürs Theater: Eine bemerkenswerte Aktivität der Pariser Oper." *Musica* 33, no. 5 (1979):455–56.

———. "Surrealismus in der Musik." *Melos: Zeitschrift für neue Musik* 31 (December 1964):381–89.

G. K. [Mme Georges Kinen]. "Les Concerts." *Revue musicale S.I.M.* 8 (July / August 1912):66–67.

———. "Concerts Divers." *Revue musicale S.I.M.* 9 (15 April 1913):56–57.

Kerner, Leighton. "'Parade'—Elle Marche." *Village Voice* 26 no. 11 (11–17 March 1981):70.

———. "Satie Among the Coffee Spoons." *Village Voice* 24 no. 26 (25 June 1979):90.

Kisling, Moïse. "Souvenir de Satie." *La Revue musicale* 214 (June 1952):107–10.

Klein, Lothar. "Twentieth Century Analysis: Essays in Miniature." *Music Educators Journal* 53 (1966):25–26.

Koch, Gerhard R. "Im Banalen liegt die Ewigkeit." *Hi Fi Stereophonie* 15 (November 1976):1264–66.

———. "Sehr jung auf dieser sehr alten Welt: Ein Versuch über Erik Satie." *Musica* 30, no. 4 (1976):301–4.

Koechlin, Charles. "Erik Satie." *La Revue musicale* 5 (March 1924):193–207.

———. "Situation actuelle de la musique en France." *La Revue internationale de musique* 1 (March / April 1938):40–54.

Kolodin, Irving. "Music to My Ears." *Saturday Review* 48 (23 January 1965):38.

La Grange, Henri-Louis de. "Satie revisité." *Contrepoints,* no. 6 (1949):171–72.

Laloë, Marcel. "Erik Satie." *Les Réverbères,* no. 1 (April 1938):8.

Lambert, Constant. "Erik Satie et la musique abstraite." *La Revue musicale* 214 (June 1952):101–6.

Landormy, Paul. "Le Déclin de l'Impressionisme." *La Revue musicale* 2 (February 1921):97–113.

———. "Le Groupe des Six." *Revue de Genève* 3, no. 15 (September 1921):393–409.

Lanza Tomasi, Gioacchino. "Erik Satie et la musica del surrealismo." In *Studi sul surrealismo.* Rome: Officina Edizione, 1976, 218–65.

Le Flem, Paul. "Les Concerts: Mme J. Mortier." *Le Courrier musical* 23 (15 January 1921):29–30.

Léger, Fernand. "Satie inconnu." *La Revue musicale* 214 (June 1952):137–38.

Leiris, Michael. "L'Humour d'Erik Satie." *La Nouvelle revue française* 26 (1938):163–64.

Le Masle, Robert. "Chroniques: D'Angleterre: Anniversaires 3: Erik Satie évoqué et interprété à Londres." *Contrepoints,* no. 1 (1946):119–21.

Leroi, Pierre. "Les Concerts: Festival Erik Satie." *Le Courrier musical* 22 (August / September 1920):233.

———. "Les Concerts: Mme Marthe Martine." *Le Courrier musical* 24 (1 April 1922):122.

Lieberman, William S. "Picasso and the Ballet." *Dance Index* 5 (November / December 1946):261–308.

C. L. [Clarence Lucas]. "In Memoriam Erik Satie." *Musical Courier* 99 (10 August 1929):24.

Luten, C. J. "Maurice Abravanel's Homage to Erik Satie." *American Record Guide* 35 (October 1968):119.

———. "Satie: *Parade, Relâche, Gymnopédies* Nos. 1 & 3." *American Record Guide* 35 (October 1968):118.

Lutz, Henri. "Les Concerts: Pour la musique." *Le Courrier musical* 21 (1 June 1919):169.

Lyle, Wilson. "Erik Satie and Rosicrucianism." *Music Review* 42 (1981):238–42.

Macdougall, Allan Ross. "Music and Dancing in Paris." *Arts and Decoration* 21 (October 1924):35, 80.

Mangeot, André. "Concerts: Salle Gaveau." *Le Monde musical* 23 (30 January 1911):27.

———. "Erik Satie." *Le Monde musical* 44 (31 January 1933):7–9.

Mann, Michael. "Reaction and Continuity in Musical Composition." *Music Review* 15 (1954):39–46.

Maré, Rolf de. "The Swedish Ballet and the Modern Aesthetic." *Little Review* 11 (1925–26):24–28.

Maritain, Raissa. "A Handful of Musicians." *Commonweal* 39 (29 October 1943):32–35.

Marks, Martin. "The Well-Furnished Film: Satie's Score for *Entr'acte.*" *Canadian University Music Review,* no. 4 (1983):245–77.

Markus, Wim. "Axel or the Rejection of Life." *Key Notes,* no. 6 (1977):19–32.

Marnold, Jean. "Revue de la quinzaine: Musique." *Mercure de France* 123 (1917):132–37, 139 (1920):782–91; 175 (1924):524–31.

Martin, Marianne W. "The Ballet *Parade*: A Dialogue Between Cubism and Futurism." *Art Quarterly,* new series 1, no. 2 (Spring 1978):85–111.

Marval, Louis de. "À propos d'Erik Satie." *Schweizerische Musikzeitung/Revue musicale suisse* 107, no. 6 (November / December 1967):340–42.

Marvy, Luc. "Concerts: Société Nationale." *Le Monde musical* 26 (15 April 1914):120.

Massot, Pierre de. "Quelques propos et souvenirs sur Erik Satie." *La Revue musicale* 214 (June 1952):125–28.

———. "'Soirée de Paris.'" *Little Review* 10 (1924–25):24–27.

Mayr, W. "Entretien avec Erik Satie." *Le Journal littéraire*, no. 24 (October 1924):11.

Mellers, Wilfrid H. "The Classicism of Erik Satie." *Listener* 18 (11 August 1937):318.

———. "Erik Satie and the 'Problem' of Contemporary Music." *Music and Letters* 23 (1942):210–27.

———. "Erik Satie et la musique 'fonctionelle.'" *La Revue musicale* 214 (June 1952):33–37.

Mesens, E. L. T. "Hommage à Erik Satie." *Sélection: Chronique de la vie artistique et littéraire* 3, no. 10 (August 1924):535–38.

———. "Le souvenir d'Erik Satie." *La Revue musicale* 214 (June 1952):147–51.

Messiaen, Alain. "Les Musiciens devant Dieu: Erik Satie." *Les Amis de Saint-François: Revue de doctrine, de littérature et d'art* 9, no. 3 (May / June 1968):102–6.

Michaut, Pierre. "Cocteau and the Ballet." *Adelphi* 29 (February 1953):112–18.

Milhaud, Darius. "Chronique musicale." *Intentions* 2, no. 20 (December 1923):17–18.

———. "Les Concerts: Festival Erik Satie." *Le Courrier musical* 23 (15 January 1921):28.

———. "The Day after Tomorrow." *Modern Music* 3 (November / December 1925):22–24.

———. "Les dernières oeuvres d'Erik Satie et les premières oeuvres d'Henri Sauguet." *Les Feuilles libres* 5, no. 37 (September / October 1924):46–48.

———. "Erik Satie et l'Art de la Fugue." *Musique: Revue mensuelle de critique d'histoire, d'esthétique et d'information musicales* 3, no. 4 (15 January 1930):145–47.

———. "Lettre de Darius Milhaud." *La Revue musicale* 214 (June 1952):153.

———. "Notes sur Erik Satie." In *Oeuvres nouvelles*. New York: Maison Français, 1946, 91–108.

———. "Werdegang von Erik Satie." *Anbruch: Monatsschrift für moderne Musik* 12 (April / May 1930):144–45.

Mueller, John. "Films: 'Relâche' and 'Entr'acte.'" *Dance Magazine* 51 (July 1977):102–3.

Myers, Rollo H. "A Music Critic in Paris in the Nineteen-Twenties: Some Personal Recollections." *Musical Quarterly* 63 (1977):524–44.

———. "Erik Satie and 'Socrate.'" *Listener* 30 (9 June 1949):996.

———. "Esoterick Satie." *Music and Musicians* 27 (July 1979):74–75.

———. "Importance de Satie dans la musique contemporaine." *La Revue musicale* 214 (June 1952):77–81.

————. "Note sur 'Socrate.'" *La Revue musicale* 214 (June 1952):81–84.

————. "Poet or Buffoon?" *Radio Times,* 13 August 1937, 11.

————. "Quelques reflexions sur le Rôle de la Musique dans le Ballet contemporaine." *Polyphonie: Revue musicale trimestrielle* 1 (1947–48):66–70.

————. "The Significance of Satie: A Centenary Tribute." *Music and Musicians* 14 (May 1966):16–17, 41.

————. "Some Recent Satie Publications." *Musical Times* 111 (January 1970):32–33.

————. "The Strange Case of Erik Satie." *Musical Times* 86 (July 1945):201–3.

"Necrologie: Erik Satie." *Le Ménestrel* 87 (10 July 1925):312.

Neill, Edward. "Erik Satie." *Musicalia: International Music Review* 1 (June 1970):4–11.

"Nos Echos—*Relâche.*" *Le Journal littéraire,* no. 33 (6 December 1924):4.

"Notes sur les concerts: La S.M.I." *Le Guide du concert* 2 (14 January 1911):156–57.

"Notes sur les concerts: S.M.I." *Le Guide du concert* 5 (10 January 1914):203–4.

Nyman, Michael. "Cage and Satie." *Musical Times* 114 (December 1973):1227–29.

Op de Coul, Paul. "Satie und Péladan: Ein Beitrag zur Biographie des junger Erik Satie." *Bericht über den Internationalen Musikwissenschaftlichen Kongress Berlin 1974,* Hellmut Kühn and Peter Nitsche, eds. Kassel: Bärenreiter-Verlag, 1980, 195–207.

Orban, Marcel. "Les Concerts: Au Vieux-Colombier." *Le Courrier musical* 20 (1 January 1918):17.

————. "Les Concerts: Société Musicale Indépendante." *Le Courrier musical* 19 (June 1917):257.

————. "La Quinzaine: Société Musicale Indépendante." *Le Courrier musical* 14 (1 February 1911):100.

Pâris, Alain. "À la recherche d'Erik Satie." *Le Courrier musical de France* 52 (1975):130–31.

Pearsall, Ronald. "Satie Forty Years After." *Musical Opinion* 88 (March 1965):335.

————. "The Sophistication of the Graceful." *Music Review* 23 (1962):205–7.

Pernaud, Georges. "Erik Satie inconnu à cinquante ans." *À la page: L'Hebdomadaire des jeunes,* no. 24 (June 1966):898–907.

Peterkin, Norman. "Erik Satie's 'Parade.'" *Musical Times* 60 (August 1919):426–27.

Petit, Raymond. "Music Written for French Films." *Modern Music* 3 (March / April 1926):32–36.

Phelps, Robert. "The Re-sounding Triumph of a Whimsical Composer: Erik Satie, 1866–1925." *Vogue* 157, no. 9 (May 1971):156.

Picabia, Francis. "Entr'acte." *This Quarter,* 1, no. 3 (1927):301–2.

Polignac, Princesse Edmond de. "Memoirs." *Horizon* 12 (August 1945):110–41.

Politis, Hélène. "Sermons humoristiques (Les *Écrits* d'Erik Satie)." In *Écrit pour Vladimir Jankélévitch.* Paris: Flammarion, 1978, 83–105.

Porter, David H. "Recurrent Motifs in Erik Satie's *Sports et Divertissements.*" *Music Review* 39 (1978):227–30.

Potamkin, Harry Alan. "René Clair and Film Humor." *Hound and Horn* 6, no. 1 (October / December 1932):114–23.

Poueigh, Jean. "Concerts et Récitals: À Travers la Quinzaine." *Revue musicale S.I.M.* 10 (1 February 1914):55–57.

Poulenc, Francis. "La musique de piano d'Erik Satie." *La Revue musicale* 214 (June 1952):23–26.

"Précisions sur le 'cas Eric Satie.'" *Dissonances: Revue musicale indépendante* 4 (June 1931):159–60.

Prieberg, Fred K. "Erik Satie." *Musica* 9 (1955):366–69.

"Programme annotés des concerts: Société Olenine d'Alheim." *Le Guide du concert* 7 (29 April 1921):440.

Prunières, Henry. "Les Ballets Russes: *La Pastorale* de Georges Auric—*Jack in the Box* d'Eric Satie." *La Revue musicale* 7 (July 1926):56–58.

———. "Chroniques et Notes: *Socrate* d'Erik Satie." *La Revue musicale* 4 (February 1923):65–66.

———. "Erik Satie: à propos de Socrate." *Nouvelle revue française* 14 (1920):605–8.

———. "Erik Satie (1866–1925)." *Il Pianoforte* 6 (August / September 1925):254–57.

———. "The Failure of Success." *Musical Digest* 8 (28 July 1925):5.

Puccini, Gianni. "*Entr'acte.*" *Cinema: Quindicinale di divulgazione cinematografica* 3, no. 60 (1938):385–86.

Rašín, Vera. "'Les Six' and Jean Cocteau." *Music and Letters* 38 (1957):164–69.

Rathert, Wolfgang and Andreas Traub. "Zu einer bislang unbekannten Ausgabe des 'Socrate' von Erik Satie." *Die Musikforschung* 38 (1985):118–21.

Ravel, Maurice. "Contemporary Music." *Rice Institute Pamphlet* 15 (1928):131–45.

Renshaw, Rosette. "Erik Satie (1866–1925)." *La Nouvelle revue canadienne* 1 (1951):76–80.

"Les Revues et la Presse: Erik Satie." *La Revue musicale* 2 (February 1921):181.

"Les Revues et la Presse: Mots d'Erik Satie." *La Revue musicale* 3 (August 1922):189.

"Les Revues et la Presse: *Parade.*" *La Revue musicale* 2 (March 1921):282–83.

"Les Revues et la Presse: Une appréciation italienne du *Socrate* d'Erik Satie." *La Revue musicale* 2 (June 1921):280.

Rey-Andreu, Étienne. "Musique Nouvelles: Musique de Piano." *Le Courrier musical* 24 (15 March 1922):109.

Ringo, James. "Delicately Molded Sensuality, Bordering on the Pornographic." *American Record Guide* 37 (January 1971):310–12.

———. "The Real Thing—Satie and William Masselos." *American Record Guide* 36 (May 1970):692–94.

Roberts, W. Wright. "The Problem of Satie." *Music and Letters* 4 (1923):313–20.

Rogers, M. Robert. "Jazz Influence on French Music." *Musical Quarterly* 21 (1935):53–68.

Roland-Manuel [Roland-Alexis Manuel Lévy]. "Adieu à Satie." *Revue pleyel,* no. 15 (December 1924):21–22.

———. "Satie tel que je l'ai vu." *La Revue musicale* 214 (June 1952):9–11.

———. "Silhouettes d'Artistes: Erik Satie." *L'Écho Musical: Revue Mensuelle Illustré* 2 (April 1913):1–3.

Rorem, Ned. "Notes on Parade." *Opera News* 45 (28 February 1981):8–18.

Rostand, Claude. "Cocteau: ein Leben mit der Musik." *Melos: Zeitschrift für neue Musik* 31 (February 1964):48–52.

———. "Jean Cocteau et la musique." *La Table ronde* 94 (1955):84–90.

———. "Picasso et la musique." *Schweizerische Musikzeitung/Revue musicale suisse* 101, no. 6 (November / December 1961):374–77.

Roy, Jean. "Erik Satie: Le mythe et la réalité." *Panorama de la musique,* no. 29 (May / June 1979):6–9.

———. "L'original Erik Satie." *Musica: Revue mensuelle,* no. 138 (September 1965):13–15.

———. "Satie poète." *La Revue musicale* 214 (June 1952):55–57.

———. "Tout autour d'une lettre: Erik Satie." *Journal musical français: Musica-Disques,* no. 174 (November 1968):44–45.

Ruppel, K. H. "Monsieur le Pauvre." *Melos: Zeitschrift für neue Musik* 33 (July / August 1966):205–9.

H. R. [Harold Rutland]. "Homage to Erik Satie." *Musical Times* 98 (December 1957):682.

———. "Notes and Comments." *Musical Times* 98 (December 1957):665.

H. S. [Hubert Saal]. "The Parade Goes On." *Newsweek* 81 (2 April 1973): 61–62.

Sabatier, François. "Pour le Cinquantenaire de la mort d'Erik Satie." *Jeunesse et orgue* 25 (September 1975):5–6.

E. S. [Eric Salzman]. "Satie: *Socrate.*" *Stereo Review* 24 (June 1970):90.

Sandro, Paul. "Parodic Narration in 'Entr'acte.'" *Film Criticism* 4, no. 1 (Fall 1979):44–55.

Sanouillet, Michel. "Erik Satie et son 'violon d'encre.'" *Travaux de linguistique et de littérature publiés par le centre de philogie et de littérature romanes de l'Université de Strasbourg* 7, no. 2 (1969):167–80.

Santi, Piero. "Il 'Point de Départ' di Satie." *Chigiana: Rassegna annuale di studi musicologia* 23 (1966):183–99.

Sasser, William G. "Le développement du style d'Erik Satie." *La Revue musicale*

214 (June 1952):111–17.

Satie, Conrad. "Erik Satie." *Le Coeur* 2, no. 10 (June 1895):2–3.

"Satie-ana." *La Revue musicale* 5 (March 1924):224–28.

"Satie Applauded: A Happening in South Dakota." *Clavier* 8 (March 1969):34.

Sauguet, Henri. "Erik Satie." *Le Courrier musical de France* 52 (1975):129.

———. "Quelques extraits des souvenirs." *La Revue musicale* 361–63 (1983): 225–49.

———. "Souvenirs et réflexions autour d'Erik Satie." *La Revue musicale* 214 (June 1952):95–99.

Saunders, William. "Erik Satie." *Musical News* 53 (1 September 1917):131–33.

———. "Erik Satie's Forms and Harmonies." *Musical News* 53 (8 September 1917):147–48.

Savinio, Alberto. "Erik Satie." In *Scatola sonora*. Turin: Giulio Einaudi, 1977, 279–83.

Schloezer, Boris de. "Les Ballets russes: Eric Satie." *La Nouvelle revue française* 25 (1925):247–52.

———. "Réflexions sur la musique: Le cas Satie." *La Revue musicale* 5 (August 1924):173–76.

Schmitt, Florent. "Erik Satie." *Montjoie!* (14 March 1913):11–12.

Schneider, Édouard. "La Quinzaine: Concerts de la S.M.I." *Le Courrier musical* 15 (1 July 1912):403.

"Scritti di Erik Satie." *Musicalia: International Music Review* 1 (1970):12–13.

Shattuck, Roger. "Erik Satie, Composer to the School of Paris." *Art News Annual* 27 (1958):65–68; 186–91.

———. "Satie et la musique de placard." *La Revue musicale* 214 (June 1952):47–54.

Skulsky, Abraham. "Erik Satie." *Musical America* 70 (15 November 1950):5, 32, 36.

———. "Satie Controversy." *Musical America* 70 (15 December 1950):12.

Schnebel, Dieter. "Gothische Tänze, Schlaffe Präludien (für einen Hund), Sport und Vergnügen." *Musik-Konzepte*, no. 11 (January 1980):64–65.

Socanne, Pierre. "Sur Erik Satie." *Le Guide du concert* 13 (7 January 1927):377–79.

Sonnedecker, Shirley and Donald. "The Unappreciated Erik Satie." *Music Journal* 16 (1958):44, 97.

Stuckenschmidt, Hans-Heinz. "Erik Satie." *Anbruch: Monatsschrift für moderne Musik* 11 (February 1929):60–64; reprinted in *Der Auftakt* 14, nos. 1–2. (1934):6–9.

Terenzio, Vincenzo. "Erik Satie: un bilancio." *Musica d'oggi* 6 (July / August 1963):156–60.

Terpander. "Erik Satie's 'Trois Petites pièces montées' (1919)." *Gramophone* 12 (January 1935):321–22.

"Texte d'Erik Satie." *Empreintes,* nos. 7–8. (May / June / July 1950):98.

"Textes d'Erik Satie." *La Revue musicale* 214 (June 1952):61–71.

Thomson, Virgil. "A Little about Movie Music." *Modern Music* 10 (1933):188–91.

———. "How Modern Music Gets That Way." *Vanity Fair* 24 (April 1925):46, 102.

———. "In the Theater." *Modern Music* 14 (1937):101–5.

———. "Now in Paris." *Modern Music* 10 (1933):141–48.

———. "La place de Satie dans la musique du xxe siècle." *La Revue musicale* 214 (June 1952):13–15.

———. "Satie: 'Socrate.'" *Musical Quarterly* 39 (1953):147–49.

Tiénot, Yvonne, and O. d'Estrade-Guerra. "Debussy et Erik Satie." *Revue musicale de suisse romande* 15 (June / July 1962):86.

Udine, Jean d'. "Couleurs, mouvements et sons: Les Ballets russes, en 1917." *Le Courrier musical* 19 (June 1917):237–41.

Vallas, Léon. "Concerts de la semaine: Glanes." *Le Guide du concert* 11 (14 November 1924):144.

Veen, Jan van der. "Erik Satie." *Mens en Melodie* 8 (December 1953):389–94.

———. "De fauteuil van Sokrates: Erik Satie en de funktionele muziek." In *Orfeus onder de stervelingen*. The Hague: Bert Bakker / Daamen nv, 1968, 11–63.

Vermeulen, Ernst. "Chabrier, Rossini en Clementi als voorlopers van Satie." *Mens en Melodie* 31 (March 1976):79–82.

Vernazza, Marcelle. "Erik Satie's Music for Children." *Clavier* 18 (January 1979):39–40.

Vianis, Paul. "À la vanvole." *Le Guide du concert* 6 (17 and 24 April 1920):219.

Vidal, Max. "La Quinzaine musicale: Société Nationale." *Le Courrier musical* 16 (1 May 1913):266.

Vuillermoz, Émile. "The Legend of the Six." *Modern Music* 1 (February 1924):15–19.

Walker, Robert. "Children's Pieces for Piano." *Music in Education* 40 (January / February 1976):24.

Wehmeyer, Grete. "Erik Satie und die Künstler." V., In *Vom Klang der Bilder: Die Musik in der Kunst des 20. Jahrhunderts,* edited by Karin V. Maur. Munich: Prestel-Verlag, 1985, 384–89.

———. "Saties Instananeismus." In *Festschrift Karl Gustav Fellerer* (Musicae Scientiae Collectanea), edited by Heinrich Hüschen. Cologne: Arno-Volk-Verlag, 1973, 626–39.

———. "Satie und das Werden der Multimedia-Idee." *Österreichische Musikzeitschrift* 30 (1975):401–8.

Wilheim, András. "Erik Satie's Gregorian Paraphrases." *Studia Musicologica Academiae Scientiarum Hungaricae* 25 (1983):229–37.

Viñes, Ricardo. "Tres Aristocrates del sonido." *Ilerda: Revista de Investigaciones Ieridanas* 6, nos. 10–11 (1948):69–80.

Volta, Ornella. "Erik Satie—L'os à moelle." *Revue internationale de musique française,* no. 23 (June 1987):7–98.

Zacher, Gerd. "Beobachtungen an Erik Saties 'Messe des pauvres.'" *Musik-Konzepte,* no. 11 (January 1980):48–63.

Newspaper Articles

Achard, Paul. "Les Spectacles: Les Adieux des Ballets suédois." *L'Éclair,* 31 December 1924, 4.

Apollinaire, Guillaume. "'Parade' et l'esprit nouveau." *Excelsior,* 11 May 1917, 5.

Auric, Georges. "Les Ballets suédois." *Les Nouvelles littéraires,* 6 December 1924, 7.

———. "Les Concerts 'Soirées de Paris.'" *Les Nouvelles littéraires,* 24 May 1924, 7.

———. Les Concerts: Le souvenir d'Erik Satie." *Marianne,* 8 December 1937, 18.

———. "Erik Satie." *Les Nouvelles littéraires,* 11 July 1925, 1.

———. "La Musique." *Les Nouvelles littéraires,* 30 June 1923, 5; 17 November 1923, 3; 26 April 1924, 7; 21 June 1924, 7; 19 December 1925, 4.

———. "La Musique: Hommage à Erik Satie." *Les Lettres françaises,* 7 July 1945, 5.

———. "Notes justes." *Gringoire,* 5 July 1929, 9.

———. "'Relâche,' les Ballets suédois." *Les Nouvelles littéraires,* 13 December 1924, 7.

Azaïs, Marcel. "Chronique Musicale: Au Champs-Élysées—L'École d'Arcueil, Les Ballets suédois." *L'Action française,* 6 November 1923, 2.

———. "Chronique Musicale: 'Socrate' et diverse oeuvres de M. Erik Satie." *L'Action française,* 16 January 1923, 2.

Banès, Antoine. "Les Concerts: Festival Erik Satie." *Le Figaro,* 9 June 1920, 4.

———. "Théâtre des Champs-Élysées: Ballets russes." *Le Figaro,* 26 December 1920, 3.

Barnes, Clive. "Dance: Joffrey Revives 'Parade,' Diaghilev Work." *New York Times,* 24 March 1973, 19.

———. "Picasso Led the Parade." *New York Times,* 8 April 1973, Section 2, 16.

Bénard-Sesboüé, Elisabeth. "Erik Satie chez les belges." *La Renaissance politique, littéraire, artistique,* 19 April 1924, 14.

Bex, Maurice. "La Musique: Erik Satie." *Candide,* 12 January 1933, 14.

Billy, André. "Les Ballets russes: 'Parade.'" *Bonsoir,* 25 December 1920, 3.

Boucher, Maurice. "La Musique: Les Ballets suédois—:'Relâche.'" *L'Avenir,* 9 December 1924, 2.

Bret, Gustave. "Musique: Erik Satie." *L'Intransigeant,* 15 January 1933, 6.

Briant, Théophile. "Erik Satie et Vincent Hyspa." *Le Goéland,* 22 April 1937, 2.

Brissac, Jacques. "L'Esprit d'Erik Satie." *Le Soir,* 4 July 1925, 3.

Brunel, Raoul. "Spectacles: Les Ballets suédois." *L'Oeuvre,* 28 October 1923, 7.

———. "Spectacles: 'Jack-in-the-Box' d'Erik Satie." *L'Oeuvre,* 6 June 1926, 5.

Brussel, Robert. "Mort d'Erik Satie." *Le Figaro,* 3 July 1925, 1.

———. "Pour la tombe du solitaire d'Arcueil: Un monument d'Erik Satie." *Le Figaro,* 16 May 1926, 2.

Bruyr, José. "Le compositeur le moins souvent joué." *Temps présent,* 25 October 1946, 5.

Caby, Robert. "La commémoration de la mort d'Erik Satie aujourd'hui à Arcueil-Cachan." *L'Humanité,* 30 June 1929, 4.

———. "Erik Satie: 'Le plus grand musicien du monde.'" *Le Monde,* 1 December 1928, 8.

———. "Il y a vingt-cinq ans mourait Erik Satie, 'musicien médiéval' aux prises avec les hommes, les rêves et le démon." *Le Figaro littéraire,* 24 June 1950, 6.

Chalupt, René. "Erik Satie est mort." *Comoedia,* 3 July 1925, 1.

———. "La Musique." *Les Nouvelles littéraires,* 28 October 1922, 4.

Charpentier, Raymond. "À Honfleur." *Arts,* 4 August 1950, 7.

Chennevière, Georges. "La Musique." *L'Humanité,* 13 March 1924, 2.

Clair, René. "La première d'*Entr'acte.*" *Le Figaro littéraire,* 26 June–2 July 1967, 38–39.

Cocteau, Jean. "Avant 'Parade.'" *Excelsior,* 18 May 1917, 5.

———. "'Parade.'" *Comoedia,* 21 December 1920, 1.

———. "Pour la tombe d'Erik Satie." *Comoedia,* 17 May 1926, 1.

———. "La Reprise de 'Parade.'" *Paris-Midi,* 21 December 1920, 2.

Coeuroy, André. "La Musique: Erik Satie." *Gringoire,* 6 January 1933, 9.

Collet, Henri. "Un livre de Rimsky et un livre de Cocteau: les Cinq russes, les Six français et Erik Satie." *Comoedia,* 16 January 1920, 2.

———. "Oeuvres d'Erick [*sic*] Satie, Darius Milhaud, Louis Durey et Georges Auric." *Comoedia,* 17 September 1920, 2.

———. "Les 'Six' français: Darius Milhaud, Louis Durey, Georges Auric, Arthur Honegger, Francis Poulenc, et Germaine Tailleferre." *Comoedia,* 23 January 1920, 2.

"Commémoration de la mort d'Erik Satie—Une cérémonie et un concert à Arcueil." *Le Soir,* 30 June 1929, 2.

"Composer Erik Satie—Joker or Pioneer?" *Times* (London), 25 October 1966, 16.

Contamine de Latour, J. P. "Erik Satie intime." *Comoedia,* 3 August 1925, 2; 5 August 1925, 3; 6 August 1925, 2.

"Courrier des Théâtres: Théâtre des Champs-Élysées." *Comoedia,* 29 November 1924, 5.

"Courrier Théâtral et Musical: Pour Erik Satie." *Comoedia,* 4 May 1926, 5.

"Courrier Théâtral et Musical: La tombe de Satie." *Comoedia,* 8 July 1926, 5.

Dambly, Paul. "Premières Représentations: Les Ballets suédois—'Relâche.'" *Le Petit journal,* 9 December 1924, 4.

Dautun, Yves. "Un grand musicien méconnu: Erik Satie." *Le Petit parisien,* 20 August 1929, 6.

———. "Le Solitaire d'Arcueil." *Le Petit parisien,* 28 July 1928, 5.

Delaune, H. "'Le plus original de nos compositeurs': Erik Satie." *La Croix,* 12 July 1959, 5.

Devaise, Georges. "Les Disques: Erik Satie." *Gringoire,* 22 October 1937, 15.

Dezarnaux, Robert. "Les Théâtres: Aux Ballets suédois—:'Relâche.'" *La Liberté,* 6 December 1924, 2.

Downes, Olin. "Passing of Satie and His Cult—An Aged Plotter of Revolution." *New York Times,* 6 September 1925, Section 7, 7.

———. "Satie—'Fantasist.'" *New York Times,* 8 March 1953, Section 2, 7.

"En l'honneur d'Erik Satie." *Le Petit journal,* 1 July 1929, 2.

"Epaves et Coquillages: Erik Satie et l'arrivisme." *Le Goéland,* 15 February 1938, 1.

"Erik Satie." *Le Soir,* 4 July 1925, 3.

"Erik Satie d'Iéna." *Paris-Midi,* 1 December 1937, 2.

"Erik Satie Dies at 56 [*sic*]: Founder of 'Les Six'." *New York Times,* 4 July 1925, 11.

"Erik Satie est mort." *L'Écho de Paris,* 3 July 1925, 3.

"Erik Satie est mort." *L'Éclair,* 3 July 1925, 1.

M.F., "Les obsèques d'Erik Satie à l'église d'Arcueil." *Comoedia,* 7 July 1925, 1.

Frétaval, Jean. "Carnet du Lecteur." *Le Figaro,* 13 January 1933, 5.

Flament, Albert. "'Jack-in-the-Box': La pierre de Satie." *L'Intransigeant,* 17 May 1926, 1.

"G." "Un festival pour la tombe d'Erik Satie à Arcueil." *Comoedia,* 13 May 1926, 1.

Gandrey-Rety, Jean. "Au Théâtre des Champs-Élysées: 'Relâche.'" *Comoedia,* 6 December 1924, 2.

Georges, André. "La Musique: Autour de 'L'École d'Arcueil.'" *Les Nouvelles littéraires,* 4 April 1925, 7.

———. "La Musique: Les Concerts." *Les Nouvelles littéraires,* 29 December 1923, 3.

———. "La Musique: Wagner et un autre." *Les Nouvelles littéraires,* 15 April 1933, 10.

Givrey, R. de. "Au Théâtre des Champs-Élysées: Les dernières représentations à Paris des Ballets suédois." *Bonsoir,* 28 October 1923, 3.

Grass-Mick, Augustin. "Pour Commémorer de souvenir d'Erik Satie." *Arts: Beaux-Arts, Littérature, Spectacles,* 4 August 1950, 1, 7.

"L'Habilleuse." "Les Spectacles: En scène!" *Candide,* 2 December 1937, 19.

Hahn, Reynaldo. "Chronique Musicale." *Le Figaro,* 9 December 1937, 5.

Henahan, Donal. "Lovely Morsels Heard in Satie Retrospective." *New York Times,* 19 April 1974, 21.

Hermant, Abel. "Les Ballets russes." *Excelsior,* 20 May 1917, 13.

Herrand, Marcel. "L'Humour d'Erik Satie." *Le Figaro,* 23 November 1937, 5.

Hirsbrunner, Theo. "Erik Satie und das Musikleben seiner Zeit." *Der kleine Bund: Beilage für Literatur und Kunst,* 16 April 1972, 1–2.

———. "Jugend und Avantgarde." *Der kleine Bund: Beilage für Literatur und Kunst,* 15 April 1973, 1.

H. H. [Horace Horsnell]. "The Russian Ballet—'Parade' and 'Jack in the Box.'" *Observer* (London), 11 July 1926, 13.

"Intérim." "'Relâche' ou la malechance de Picabia." *L'Éclair,* 29 November 1924, 4.

Jeanne, René. "Le Cinéma aux Ballets suédois." *Les Nouvelles littéraires,* 13 December 1924, 7.

Kerdyk, René. "Quand Erik Satie écrivait à Vincent Hyspa." *Paris-Midi,* 17 May 1937, 2.

Kisselgoff, Anna. "So Talked About—But Never Seen." *New York Times,* 18 March 1973, Section 2, 24.

Koechlin, Charles. "À la mémoire d'Erik Satie." *Journal des débats,* 16 May 1926, 3.

Kramer, Hilton. "Picasso's Cubist Images Still Dominate 'Parade.'" *New York Times,* 24 March 1973, 19.

Laloy, Louis. "Au Théâtre des Champs-Élysées—Reprises de 'Parade.'" *Comoedia,* 23 December 1920, 1.

———. "L'enchantement des Ballets russes." *Le Figaro,* 12 May 1926, 1.

———. "'Mercure' aux Ballets russes." *Comoedia,* 2 June 1927, 1.

Landormy, Paul. "Les Ballets suédois." *La Victoire,* 30 October 1924, 2.

———. "Le cas Satie." *La Victoire,* 16 September 1924, 2.

———. "Les Concerts." *La Victoire,* 29 November 1921, 2.

———. "Erik Satie." *La Victoire,* 18 March 1924, 2.

Lannes, Roger. "Souvenirs d'une croisade—Darius Milhaud a évoqué hier Erik Satie." *L'Intransigeant,* 12 December 1938, 2.

Le Borne, Fernand. "Le Théâtre à Paris: Théâtre des Champs-Élysées—Les Ballets suédois—'Relâche.'" *Le Petit parisien,* 19 December 1924, 6.

Levinson, André. "Au Théâtre des Champs-Élysées: Le Spectacle." *Comoedia,* 6 December 1924, 2.

Malherbe, Henry. "Chronique Musicale." *Le Temps,* 19 May 1926, 3.

———. "Chronique Musicale: Au Théâtre des Champs-Élysées—Ballets suédois." *Le Temps,* 10 December 1924, 3.

———. "La Musique: Erik Satie." *Le Temps,* 16 December 1932, 3.

Marchès, Léo. "Erik Satie." *Le Petit bleu,* 5 and 6 July 1925, 3.

Maré, Rolf de. "À propos de 'Relâche.'" *Comoedia,* 27 November 1924, 2.

Marjorie, Odette. "Une plaque sur la demeure d'Erik Satie." *L'Intransigeant,* 2 July 1929, 6.

Massot, Pierre de. "Hommes d'aujourd'hui: Erik Satie." *L'Ère nouvelle,* 14 September 1924, 2.

———. "Vingt cinq minutes avec: Erik Satie." *Paris-Journal,* 30 May 1924, 2.

Mellers, Wilfrid H. "Small Sincerities." *Times Literary Supplement,* 7 November 1975, 1334.

Messager, André. "Chronique Théâtrale—Les Premières—Ballets russes—'Jack-in-the-Box' d'Erik Satie." *Le Figaro,* 7 June 1926, 3.

———. "Figaro-Théâtre—Les Premières—Théâtre des Champs-Élysées: 'Relâche.'" *Le Figaro,* 9 December 1924, 5.

———. "La Musique: Le Festival Erik Satie au profit de sa tombe." *Comoedia,* 19 May 1926, 3.

Mila, Massimo. "Tanti giovani a Barga per Scarlatti e Satie." *La Stampa* (Turin), 29 July 1975, 6.

Milhaud, Darius. "Les Ballets Russes à Monte-Carlo." *Paris-Journal,* 15 February 1924, 1.

———. "Les derniers jours d'Erik Satie." *Le Figaro littéraire,* 23 April 1949, 5.

"Mort du compositeur Erik Satie." *La Lanterne,* 3 July 1925, 3.

"Music: A Long, Long, Long Night (and Day) at the Piano—Satie's 'Vexations' Played 840 Times by Relay Team." *New York Times,* 11 September 1963, 45, 48.

"La Musique: Un festival Erik Satie." *Comoedia,* 27 June 1935, 2.

"On a célébré dimanche à Arcueil le souvenir d'Erik Satie." *Paris-Soir,* 3 July 1929, 5.

"Paris Week by Week: Erik Satie." *Observer* (London), 8 May 1921, 7.

Petridis, Petro J. "Erik Satie's New Ballet." *Christian Science Monitor,* 10 January 1925, 16.

Picabia, Francis. "Erik Satie." *L'Ère nouvelle,* 8 July 1925, 3.

———. "Erik Satie." *Paris-Journal,* 27 June 1924, 1.

———. "Instantanéisme." *Comoedia,* 21 November 1924, 4.

———. "Pourquoi j'ai écrit 'Relâche.'" *Le Siècle,* 27 November 1924, 4.

———. "Pourquoi 'Relâche' a fait relâche." *Comoedia,* 2 December 1924, 1.

Picard, Gaston. "L'écrivain chez Erik Satie." *Le Figaro: Supplement littéraire,* 11 July 1925, 2.

Pinzauti, Leonardo. "Socrate di Satie." *La Nazione* (Florence), 29 July 1975, 9.

Pioch, Georges. "La chance d'Erik Satie." *Paris-Soir,* 5 July 1925, 1–2.

———. "La Musique: Erik Satie, sa gloire et ses meilleurs ennemis." *Le Soir,* 12 July 1929, 2.

Polaczek, Dietmar. "Der nüchterne Magier: Zur Aufführung des Gesamtwerks von Erik Satie in Paris." *Frankfurter Allgemeine Zeitung,* 14 May 1979, 21.

———. "Besser als die Wirklichkeit: Der Komponist Erik Satie." *Frankfurter Allgemeine Zeitung,* 26 May 1979, Supplement: Bilder und Zeiten, 6.

"Pour commémorer la mort d'Erik Satie: Une cérémonie et un concert à Arcueil." *Comoedia,* 30 June 1929, 2.

Prim, Jean-L. "Les Spectacles—Les Théâtres: Erik Satie Salle d'Iéna." *L'Ordre,* 2 December 1937, 3–4.

Radiguet, Raymond. "*Parade.*" *Le Gaulois,* 25 December 1920, 4.

Richard, Marius. "Une Controverse musicale: Claude Debussy et Erik Satie." *La Liberté,* 13 January 1932, 2.

Roland-Manuel [Roland-Alexis Manuel Lévy]. "La Quinzaine musicale: Les Ballets suédois." *L'Éclair,* 9 December 1924, 2.

———. "La Quinzaine musicale: L'École d'Arcueil." *L'Éclair,* 29 October 1923, 3.

———. "La Quinzaine musicale: Le 'Socrate' de M. Erik Satie—Concerts Pasdeloup et Lamoureux." *L'Éclair,* 23 February 1920, 3.

Rollot, Jean. "Un jeune groupement théâtral honore la mémoire d'Eric Satie, musicien humoriste." *L'Intransigeant,* 30 November 1937, 3.

Roussel, Albert. "À propos d'un récent festival." *Le Gaulois,* 12 June 1926, 3.

Sauguet, Henri. "Vive Satie!" *La Bataille,* 5 July 1945, 4.

Schaeffner, André. "La Musique: De Markevitch à Satie." *Beaux-Arts,* 14 July 1933, 5.

Schneider, Louis. "'Closed,' Name of Play, Puzzle to Theatre Crowd." *New York Herald* (Paris), 28 November 1924, 4.

———. "Le Gaulois au Théâtre—Mort d'Erik Satie." *Le Gaulois,* 4 July 1925, 5.

———. "Le Gaulois au Théâtre—Les Premières—Théâtre Sarah-Bernhardt (Ballets russes)—*Jack in the Box,* ballet d'Erik Satie." *Le Gaulois,* 6 June 1926, 5.

———. "Music in Paris." *New York Herald* (Paris), 6 December 1924, 4.

———. "Musique." *Le Petit parisien,* 3 January 1933, 5.

Schonberg, Harold C. "Unobserved Anniversary." *New York Times,* 24 April 1966, Section 2, 13.

Shattuck, Roger. "Music and Mobiles—When Calder and Satie Joined Forces." *New York Times,* 6 November 1977, Section 2, 1, 31.

Sordet, Dominique. "La Semaine musicale." *L'Écho national,* 8 January 1923, 3.

"Souvenirs: Erik Satie." *Comoedia,* 4 July 1925, 1.

Stuckenschmidt, Hans Heinz. "Erik Satie." *Vossische Zeitung,* 11 December 1926, 5.

C. T. "Théâtres—Soirée Erik Satie." *Le Temps,* 4 December 1937, 5.

F. T. [Francis Toye]. "A Satie Festival: Music without Merit but Dancing Excellent." *Morning Post* (London), 6 July 1926, 7.

L. T. "Les Lettres: Deux autographes d'Erik Satie." *L'Ordre,* 16 March 1933, 2.

"Le Théâtre: Les Échos." *Candide,* 9 July 1925, 7.

Vuillermoz, Émile. "La Musique: Ballets suédois." *Excelsior,* 29 October 1923, 3.

———. "Les Théâtres: Ballets suédois." *Excelsior,* 6 December 1924, 5.

Catalog of Musical Works

Satie's principal publishers are the Paris houses of Salabert (which in 1941 acquired the Rouart-Lerolle catalog as well as the rights to works originally published by Alfred Satie, Bellon Ponscarme, Dupré, and Baudoux) and Max Eschig (which reissued works originally published by Demets and Éditions de la Sirène). Four stage works—*Geneviève de Brabant, Jack in the Box, Cinq Grimaces pour "Le Songe d'une nuit d'été,"* and *Mercure*—are published by Universal Edition of Vienna. Dates of first publication are given where known. Only the most frequently performed or historically important of the numerous transcriptions of Satie's works have been cited. Titles in quotation marks were assigned by the editors and did not originate with the composer.

1884   *Allegro* for piano. Unpublished sketch. Dated Honfleur, 9 September 1884. Facsimile in Alan M. Gillmor, "Erik Satie and the Concept of the Avant-Garde" (Ph.D. diss., University of Toronto, 1972), plate 3.

1885   *Valse-ballet* for piano, "Op. 62." Published in *La Musique des familles,* 17 march 1887. Salabert, 1975, as *"Deux Oeuvres de jeunesse,"* no. 1.

                Fantaisie-valse for piano. Published in *La Musique des familles,* 28 July 1887. Salabert, 1975, as *"Deux Oeuvres de jeunesse,"* no. 2.

1886   *Ogives* (4) for piano. Published for the author by Dupré, 1889. Paris: Le Chant du Monde / Hamburg: Sikorski, 1965.

                "Trois mélodies de 1886" (J. P. Contamine de Latour) for voice and piano.

                    1. *Les Anges* (published by Alfred Satie as *Trois mélodies,* "Op. 20, No. 1," 1887)
                    2. *Élégie* (published by Alfred Satie as "Op. 19," 1887)
                    3. *Sylvie* (published by Alfred Satie as *Trois mélodies,* "Op. 20, No. 3," 1887)

                Salabert, 1968. For voice and orchestra by Robert Caby, Salabert, 1968.

Les Fleurs (J. P. Contamine de Latour) for voice and piano. Published by Alfred Satie as *Trois mélodies,* "Op. 20, no. 2," 1887. Salabert, 1968, as "*Trois autres mélodies,*" no. 3. For voice and orchestra by Robert Caby, Salabert, 1968.

1887   *Chanson* (J. P. Contamine de Latour) for voice and piano. Published by Alfred Satie as "Op. 52," 1887. Salabert, 1968, as "*Trois autres mélodies,*" no. 1.

          Trois Sarabandes for piano. No. 1 published in *Revue musicale S.I.M.* 7 (15 March 1911):33–34. Rouart-Lerolle, 1911; Salabert. For orchestra by Robert Caby, Salabert, 1968. For two guitars by Peter Kraus, Salabert. No. 1 for brass quintet by René Bertholet, Salabert, 1973.

1888   *Trois Gymnopédies* for piano.
          1. *Lent et douloureux* (published in *La Musique des familles,* 18 August 1888)
          2. *Lent et triste*
          3. *Lent et grave*
          No. 3 published for the author by Dupré, 1888. Nos. 1 and 2 published for the author by Dupré, 1895. Nos. 1–3, Baudoux, 1898; Rouart-Lerolle, 1911; Salabert; revised edition, Salabert, 1969. Nos. 1 and 3 for orchestra by Claude Debussy, Baudoux, 1898; Salabert; revised edition, London: Eulenburg, 1980. Nos. 1–3 for orchestra by David Diamond, 1949 (unpublished). No. 2 for orchestra by Roland-Manuel, Salabert, 1965. For flute (or oboe) and piano by Robin de Smet, London: Fentone Music, 1976. No. 1 for guitar by Francis Kleynjans, Salabert, 1983. No. 1 for ten-string guitar by Pierre Laniau, Salabert, 1982.

1889   *Gnossienne* ("No. 5") for piano. Salabert, 1968. For orchestra by Robert Caby, Salabert, 1968. For guitar by Francis Kleynjans, Salabert, 1982. For two guitars by Peter Kraus, Salabert.

          Chanson hongroise for piano. Unfinished sketch. Published in Grete Wehmeyer, *Erik Satie* (Regensburg: Gustav Bosse Verlag, 1974), 32.

1890   *Trois Gnossiennes* for piano. Nos. 1 and 3 (titled nos. 1 and 2) published in *Le Figaro musical* (September 1893). No. 2 (titled no. 6) published in facsimile in *Le Coeur* (September / October 1893). Rouart-Lerolle, 1913; Salabert. For orchestra by John Lanchbery, Salabert. For orchestra by Willem Frederik Bon,

Amsterdam: Donemus, 1977. No. 3 for orchestra by Francis Poulenc, Salabert, 1949. For guitar by Francis Kleynjans, Salabert, 1982. For ten-string guitar by Pierre Laniau, Salabert, 1982. For two guitars by Peter Kraus, Salabert, 1981.

Danse for small orchestra. Unpublished (incorporated into *Trois Morceaux en forme de poire*). Transcription in Patrick Gowers, "Erik Satie: His Studies, Notebooks and Critics" (Ph.D. diss., University of Cambridge, 1966), 2:32–40.

1891

"Gnossienne" ("No. 4") for piano. Salabert, 1968. For orchestra by Robert Caby, Salabert, 1968. For guitar by Francis Kleynjans, Salabert. For ten-string guitar by Pierre Laniau, Salabert, 1982. For two guitars by Peter Kraus, Salabert.

"Première pensée Rose + Croix" for piano. Salabert, 1968. For orchestra by Robert Caby, Salabert, 1968.

Le Fils des étoiles for piano (originally for flutes and harps). Incidental music for Joséphin Péladan's "Chaldean Pastoral" *Le Fils des étoiles.* Salabert, 1973.

Le Fils des étoiles (Preludes).
1. Act 1: *La Vocation*
2. Act 2: *L'Initiation*
3. Act 3: *L'Incantation*
Baudoux, 1896; Rouart-Lerolle, 1920; Salabert; revised edition, Salabert, 1972. Nos. 1 and 3 for orchestra by Roland-Manuel, Salabert, 1962. No. 1 for orchestra by Maurice Ravel, 1911 (lost).

Hymne pour le "Salut Drapeau" for voice and piano. Incidental music for Joséphin Péladan's play *Le Prince de Byzance.* Salabert, 1968. For orchestra or for orchestra and female chorus (ad. lib.) by Robert Caby, Salabert, 1968.

Leit-Motif du Panthée, printed in Joséphin Péladan's novel *Le Panthée* (Paris: Dentu, 1892).

1892

Sonneries de la Rose + Croix for piano.
1. *Air de l'Ordre*
2. *Air du Grand Maître*
3. *Air du Grand Prieur*
Published for the Rose + Croix by Dupré, 1892; Rouart-Lerolle, 1910; Salabert, 1971.

Quatre Préludes for piano.
   1. *Fête donnée par des Chevaliers Normands en l'Honneur d'une jeune Demoiselle (XIe siècle)* (1884?)
   2. *Prélude d'Eginhard* (1893?)
   3. *Premier Prélude du Nazaréen* (incidental music for Henri Mazel's play *Le Nazaréen*)
   4. *Deuxième Prélude du Nazaréen* (incidental music for Henri Mazel's play *Le Nazaréen*)
Rouart-Lerolle, 1929; Salabert. Nos. 1 and 3 for orchestra by Francis Poulenc, Salabert, 1949. No. 2 for orchestra by Robert Caby, Salabert, 1968. No. 2 for orchestra by John Lanchbery, Salabert. No. 3 for ten-string guitar by Pierre Laniau, Salabert, 1982.

Uspud, "Christian ballet in three acts" (with J. P. Contamine de Latour) for piano. Excerpts privately printed in 1893 and in 1895. Salabert, 1970. For orchestra by Robert Caby, Salabert, 1970.

1893   *Danses gothiques (Neuvaine pour le plus grand calme et la forte tranquillité de mon Âme)* for piano.
   1. *À l'occasion d'une grande peine* (published in *Revue musicale S.I.M.* 7 (15 March 1911):39–40)
   2. *Dans laquelle les Pères de la Très Véritable et Très Sainte Église sont invoqués*
   3. *En faveur d'un malheureux*
   4. *À propos de Saint Bernard et de Sainte Lucie*
   5. *Pour les pauvres trépassés*
   6. *Où il est question du pardon des injures reçues*
   7. *Par pitié pour les ivrognes, honteux, débauchés, imparfaits, désagréables, et faussaires en tous genres*
   8. *En le haut honneur du vénéré Saint Michel, le gracieux Archange*
   9. *Après avoir obtenu la remise de ses fautes*
Rouart-Lerolle, 1929; Salabert.

1894   *Prélude de La Porte héroïque du ciel* for piano. Incidental music for Jules Bois's play *La Porte héroïque du ciel.* Published in facsimile in *Le Coeur* (March 1894). Published in Jules Bois, *La Porte héroïque du ciel* (Paris: Librairie de l'Art Indépendant, 1894, 20–21). Rouart-Lerolle, 1912; Salabert, 1968. For orchestra by Roland-Manuel, Rouart-Lerolle, 1912; Salabert.

1895   *Messe des pauvres* for piano or organ with small choir SB ad lib. (1892?–95)

1. *Kyrie eleison*
2. *Dixit Domine*
3. *Prière des Orgues* (published in facsimile in *Le Coeur* [June 1895])
4. *Commune qui mundi nefas* (excerpts privately printed in 1895)
5. *Chant ecclésiastique*
6. *Prière pour les voyageurs et les marins en danger de mort, à la très bonne et très auguste Vierge Marie, mère de Jésus*
7. *Prière pour le salut de mon âme*

Rouart-Lerolle, 1929; Salabert. For orchestra and small choir SB ad lib. by David Diamond, Salabert, 1950.

"Pages mystiques" for piano (1893–95)
1. *"Prière"*
2. *Vexations* (published in facsimile in *Contrepoints,* no. 6 [1949])
3. *"Harmonies"* (ca. 1905–8?)

Eschig, 1969.

1897   *Gnossienne* ("No. 6") for piano. Salabert, 1968. For orchestra by Robert Caby, Salabert, 1968. For two guitars by Peter Kraus, Salabert.

Danse de travers for piano. Salabert, 1970.

Pièces froides for piano.
1. *Airs à faire fuir* (3)
2. *Danses de travers* (3)

Rouart-Lerolle, 1912; Salabert, 1973. For two guitars by Peter Kraus, Salabert, 1981.

Caresse (ca. 1897) for piano. Salabert, 1968.

Je te veux (Henry Pacory) for voice and piano. Baudoux, 1902; Bellon Ponscarme, 1903; Rouart-Lerolle; Salabert. For solo piano, Bellon Ponscarme, 1904; Rouart-Lerolle; Salabert. For small orchestra, Rouart-Lerolle, 1919; Salabert, 1978. For ten-string guitar by Pierre Laniau, Salabert, 1982.

1899–1900   *Jack in the Box* for piano. Incidental music for a pantomime by Jules Dépaquit.
1. *Prélude*
2. *Entr'acte*
3. *Final*

Universal Edition, 1929. For orchestra by Darius Milhaud, Universal Edition, 1929.

ca. 1900   *Geneviève de Brabant* for solo voices, chorus, and piano. Miniature opera for marionettes on a libretto by Lord Cheminot (J. P. Contamine de Latour).
1. *Prélude*
  Act 1
2. *Choeur*
3. *Entrée des soldats*
  Act 2
4. *Entr'acte*
5. *Air de Geneviève*
6. *Sonnerie de cor*
7. *Entrée des soldats*
  Act 3
8. *Entr'acte*
9. *Choeur*
10. *Air de Golo*
11. *Entrée des soldats*
12. *Cortège*
13. *Entrée des soldats*
14. *Petit air de Geneviève*
15. *Choeur final*
Universal Edition, 1930. New edition with the original libretto of Lord Cheminot (J. P. Contamine de Latour), 1986. For solo voices, chorus, and orchestra by Roger Désormière, Universal Edition, 1930.

L'Omnibus automobile (Vincent Hyspa) for voice and piano (ca 1900-6). *L'Album musical,* no. 33 (March 1906). Salabert, 1976.

Un Dîner à l'Élysée (Vincent Hyspa) for voice and piano (ca. 1900). Published in Vincent Hyspa, *Chansons d'humour* (Paris: Enoch, 1903), 108–13.

Le Veuf (Vincent Hyspa) for voice and piano (ca. 1900–2) (two versions). Unpublished (one version incorporated into *Trois Morceaux en forme de poire*). Transcription of both versions in Patrick Gowers, "Erik Satie: His Studies, Notebooks and Critics" (Ph.D. diss., University of Cambridge, 1966), 2:169–72; and in facsimile in Steven M. Whiting, "Erik Satie and Parisian Musical Entertainment, 1888 to 1909" (M.A. thesis, University of Illinois, 1984), 150–51, 153–54.

Légende californienne (J. P. Contamine de Latour - words lost) for voice and piano (ca. 1900). Excerpt published in Nigel Wilkins, ed. and trans. *The Writings of Erik Satie* (London: Eulenburg, 1980), 155.

Imperial-Oxford (J. P. Contamine de Latour - words lost) for voice and piano (ca. 1900–5). Excerpt published in Nigel Wilkins, ed. and trans. *The Writings of Erik Satie* (London: Eulenburg, 1980), 153.

Poudre d'or for piano (ca. 1900). Baudoux, 1902; Rouart-Lerolle; Salabert. For small orchestra, Salabert, 1978.

Le Piccadilly for piano (ca. 1900–4). Alexis Rouart, 1907; Salabert, 1975. For small orchestra, Alexis Rouart, 1907; Salabert.

Rêverie du pauvre for piano (1900). Salabert, 1968.

Petite ouverture à danser for piano (ca. 1900). Salabert, 1968. For orchestra by Robert Caby, Salabert, 1968. For guitar by Francis Kleynjans, Salabert, 1982.

Petite musique de clown triste for piano (1900). Eschig, 1980.

Verset laïque et sompteux for piano (1900). Published in facsimile in Ornella Volta, *L'Ymagier d'Erik Satie* (Paris: Éditions Van de Velde, 1979), 40.

1901   *The Dreamy Fish (Le Poisson Rêveur)—Esquisse* for piano. Music for a story by Lord Cheminot (J. P. Contamine de Latour). Salabert, 1968. For piano and orchestra by Robert Caby, Salabert, 1970.

ca. 1902 *Tendrement* (Vincent Hyspa) for voice and piano. Baudoux, 1902; Bellon Ponscarme, 1903; Rouart-Lerolle; Salabert. For small orchestra under the title *Illusion,* Salabert, 1979.

1903   *Trois Morceaux en forme de poire* for piano four hands.
     1. *Manière de commencement*
     2. *Prolongation de même*
     3. *1. Lentement*
     4. *2. Enlevé*
     5. *3. Brutal*
     6. *En plus*
     7. *Redite*
    No. 3 and excerpt of no. 4 (mm. 1–32) published in *Revue mu-*

sicale S.I.M. 7 (15 March 1911):35–38. Rouart-Lerolle, 1911; Salabert. For orchestra by Roger Désormière, Salabert, 1950.

1904   *La Diva de l'Empire* (Dominique Bonnaud and Numa Blès) "American Intermezzo" for voice and piano. Bellon Ponscarme, 1904; Rouart-Lerolle, 1919; Salabert, 1976. For solo piano by Hans Ourdine, Rouart-Lerolle, 1919; Salabert. For small orchestra, Rouart-Lerolle, 1919; Salabert, 1978. For ten-string guitar by Pierre Laniau, Salabert, 1982.

1905   *Pousse l'Amour,* operetta in collaboration with Maurice de Féraudy and Jean Kolb. Fragments. Unpublished.

"Trois mélodies sans paroles" for voice and piano (ca. 1905).
            1. *Rambouillet*
            2. *Les Oiseaux*
            3. *Marienbad*
Salabert, 1978.

Chez le docteur (Vincent Hyspa) for voice and piano (ca. 1905–6). *L'Album musical* no. 33 (March 1906). Salabert, 1976.

1905–1906   *Allons-y Chochotte* (D. Durante) for voice and piano. Salabert, 1978.

1906   *"Chanson médiévale"* (Catulle Mendès) for voice and piano. Salabert, 1968, as *"Trois autres mélodies,"* no. 2.
For voice and orchestra by Robert Caby, Salabert, 1968.

Passacaille for piano. Rouart-Lerolle, 1929, Salabert. For orchestra by David Diamond, Salabert, 1950.

Prélude en tapisserie for piano. Rouart-Lerolle, 1929; Salabert.

1906–1908   *"Douze petits chorals"* for piano. Salabert, 1968.

1906–1913   *"Musiques intimes et secrètes"* for piano.
            1. *"Nostalgie"*
            2. *"Froide songerie"*
            3. *Fâcheux exemple*
Salabert, 1968. For ten-string guitar by Pierre Laniau, Salabert, 1982.

"Six Pièces de la période 1906–1913" for piano.
            1. *Désespoir agréable* (1908)
            2. *Effronterie*

     3. *Poésie* (ca. 1913)
     4. *"Prélude canin"* (ca. 1910)
     5. *Profondeur*
     6. *Songe-creux*
Salabert, 1968. No. 4 for orchestra by Robert Caby,
Salabert, 1968. No. 6 for two guitars by Peter Kraus,
Salabert, 1981.

1908–1912   *Aperçus désagréables* for piano four hands.
     1. *Pastorale* (1912)
     2. *Choral* (1908)
     3. *Fugue* (1908)
Demets, 1913; Eschig, 1967.

1910–1911   *Nouvelles Pièces froides* for piano.
     1. *Sur un mur*
     2. *Sur un arbre*
     3. *Sur un pont*
Salabert, 1968. For two guitars by Peter Kraus, Salabert.

    Deux Rêveries nocturnes for piano.
     1. *Pas vite*
     2. *Très modérément*
Salabert, 1968. For two guitars by Peter Kraus, Salabert.

1897–1914   *"Carnet d'Esquisses et de Croquis"* for piano.
     1. *Air* (1914)
     2. *Essais*
     3. *Notes*
     4. *Notes*
     5. *Le Prisonnier maussade*
     6. *Esquisses ("Le Grand Singe")*
     7. *Exercices*
     8. *Notes*
     9. *Harmonies*
    10. *Songerie vers "Jack"* (1897)
    11. *Bribes*
    12. *Choral*
    13. *Exercices*
    14. *Exercices*
    15. *Exercices*
    16. *Exercices*
    17. *Esquisse & Sketch Montmartrois 1 & 2*
    18. *Essais (Arrière-Propos)*

19. *Petite Danse*
Salabert, 1968.

1911   *En Habit de cheval* for piano four hands.
            1. *Choral*
            2. *Fugue litanique*
            3. *Autre choral*
            4. *Fugue de papier*
            Rouart-Lerolle, 1911; Salabert. For orchestra, Rouart-Lerolle,
            1912; Salabert.

1912   *Préludes flasques (pour un chien)* for piano.
            1. *Voix d'intérieur*
            2. *Idylle cynique*
            3. *Chanson canine*
            4. *Avec camaraderie*
            Eschig, 1967.

            Véritables Préludes flasques (pour un chien) for piano.
            1. *Sévère réprimande*
            2. *Seul à la maison*
            3. *On joue*
            Demets, 1912; Eschig.

1913   *Le Piège de Méduse,* "lyric comedy in one act by M. Erik Satie
            with dance music by the same gentleman." Deluxe edition with
            illustrations by Georges Braque, Paris: Galerie Simon, 1921.

            Le Piège de Méduse, seven little dances.
            1. *Quadrille*
            2. *Valse*
            3. *Pas vite*
            4. *Mazurka*
            5. *Un peu vif*
            6. *Polka*
            7. *Quadrille*
            For piano, Salabert, 1954. For clarinet, trumpet, trombone, vi-
            olin, cello, double bass, and percussion, Salabert, 1968.

            Descriptions automatiques for piano.
            1. *Sur un vaisseau*
            2. *Sur une lanterne*
            3. *Sur un casque*
            Demets, 1913; Eschig.

Embryons desséchés for piano.
 1. *d'Holothurie*
 2. *d'Edriophthalma*
 3. *de Podolphthalma*
Demets, 1913; Eschig. For orchestra, Eschig.

Croquis et agaceries d'un gros bonhomme en bois for piano.
 1. *Tyrolienne turque*
 2. *Danse maigre (à la manière de ces messieurs)*
 3. *Españaña*
Demets, 1913; Eschig.

Chapitres tournés en tous sens for piano.
 1. *Celle qui parle trop*
 2. *Le Porteur de grosses pierres*
 3. *Regret des Enfermés (Jonas et Latude)*
Demets, 1913; Eschig.

Vieux sequins et vieilles cuirasses for piano.
 1. *Chez le marchand d'or (Venise XIIIᵉ Siècle)*
 2. *Danse cuirassée (Période grecque)*
 3. *Défaite des Cimbres (Cauchemar)*
Demets, 1913; Eschig.

Enfantines for piano.
 I. *Menus propos enfantins*
   1. *Chant guerrier du roi des haricots*
   2. *Ce qui dit la petite princesse des Tulipes*
   3. *Valse du Chocolat aux amandes*
 II. *Enfantillages pittoresques*
   1. *Petit prélude à la journée*
   2. *Berceuse*
   3. *Marche du grand escalier*
 III. *Peccadilles importunes*
   1. *Être jaloux de son camarde qui a une grosse tête*
   2. *Lui manger sa tartine*
   3. *Profiter de ce qu'il a des cors aux pieds pour lui prendre son cerceau*
Demets, 1914; Eschig.

"*Trois Nouvelles Enfantines*" for piano.
 1. *Le Vilain petit vaurien*
 2. *Berceuse*
 3. *La Gentille toute petite fille*
Eschig, 1972.

Les Pantins dansent for piano. Published in *Montjoie!* (January 1914). Rouart-Lerolle, 1929; Salabert. For orchestra, Salabert, 1967; excerpt of orchestral score in facsimile in *Montjoie!* (November–December 1913). For ten-string guitar by Pierre Laniau, Salabert, 1983.

1914

Choses vues à droite et à gauche (sans lunettes) for violin and piano.
   1. *Choral hypocrite*
   2. *Fugue à tâtons*
   3. *Fantaisie musculaire*
Rouart-Lerolle, 1916; Salabert. No. 1 for chamber orchestra by David Diamond, 1932. Unpublished.

Sports et divertissements for piano.
   1. *Choral inappétissant*
   2. *La Balançoire*
   3. *La Chasse*
   4. *La Comédie italienne*
   5. *Le Reveil de la Mariée*
   6. *Colin-Maillard*
   7. *La Pêche*
   8. *Le Yachting*
   9. *Le Bain de mer*
  10. *Le Carnaval*
  11. *Le Golf*
  12. *La Pieuvre*
  13. *Les Courses*
  14. *Les Quatres Coins*
  15. *Le Pique-Nique*
  16. *Le Water-Chute*
  17. *Le Tango perpétuel*
  18. *Le Traîneau*
  19. *Le Flirt*
  20. *Feu d'artifice*
  21. *Le Tennis*
Deluxe limited edition with illustrations by Charles Martin, Paris: Vogel, 1923 (reprint New York: Dover, 1982); Salabert, 1964 (French version); Salabert, 1975 (English version). Nos. 1–7 arranged for three B-flat clarinets and one bass clarinet by John S. Davidson. Salabert, 1975.

Heures séculaires et instantanées for piano.
   1. *Obstacles venimeux*

2. *Crépuscule matinal (de midi)*
3. *Affolements granitiques*
Demets, 1916; Eschig.

Les Trois Valses distinguées du précieux dégoûté for piano.
1. *Sa taille*
2. *Son binocle*
3. *Ses jambes*
Rouart-Lerolle, 1916; Salabert.

Trois Poèmes d'amour (Erik Satie) for voice and piano.
1. *Ne suis que grain de sable*
2. *Suis chauve de naissance*
3. *Ta parure est secrète*
Rouart-Lerolle, 1916; Salabert.

1915   *Cinq Grimaces pour "Le Songe d'une nuit d'été"* for orchestra.
Incidental music for Jean Cocteau's unrealized production of
Shakespeare's *A Midsummer Night's Dream*.
1. *Préambule*
2. *Coquecigrue*
3. *Chasse*
4. *Fanfaronnade*
5. *Pour sortir*
Universal Edition, 1929. For piano by Darius Milhaud, Universal
Edition, 1929.

Avant-dernières pensées for piano.
1. *Idylle*
2. *Aubade*
3. *Méditation*
Rouart-Lerolle, 1916; Salabert.

1916   *Trois mélodies* for voice and piano.
1. *La Statue de bronze* (Léon-Paul Fargue)
2. *Daphénéo* (M. God [Mimie Godebska])
3. *Le Chapelier* (René Chalupt, after Lewis Carroll's *Alice in
Wonderland*)
Rouart-Lerolle, 1917; Salabert. For voice and orchestra by Robert Caby, Salabert, 1968.

1916–1917 *Parade*, "realistic ballet in one scene" (with Jean Cocteau, Léonide Massine, and Pablo Picasso) for orchestra.
1. *Choral - Prélude du rideau rouge - Prestidigitateur chinois*

>   2. *Petite fille américaine*
>   3. *Acrobates*
>   4. *Final - Suite au Prélude du rideau rouge*
> Rouart-Lerolle, 1917; Salabert, 1960; miniature score 1979. For piano four hands (omitting *Choral*), Rouart-Lerolle, 1917; Salabert.
>
> *Rag-Time Parade* (extract from no. 2) for piano by Hans Ourdine, Rouart-Lerolle, 1919; Salabert.
>
> *Rag-Time Parade* for small orchestra, Rouart-Lerolle, 1919; Salabert.
>
> *Sonatine bureaucratique* for piano.
>   1. *Allegro*
>   2. *Andante*
>   3. *Vivace*
> Paris: S. Chapelier, 1917; L. Philippo, 1954; Combre, 1975; Salabert, 1976.

1917–1918   *Socrate,* "symphonic drama in three parts with voice" (on the Dialogues of Plato translated by Victor Cousin) for voice(s) and orchestra.
>   1. *Portrait de Socrate* (from *Symposium*)
>   2. *Les Bords de l'Illissus* (from *Phaedrus*)
>   3. *Mort de Socrate* (from *Phaedo*)
> Eschig, 1950. Piano / vocal score, Éditions de la Sirène, 1919; Eschig, 1973. Arranged for two pianos by John Cage, Eschig, 1984.

1919   *Nocturnes* (5) for piano. Rouart-Lerolle, 1919 (nos. 1–3); Salabert; Demets, 1920 (nos. 4–5); Eschig.
>
> *Trois Petites pièces montées* for small orchestra.
>   1. *De l'enfance de Pantagruel (Rêverie)*
>   2. *Marche de Cocagne (Démarche)*
>   3. *Jeux de Gargantua (Coin de Polka)*
> Éditions de la Sirène, 1921; Eschig, 1977. For piano four hands, Éditions de la Sirène, 1921; Eschig. No. 1 for piano solo, Éditions de la Sirène, 1921; Eschig, 1968.

1920   *Premier Menuet* for piano. Éditions de la Sirène, 1921; Eschig.
>
> *La Belle Excentrique,* "serious fantasy" for small orchestra (for Mlle Caryathis).
>   1. *Grande Ritournelle*

    2. *Marche Franco-Lunaire*
    3. *Valse du "Mystérieux baiser dans l'oeil"*
    4. *Cancan Grand-Mondain*
Éditions de la Sirène, 1922; Eschig, 1950. For piano four hands,
Éditions de la Sirène, 1922; Eschig, 1950; revised edition by Or-
nella Volta, 1987.

Musique d'ameublement
    1. *Chez un Bistrot*
    2. *Un Salon*
Unpublished.

Quatre petites mélodies for voice and piano.
    1. *Élégie* (Alphonse de Lamartine)
    2. *Danseuse* (Jean Cocteau)
    3. *Chanson* (anonymous 18th-century)
    4. *Adieu* (Raymond Radiguet)
Éditions de la Sirène, 1922; Eschig.

1921   *Sonnerie pour réveiller le bon gros Roi des Singes (lequel ne dort toujours que d'un oeil)* for two trumpets. Published in facsimile in *Fanfare* (1 October 1921). Published as *Carillon: For Awakening the Good Fat Monkey King (Who Always Sleeps with One Eye Open)*. Bulle, Switzerland: Éditions BIM, 1981.

1923   *Ludions* (Léon-Paul Fargue) for voice and piano.
    1. *Air du rat*
    2. *Spleen*
    3. *La Grenouille américaine*
    4. *Air du poète* (published in facsimile in *Les Feuilles libres* 5 [January–February 1924]; and in *The Transatlantic Review* 1 [May 1924])
    5. *Chanson du chat*
Rouart-Lerolle, 1926; Salabert.

Musique d'Ameublement for small orchestra.
    1. *Tenture de cabinet préfectoral* (1923)
    2. *Tapisserie en fer forgé* (1917–23)
    3. *Carrelage phonique* (1917–23) (published in facsimile in John Cage, *Notations* [New York: Something Else Press, 1969])
Salabert, 1975.

Recitatives for Charles Gounod's *Le Médecin malgré lui*. Unpublished.

1924   *Mercure,* "plastic poses in three tableaux" (with Léonide Massine
         and Pablo Picasso) for orchestra.
         1. *Marche Ouverture*
            First Tableau
         2. *La Nuit*
         3. *Danse de tendresse*
         4. *Signes du Zodiaque*
         5. *Entrée de Mercure*
            Second Tableau
         6. *Danses des Grâces*
         7. *Bain des Grâces*
         8. *Fuite de Mercure*
         9. *Colère de Cerbère*
            Third Tableau
         10. *Polka des Lettres*
         11. *Nouvelle Danse*
         12. *Le Chaos*
         13. *Rapt de Proserpine*
         Universal Edition, 1930. Piano reduction, Universal Edition,
         1930.

         Relâche, "instantaneous ballet in two acts, a cinematographic
         entr'acte, and 'the tail of the dog'" (with Francis Picabia and Jean
         Börlin) for orchestra.
         1. *Ouverture*
         2. *Projection - Rideau*
            Act 1
         3. *Entrée de la Femme*
         4. *Musique entre l'entrée de la Femme et sa "Danse sans
            musique"*
         5. *Entrée de l'Homme*
         6. *Danse de la Porte tournante*
         7. *Entrée des Hommes*
         8. *Danse des Hommes*
         9. *Danse de la Femme*
         10. *Final*
            Act 2
         11. *Musique de Rentrée*
         12. *Rentrée des Hommes*
         13. *Rentrée de la Femme*
         14. *Les Hommes se dévêtissent*
         15. *Danse de l'Homme et de la Femme*
         16. *Les Hommes regagnent leur place et retrouvent leurs
            pardessus*

17. *Danse de la Brouette*
18. *Danse de la Couronne*
19. *Le Danseur dépose la Couronne sur la tête d'une spectatrice*
20. *La Femme rejoint son fauteuil*
21. *Petite Danse Finale (La Queue du Chien)*

Rouart-Lerolle, 1926; Salabert. Piano reduction, Rouart-Lerolle, 1926; Salabert. For piano four hands by Darius Milhaud, Rouart-Lerolle, 1926; Salabert.

Cinéma: Entr'acte symphonique de "Relâche" for orchestra.
1. *Cheminées, ballons qui explosent*
2. *Gants de boxe et allumettes*
3. *Prises d'air, jeux d'échecs et bateaux sur les toits*
4. *La Danseuse et figures dans l'eau*
5. *Chasseur, et début de l'enterrement*
6. *Marche funèbre*
7. *Cortège au ralenti*
8. *La Poursuite*
9. *Chûte du cerceuil et sortie de Börlin*
10. *Final (écran crevé et fin)*

Rouart-Lerolle, 1926; Salabert. For piano four hands by Darius Milhaud, Rouart-Lerolle, 1926; Salabert. For piano solo, Salabert, 1972. Revised version for orchestra, Salabert.

ARRANGEMENTS OF WORKS OF OTHER COMPOSERS

Alfred Verley, *Pastels sonores* (for piano?)
1. "Cloches dans la vallée"
2. "L'Aurore aux doigts de rose"

No. 2 transcribed for piano four hands by Erik Satie. Paris: Chez l'Auteur: 86bis Boulevard Victor-Hugo, Neuilly, 1916.
No. 2 orchestrated by Erik Satie; eleven pages (plus title page) in full score for piccolo, flutes, oboe, English horn, B-flat clarinets, bassoons, horns, trumpets, 2 trombones, tuba, timpani, tambour de Basque, cymbals, harp, strings. Unpublished. Manuscript in the Bibliothèque Nationale, Département de Musique, MS 10.034.

ARRANGEMENTS FOR STRING QUARTET OF SATIE WORKS

Quatuor intime et secret (sur 16 pièces d'Erik Satie) arranged for string quartet by Robert Caby. Salabert, 1979.
I. *Choral* (from *Douze petits chorals*, no. 6[(2)])
II. *Désespoir agréable* (from *Six pièces de la période 1906–1913*, no. 1)
III. *Nostalgie* (from *Musiques intimes et secrètes*, no. 1)

IV. *Poésie* (from *Six pièces de la période 1906–1913,* no. 3)

 V. *Songerie vers "Jack"* (from *Carnet d'Esquisses et de Croquis,* no. 10)

VI. *Nostalgie* (transposed version of no. III)

VII. *Songe-Creux* (from *Six pièces de la période 1906–1913,* no. 6)

VIII. *Fâcheux exemple* (from *Musiques intimes et secrètes,* no. 3)

 IX. *Profondeur* (from *Six pièces de la période 1906–1913,* no. 5)

 X. *Froide songerie* (from *Musiques intimes et secrètes,* no. 2)

XI. *Rêverie du pauvre*

XII. *Harmonies delectables* (from *Carnet d'Esquissese et de Croquis,*
        No. 9 and *Pages mystiques,* no. 3[(2)]

XIII. *Songe creux* (repeat of no. VII)

XIV. *Mouvement de Polka* (from *Carnet d'Esquisses et de Croquis,* no. 4)

 XV. *Le Grand Singe* (from *Carnet d'Esquisses et de Croquis,* no. 6)

XVI. *Petite Danse* (from *Carnets d'Esquisses et de Croquis,* no. 17)

Discography

For a comprehensive listing, substantially complete to 1969, consult Jeffrey Cobb's discography in Pierre-Daniel Templier, *Erik Satie,* translated by Elena L. French and David S. French (Cambridge, Mass.: MIT Press, 1969), 117–27. The following discography lists mainly those recordings issued, or reissued, since ca. 1969, although pre-1969 recordings still in print, or of special historical significance, have been retained. Many recordings—e.g., EMI/Angel, RCA Victor, Columbia—are released simultaneously, or nearly simultaneously, in several countries—France, Great Britain, Japan, United States. In most such cases only the most current domestic release has been cited in order to make the discography less unwieldly. For selective discographies, see also Anne Rey, *Erik Satie* (Paris: Éditions de Seuil, 1974), 186–91; Ornella Volta, *Erik Satie* (Paris: Éditions Seghers/Humour, 1979), 151–55; and Vincent Lajoinie, *Erik Satie* (Lausanne: Éditions l'Age d'Homme, 1985), 439–43. All items listed below are 33 1/3-rpm disc recordings unless otherwise indicated.

Allegro (piano solo)
> Jean-Pierre Armengaud, piano. Le Chant du Monde LDX 78.805; LDC 278.805 (compact disc).

Allons-y Chochotte (voice and piano)
> Bruno Laplante, baritone; Marc Durand, piano. Calliope CAL 1884.

Aperçus désagréables (piano four hands)
> 1. *Pastorale*
> 2. *Choral*
> 3. *Fugue*
> Jean-Joël Barbier and Jean Wiéner, piano. Boîte à Musique CALB 64-68.
> Aldo Ciccolini, piano (both parts). Angel S-36459.
> Jacques Février and Francis Poulenc, piano. Musicdisc 30 RC 717.
> Frank Glazer and Richard Deas, piano. Candide CE 31041.
> Wyneke Jordans and Leo Van Doeselaar, piano. Etcetera ETC 1015; KTC-1015 (compact disc).
> Yuji Takahashi and Alain Planès, piano. Denon C37-7487 (compact disc).

Avant-dernières pensées (piano solo)
> 1. *Idylle*

2. *Aubade*

3. *Méditation*

Laurence Allix, piano. Musical Heritage Society MHS 1978/79; Pye Ensayo
   NEL 2004; Ensayo 3402 (compact disc).

Jean-Joël Barbier, piano. Boîte à Musique LD 5762.

Werner Bärtschi, piano. Ex Libris EL 16965.

Angela Brownridge, piano. EMI EMX 412071-1.

Aldo Ciccolini, piano. Angel S-36482; EMI/Angel CDC7 47474-2 (compact
   disc).

France Clidat, piano. Forlane UCD-10514 (compact disc).

Evelyne Crochet, piano. Philips PHS900-179.

Philippe Entremont, piano. CBS IM-37247.

Jacques Février, piano. Everest 3221.

Frank Glazer, piano. Vox SVBX 5422.

John McCabe, piano. Saga 5472.

Roland Pöntinen, piano. Bis LP-317; CD-317 (compact disc).

Francis Poulenc, piano. Boîte à Musique LD 023; Columbia ML 4399; Odyssey
   Y 33792.

Bill Quist, piano. Windham Hill WH-1008, WD-1008 (compact disc).

Yuji Takahashi, piano. Denon C37-7486 (compact disc).

Daniel Varsano, piano. CBS M-36694; CBS MK 36694 (compact disc).

Mark Zeltser, piano. CBS 76677.

La Belle Excentrique (orchestra)

1. *Grande Ritournelle*

2. *Marche Franco-Lunaire*

3. *Valse du "Mystérieux baiser dans l'oeil"*

4. *Cancan Grand-Mondain*

Ensemble "Die Reihe" conducted by Friedrich Cerha. Candide CE 31018.

The London Festival Players conducted by Bernard Hermann. (Nos. 1 and 3)
   London SPC 21094.

Utah Symphony Orchestra conducted by Maurice Abravanel. (No. 1) Van-
   guard/Cardinal VCS 10037/38.

Version for piano four hands

Jean-Joël Barbier and Jean Wiéner, piano. Boîte à Musique C 111.

Chantal de Buchy and Théodore Paraskivesco, piano. PG Records PG-7657;
   PG PCD-7657 (compact disc).

Aldo Ciccolini, piano (both parts). Angel S-36459.

Aldo Ciccolini and Gabriel Tacchino, piano. EMI/Angel CDC7 47474-2 (compact disc).

Jacques Février and Francis Poulenc, piano. Musicdisc 30 RC 717.

Wyneke Jordans and Leo Van Doeselaar, piano. Etcetera ETC 1015; KTC-
   1015 (compact disc).

Yuji Takahashi and Alain Planès, piano (with Yuji Murai, clarinet and Koji Okazaki, bassoon). Denon C37-7487 (compact disc).

Carnet d'esquisses et de croquis (piano solo)
Aldo Ciccolini, piano. Angel S-36774.

Caresse (piano solo)
Werner Bärtschi, piano. Ex Libris EL 16965.

Version for ten-string guitar by Pierre Laniau
Pierre Laniau, guitar. EMI C 069-73127.

Chapitres tournés en tous sens (piano solo)
1. *Celle qui parle trop*
2. *Le Porteur de grosses pierres*
3. *Regret des Enfermés (Jonas et Latude)*
Jean-Joël Barbier, piano. Boîte à Musique LD 5779.
Aldo Ciccolini, piano. Angel S-36459.
Frank Glazer, piano. Vox SVBX 5422.
Peter Lawson, piano. Classics for Pleasure CFP 40329.
William Masselos, piano. MGM E-3154; (No. 1) RCA Victor LSC-3127.
John McCabe, piano. Saga 5472.

Chez le docteur (voice and piano)
Bruno Laplante, baritone; Marc Durand, piano. Calliope CAL 1884.

Choses vues à droite et à gauche (sans lunettes) (violin and piano)
1. *Choral hypocrite*
2. *Fugue à tâtons*
3. *Fantaisie musculaire*
Clara Bonaldi, violin; Sylvaine Billier, piano. Arion ARN 30 A 137.
Kenneth Goldsmith, violin; John Jensen, piano. TR Records, TRC-111.
Gidon Kremer, violin; Elena Kremer, piano. Philips 9500 912.
Keiko Mizuno, violin; Yuji Takahashi, piano. Denon C37-7486 (compact disc).
Yan Pascal, violin; Aldo Ciccolini, piano. Angel S-36713.
Steven Staryk, violin; Joseph Schwartz, piano. CBC Radio Canada SM 172.
Millard Taylor, violin; Frank Glazer, piano. Candide CE 31041.

Cinq Grimaces pour "Le Songe d'une nuit d'été"
1. *Préambule*
2. *Coquecigrue*
3. *Chasse*
4. *Fanfaronnade*
5. *Pour Sortir*
Utah Symphony Orchestra conducted by Maurice Abravanel. Vanguard/Cardinal VCS 10037/38.

Version for piano solo by Darius Milhaud
   John McCabe, piano. Saga 5472.

Version for organ by Oskar Gottlieb Blarr
   Oskar Gottlieb Blarr, organ. Schwann Musica Mundi VMS 2094.

Croquis et agaceries d'un gros bonhomme en bois (piano solo)
   1. *Tyrolienne turque*
   2. *Danse maigre (à la manière de ces messieurs)*
   3. *Españaña*
   Jean-Joël Barbier, piano. Boîte à Musique LD 5762.
   Aldo Ciccolini, piano. Angel S-36482; EMI/Angel CDC7 47474-2 (compact
      disc).
   Philippe Entremont, piano. CBS IM-37247.
   Jacques Février, piano. Everest 3221.
   Frank Glazer, piano. Vox SVBX 5422.
   Peter Lawson, piano. Classics for Pleasure CFP 40329.
   William Masselos, piano. (No. 3) RCA Victor LSC-3127.
   Francis Poulenc, piano. (Nos. 1 and 2) Boîte à Musique LD 023; Columbia ML
      4399; Odyssey Y 33792.

Danses gothiques (piano solo)
   Aldo Ciccolini, piano. Angel S-36811.
   Frank Glazer, piano. Vox SVBX 5422.
   Reinbert de Leeuw, piano. Philips 9500 880; 412 243-2 (compact disc).

Descriptions automatiques (piano solo)
   1. *Sur un vaisseau*
   2. *Sur une lanterne*
   3. *Sur un casque*
   Jean-Joël Barbier, piano. Boîte à Musique LD 5762.
   Werner Bärtschi, piano. Ex Libris EL 16965.
   Aldo Ciccolini, piano. Angel S-36459.
   Philippe Entremont, piano. CBS IM-37247.
   Frank Glazer, piano. Vox SVBX 5422.
   Francis Poulenc, piano. Boîte à Musique LD 023; Columbia ML 4399; Odyssey
      Y 33792.
   Yuji Takahashi, piano. Denon C37-7486 (compact disc).

Deux rêveries nocturnes (piano solo)
   Jean-Joël Barbier, piano. Boîte à Musique C 111.
   Aldo Ciccolini, piano. Angel S-36714.
   Evelyne Crochet, piano. Philips PHS900-179.
   John McCabe, piano. Saga 5472.

Version for two guitars by Peter Kraus
   Peter Kraus and Mark Bird, guitars. Orion ORS 74163.

La Diva de l'Empire (voice and piano)
Elly Ameling, soprano; Dalton Baldwin, piano. HMV ASD 2902.
Elly Ameling, soprano; Rudolf Jansen, piano. Philips 412 216-1PH; 412 216-2PH (compact disc).
Richard Beilharz, baritone; Adelheid Lechler, piano. RBM Musikproduktion Mannheim RBN 3078.
Elaine Bonazzi, mezzo-soprano; Frank Glazer, piano. Candide CE 31041.
Régine Crespin, soprano; Philippe Entremont, piano. CBS 36666.
Meriel Dickinson, mezzo-soprano; Peter Dickinson, piano. Unicorn RHS 338.
Bianca-Cornelia Fink, soprano; Christoph Weinhart, piano. RCA Victor VL30 405AG.
Bruno Laplante, baritone; Marc Durand, piano. Calliope CAL 1884.
Yolanda Marcoulescou, soprano; Katja Phillabaum, piano. Orion ORS 76240.
Valerie Masterson, soprano; Roger Vignoles, piano. Pearl SHE 590.
Mady Mesplé, soprano; Aldo Ciccolini, piano. Arabesque 8053L.

Version for solo piano
Laurence Allix, piano. Musical Heritage Society MHS 1978/79; Pye Ensayo NEL 2004; Ensayo 3402 (compact disc).
William Masselos, piano. MGM E-3154.

Version for ten-string guitar by Pierre Laniau
Pierre Laniau, guitar. EMI C 069-73127.

Douze petits chorals (piano)
Aldo Ciccolini, piano. Angel S-36811.
Gerd Zacher, organ. Wergo 60058.

The Dreamy Fish (Le Poisson Rêveur) (piano solo)
Jean-Pierre Armengaud, piano. Le Chant du Monde LDX 78.805; LDC 278.805 (compact disc).

Version for piano and orchestra by Robert Caby
Georges Pludermacher, piano, with Rhenish Philharmonic conducted by Pierre Stoll. Cybelia 676.

Embryons desséchés (piano solo)
1. *d'Holothurie*
3. *d'Edriophthalma*
3. *de Podolphthalma*
Jean-Joël Barbier, piano. Boîte à Musique LD 5779.
Werner Bärtschi, piano. Ex Libris EL 16965.
Angela Brownridge, piano. EMI EMX 412071-1.
Aldo Ciccolini, piano. Angel S-36485; EMI/Angel CDC7 47474-2 (compact disc).
France Clidat, piano. Forlane UCD-10514 (compact disc).
Jacques Février, piano. Everest 3221.

Frank Glazer, piano. Vox SVBX 5422.
William Masselos, piano. MGM E-3154; RCA Victor LSC-3127.
Roland Pöntinen, piano. Bis LP-317; CD-317 (compact disc).
Pascal Rogé, piano. London 410-220-2DH (compact disc).
Yuji Takahashi, piano. Denon C37-7486 (compact disc).
Daniel Varsano, piano. CBS M-36694; CBS MK 36694 (compact disc).

Version for orchestra
Ensemble "Die Reihe" conducted by Friedrich Cerha; Marie-Thérèse Escribano, narrator. Candide CE 31018.

Enfantines (piano solo)
1. *Menus propos enfantins*
2. *Enfantillages pittoresques*
3. *Peccadilles importunes*
Jean-Joël Barbier, piano. Boîte à Musique LD 5779.
Aldo Ciccolini, piano. Angel S-36485.
Frank Glazer, piano. Vox SVBX 5422.
Charles Miles, piano. (Nos. 1 and 2) Musical Heritage Society MHS 1475/76.
Marga Richter, piano. MGM E-3181.

En Habit de cheval (piano four hands)
1. *Choral*
2. *Fugue litanique*
3. *Autre choral*
4. *Fugue de papier*
Jean-Joël Barbier and Jean Wiéner, piano. Boîte à Musique CALB 64-68.
Aldo Ciccolini, piano (both parts). Angel S-36459.
Jacques Février and Francis Poulenc, piano. Musicdisc 30 RC 717.
Frank Glazer and Richard Deas, piano. Candide CE 31041.
Arthur Gold and Robert Fizdale, piano. Columbia ML 4854.
Wyneke Jordans and Leo Van Doeselaar, piano. Etcetera ETC 1015; KTC-
1015 (compact disc).

Version for orchestra
French National Radio and Television Orchestra conducted by Manuel Rosenthal. Everest 3234; Adès 14082-2 (compact disc).
Utah Symphony Orchestra conducted by Maurice Abravanel. Vanguard/Car-
dinal VCS 10037/38.

Version for organ by Oskar Gottlieb Blarr
Oskar Gottlieb Blarr, organ. Schwann Musica Mundi VMS 2094.

Fantaisie-valse (piano solo)
Angela Brownridge, piano. EMI EMX 412071-1.

Le Fils des étoiles (piano solo)
1. Prelude, Act 1: *La Vocation*

2. Prelude, Act 2: *L'Initiation*
3. Prelude, Act 3: *L'Incantation*
Laurence Allix, piano. (No. 3) Musical Heritage Society MHS 1978/79; Pye Ensayo NEL 2004.
Jean-Joël Barbier, piano. (No. 1) Boîte à Musique 5.093; (Nos. 2 and 3) Boîte à Musique CALB 64-68.
Aldo Ciccolini, piano. Angel S-36714.
Peter Lawson, piano. (No. 2) Classics for Pleasure CFP 40329.
John McCabe, piano. Saga 5472.
Charles Miles, piano. (Nos. 1 and 2) Musical Heritage Society MHS 1475/76.
Bill Quist, piano. (Nos. 1 and 2) Windham Hill WH-1008, WD-1008 (compact disc).

Version of nos. 1 and 3 for orchestra by Roland-Manuel.
Utah Symphony Orchestra conducted by Maurice Abravanel. Vanguard/Cardinal VCS 10037/38.

Version for organ by Oskar Gottlieb Blarr
Oskar Gottlieb Blarr, organ. Schwann Musica Mundi VMS 2094.

Geneviève de Brabant (miniature opera for marionettes) (orchestrated by Roger Désormière)
Orchestre de Paris and Chorus of the National Theatre Opera conducted by Pierre Dervaux. Mady Mesplé, soprano (Geneviève); Jean-Christophe Benoit, baritone (Golo); Pierre Bertin, narrator. Arabesque 8053-L.
Orchestre Symphonique de Radio-Télé Luxembourg and Chorale "Uelzecht" d'Esch-sur-Alzette conducted by Roland Douatte. Renée Bertemes-Roeder, soprano (Geneviève); Alphonse Kontz, baritone (Golo). Musicdisc 30 RC 676.
"Air de Geneviève" (act 2) and "Petit air de Geneviève" (act 3). Meriel Dickinson, mezzo-soprano; Peter Dickinson, piano. Unicorn RHS 338.

(6) *Gnossienees*
Laurence Allix, piano. (Nos. 1–3) Musical Heritage Society MHS 1978/79; Pye Ensayo NEL 2004; (Nos. 1–6) Ensayo 3402 (compact disc).
Jean-Joël Barbier, piano. (Nos. 1–3) Boîte à Musique 5.093; (Nos. 4–6) Boîte à Musique C III; (Nos. 1–6) Accord 149564 (compact disc).
Werner Bärtschi, piano. (Nos. 1–3) Ex Libris EL 16965.
André Bernot, piano. (Nos. 1–3) Club de L'Echiquier CED 30 C 2M.
Nathalie Béra-Tagrine, piano. (No. 1) Pianissime 2002.
Angela Brownridge, piano. (Nos. 1–3) EMI EMX 413071-1.
Chantal de Buchy, piano. PG Records PG-7657; PG PCD-7657 (compact disc).
Aldo Ciccolini, piano. (Nos. 1–3) Angel S-36482; (Nos. 4–6) Angel S-36714; (Nos. 1–6) EMI/Angel CDC7 47474-2 (compact disc).
France Clidat, piano. (Nos. 1–4) Forlane UCD-10514 (compact disc).
Evelyne Crochet, piano. Philips PHS900-179.

Peter Dickinson, piano. (No. 2) Unicorn RHS 338.
Philippe Entremont, piano. (Nos. 1–3) CBS IM-37247.
Jacques Février, piano. (No. 1) Everest 3221.
Frank Glazer, piano. (Nos. 1–3) Vox SVBX 5422.
Peter Lawson, piano. (Nos. 2 and 4) Classics for Pleasure CFP 40329.
Reinbert de Leeuw, piano. Philips 9500 880; 412 243-2 (compact disc).
William Masselos, piano. (Nos. 1–3) MGM E-3154; (Nos. 1–3) RCA Victor LSC-3127.
John McCabe, piano. (Nos. 1, 4 and 5) Saga 5387; (Nos. 2 and 3) Saga 5472.
Charles Miles, piano. Musical Heritage Society MHS 1475/76.
Francis Poulenc, piano. (No. 3) Boîte à Musique LD 023; Columbia ML 4399; Odyssey Y 33792.
Bill Quist, piano. (Nos. 1–3) Windham Hill WH-1008; WD-1008 (compact disc).
Pascal Rogé, piano. (Nos. 1–3) London 410-220-2DH (compact disc).
Roland Pöntinen, piano. Bis LP-317; CD-317 (compact disc).
Yuji Takahashi, piano. (Nos. 1–3) Denon C37-7485 (compact disc).
Daniel Varsano, piano. (Nos. 1–5) CBS M-36694; CBS MK 36694 (compact disc).

Version of nos. 1–3 for orchestra by John Lanchbery
Orchestra of the Royal Opera House, Covent Garden conducted by John Lanchbery. Angel S-37580.

Version of no. 3 for orchestra by Francis Poulenc
English Chamber Orchestra conducted by Aviva Einhorn. Pinnacle/Aurora AUR5065; Ensayo ENY 812(K).
Utah Symphony Orchestra conducted by Maurice Abravanel. Vanguard/Cardinal VCS 10037/38.

Version of nos. 1–4 for ten-string guitar
Paul Chiaro, guitar. (Nos. 1–3) Towerhill T-1015.
Pierre Laniau, guitar. EMI C 069-73127.
Vincenzo Macaluso, guitar. (Nos. 1–3) Klavier KS 523.

Version of nos. 1–6 for two guitars by Peter Kraus
Peter Kraus and Mark Bird, guitars. Orion ORS 74163.

Version of no. 4 for flute and harp
Roger Bourdin, flute; Annie Challan, harp. Arion ARN 38356.

(3) *Gymnopédies*
Laurence Allix, piano. Musical Heritage Society MHS 1978/79; Pye Ensayo NEL 2003; Fidelio 3320; Ensayo 3402 (compact disc).
Jean-Joël Barbier, piano. Boîte à Musique 5.093; Accord 149564 (compact disc).
André Bernot, piano. Club de l'Echiquier CED 30 C 2M.
Angela Brownridge, piano. EMI EMX 412071-1.

Chantal de Buchy, piano. PG Records PG-7657; PG PCD-7657 (compact disc).

Aldo Ciccolini, piano. Angel S-36482; EMI/Angel CDC7 47474-2 (compact disc).

France Clidat, piano. Forlane UCD-10514 (compact disc).

Evelyne Crochet, piano. Philips PHS900-179.

Peter Dickinson, piano. (No. 1) Unicorn RHS 338.

Marylène Dosse, piano. (No. 1) Turnabout TV 34765.

Philippe Entremont, piano. CBS IM-37247; Columbia M-32070.

Morton Estrin, piano. (No. 1) Connoisseur Society CSQ 2065.

Albert Ferber, piano. (No. 1) Meridian E77018.

Jacques Février, piano. (No. 1) Everest 3221.

Frank Glazer, piano. Vox SVBX 5422.

Pierre Huybregts, piano. Educo 3091.

Peter Lawson, piano. Classics for Pleasure CFP 40329.

Reinbert de Leeuw, piano. Philips 9500 870.

William Masselos, piano. MGM E-3154; RCA Victor LSC-3127.

John McCabe, piano. Saga 5387.

Charles Miles, piano. Musical Heritage Society MHS 1475/76.

Cécile Ousset, piano. Angel DS-38104.

Leonard Pennario, piano. (No. 1) Angel S-37303.

Roland Pöntinen, piano. Bis LP-317; CD-317 (compact disc).

Francis Poulenc, piano. (No. 1) Boîte à Musique LD 023; Columbia ML 4399; Odyssey Y 33792.

Bill Quist, piano. Windham Hill WH-1008; WD-1008 (compact disc).

Pascal Rogé, piano. London 410-220-2DH (compact disc).

Yuji Takahashi, piano. Denon C37-7485 (compact disc).

Daniel Varsano, piano. CBS M-36694; CBS MK 36694 (compact disc).

Ilana Vered, piano. (No. 1) London SPC 21156.

Version of nos. 1 and 3 for orchestra by Claude Debussy

City of Birmingham Symphony Orchestra conducted by Louis Frémaux. Angel/EMI Q4ASD 2989.

Concert Arts Orchestra conducted by Vladimir Golschmann. Capitol CTL 7055; Capitol P 8244.

English Chamber Orchestra conducted by Aviva Einhorn. Pinnacle/Aurora AUR5065; Ensayo ENY 812(K).

Frank Pourcel and His Orchestra. Angel DS-37751.

Hague Philharmonic Orchestra conducted by Willem van Otterloo. Philips SBR 6234.

Hallé Orchestra conducted by Maurice Handford. Classics for Pleasure CFP 40320.

London Philharmonic Orchestra conducted by Bernard Hermann. London SPC 21062.

London Symphony Orchestra conducted by André Previn. RCA Victor LSC-2945.

National Philharmonic conducted by Charles Gerhardt. RCA Victor AGLI-4948.

Orchestra of the Royal Opera House, Covent Garden, conducted by John Lanchbery. Angel S-37580.

Orchestre Philharmonique de Monte-Carlo conducted by Lawrence Foster. Erato ERA 9271; ECD 88103 (compact disc).

Orchestre de la Radio Suisse italienne conducted by Roland Douatte. Music-disc RC 708.

Paris Conservatoire Orchestra conducted by Louis Auriacombe. Angel S-36486.

Royal Philharmonic conducted by Philippe Entremont. CBS M-30294; (No. 3) Columbia M-31349.

St. Louis Symphony conducted by Leonard Slatkin. Telarc DG-10059; CD-80059 (compact disc).

Utah Symphony Orchestra conducted by Maurice Abravanel. Vanguard/Cardinal VCS 10037/38; Vanguard VSD-71275.

Violins of Versailles conducted by André Durand. Stanyan Records (Q)SRQ4000.

Version of no. 2 for orchestra by Richard Jones
Concert Arts Orchestra conducted by Vladimir Golschmann. Capitol P 8244.

Version of no. 2 for orchestra by Roland-Manuel
Orchestra of the Royal Opera House, Covent Garden, conducted by John Lanchbery. Angel S-37580.

Version of no. 3 for violin and orchestra by Arthur Harris
Issac Stern, violin with Columbia Symphony Orchestra conducted by Frank Brieff. Columbia M-31425.

Version of no. 3 for saxophone and orchestra by Michel Colombier
Branford Marsalis, soprano saxophone with English Chamber Orchestra conducted by Andrew Litton. CBS M42122; CBS MK-42122 (compact disc).

Version of nos. 1–3 for guitar
Christopher Parkening, guitar. Angel S-36053.
Liona Boyd, guitar. (No. 1) Columbia M-35137; CBS 37788.
Paul Chiaro, guitar. Towerhill T-1015.

Version of nos. 1–3 for ten-string guitar
Pierre Laniau, guitar. (No. 1) EMI C 069-73127.
Vincenzo Macaluso, guitar. (Nos. 2 and 3) Klavier KS-508.

Version of nos. 1–3 for two guitars by Peter Kraus
Peter Kraus and Mark Bird, guitars. Orion ORS 74163.

Version of no. 1 for flute and guitar
André-Gilles Duchemin, flute; Peter McCutcheon, guitar. Pro-Culture PPC 7002.

Version of nos. 1 and 3 for flute and harp
  Robert Aitken, flute; Erica Goodman, harp. ERA Records Era 101.
  Roger Bourdin, flute; Annie Challan, harp. (No. 1) Arion 30 A 113.
  Ransom Wilson, flute; Nancy Allen, harp. (No. 1) Angel S-37398.

Version of no. 1 for flute, cello, and piano
  Bowkun Trio (Sandra Bowkun, flute; Julia Bowkun, cello; Ellen Meyer, piano).
  Duke Street Records DSR 31013.

Version of nos. 1 and 2 for English horn and piano by Patricia Stenberg
  Patricia Stenberg, English horn; Gary Wolf, piano. Golden Crest RE 7039.

Version of no. 1 for harmonica, piano, and harp
  Tommy Reilly, harmonica; James Moody, piano; Skaila Kanga, harp. Argo
  ZK55.

Version of no. 1 for string quartet
  San Francisco String Quartet. 1750 Arch Records S-1783.

Version of no. 2 for two pianos
  Arthur Whittemore and Jack Lowe, duo-pianists. RCA Victor LM-1926.

Version of no. 1 for brass ensemble by Richard Harvey
  Philip Jones Brass Ensemble. London LDR-71094-1; Decca 410 125-1.

Version of nos. 1–3 for brass ensemble by Brian Raby
  Welsh Brass Consort conducted by György Fischer. Nimbus 45006 (12-inch,
  45 rpm).

Version of no. 1 for saxophone quartet by Hywel Lewis
  English Saxophone Quartet. A531 (English Saxophone Quartet)

Heures séculaires et instananées (piano solo)
  1. *Obstacles venimeux*
  2. *Crépuscule matinal (de midi)*
  3. *Affolements granitiques*
  Jean-Joël Barbier, piano. Boîte à Musique LD 5779.
  Aldo Ciccolini, piano. Angel S-36482.
  Frank Glazer, piano. Vox SVBX 5422.
  Peter Lawson, piano. Classics for Pleasure CFP 40329.

Hymne pour le "Salut Drapeau" (voice and piano)
  Meriel Dickinson, mezzo-soprano; Peter Dickinson, piano. Unicorn RHS 338.
  Marjanne Kweksilber, soprano; Reinbert de Leeuw, piano. Philips 9500 934.

Jack in the Box (piano solo)
  Jean-Joël Barbier, piano. Boîte à Musique
  Angela Brownridge, piano. EMI EMX 412071-1.
  Aldo Ciccolini, piano. Angel S-36774.
  Jay Vrana, piano. Pinnacle/Supraphon 111 1721/2.

Version for orchestra by Darius Milhaud
  Monte Carlo National Opera Orchestra conducted by Igor Markevitch. Pearl
    SHE-554/5; Varèse VC 81097.
  London Festival Players conducted by Bernard Hermann. London SPC 21094.
  Orchestra of the Royal Opera House, Covent Garden, conducted by John
    Lanchbery. Angel S-37580.
  Utah Symphony Orchestra conducted by Maurice Abravanel. Vanguard/Car-
    dinal VCS 10037/38.

Je te veux (voice and piano)
  Elly Ameling, soprano; Dalton Baldwin, piano. HMV ADS 2902.
  Elaine Bonazzi, mezzo-soprano; Frank Glazer, piano. Candide CE 31041.
  Régine Crespin, soprano; Philippe Entremont, piano. CBS 36666.
  Meriel Dickinson, mezzo-soprano; Peter Dickinson, piano. Unicorn RHS 338.
  Bruno Laplante, baritone; Marc Durand, piano. Calliope CAL 1884.
  Yolanda Marcoulescou, soprano; Katja Phillabaum, piano. Orion ORS 76240.
  Jessye Norman, soprano; Dalton Baldwin, piano. Philips 9500 356; Philips 416
    445-2PH (compact disc).
  Jennie Tourel, mezzo-soprano; Georges Reeves, piano. Columbia ML 4158;
    Odyssey Y 232880.

Version for piano solo
  Jean-Pierre Armengaud, piano. Le Chant du Monde LDX 78.805; LDC
    278.805 (compact disc).
  Jean-Joël Barbier, piano. Boîte à Musique CALB 64-68; Accord 149564 (com-
    pact disc).
  Werner Bärtschi, piano. Ex Libris EL 16965.
  Angela Brownridge, piano. EMI EMX 412071-1.
  Peter Dickinson, piano. Unicorn RHS 338.
  Philippe Entremont, piano. CBS IM-37247.
  John McCabe, piano. Saga 5472.
  Pascal Rogé, piano. London 410-220-2DH (compact disc).
  Yuji Takahashi, piano. Denon C37-7485 (compact disc).

Version for ten-string guitar by Pierre Laniau
  Pierre Laniau, guitar. EMI C 069-73127.

Ludions (voice and piano)
  1. *Air du rat*
  2. *Spleen*
  3. *La Grenouille américaine*
  4. *Air du poète*
  5. *Chanson du chat*
  Elly Ameling, soprano; Rudolf Jansen, piano. Philips 412 628-IPH; 412 628-
    2PH (compact disc).

Richard Beilharz, baritone; Adelheid Lechler, piano. (Nos. 2 and 3) RBM Mu-
sikproduktion Mannheim RBM 3078.
Elaine Bonazzi, mezzo-soprano; Frank Glazer, piano. Candide CE 31041.
Régine Crespin, soprano; Philippe Entremont, piano. (No. 5) CBS 36666.
Hugues Cuenod, tenor; Geoffrey Parsons, piano. Nimbus 2112; NIM 5027
(compact disc).
Carol Kimball, mezzo-soprano; Thomas Grubb, piano. Orion ORS 82422.
Marjanne Kweksilber, soprano; Reinbert de Leeuw, piano. Philips 9500 934.
Bruno Laplante, baritone; Marc Durand, piano. Calliope CAL 1884.
Mady Mesplé, soprano; Aldo Ciccolini, piano. Angel S-36713.

Mercure (ballet)
The London Festival Players conducted by Bernard Hermann. London SPC
21094.
Orchestre de Paris conducted by Pierre Dervaux. Angel S-36846.
Utah Symphony Orchestra conducted by Maurice Abravanel. Vanguard/Car-
dinal VCS 10037/38; Vanguard VSD-71275.

Messe des pauvres (piano or organ with small choir SB ad lib.)
1. *Kyrie eleison*
2. *Dixit Domine*
3. *Prière des Orgues*
4. *Commune qui mundi nefas*
5. *Chant ecclésiastique*
6. *Prière pour les voyageurs et les marins en danger de mort, à la très bonne et
très auguste Vierge Marie, mère de Jésus*
7. *Prière pour le salut de mon âme*
Gaston Litaize, organ, with Chorus of René Duclos directed by Jean Laforge.
Arabesque 8053-L.
Marilyn Mason, organ, with The Randolph Singers. Counterpoint/Esoteric
Records CPT-510.
Klaus Martin Ziegler, organ, with Martinskantorei, Kassel. (Nos. 1, 3, 5, and
7) Psallite 89/25096PET.

Musique d'ameublement (chamber orchestra)
1. *Tenture de cabinet préfectoral*
2. *Tapisserie en fer forgé*
3. *Carrelage phonique*
Ensemble Ars Nova conducted by Marius Constant. Erato STU 71336; Musical Heritage Society MHS-4700.

Musiques intimes et secrètes (piano solo)
1. *Nostalgie*
2. *Froide songerie*
3. *Fâcheux exemple*
Aldo Ciccolini, piano. Angel S-36774.

Version for ten-string guitar by Pierre Laniau
Pierre Laniau, guitar. (Nos. 1 and 3) EMI C 069-73127.

(5) *Nocturnes* (piano solo)
Jean-Joël Barbier, piano. Boîte à Musique LD 5762.
Werner Bärtschi, piano. Ex Libris EL 16965.
André Bernot, piano. Club de l'Echiquier CED 30 C 2M.
Aldo Ciccolini, piano. (Nos. 1–3) Angel S-36482; (Nos. 4–5) Angel S-36774;
    (Nos. 1–5) EMI/Angel CDC7 47474-2 (compact disc).
France Clidat, piano. (Nos. 1–3) Forlane UCD-10514 (compact disc).
Philippe Entremont, piano. (No. 1) CBS IM-37247.
Fred Fisher, piano. (Nos. 1–3) Spectrum SR-132.
Frank Glazer, piano. Vox SVBX 5422.
Peter Lawson, piano. (Nos. 2 and 4) Classics for Pleasure CFP 40329.
William Masselos, piano. (No. 3) RCA Victor LSC-3127; (No. 5) MGM E-
    3154.
John McCabe, piano. (No. 1) Saga 5387; (Nos. 3 and 5) Saga 5472.
Charles Miles, piano. (Nos. 1–3) Musical Heritage Society MHS 1475/76.
Bill Quist, piano. (Nos. 1–3) Windham Hill WH-1008; WD-1008 (compact disc).
Pascal Rogé, piano. (No. 4) London 410-220-2DH (compact disc).
Yuji Takahashi, piano. Denon C37-7486 (compact disc).
Daniel Varsano, piano. (No. 1) CBS M-36694; CBS MK 36694 (compact disc).

Version of nos. 1–3 for guitar
Paul Chiaro, guitar. Towerhill T-1015.

Version of nos. 4–5 for ten-string guitar
Vincenzo Macaluso, guitar. Klavier KS 523.

Nouvelles pièces froides (piano solo)
    1. *Sur un mur*
    2. *Sur un arbre*
    3. *Sur un pont*
Jean-Joël Barbier, piano. Boîte à Musique C 111.
Werner Bärtschi, piano. Ex Libris EL 16965.
Aldo Ciccolini, piano. Angel S-36714.
Evelyne Crochet, piano. Philips PHS900-179.
Peter Lawson, piano. Classics for Pleasure CFP 40329.

Version for two guitars by Peter Kraus
Peter Kraus and Mark Bird, guitars. Orion ORS 74163.

(4) *Ogives* (piano solo)
Jean-Joël Barbier, piano. (Nos. 1 and 4) Boîte à Musique 5.093; Accord 149564
    (compact disc); (Nos. 2 and 3) Boîte à Musique CALB 64-68.
Aldo Ciccolini, piano. Angel S-36811.
Fred Fisher, piano. Spectrum SR-132.

Frank Glazer, piano. Vox SVBX 5422.

Reinhert de Leeuw, piano. Philips 9500 870.

Bill Quist, piano. (Nos. 1 and 2) Windham Hill WH-1008; WD-1008 (compact disc).

Version of nos. 1 and 4 for two guitars
Peter Kraus and Mark Bird, guitars. Orion ORS 74163.

Version of no. 1 for two marimbas
Emmanuel Séjourné and Jean-Louis Hennequin, marimbas. Auvidis AV4723.

L'Omnibus automobile (voice and piano)
Régine Crespin, soprano; Philippe Entremont, piano. CBS 36666.
Bruno Laplante, baritone; Marc Durand, piano. Calliope CAL 1884.

Pages mystiques (piano solo)
1. *Prière*
2. *Vexations*
3. *Harmonies*
Aldo Ciccolini, piano. Angel S-36811.
Michel Dalberto, piano. (No. 2 - ten times) Erato STU 71336; Musical Heritage Society MHS-4700.
Peter Dickinson, piano. (No. 2 - once but with locking groove on final chord) Unicorn RHS 338.
Reinbert de Leeuw, piano. (No. 1) Philips 9500 881; (No. 2 - thirty-five times) Philips 410-435-1.

Les Pantins dansent (piano solo)
Jean-Pierre Armengaud, piano. Le Chant du Monde LDX 78.805; LDC 278.805 (compact disc).
Aldo Ciccolini, piano. Angel S-36485.
Frank Glazer, piano. Vox SVBX 5422.
John McCabe, piano. Saga 5472.

Version for orchestra
Ensemble "Die Reihe" conducted by Friedrich Cerha. Candide CE 31018.
Lamoureux Concerts Orchestra conducted by Aldo Ciccolini. Angel S-36713.

Version for ten-string guitar by Pierre Laniau
Pierre Laniau, guitar. EMI C 069-73127.

Parade (ballet)
French National Radio and Television Orchestra conducted by Manuel Rosenthal. Everest 3234; Adès 16022; Adès 14082-2 (compact disc).
London Symphony Orchestra conducted by Antal Dorati. Mercury SR90435; Philips 838 434 LY; Philips SAL3637.
Monte-Carlo Opera Orchestra conducted by Louis Frémaux. Deutsche Grammophon SLPM 138 649; DG 2543807; DG 17-512; DG 135146.

Orchestra of Radio Luxembourg conducted by Louis de Froment. Candide CE 31018.

Orchestre Symphonique de Radio-Télé Luxembourg conducted by Roland Douatte. Musicdisc 30 RC 676.

Paris Conservatoire Orchestra conducted by Louis Auriacombe. Angel S-36486.

Royal Philharmonic Orchestra conducted by Philippe Entremont. CBS M-30294.

Utah Symphony Orchestra conducted by Maurice Abravanel. Vanguard/Cardinal VCS 10037/38; Vanguard VSD-71275.

Version for piano four hands
Wyneke Jordans and Leo Van Doeselaar, piano. Etcetera ETC 1015; KTC-1015 (compact disc).
Yuji Takahashi and Alain Planès, piano. Denon C37-7487 (compact disc).

Rag-Time Parade
New England Conservatory Ragtime Ensemble conducted by Gunther Schuller. Golden Crest CRS-31042.

Version of *Rag-Time Parade* for piano solo
John McCabe, piano. Saga 5387.
Yuji Takahashi, piano. Denon C37-7485 (compact disc).

Passacaille (piano solo)
Laurence Allix, piano. Musical Heritage Society MHS 1978/79; Pye Ensayo NEL 2003; Fidelio 3328; Ensayo 3402 (compact disc).
Jean-Joël Barbier, piano. Boîte à Musique CALB 64-68.
Aldo Ciccolini, piano. Angel S-36485.
Frank Glazer, piano. Vox SVBX 5422.
Peter Lawson, piano. Classics for Pleasure CFP 40329.
John McCabe, piano. Saga 5387.

Version for guitar
Paul Chiaro, guitar. Towerhill 1015.

Petite musique de clown triste (piano solo)

Version for ten-string guitar by Pierre Laniau
Pierre Laniau, guitar. EMI C 069-73127.

Petite ouverture à danser (piano solo)
Jean-Joël Barbier, piano. Boîte à Musique CALB 64-68.
Aldo Ciccolini, piano. Angel S-36714.
Evelyne Crochet, piano. Philips PHS900-179.
Reinbert de Leeuw, piano. Philips 9500 880; 412 243-2 (compact disc).

Le Piccadilly (piano solo)
Jean-Joël Barbier. Boîte à Musique CALB 64-68; Accord 149564 (compact disc).
Angela Brownridge, piano. EMI EMX 412071-1.
Peter Dickinson, piano. Unicorn RHS 338.
Pascal Rogé, piano. London 410-220-2DH (compact disc).

Pièces froides (piano solo)
1. *Airs à faire fuir* (3)
2. *Danses de travers* (3)
Laurence Allix, piano. Musical Heritage Society MHS 1978/79; Pye Ensayo NEL 2004.
Jean-Pierre Armengaud, piano. Le Chant du Monde LDX 78.805; LDC 278.805 (compact disc).
Jean-Joël Barbier, piano. (No. 1) Boîte à Musique 5.093; (No. 2) Boîte à Musique LD 5762; (Nos. 1 and 2) Accord 149564 (compact disc).
Werner Bärtschi, piano. Ex Libris EL 16965.
André Bernot, piano. Club de l'Echiquier CED 30 C 2M.
Aldo Ciccolini, piano. Angel S-36485.
Peter Dickinson, piano. (No. 1/2) Unicorn RHS 338.
Jacques Février, piano. (No. 1/1; No. 2/1) Everest 3221.
Frank Glazer, piano. Vox SVBX 5422.
Reinbert de Leeuw, piano. Philips 9500 881.
John McCabe, piano. (No. 1) Saga 5472.
Charles Miles, piano. Musical Heritage Society MHS 1475/76.
Roland Pöntinen, piano. Bis LP-317; CD-317 (compact disc).
Yuji Takahashi, piano. Denon C37-7485 (compact disc).

Version of no. 1 for two guitars by Peter Kraus
Peter Kraus and Mark Bird, guitars. Orion ORS 74163.

Version of no. 1/2 for English horn and piano by Patricia Stenberg
Patricia Stenberg, English horn; Gary Wolf, piano. Golden Crest RE 7039.

Le Piège de Méduse (lyric comedy in one act)
Lamoureux Concerts Orchestra conducted by Aldo Ciccolini. Pierre Bertin (Baron Méduse); Hubert Deschamps (Polycarpe); Joseph-Marie Falcucci (Astolpho); Marie Laurence (Frisette). Angel S-36713.

Suite for orchestra
Ensemble "Die Reihe" conducted by Friedrich Cerha. Candide CE 31018.

Suite for piano solo
Jean-Pierre Armengaud, piano. Le Chant du Monde LDX 78.805; LDC 278.805 (compact disc).
Werner Bärtschi, piano. Ex Libris EL 16965.

Aldo Ciccolini, piano. Angel S-36485.
Peter Lawson, piano. Classics for Pleasure CFP 40329.
William Masselos, piano. RCA Victor LSC-3127.
John McCabe, piano. Saga 5472.
Charles Miles, piano. Musical Heritage Society MHS 1475/76.

Poudre d'or (piano solo)
Jean-Joël Barbier, piano. Boîte à Musique CALB 64-68.
Angela Brownridge, piano. EMI EMX 412071-1.
Aldo Ciccolini, piano. Angel S-36811.
France Clidat, piano. Forlane UCD-10514 (compact disc).
Peter Dickinson, piano. Unicorn RHS 338.
Philippe Entremont, piano. CBS IM-37247.

Prélude de La Porte héroïque du ciel (piano solo)
Jean-Joël Barbier, piano. Boîte à Musique LD 5762.
Werner Bärtschi, piano. Ex Libris EL 16965.
Aldo Ciccolini, piano. Angel S-36774; Angel S-36713.
France Clidat, piano. Forlane UCD-10514 (compact disc).
Frank Glazer, piano. Vox SVBX 5422.
Reinbert de Leeuw, piano. Philips 9500 880; 412 243-2 (compact disc).
John McCabe, piano. Saga 5472.
Francis Poulenc, piano. Boîte à Musique LD 023.
Bill Quist, piano. Windham Hill WH-1008; WD-1008 (compact disc).
Yuji Takahashi, piano. Denon C37-7485 (compact disc).

Prélude en tapisserie (piano solo)
Laurence Allix, piano. Musical Heritage Society MHS 1978/79; Pye Ensayo
    NEL 2003; Fidelio 3328; Ensayo 3402 (compact disc).
Jean-Joël Barbier, piano. Boîte à Musique CALB 64–68.
Angela Brownridge, piano. EMI EMX 412071-1.
Aldo Ciccolini, piano. Angel S-36485.
Frank Glazer, piano. Vox SVBX 5422.
Pascal Rogé, piano. London 410-220-2DH (compact disc).

Préludes flasques (pour un chien) (piano solo)
    1. *Voix d'intérieur*
    2. *Idylle cynique*
    3. *Chanson canine*
    4. *Avec camaraderie*
Jean-Joël Barbier, piano. Boîte à Musique LD 5779.
Chantal de Buchy, piano. PG Records PG-7657; PG PCD-7657 (compact disc).
Aldo Ciccolini, piano. Angel S-36485.
Pascal Rogé, piano. London 410-220-2DH (compact disc).
Yuji Takahashi, piano. Denon C37-7486 (compact disc).

Première pensée Rose + Croix (piano solo)
Aldo Ciccolini, piano. Angel S-36714.
Evelyne Crochet, piano. Philips PHS900-179.
John McCabe, piano. Saga 5472.

Version for organ by Oskar Gottlieb Blarr
Oskar Gottlieb Blarr, organ. Schwann Musica Mundi VMS 2094.

Premier Menuet (piano solo)
Jean-Joël Barbier, piano. Boîte à Musique CALB 64-68.
Aldo Ciccolini, piano. Angel S-36774.
Frank Glazer, piano. Vox SVBX 5422.

Quartre petites mélodies (voice and piano)
  1. *Élégie*
  2. *Danseuse*
  3. *Chanson*
  4. *Adieu*
Elaine Bonazzi, mezzo-soprano; Frank Glazer, piano. Candide CE 31041.
Nicolai Gedda, tenor; Aldo Ciccolini, piano. Angel S-36713.
Marjanne Kweksilber, soprano; Reinbert de Leeuw, piano. Philips 9500 934.
Bruno Laplante, baritone; Marc Durand, piano. Calliope CAL 1884.

Quatre Préludes (piano solo)
  1. *Fête donnée par des Chevaliers Normands en l'Honneur d'une jeune Demoi-
     selle (XIᵉ siècle)*
  2. *Prélude d'Eginhard*
  3. *Premier Prélude du Nazaréen*
  4. *Deuxième Prélude du Nazaréen*
Jean-Joël Barbier, piano. (No. 1) Boîte à Musique LD 5762; (Nos. 2 and 3)
     Boîte à Musique CALB 64-68.
Aldo Ciccolini, piano. Angel S-36714.
Frank Glazer, piano. Vox SVBX 5422.
Reinbert de Leeuw, piano. Philips 9500 881.
Charles Miles, piano. (Nos. 2 and 3) Musical Heritage Society MHS 1475/76.
Mats Persson, piano. (No. 4) Caprice CAP 1071.
Francis Poulenc, piano. (No. 1) Boîte à Musique LD 023.
Bill Quist, piano. (Nos. 1 and 2) Windham Hill WH-1008; WD-1008 (compact
     disc).

Version of no. 3 for organ by Oskar Gottlieb Blarr
Oskar Gottlieb Blarr, organ. Schwann Musica Mundi VMS 2094.

Version of nos. 1 and 3 for orchestra by Francis Poulenc
Orchestra of the Royal Opera House, Covent Garden, conducted by John
     Lanchbery. Angel S-37580.

Utah Symphony Orchestra conducted by Maurice Abravanel. Vanguard/Cardinal VCS 10037/38.

Version of no. 2 for orchestra by John Lanchbery
Orchestra of the Royal Opera House, Covent Garden, conducted by John Lanchbery. Angel S-37580.

Version of no. 3 for ten-string guitar by Pierre Laniau
Pierre Laniau, guitar. EMI C 069-73127.

Relâche (ballet)
Orchestre Symphonique de Radio-Télé Luxembourg conducted by Roland Douatte. Musicdisc 30 RC 676.
Paris Conservatoire Orchestra conducted by Louis Auriacombe. Angel S-36486.
Royal Philharmonic Orchestra conducted by Philippe Entremont. CBS M-30294.
Utah Symphony Orchestra conducted by Maurice Abravanel. Vanguard/Cardinal VCS 10037/38; Vanguard VSD-71275.

Cinéma: Entr'acte symphonique de "Relâche" (orchestra)
Ensemble Ars Nova conducted by Marius Constant. Erato STU 71336; Musical Heritage Society MHS-4700.
Ensemble "Die Reihe" conducted by Friedrich Cerha. Candide CE 31018.

Version for piano solo
Jean-Pierre Armengaud, piano. Le Chant du Monde LDX 78.805; LDC 278.805 (compact disc).

Version for piano four hands by Darius Milhaud
Yuji Takahashi and Alain Planès, piano. Denon C37-7487 (compact disc).

Rêverie du pauvre (piano solo)
John McCabe, piano. Saga 5472.

(3) *Sarabandes* (piano solo)
Laurence Allix, piano. Musical Heritage Society MHS 1978/79; Pye Ensayo NEL 2003; Fidelio 3328; Ensayo 3402 (compact disc).
Jean-Joël Barbier, piano. Boîte à Musique LD 5762; Accord 149564 (compact disc).
Aldo Ciccolini, piano. Angel S-36485.
Jacques Février, piano. (No. 1) Everest 3221.
Frank Glazer, piano. Vox SVBX 5422.
Reinbert de Leeuw, piano. Philips 9500 870.
John McCabe, piano. (Nos. 1 and 3) Saga 5387.
Roland Pöntinen, piano. (No. 3) Bis LP-317; CD-317 (compact disc).
Francis Poulenc, piano. (No. 2) Boîte à Musique LD 023; Columbia ML 4399; Odyssey Y 33792.

Bill Quist, piano. Windham Hill WH-1008; WD-1008 (compact disc).
Daniel Varsano, piano. (Nos. 1 and 3) CBS M-36694; CBS MK 36694 (compact disc).

Version for guitar
Paul Chiaro, guitar. Towerhill T-1015.

Version for two guitars by Peter Kraus
Peter Kraus and Mark Bird, guitars. Orion ORS 74163.

Six pièces de la période 1906–1913 (piano solo)
1. *Désespoir agréable*
2. *Effronterie*
3. *Poésie*
4. *Prélude canin*
5. *Profondeur*
6. *Songe-creux*
Jean-Joël Barbier, piano. (No. 6) Boîte à Musique C 111.
Aldo Ciccolini, piano. Angel S-36774.
Evelyne Crochet, piano. (Nos. 1–2; 4–6) Philips PHS900–179.
John McCabe, piano. Saga 5387.

Version of nos. 1 and 6 for ten-string guitar by Pierre Laniau
Pierre Laniau, guitar. EMI C 069-73127.

Version of no. 6 for two guitars by Peter Kraus
Peter Kraus and Mark Bird, guitars. Orion ORS 74163.

Socrate (symphonic drama in three parts with voice)
Ensemble "Die Reihe" conducted by Friedrich Cerha. Michèle Bedard, Marie-Thérèse Escribano, Emiko Liyama, Gerlinde Lorenz, sopranos. Candide CE 31024.
Orchestra conducted by Henri Sauguet. Anne Laloë, soprano. Le Chant du Monde LDX-A-8292.
Orchestre de Paris conducted by Pierre Dervaux. Andrée Esposito, Andréa Guiot, Mady Mesplé, sopranos; Danielle Millet, mezzo-soprano. Angel S-36846.
Paris Philharmonic Orchestra conducted by René Leibowitz. Anne-Marie Carpenter, Violette Journeaux, Janine Lindenfelder, Simone Pèbordes, sopranos. Counterpoint/Esoteric CPT-510.

Version for voice and piano
Hugues Cuenod, tenor; Geoffrey Parsons, piano. Nimbus 2104; NIM 5027 (compact disc).

Part 3 (*La Morte de Socrate*) only
French National Radio and Television Orchestra conducted by Manuel Rosen-

thal. Denise Monteil, soprano. Everest 3234; Adès 16022; Adès 14082-2 (compact disc).

Sonatine bureaucratique (piano solo)
Jean-Joël Barbier, piano. Boître à Musique LD 5779.
Werner Bärtschi, piano. Ex Libris EL 16965.
Aldo Ciccolini, piano. Angel S-36811; EMI/Angel CDC7 47474-2 (compact disc).
Frank Glazer, piano. Vox SVBX 5422.
Peter Lawson, piano. Classics for Pleasure CFP 40329.
John McCabe, piano. Saga 5387.
Roland Pöntinen, piano. Bis LP-317; CD-317 (compact disc).
Pascal Rogé, piano. London 410-220-2DH (compact disc).
Yuji Takahashi, piano. Denon C37-7486 (compact disc).
Daniel Varsano, piano. CBS M-36694; CBS MK 36694 (compact disc).

Sonneries de la Rose-Croix (piano solo)
1. *Air de l'Ordre*
2. *Air du Grand Maître*
3. *Air du Grand Prieur*
Jean-Joël Barbier, piano. (Nos. 1 and 3) Boîte à Musique 5.093; (No. 2) Boîte à Musique CALB 64-68.
Werner Bärtschi, piano. Ex Libris EL 16965.
Aldo Ciccolini, piano. Angel S-36714.
Reinbert de Leeuw, piano. Philips 9500 881.

Sonnerie pour réveiller le bon gros Roi des Singes (lequel ne dort toujours que d'un oeil) (two trumpets)
Dallas Trumpets. Crystal Records 5230.
Ensemble Ars Nova conducted by Marius Constant. Erato STU 71336; Musical Heritage Society MHS-4700.

Sports et divertissements (piano solo)
Laurence Allix, piano. Musical Heritage Society MHS 1978/79; Pye Ensayo NEL 2003; Fidelio 3328; Ensayo 3402 (compact disc).
Jean-Pierre Armengaud, piano. Le Chant du Monde LDX 78.805; LDC 278.805 (compact disc).
Jean-Joël Barbier, piano. Boîte à Musique 5.093.
Werner Bärtschi, piano. Ex Libris EL 16965.
Angela Brownridge, piano. (excerpts–*Le Golf; Les Courses; Le Pique-Nique; Le Water-Chute; Le Tango; Le Traîneau; Le Feu d'artifice; Le Tennis*) EMI EMX 412071-1.
Chantal de Buchy, piano. PG Records PG 7657; PG PCD-7657 (compact disc).
Aldo Ciccolini, piano. Angel S-36459.

France Clidat, piano. Forlane UCD-10514 (compact disc).
Frank Glazer, piano. Vox SVBX 5422.
John Jensen, piano; Odette deLécluse, narrator. TR Records TRC-111.
Grant Johannesen, piano; Mildred Natwick, narrator. Golden Crest CRS-4133.
William Masselos, piano. MGM E-3154; RCA Victor LSC-3127.
John McCabe, piano. Saga 5387.
Yuji Takahashi, piano. Denon C37-7486 (compact disc).

Tendrement (voice and piano)
Elaine Bonazzi, mezzo-soprano; Frank Glazer, piano. Candide CE 31041.
Régine Crespin, soprano; Philippe Entremont, piano. CBS 36666.
Meriel Dickinson, mezzo-soprano; Peter Dickinson, piano. Unicorn RHS 338.
Nicolai Gedda, tenor; Aldo Ciccolini, piano. Angel S-36713.
Bruno Laplante, baritone; Marc Durand, piano. Calliope CAL 1884.
Yolanda Marcoulescou, soprano; Katja Phillabaum, piano. Orion ORS 76240.

Trois autres mélodies (voice and piano)
1. *Chanson*
2. *Chanson médiévale*
3. *Les Fleurs*
Meriel Dickinson, mezzo-soprano; Peter Dickinson, piano. Unicorn RHS 338.
Marjanne Kweksilber, soprano; Reinbert de Leeuw, piano. Philips 9500 034.
Bruno Laplante, baritone; Marc Durand, piano. Calliope CAL 1884.
Mady Mesplé, soprano; Aldo Ciccolini, piano. Arabesque 8053-L.

Trois Mélodies (voice and piano)
1. *La Statue de bronze*
2. *Daphénéo*
3. *Le Chapelier*
Jane Bathori, soprano; Darius Milhaud, piano. Voix Illustres (Pathé) 50.030.
Pierre Bernac, baritone; Francis Poulenc, piano. Columbia ML 4484; Odyssey
    32160135; Odyssey 32260009.
Elaine Bonazzi, mezzo-soprano; Frank Glazer, piano. Candide CE 31041.
Christiane Castelli, soprano; Hélène Boschi, piano. Chant du Monde LDA
    4003.
Régine Crespin, soprano; Philippe Entremont, piano. CBS 36666.
Hugues Cuenod, tenor; Geoffrey Parsons, piano. Nimbus NIM 5027 (compact
    disc).
Marjanne Kweksilber, soprano; Reinbert de Leeuw, piano. Philips 9500 934.
Bruno Laplante, baritone; Marc Durand, piano. Calliope CAL 1884.
Yolanda Marcoulescou, soprano; Katja Phillabaum, piano. Orion ORS 76240.
Mady Mesplé, soprano; Aldo Ciccolini, piano. (Nos. 2 and 3) Arabesque 8053-L.
Jessye Norman, soprano; Dalton Baldwin, piano. Philips 9500 356; 416 445-
    2PH (compact disc).

Jennie Tourel, mezzo-soprano; Leonard Bernstein, piano. (No. 3) Columbia M-32231.

Jennie Tourel, mezzo-soprano; George Reeves, piano. (No. 3) Columbia ML 4158; Odyssey Y 232880.

Trois mélodies de 1886 (voice and piano)
1. *Les Anges*
2. *Élégie*
3. *Sylvie*
Meriel Dickinson, mezzo-soprano; Peter Dickinson, piano. Unicorn RHS 338.
Marjanne Kweksilber, soprano; Reinbert de Leeuw, piano. Philips 9500 934.
Bruno Laplante, baritone; Marc Durand, piano. Calliope CAL 1884.
Mady Mesplé, soprano; Aldo Ciccolini, piano. Arabesque 8053-L.

Trois mélodies sans paroles (voice and piano)
1. *Rambouillet*
2. *Les oiseaux*
3. *Marienbad*
Bruno Laplante, baritone; Marc Durand, piano. Calliope CAL 1884.

Trois Morceaux en forme de poire (piano four hands)
James Anagnoson and Leslie Kinton, piano. Jubal 5002.
Georges Auric and Jacques Février, piano. Everest 3221; Adès 16022; Adès 14082-2 (compact disc).
Jean-Joël Barbier and Jean Wiéner, piano. Boîte à Musique C 111.
Hélène Boschi and Serge Nigg, piano. Chant du Monde LDA 4003.
Robert and Gaby Casadesus, piano. Columbia ML 4246; Columbia ML 5273; Columbia MS-6323.
Aldo Ciccolini, piano (both parts). Angel S-36482.
Aldo Ciccolini and Gabriel Tacchino, piano. EMI/Angel CDC7 47474-2 (compact disc).
Bracha Eden and Alexander Tamir, piano. London CS6754; Decca SXL 6551.
Jacques Février and Francis Poulenc, piano. Musicdisc 30 RC 717.
Frank Glazer and Richard Deas, piano. Candide CE 31041.
Christian Ivaldi and Noel Lee, piano. Conifer/Arion ARN 336025.
Wyneke Jordans and Leo Van Doeselaar, piano. Etcetera ETC 1015; KTC-1015 (compact disc).
Yuji Takahashi and Alain Planès, piano. Denon C37-7487 (compact disc).

Version for piano solo
Laurence Allix piano. Musical Heritage Society MHS 1978/79; Pye Ensayo NEL 2004; Ensayo 3402 (compact disc).

Version for orchestra by Roger Désormière
Orchestra of the Royal Opera House, Covent Garden, conducted by John Lanchbery. Angel S-37580.

Utah Symphony Orchestra conducted by Maurice Abravanel. Vanguard/Cardinal VCS 10037/38.

Trois Petites pièces montées (orchestra)
1. *De l'enfance de Pantagruel (Rêverie)*
2. *Marche de Cocagne (Démarche)*
3. *Jeux de Gargantua (Coin de Polka)*
Ensemble "Die Reihe" conducted by Friedrich Cerha. Candide CE 31018.
French National Radio and Television Orchestra conducted by Manuel Rosenthal. Everest 3234; Adès 16022; Adès 14082-2 (compact disc).

Version for piano four hands
Wyneke Jordans and Leo Van Doeselaar, piano. Etcetera ETC 1015; KTC–1015 (compact disc).

Version of no. 1 for piano solo
Aldo Ciccolini, piano. Angel S-36485.
Frank Glazer, piano. Vox SVBX 5422.

Trois Poèmes d'amour (voice and piano)
1. *Ne suis que grain de sable*
2. *Suis chauve de naissance*
3. *Ta parure est secrète*
Gabriel Bacquier, baritone; Aldo Ciccolini, piano. Angel S-36713.
Elaine Bonazzi, mezzo-soprano; Frank Glazer, piano. Candide CE 31041.
Marjanne Kweksilber, soprano; Reinbert de Leeuw, piano. Philips 9500 934.
Bruno Laplante, baritone; Marc Durand, piano. Calliope CAL 1884.

Les Trois valses distinguées du précieux dégoûté (piano solo)
1. *Sa Taille*
2. *Son binocle*
3. *Ses jambes*
Laurence Allix, piano. Musical Heritage Society MHS 1978/79; Pye Ensayo NEL 2003; Fidelio 3328; Ensayo 3402 (compact disc).
Jean-Joël Barbier, piano. Boîte à Musique LD 5779.
Werner Bärtschi, piano. Ex Libris EL 16965.
Angela Brownridge, piano. EMI EMX 412071-1.
Aldo Ciccolini, piano. Angel S-36482.
France Clidat, piano. Forlane UCD-10514 (compact disc).
Evelyne Crochet, piano. Philips PHS900-179.
Philippe Entremont, piano. CBS IM-37247.
Frank Glazer, piano. Vox SVBX 5422.
John McCabe, piano. Saga 5472.
Roland Pöntinen, piano. Bis LP-317; CD-317 (compact disc).
Bill Quist, piano. Windham Hill WH-1008; WD-1008 (compact disc).
Yuji Takahashi, piano. Denon C37-7486 (compact disc).

Daniel Varsano, piano. CBS M-36694; CBS MK 36694 (compact disc).

Valse-ballet (piano solo)
  Jean-Pierre Armengaud, piano. Le Chant du Monde LDX 78.805; LDC 278-805 (compact disc).
  Angela Brownridge, piano. EMI EMX 412071-1.
  John McCabe, piano. Saga 5472.

Véritables préludes flasques (pour un chien) (piano solo)
  1. *Sévère réprimande*
  2. *Seul à la maison*
  3. *On joue*
  Jean-Joël Barbier, piano. Boîte à Musique LD 5779.
  Werner Bärtschi, piano. Ex Libris EL 16965.
  Chantal de Buchy, piano. PG Records PG-7657; PG PCD-7657 (compact disc).
  Aldo Ciccolini, piano. Angel S-36459; EMI/Angel CDC7 47474-2 (compact disc).
  Frank Glazer, piano. Vox SVBX 5422.
  William Masselos, piano. MGM E-3154; RCA Victor LSC-3127.
  John McCabe, piano. Saga 5387.
  Roland Pöntinen, piano. Bis LP-317; CD-317 (compact disc).
  Yuji Takahashi, piano. Denon C37-7486 (compact disc).

Version for ten-string guitar
  Vincenzo Macaluso, guitar. Klavier KS 523.

Verset laïque et somptueux (piano solo)
  Jean-Pierre Armengaud, piano. Le Chant du Monde LDX 78.805; LDC 278.805 (compact disc).

Vieux sequins et vieilles cuirasses (piano solo)
  1. *Chez le marchand d'or (Venise XIIIe Siècle)*
  2. *Danse cuirassée (Période grecque)*
  3. *Défaite des Cimbres (Cauchemar)*
  Jean-Joël Barbier, piano. Boîte à Musique LD 5779.
  Werner Bärtschi, piano. Ex Libris EL 16965.
  Aldo Ciccolini, piano. Angel S-36459.
  Frank Glazer, piano. Vox SVBX 5422.
  William Masselos, piano. (No. 2) RCA Victor LSC-3127.
  John McCabe, piano. Saga 5387.
  Pascal Rogé, piano. London 410-220-2DH (compact disc).

*   *   *

FREE ARRANGEMENTS

The Camarata Contemporary Chamber Group - *The Music of Erik Satie: The Velvet Gentleman*. Deram DES 18036.

Avant-dernières pensées
Embryons desséchés
Enfantines:
    2. *Enfantillages pittoresques* (no. 1)
    3. *Peccadilles importunes* (nos. 1 and 3)
Gnossiennes (nos 1–3)
Gymnopédies (nos. 1–3)
Heures séculaires et instantanées
Nocturnes (nos. 1–3)
Passacaille
Pièces froides
    1. *Airs à faire fuir* (nos. 1–3)

The Camarata Contemporary Chamber Orchestra - *The Music of Erik Satie: Through the Looking Glass.* Deram DES 18052.
Le Fils des étoiles (Prelude, act 1)
Gnossiennes (nos. 4–6)
Gymnopédie (no. 1)
Parade
Prélude de La Porte héroïque du ciel
Quatre Préludes (nos. 1 and 3 - orchestral version by Francis Poulenc)
Sarabandes (nos. 2 and 3)

The Moog Synthesizer with the Camarata Contemporary Chamber Orchestra - *The Electronic Spirit of Erik Satie.* Deram XDES 18066.
Chapitres tournés en tous sens
Cinq Grimaces pour "Le Songe d'une nuit d'été"
Croquis et agaceries d'un gros bonhomme en bois
Préludes flasques
Sports et divertissements
Trois Petites pièces montées
    1. *De l'enfance de Pantagruel (Rêverie)*
    3. *Jeux de Gargantua (Coin de Polka)*
Trois valses distinguées du précieux dégoûté

Vienna Art Orchestra - Mathias Rüegg, leader, conductor, arranger - *The Minimalism of Erik Satie.* Hat Art 2005.
Reflections on Aubade
Reflections on Méditation
Reflections on Sévère réprimande
Reflections on Idylle
Gymnopédie No. 3
Gnossienne No. 3
Reflections on Gnossienne No. 2
Reflections on Gnossienne No. 1
Satie ist mir im Traum 3x nicht erschienen

Vexations 1801
Vexations 1611
Vexations 2105

Danceries Ensemble - Ichiro Okamoto, leader, arranger - *Erik Satie: Danceries.*
Denon 33CP-1289 (compact disc).
  Chanson médiévale (instrumental version)
  La Diva de l'Empire
  Je te veux
  Tendrement
  La Belle Excentrique
  Trois mélodies sans paroles
  Trois Gymnopédies
  Ludions
  Trois petities piéces montées
  Chanson médiévale (vocal version)

Gymnopédie (no. 1)
  Blood, Sweat and Tears - "Variations on a Theme by Eric Satie." Columbia
    WPC-9720.
  Canadian Brass and Friends - *Unexplored Territory.* Moss Music Group MMG-
    119 - CBC Series.
  James Galway, flute; Cleo Lane, soprano - *Sometimes When We Touch.* RCA
    Victor ARL1-3628.
  Ayako Shinozaki, harp; Ensemble Lunaire (arranged by Yasuo Minami). Denon
    C37-7066 (compact disc).
  Ruth White - arranged and realized on the Moog Synthesizer and other elec-
    tronics by Ruth White. Angel S-36042.

Gymnopédie (no. 2)
  Herbie Mann, flute; Bill Evans, piano; Chuck Israels, bass; Paul Motian,
    drums. Atlantic LP 1426; Atlantic 2SA-300.
  Werner Muller and His Orchestra. London SP 44166.

Gymnopédie (No. 3)
  Ayako Shinozaki, harp; Ensemble Lunaire (arranged by Yasuo Minami). Denon
    C37–7066 (compact disc).

Index

Abd-el-Kader, 152
Aeschylus, 219
Alain, Jehan, 104
Album musical, L', 115
Alcibiades, 220–21
Alkan, Valentin, 150
Allais, Alphonse, 59, 60, *65–69*, 107, 262, 270n20; "Anaemic Young Girls Going to their First Communion through a Blizzard," 66; "Drunkards Dancing in a Fog," 66; *Funeral March,* 66, 270n20; "Imprudential Assurance Company, The," 67; "Negroes Fighting in a Cave at Night," 66; "Personal Column," 67–68
Andersen, Hans Christian, 14
André, Émile, 54
Andrea, Johann Valentin, 74; *Fama Fraternatis of the Meritorious Order of the Rosy Cross,* 74
Ansermet, Ernest, 197, 205
Anton, Jane Leslie. *See* Satie, Jane Leslie
Apollinaire, Guillaume, 197, 208–9, 267n5
Après dîner, 247, 287n24, 287n27
Aragon, Louis, 238, 246, 286n6
Argyropoulo, Madame Hélène, 217
Art et critique, 92
Art moderne, 106
Artois, Charles-Philippe, comte d'. *See* Charles X
Ashton, Sir Frederick, 40, 47; *Monotones I,* 47; *Monotones II,* 40
Astruc, Gabriel, 192

"As-tu vu la cantinière," 251
Athenaeus, 41
"Au clair de la lune," 181
Audran, Edmond, 9, 162–63; *La Mascotte,* 162–64, 169
Auric, Georges, 126, 191, 197, 209–12, 230, 242–44, 260; *Adieu, New York!,* 212, 230; *Fâcheux, Les,* 243–44
Auriol, George, 8, 59, 107
"Aux champs (en marchant)," 152–54
Avenir d'Arcueil-Cachan, L', 143
Avril, Jane, 53
Axsom, Richard H., 200, 282n20

Bach, Johann Sebastian, 15, 86, 134, 136–37, 183, 286n6; *Art of the Fugue,* 137
Balanchine, George, 119
Balguerie, Suzanne, 218, 220
Bancroft, David, 211
Barbey d'Aurevilly, Jules, 72
Barnetche, Eugénie. *See* Satie-Barnetche, Eugénie
Bartók, Béla, 234
Bathori, Jane (Jeanne-Marie Berthier), 216–18, 220, 242
Baudelaire, Charles, 29, 73
Beach, Sylvia, 242
Beaumont, comte Étienne de, 124, 197, 217, 230, 245, 258
Beaumont, comtesse Étienne de (Édith), 197
Beethoven, Ludwig van, 3, 10, 78, 86, 94, 161; Piano Sonata, op. 26, 10; String Quartet, op. 131, 78; String Quartet, op. 135, 78; Symphony no. 5, 161

Dukas, Paul, 4, 11, 138, 176, 234; *Sorcerer's Apprentice, The,* 4, 11
Dumas, Alexandre [Dumas *père*], 13–14; *Mémoires,* 14
Dumesnil, Maurice, 274n9
Dunstable, John, 86
Duparc, Henri, 5
Durey, Louis, 209, 211–12, 259, 263–64
Durrell, Lawrence, 263; *Clea (Alexandria Quartet),* 263
Dussek, Jan Ladislav, 9
Duvernoy, Henri, 10, 17

Echecrates, of Phlius, 227
Écho de Paris, 92
Éclair, L', 217
Écorcheville, Jules, 144, 146
Edwards, Alfred, 190
Edwards, Misia. *See* Sert, Misia
Einstein, Albert, 257
Éluard, Paul, 239, 286n6
Emerson, Ralph Waldo, 150
Eno, Brian, 234
Ernst, Alfred, 5–6, 93
Euripides, 216
Evans, Peter, 103
Excelsior, 197, 257

Fanfare, 219, 233
Fantin-Latour, Henri, 5
Fargue, Léon-Paul, 69, 185, 191, 209, 241–42
Fauré, Gabriel, 3–4, 9, 11, 24–25, 216, 229; *Souvenirs de Bayreuth* (Fauré/Messager), 24–25
Féraudy, Maurice de, 133; *Pousse l'Amour* (Féraudy/Kolb), 133
Festin, Le, 188
Feuilles libres, Les, 13, 237, 240, 256
Feure, Georges de, 60, 106
Figaro, Le, 92, 257
Fissot, Alexis-Henri, 10
Flaubert, Gustave, 14, 36, 41, 58, 73–74, 98; *Salammbô,* 36, 41, 73; *Tentation de Saint-Antoine,*

La, 36, 73, 98
Foch, Marshal Ferdinand, 286n6
Folle, La. *See* Avril, Jane
"For He's a Jolly Good Fellow," 157
Forain, Jean-Louis, 59
Fort, Paul, 145
Fournier, Gabriel, 205
Fragerolle, Georges, 58, 60; *Journey to the Star, The,* 58
France, Anatole (Jacques Anatole Thibault), 58, 286n6
Franck, César, 3, 5–6, 15, 61, 64–65, 78, 92, 134
Fratellini, Albert, François, and Paul, 190
"Frère Jacques," 181
Fresnaye, Roger de la, 191
Freund, Marya, 218, 220, 261
Friis, Inge, 248
Fumet, Dynam-Victor, 60–65, 262, 269n13; *Enlisements d'en haut, Les,* 62–63, 269n13
Fumet, Raphaël, 269n14
Fumet, Stanislas, 62, 64, 269n13

Gallez, Douglas W., 288n32
Galway, James, 40
Gandara, Antonio de la, 57
Gandry-Rety, Jean, 257
Garrigue, Henri, 17
Gaulois, Le, 114, 119
Gauthier-Villars, Henri [pseud. Willy], 69, 92–94; "Lettres de l'Ouvreuse, Les," 93
Gautier, Judith, 74
Gide, André, 217
Gil Blas, 90, 92, 145
Gil Blas illustré, 59
Giselle (Adolphe Adam), 197
Glass, Philip, 48
Glazunov, Alexander, 187–88
Gleizes, Albert, 190, 196
Glinka, Mikhail, 187–88; *Russlan and Ludmilla,* 187
Gluck, Christoph Willibald von, 134
Godebska, Ida, 185, 190–91
Godebska, Mimie, 185–86
Godebska, Misia (Marie). *See* Sert,